XHTML
Introductory

Don Gosselin

THOMSON
COURSE TECHNOLOGY™

Australia • Canada • Mexico • Singapore • Spain • United Kingdom • United States

THOMSON

COURSE TECHNOLOGY

XHTML Introductory
by Don Gosselin

Executive Editor:
Jennifer Locke

Acquistions Editor:
Bill Larkin

Product Manager:
Alyssa Pratt

Development Editors:
Marilyn Freedman and Ann Shaffer

Associate Product Manager:
Janet Aras

Editorial Assistant:
Christy Urban

Senior Marketing Manager:
Angela Laughlin

Production Editor:
Melissa Panagos

Cover Designer:
Joseph Lee, Black Fish Design

Compositor:
GEX Publishing Services

Manufacturing Coordinator:
Laura Burns

BRIEF
Contents

TABLE OF
Contents

Preface

HTML is one of the most widely used technologies on the Internet; it is essentially the key ingredient for building most types of Web pages. However, the HTML language is no longer being developed and will eventually be replaced by Extensible HTML, or XHTML for short. Although XHTML will eventually replace HTML, it will be some time before Web browsers and other software are capable of using it. Furthermore, much of the XHTML syntax is identical to the syntax in HTML. This means that Web page developers can use their same core HTML skills to develop XHTML pages.

XHTML Introductory provides an introduction to authoring Web pages with XHTML. If you are a new or beginner Web page author, this book introduces you to the basics of building structured Web pages with XHTML. You will learn why XHTML was developed as well as the skills you need for building basic Web pages. You will also learn how to link and publish your Web pages and how to add text and images. You will also examine some more advanced Web page techniques including how to create frames, tables, and forms. Finally, you will learn how to format and design your Web pages using Cascading Style Sheets (or CSS).

This book assumes no prior knowledge of HTML, XHTML, or CSS. Each chapter provides clear, non-technical explanations of the important concepts and techniques of a particular language or tool. The focus, however, is on learning by doing as you complete typical Web authoring tasks, such as adding tables to your Web pages. In the tasks, Hands-on Projects, and Case Projects throughout the book, you create many different applications ranging from simple Web pages that link to other Web pages, forms that you can use to interact with visitors to your Web site, and Web pages designed with CSS.

The Approach

This book introduces a variety of techniques, focusing on what you need to know to start authoring Web pages. In each chapter, you perform tasks that let you use a particular technique to build and create Web pages, or the pieces of a Web page, such as tables and forms. In addition to step-by-step tasks, each chapter includes a Chapter Summary, Review Questions, Hands-on Projects, and Case Projects that highlight major concepts and let you practice the techniques you learn. The Hands-on Projects are guided activities that reinforce the skills you learn in the chapter and build on your learning experience by providing additional ways to apply your knowledge in new situations. At the end of each chapter, you will also complete Case Projects that let you use the skills you learned in the chapter to author a Web page on your own.

Overview of This Book

The examples and exercises in this book will help you achieve the following objectives:

- Understand Web page authoring using HTML and XHTML
- Add document structure to your Web pages
- Link and publish basic Web pages
- Add text and images to your Web pages
- Structure your Web pages with frames
- Organize your information with tables
- Interact with visitors to your Web pages via forms
- Format your Web pages with CSS

XHTML Introductory presents eight chapters that cover specific aspects of XHTML. **Chapter 1** covers HTML and XHTML, languages that provide the basic building blocks for authoring Web pages, along with the differences between the two languages. **Chapter 2** discusses how to add basic document structure to your Web pages. **Chapter 3** focuses on linking and publishing your Web pages. **Chapter 4** explains how to add text and images to your Web pages. **Chapter 5** teaches you how to divide your Web pages using frames. **Chapter 6** discusses organizing data on Web pages using tables. **Chapter 7** introduces the use forms to gather information from visitors to your Web site. Finally, **Chapter 8** shows how to format Web pages using CSS.

Features

XHTML Introductory is a superior textbook because it also includes the following features:

- **Chapter Objectives**: Each chapter in this book begins with a list of the important concepts to be mastered within the chapter. This list provides you with a quick reference to the contents of the chapter as well as a useful study aid.

- **Illustrations and Tables**: Illustrations help you visualize common components and relationships. Tables list conceptual items and examples in a visual and readable format.

- **Tips**: These helpful asides provide you with practical advice and proven strategies related to the concept being discussed.

- **Notes**: Notes provide additional helpful information on specific techniques and concepts.

- **Cautions**: These short warnings point out troublesome issues that you need to watch out for when developing Web pages.

- **Chapter Summaries**: These brief overviews of chapter content provide a helpful way to recap and revisit the ideas covered in each chapter.

- **Review Questions**: This set of approximately 15 to 20 review questions reinforce the main ideas introduced in each chapter. These questions help determine whether or not you have mastered the concepts covered in the chapter.

 Hands-on Projects: Although it is important to understand the concepts behind Web design topics, no amount of theory can improve on real-world experience. To this end, along with conceptual explanations, each chapter provides Hands-on Projects related to each major topic aimed at providing you with practical experience. Some of these include researching information from people, printed resources, and the Internet, as well as installing and using some of the technologies discussed. Because the Hands-on Projects ask you to go beyond the boundaries of the text itself, they provide you with practice implementing Web design skills in real-world situations.

 Case Projects: The Case Projects at the end of each chapter are designed to help you apply what you have learned to business situations much like those you can expect to encounter as a Web designer. They give you the opportunity to independently synthesize and evaluate information, examine potential solutions, and make recommendations, much as you would in an actual design situation.

Teaching Tools

The following supplemental materials are available when this book is used in a classroom setting. All of the teaching tools available with this book are provided to the instructor on a single CD-ROM.

Electronic Instructor's Manual. The Instructor's Manual that accompanies this textbook includes:

- Additional instructional material to assist in class preparation, including suggestions for lecture topics. It is critical for the instructor to be able to help the students understand how to use the help resources and how to identify problems. The Instructor's Manual will help you identify areas that are more difficult to teach, and provide you with ideas of how to present the material in an easier fashion.

- Solutions to all end-of-chapter materials, including the Review Questions, and when applicable, Hands-on Projects and Case Projects.

ExamView®. This textbook is accompanied by ExamView, a powerful testing software package that allows instructors to create and administer printed, computer (LAN-based), and Internet exams. ExamView includes hundreds of questions that correspond to the topics covered in this text, enabling students to generate detailed study guides that include page references for further review. The computer-based and Internet testing components allow students to take exams at their computers, and also save the instructor time by grading each exam automatically.

PowerPoint Presentations. This book comes with Microsoft PowerPoint slides for each chapter. These are included as a teaching aid for classroom presentation, to make available to students on the network for chapter review, or to be printed for classroom distribution. Instructors can add their own slides for additional topics they introduce to the class.

Data Files. Files that contain all of the data necessary for the Hands-on Projects and Case Projects are provided through the Course Technology Web site at *www.course.com*, and are also available on the Teaching Tools CD-ROM.

Solution Files. Solutions to end-of-chapter Review Questions, Hands-on Projects, and Case Projects are provided on the Teaching Tools CD-ROM and may also be found on the Course Technology Web site at *www.course.com*. The solutions are password protected.

Distance Learning. Course Technology is proud to present online test banks in WebCT and Blackboard, as well as MyCourse 2.0, Course Technology's own course enhancement tool, to provide the most complete and dynamic learning experience possible. Instructors are encouraged to make the most of the course, both online and offline. For more information on how to access your online test bank, contact your local Course Technology sales representative.

ACKNOWLEDGMENTS

A text such as this represents the hard work of many people, not just the author. I would like to thank all the people who helped make this book a reality. First and foremost, I would like to thank Marilyn Freedman and Ann Shaffer, Development Editors, for helping me get the job done. Marilyn: thanks for all of your hard work and patience over the years. Ann: thanks for jumping in and taking the project to the finish line. I would also like to thank Melissa Panagos, Production Editor, for keeping the peace during the production of this book. Next, I would like to thank Alyssa Pratt, Product Manager, for taking up the reigns from Margarita Donovan. Margarita: I'll miss you always. Alyssa: you're a worthy replacement! I would also like to thank Kirsten Duerr, Senior Vice President, Publisher; Bill Larkin, Acquisitions Editor; and Harris Bierhoff, Chris Schriver, and Mark Spoto, Quality Assurance Testers.

Many, many thanks to the reviewers who provided plenty of comments and positive direction during the development of this book: Janos Fustos, The Metropolitan State College of Denver; Jeff Gullion, Des Moines Area Community College; Kris Howell, University of Southern Colorado; Donna Occhifinto, County College of Morris; Boyd Rodman, Pueblo Community College; and John Whitney, Fox Valley Technical College. You truly made this a better book.

On the personal side, I would like to thank my family and friends for their eternal patience with my crazy schedule. My most important thanks always goes to my wonderful wife, Kathy.

For many years, my loyal cat, Maybelline, kept me company while I wrote. For this reason, I dedicate this work to her for all of the long and solitary days that she made a little less lonely. Kathy, Noah (the dog), and I will miss you always.

Don Gosselin
Napa, California

Read This Before You Begin

The following information will help you as you prepare to use this textbook.

TO THE USER OF THE DATA FILES

To complete the steps and projects in this book, you will need data files that have been created specifically for this book. Your instructor may provide the data files for you. You also can obtain the files electronically from the Course Technology Web site by connecting to *www.course.com* and then searching for this book title. Note that you can use a computer in your school lab or your own computer to complete the steps and Hands-on Projects in this book.

Software Provided with this Book

A 120-day version of XMLSPY 5 Enterprise Edition is packaged with this book. XMLSPY 5 is an XML Development Environment for designing, editing, and debugging software applications involving XML, XML Schema, XSL/XSLT, SOAP, WSDL, and Web Services technologies. You can also download a complimentary 30-day evaluation copy of the XMLSPY 5 Enterprise Edition from *www.altova.com/download*.

Adobe Photoshop 7 also is packaged with this book. Note that the version provided on the CD is a 30-day trial version, so you should not install it until you are ready to begin using the program.

Using Your Own Computer

You can use a computer in your school lab or your own computer to complete the chapters, Hands-on Projects, and Case Projects in this book. To use your own computer, you will need the following:

- **A Web browser**, such as Microsoft Internet Explorer 5.0 or later, Netscape Navigator version 6.0 or later, or Opera version 5.0 or later.
- **A code-based HTML editor**, such as Macromedia Homesite, or a text editor such as Notepad (in Windows) or SimpleText (on a Macintosh).

TO THE INSTRUCTOR

To complete all the exercises and chapters in this book, your students must work with a set of user files, called a Data Disk, and download software from Web sites. The data files are included in the Instructor's Resource Kit. They may also be obtained electronically through the Course Technology Web site at *www.course.com*. Follow the instructions in the Help file to copy the user files to your server or standalone computer. You can view the Help file using a text editor, such as WordPad or Notepad.

After the files are copied, you can create Data Disks for the users, or you can tell them where to find the files so they can make their own. Make sure the files are set up correctly by having students follow the instructions in the "To the User of the Data Files" section.

Course Technology Data Files

You are granted a license to copy the data files to any computer or computer network used by individuals who have purchased this book.

Visit Our World Wide Web Site

Additional materials designed especially for this book might be available for your course. Periodically search *www.course.com* for more information and materials to accompany this text.

1

INTRODUCTION TO WEB PAGES

In this chapter, you will:

♦ Learn about the World Wide Web (WWW)
♦ Create simple Hypertext Markup Language (HTML) documents
♦ Learn about the World Wide Web Consortium (W3C)
♦ Learn about Web browsers
♦ Study how Extensible Hypertext Markup Language (XHTML) evolved
♦ Learn about the basics of Extensible Markup Language (XML)
♦ Learn why XML and HTML were combined to create XHTML

HTML became an Internet standard in 1993 with the release of version 1.0. However, many of the features that are part of today's HTML standard, such as tables, were not available until the release of HTML version 3.2 in 1996. The current HTML version 4.01 was released in 1999. HTML 4.01, however, will be the last version of the HTML language because it is being replaced with XHTML. Later in this chapter you will study some of the reasons why HTML is being replaced with XHTML.

This book discusses HTML because at the time of this writing it is still widely used for creating traditional Web pages that display in Web browsers on desktop computers and workstations. The Web is expanding to other types of media including mobile phones and Personal Digital Assistants (PDAs). You need to use XHTML for the Web pages you write to be compatible with these types of devices. Although XHTML is available now, it will take time for people who write Web pages to adapt to the new language and for all Web browsers to provide complete support for XHTML. Millions of HTML Web pages will continue to exist for a long time because it is not worth the time to convert them to XHTML. The good news is that XHTML is almost identical to HTML, which means that the techniques you use in both languages are virtually interchangeable. The biggest difference between the two languages is that XHTML documents must be well formed, or written according to specific rules, for them to be considered XHTML documents. The concept of writing well-formed XHTML documents will be a central theme throughout this book.

1

THE WORLD WIDE WEB

The **Internet** is a vast network connecting computers all over the world. The original plans for the Internet grew out of a series of memos written by J.C.R. Licklider of the Massachusetts Institute of Technology (MIT) in August 1962 discussing his concept of a "Galactic Network." Licklider envisioned a global computer network through which users could access data and programs from any site on the network. The Internet was developed in the 1960s by the Advanced Research Projects Agency (ARPA) of the U.S. Department of Defense to connect the main computer systems of various universities and research institutions that were funded by ARPA. This first implementation of the Internet was referred to as the *ARPANET*. More computers were connected to the ARPANET in the years following its initial development, although access to the ARPANET was still restricted by the U.S. government primarily to academic researchers, scientists, and the military.

Contrary to a persistent false rumor, the ARPANET was not originally designed as a communications network capable of surviving a nuclear attack. That rumor comes from a separate study on communications networks done by the RAND Corporation that did consider the threat of nuclear attack. The RAND study occurred prior to the development of the ARPANET.

Widespread development of local area networks (LANs) and the personal computer (PC) occurred in the 1980s. Although once restricted to academia, scientists, and the military, computers and networks soon became common aspects of business and everyday life. By the end of the 1980s, businesses and individual computer users began to recognize the global communications capabilities and potential of the Internet and convinced the U.S. government to allow commercial access to the Internet.

In 1990 and 1991, Tim Berners-Lee created what would become the **World Wide Web** (WWW), or the **Web**, at the European Laboratory for Particle Physics (CERN) in Geneva, Switzerland, as a way to easily access cross-referenced documents that existed on the CERN computer network. Once other academics and scientists saw the of Berners-Lee's system, the Web as we know it today was born. This method of accessing cross-referenced documents, known as **hypertext linking**, is probably the most important aspect of the Web because it allows you to quickly open other Web pages. A **hypertext link**, or **hyperlink**, contains a reference to a specific Web page that you can click to quickly open that Web page. Although you will not study hypertext links until Chapter 2, remember that they are one of the essential ingredients that allow you to easily navigate or "surf" the Web.

If you would like to learn more about the history of the Internet, the Internet Society (ISOC) maintains a list of links to Internet histories at *http://www.isoc.org/internet/history.*

A common misconception is that the Web is the Internet. However, the Web is only one *part* of the Internet, and is a means of communicating on the Internet. The Internet is also composed of other communication methods such as e-mail systems that send and receive messages. Due to its enormous influence on computing, communications, and the economy, the World Wide Web is arguably the most important part of the Internet today and is the primary focus of this book.

A document on the Web is called a **Web page** and is identified by a unique address called the **Uniform Resource Locator**, or **URL**. A URL is also commonly referred to as a **Web address**. A URL is a type of **Uniform Resource Identifier** (**URI**), which is a generic term for many types of names and addresses on the World Wide Web. A **Web site** refers to the location on the Internet of the Web pages and related files (such as graphic files) that belong to a company, organization, or individual. You display a Web page on your computer screen using a program called a **Web browser**. Currently, the most popular browser is Internet Explorer. Web pages are located and opened in a Web browser either by entering a URL in the Web browser's Address box or by clicking a hypertext link.

Given the Web's popularity, you should be familiar with Web sites, Web pages, Web browsers, URLs, and hyperlinks. To ensure that you understand the basics, examine the home page for Marin Outdoors is shown in Figure 1-1. A **home page** is the primary Web page for any given Web site. The home page in Figure 1-1 was opened in Internet Explorer by typing its URL, *http://www.marinoutdoors.com/*, in the Address box and pressing Enter.

Figure 1-1   Web page displayed by entering its URL in the Address box

Notice the buttons at the bottom of the Web page in Figure 1-1. These buttons contain hyperlinks to other Web pages on the Marin Outdoors Web site. If you click the About Us button, its hyperlink opens the URL *http://www.marinoutdoors.com/aboutmo.htm*, and the browser displays the About Us Web page shown in Figure 1-2. Notice in Figure 1-2 that the URL displayed in the Address box changes to the URL for the About Us Web page. Although the design of the Web pages in Figures 1-1 and 1-2 is similar, they are different pages that exist on the same Web site.

Figure 1-2   Web page displayed by clicking a hyperlink

 Many of the figures in this book, such as the Marin Outdoors Web pages, come from existing Web sites. If you would like to see each Web site in color, enter its URL in your Web browser's Address box and press Enter. Keep in mind, however, that the content and design of Web sites can and will change over time. The current Web sites for existing companies may not always match the figures that appear in this book.

HTML DOCUMENTS

Originally, people created Web pages using Hypertext Markup Language. **Hypertext Markup Language**, or **HTML**, is a simple language used to create the Web pages that appear on the World Wide Web. Web pages are also commonly referred to as HTML pages or documents. A **markup language** is a set of characters or symbols that define a document's logical structure or how a document should be printed or displayed. HTML is based on an older language called **Standard Generalized Markup Language**, or **SGML**, which defines the data in a document independently of how the data will be displayed. SGML separates the data in a document from the way that data is to appear. Each element in an SGML document is marked according to its type, such as paragraphs, headings, and so on. How individual elements in an SGML document are displayed depends on each target output format. A **target output format** refers to the medium in which a document will be displayed, such as a Web page or an online help system. For instance, the paragraphs in a printed help document may appear quite differently from how they appear in an online help system, although they still represent the same type of element and the same data. HTML works in the same way, except that the target output format is almost always a page in a Web browser. The HTML language was originally designed as a way of defining the elements in a document independently of how they would appear, the same as its predecessor, SGML. HTML was not intended to be used as a method of designing the actual appearance of the pages in a Web browser. HTML, however, has gradually evolved into a language that is capable of defining how elements should appear in a Web browser.

 This book uses the terms Web pages and HTML documents interchangeably.

Basic HTML Syntax

HTML documents are text documents that contain formatting instructions, called **tags**, along with the text that is to be displayed on a Web page. HTML tags range from formatting commands that make text appear in boldface or italic, to controls that allow user input, such as radio buttons and check boxes. Other HTML tags allow you to display graphic images and other objects in a document or Web page. Tags are enclosed in brackets (< >), and most consist of a starting tag and an ending tag that surround the text or other items they are formatting or controlling. The ending tag must include a forward slash (/) immediately after the opening bracket to define it as an ending tag. For example, the starting tag to make a line of text appear in boldface is **** and the ending tag is ****. Any text contained between this pair of tags appears in boldface when you open the HTML document in a Web browser. Some tags do not require an ending tag. For instance, the **<hr>** tag, which inserts a horizontal rule on a Web page, does not include an ending tag. You simply place the **<hr>** tag anywhere in an HTML document where you want the horizontal rule to appear.

 HTML documents must have a file extension of .html or .htm.

There are hundreds of HTML tags and identical XHTML tags, many of which you will learn about throughout the course of this book. Table 1-1 lists some of the more common structure and formatting tags.

Table 1-1   Common Structure and Formatting HTML Tags

HTML Tag	Description
`<b></b>`	Formats enclosed text in a bold typeface
`<body></body>`	Encloses the body of the HTML document
` `	Inserts a line break
`<center></center>`	Centers the enclosed text in the middle of the browser window
`<head></head>`	Encloses the page header and contains information about the entire page
`<hn></hn>`	Creates heading level tags, where *n* represents a number from 1 (the largest) to 6 (the smallest)
`<hr>`	Inserts a horizontal rule
`<html></html>`	Starts and ends an HTML document
`<i></i>`	Formats enclosed text in an italic typeface
`<img src="...">`	Displays an image file
`<p></p>`	Identifies enclosed text as a paragraph
`<strong></strong>`	Formats enclosed text in a strong typeface, similar to bold
`<sub></sub>`	Formats enclosed text as subscript
`<sup></sup>`	Formats enclosed text as superscript
`<u></u>`	Formats enclosed text as underlined

The goal of this section is to introduce HTML syntax briefly. In Chapters 2 and 3, you will study in detail the tags listed in Table 1.

All HTML documents begin with `<html>` and end with `</html>`. These tags tell a Web browser that the instructions between them are to be assembled into an HTML document. The opening and closing `<html>...</html>` tags are required and contain all the text and other tags that make up the HTML document.

Two other important HTML tags are the `<head>` tag and the `<body>` tag. The `<head>` tag contains information that is used by the Web browser, and you place it at the start of an HTML document, after the opening `<html>` tag. You place several tags within the `<head>...</head>` tag pair to help manage a document's content, including the `<title>` tag, which contains text that appears in a browser's title bar. A `<head>` tag pair must contain a `<title>` tag. With the exception of the `<title>` tag, elements contained in the `<head>` tag do not affect the rendering of the HTML document. The `<head>` tag pair and the tags it contains are referred to as the **document head**.

Following the document head is the `<body>` tag, which contains the document body. The `<body>` tag pair and the text and tags it contains are referred to as the **document body**. You will study the `<head>` and `<body>` tags in Chapter 2.

1

When you open an HTML document in a Web browser, the document is assembled and formatted according to the instructions contained in its tags. A Web browser's process of assembling and formatting an HTML document is called **parsing** or **rendering**. The following line is an example of how to make text appear in boldface in an HTML document:

```
<b>This text will appear in boldface in a Web browser.</b>
```

HTML is not case sensitive, so you can use `<B>` in place of `<b>`. XHTML, on the other hand, is case sensitive, and you must use lowercase letters for tags. For this reason, this book uses lowercase letters for all tags.

You use various parameters, called **attributes**, to configure many HTML tags. You place an attribute before the closing bracket of the starting tag, and separate it from the tag name or other attributes with a space. You assign a value to an attribute using the syntax *attribute="value"*. For example, you can configure the `<img>` tag, which embeds an image in an HTML document, with a number of attributes, including the **src** attribute. The **src** attribute specifies the filename of an image file or video clip. To include the **src** attribute within the `<img>` tag, you type `<img src="mygraphic.gif">`.

When a Web browser parses or renders an HTML document, it ignores nonprinting characters such as tabs and carriage returns; the final document that appears in the Web browser includes only recognized HTML tags and text. You cannot use carriage returns in the body of an HTML document to insert spaces before and after a paragraph; the browser recognizes only paragraph `<p>` and line break `<br>` tags for this purpose. Additionally, most Web browsers will ignore multiple, contiguous spaces on a Web page and replace them with a single space. Figure 1-3 shows a simple HTML document, and Figure 1-4 shows how it appears in a Web browser.

```
<html>
<head>
<title>Hello World</title>
</head>
<body>
<h1>Hello World (this is the heading 1 tag)</h1>
<h2>This line is formatted with the heading 2 tag</h2>
<center>This line is centered</center>
<p>This body text line contains several character formatting tags including
<i>italics</i>, <b>bold</b>, and <u>underline</u>. The following code line
creates a line break followed by a horizontal rule:</p>
<hr>
<img src="teddybear.gif">This line contains an image.
</body>
</html>
```

Figure 1-3   A simple HTML document

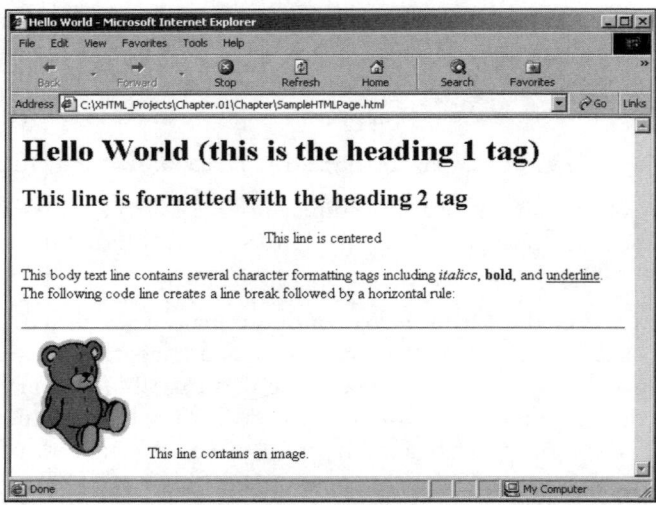

Figure 1-4   An HTML document in a Web browser

Creating an HTML Document

Because HTML documents are text files, you can create them in any text editor, such as Notepad or WordPad, or any word-processing application capable of creating simple text files. If you use a text editor to create an HTML document, you cannot view the final result until you open the document in a Web browser. However, applications called HTML editors are designed specifically for creating HTML documents. Some popular HTML editors, such as Microsoft FrontPage and Macromedia Dreamweaver, have graphical interfaces that allow you to create Web pages and immediately view the results, similar to the what-you-see-is-what-you-get (WYSIWYG) interface in word-processing programs. In addition, many current word-processing applications, including Microsoft Word and WordPerfect, allow you to save files as HTML documents.

HTML editors still create simple text files, but they automate the process of applying tags. For example, if you create a document in Word that contains boldface text, then save it as an HTML document, Word automatically adds the **...** tag to the text in the HTML text file.

What is surprising to many people who are new to creating Web pages is that you cannot use a Web browser to create an HTML document.

Any HTML editor can greatly simplify the task of creating Web pages; once your Web page creation skills increase, you will definitely want to use one. However, to become truly proficient in HTML and XHTML, you need to thoroughly understand the tags

1

and attributes that make up a Web page. HTML editors automatically add many unfamiliar tags and attributes to documents that may confuse you and distract from the learning process. For instance, if you create even the simple Web page shown in Figure 1-5 using Microsoft FrontPage, the HTML document will include the tags and attributes shown in Figure 1-6.

Figure 1-5 Simple Web page created with Microsoft FrontPage

```
<html>
<head>
<meta http-equiv="Content-Language" content="en-us">
<meta http-equiv="Content-Type" content="text/html; charset=windows-1252">
<meta name="GENERATOR" content="Microsoft FrontPage 4.0">
<meta name="ProgId" content="FrontPage.Editor.Document">
<title>Llamas are from South America</title>
</head>
<body>
<p>Llamas are from South America.</p>
</body>
</html>
```

Figure 1-6 HTML tags generated by Microsoft FrontPage

The tags and attributes shown in Figure 1-6 are not complicated; in fact, you will study all of them in Chapters 2 and 3. However, with more complex Web pages, an HTML editor will add many more tags that will be difficult for you to decipher at first. For this reason, in this book you will create Web pages using a simple text editor.

Next, you will create a simple HTML document that contains some of the tags you have seen in this section. You can use any text editor, such as Notepad or WordPad.

To create an HTML document:

1. Start your text editor and create a new document, if necessary.

2. Type the following tags to begin the HTML document. Remember that all HTML documents must begin and end with the <html>...</html> tag pair.

   ```
   <html>
   </html>
   ```

3. Add the following `<head>` and `<title>` tags between the `<html>`...`</html>` tag pair. The title will appear in your Web browser's title bar. Remember that the `<head>`...`</head>` tag pair must include the `<title>`...`</title>` tag pair. The `<title>`...`</title>` tag pair cannot exist outside the `<head>`...`</head>` tag pair.

```
<head>
<title>Web Page Example</title>
</head>
```

4. Next, add the following document body tags above the closing `</html>` tag:

```
<body>
</body>
```

5. Type the following tags and text between the `<body>`...`</body>` tag pair to create the body of the HTML document.

```
<h1>This line uses the heading 1 tag</h1>
<p>This line includes <br> a line break</p>
<p>The following line is a horizontal rule</p>
<hr>
<h2>This line uses the heading 2 tag</h2>
<h3>This line uses the heading 3 tag</h3>
<p>This <b>line</b> <i>contains</i> <sup>text</sup>
<sub>formatting</sub></p>
```

6. Save the file as **FirstWebPage.html** in the Chapter.01\Chapter folder. Some text editors automatically add their own extension to a document. Notepad, for instance, adds an extension of .txt. Be sure your document is saved with an extension of .html.

Some Web servers do not correctly interpret spaces within the name of HTML files. For example, some Web servers may not correctly interpret a filename of Hello World.html, with a space between Hello and World. For this reason, filenames in this book do not include spaces.

7. Close the **FirstWebPage.html** file and then open it in Internet Explorer or another Web browser. (You open a local HTML file in Internet Explorer by selecting Open from the File menu; other Web browsers include similar commands.) Figure 1-7 displays the FirstWebPage.html file as it appears in Internet Explorer.

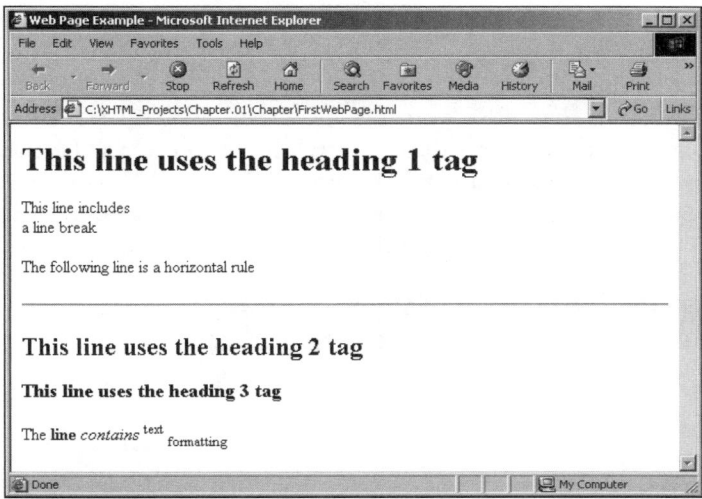

Figure 1-7   FirstWebPage.html file in Internet Explorer

8. Close your Web browser window.

Web Page Design and Authoring

Web page design, or **Web design**, refers to the visual design and creation of the documents that appear on the World Wide Web. Many businesses today—both prominent and small—have Web sites, and in the future even more businesses are likely to have a Web presence. To attract and retain visitors, and to stand out from the crowd, Web sites must be exciting and visually stimulating. Quality Web design plays an important role in attracting first-time and repeat visitors. However, the visual aspect of a Web site is only one part of the story. Equally important is the Web site content and how that content is structured.

Web design is an extremely important topic. However, this book is *not* about Web design, even though you will certainly learn many Web design concepts and techniques as you work through this book. Instead, this book teaches **Web page authoring**, which refers to the creation and assembly of the tags, attributes, and data that make up a Web page. This is a subtle, but important distinction: A book on Web design teaches the visual and graphical design aspects of creating Web pages, whereas a book on XHTML teaches the more basic concepts that you need to get started, such as how to work with tags and attributes.

 If you would like to study the topic of Web page design itself, please refer to Joel Sklar's excellent book, *Web Design*, published by Course Technology.

There are countless ways of combining the hundreds of HTML tags to create interesting Web pages. One technique that professional Web authors use to increase their HTML skill is examining the underlying HTML tags for a Web page that they admire. All Web browsers contain commands that allow you to view the underlying HTML code for a Web page that appears in the browser; in Internet Explorer you select the Source command from the View menu, which displays the underlying HTML code in Notepad. Figure 1-8 shows a partial listing of the HTML code for the Marin Outdoors About Us page, as it appears in Notepad after you select the Source command from the View menu.

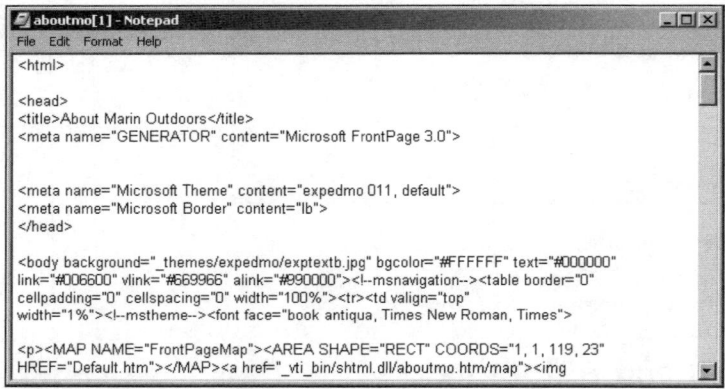

Figure 1-8   HTML code for Marin Outdoors About Us page

Most of the code used to create the Marin Outdoors home page will not mean much to you now. However, once your skills progress, you will find it useful to examine a Web page's HTML code to better understand how the tags on the page were structured, what colors were used, and so on.

The open nature of HTML allows anyone to easily see how another Web author created a Web page. However, you should *never* copy another Web page author's work and attempt to pass it off as your own. As a responsible member of the Web community, examine the HTML code behind a Web page only to improve your own skills. The potential theft of another Web page author's hard work and intellectual property is no small concern. Stealing another Web page author's code and Web page designs is unscrupulous, and in many cases illegal, especially if the work is copyrighted. Throughout this book you will examine the underlying HTML code from various published Web sites. Remember that your reasons for examining existing HTML code are to understand the techniques used to create specific elements on an a Web page to improve your own skills, not to hijack someone else's hard work.

THE W3C

As mentioned earlier, HTML was not intended to be used as a method of designing the actual appearance of the pages in a Web browser. However, once the Web grew beyond a small academic and scientific community, users began to recognize that greater interactivity and better visual design would make the Web more useful. As commercial applications of the Web grew, the demand for more interactive and visually appealing Web sites also grew.

To provide new functionality, Web browser manufacturers began to add their own tags and attributes (commonly referred to as *extensions*) to HTML. No standard existed for adding new functionality to HTML, and each browser manufacturer added new extensions and implemented new technologies as it saw fit. As a result, Web page authors began to find it necessary to write slightly different HTML code for each Web browser in which they anticipated their Web page would be opened. To address the growing need for standards, Tim Berners-Lee established the **World Wide Web Consortium**, or **W3C**, in 1994 at MIT to oversee the development of Web technology standards. The W3C has approximately 500 members around the world, including Microsoft, Netscape, IBM, and Sun Microsystems, who contribute to the study and recommendation of Web standards.

 If you would like to read more about the W3C's standardization efforts for the Web, visit their Web site at *http://www.w3c.org*.

The W3C does not release a version of a particular technology. Instead, it issues a formal recommendation for a technology, which essentially means that the technology is (or will be) a recognized industry standard.

WEB BROWSERS

At the time of this writing, Internet Explorer browsers are being used by more than 85% of the market. For this reason alone, the majority of the Web page examples in this book are presented in the latest release of Internet Explorer, version 6. Although Internet Explorer is by far the most popular browser, it is not the only browser—nor was it the first browser. NCSA Mosaic was created in 1993 at the University of Illinois and was the first program to allow users to navigate the Web using a Graphical User Interface (GUI). In 1994, Netscape released Navigator, which soon controlled 75% of the market. Netscape maintained its control of the browser market until 1996, when Microsoft entered the market with the release of Internet Explorer, and the so-called browser wars began.

 Although the NCSA Mosaic browser is no longer being developed, you can download the last version at *http://archive.ncsa.uiuc.edu/SDG/Software/Mosaic/*.

Prior to version 6, the Netscape Web browser was called Navigator or Netscape Navigator. With the release of version 6, however, Netscape dropped "Navigator" from the browser name, and now simply refers to its browser as "Netscape". For this reason, whenever this book mentions the Navigator Web browser, it is referring to versions older than version 6. However, whenever the Netscape Web browser is mentioned, we are referring to version 6 and later.

The browser wars began over Dynamic Hyper Text Markup Language (DHTML), which allows a Web page to change after it has been rendered by a browser. Examples of DHTML include the ability to position text and elements, change document background color, and create effects such as animation.

DHTML is actually a combination of HTML, Cascading Style Sheets (CSS), and JavaScript. CSS, also called style sheets, are a standard set by the W3C for managing the formatting information of Web pages. JavaScript is a programming language that you can use to control Web pages and Web browsers. You will learn about CSS in Chapter 8. The comprehensive edition of the book also includes several chapters on working with JavaScript.

Earlier versions of Internet Explorer and Navigator included DHTML tags that were incompatible. Furthermore, Microsoft and Netscape each wanted its version of DHTML to become the industry standard. To settle the argument, the W3C set out to create a platform-independent and browser-neutral version of DHTML. While the W3C was drafting a recommendation for DHTML, versions 4 of both Internet Explorer and Navigator added a number of proprietary DHTML tags that were incompatible with the other browser. These incompatibilities meant that for advanced DHTML techniques, such as animation, you had to write a different set of HTML code for each browser type. Unfortunately for Netscape, the W3C adopted the version of DHTML found in version 4 of Internet Explorer, which prompted many loyal Netscape followers to defect to Microsoft.

One great benefit of the browser wars is that it has forced the Web industry to rapidly develop and adopt advanced Web page standards (including JavaScript, CSS, and DHTML) that are consistent across browser types. And although Microsoft appears to be winning the browser wars, that does not mean they are over. Other excellent browsers exist, some of which support new technologies and functionalities sooner than Internet Explorer or Netscape. Three additional browsers that are worth noting are Amaya (*http://www.w3.org/amaya*), Mozilla (*http://www.mozilla.org*), and Opera (*http://www.opera.com*).

Most Web browsers, including Internet Explorer, Netscape, Amaya, Mozilla, and Opera, use GUIs. However, one well-known browser, Lynx, is text-based. One of the most important uses of the Lynx browser is providing Web access to users with disabilities, including users of Braille and speech devices. For more information on the Lynx browser, visit *http://www.lynx.browser.org*.

Your challenge as a Web page author is to author Web pages that are compatible with as many browser types and versions as possible. This will ensure the widest possible audience for the Web pages you create. Keep in mind that many Web users simply do not care about using the latest Web browsers and cutting-edge technology and are content with using whatever browser version is currently installed on their computer. Deciding which browsers and browser versions to support depends on the technologies you want to use on your Web site. Many Web page authors try to create their Web pages to be compatible with HTML version 3.2 and higher, which is available in Internet Explorer version 3 and Navigator version 2. However, if you intend to use CSS techniques in your Web pages, then HTML version 3.2 is an insufficient target because CSS did not appear in Navigator until version 4.5.

To make sure that your Web pages will reach a broad audience, you must test your Web pages in every browser and browser version in which you anticipate they will be opened. As a general rule of thumb, most professional Web page authors and developers ensure that their Web pages will function with Internet Explorer version 4 and higher and Netscape browsers higher than version 4. (Many Web page authors consider Netscape Navigator version 4.0 to be obsolete.) Additionally, be sure to test your Web pages in browsers for different platforms including Windows, Macintosh, Linux, and Unix.

Each Web browser may render the parts of a Web page slightly differently from other browsers. This means that in addition to testing whether the technology on your Web pages works as intended, you should also test to ensure that your Web pages display properly across different browsers and browser versions.

Another factor you must consider is monitor resolution. **Resolution** refers to the number of pixels that can be displayed on a monitor. A **pixel** (short for **pic**ture **el**ement) represents a single point on a computer screen. You can think of pixels as thousands of millions of tiny dots arranged in columns and rows on your monitor. The number of pixels available depends on a computer monitor's resolution. For example, a VGA monitor contains 640 columns by 480 rows of pixels, or about 300,000 pixels; a Super VGA monitor contains 1024 columns by 768 rows of pixels, or approximately 800,000 pixels. If you use a high resolution of 1024×768 when creating a Web page, the Web page will appear much larger in monitors set to a resolution of 800×600 or 640×480. Many Web page authors feel that all Web pages should be designed with the lowest common denominator in mind, which is currently considered to be a resolution of 640×480. Other Web page authors, however, feel that designing Web pages for a resolution of 800×600 is acceptable because of the large (and growing) number of users with monitors capable of displaying this resolution or higher. The Web page examples in this book are designed using a resolution of 800×600. Regardless of the resolution you decide to use, be sure to test the appearance of your Web pages in as many browsers and browser versions as possible.

The monitor resolutions given in this book are for Windows operating systems. Macintosh operating systems use a different scale for measuring resolution. A Windows monitor resolution of 640×480 is equivalent to a Macintosh monitor resolution of 512×384; a Windows monitor resolution of 800×600 is equivalent to a Macintosh monitor resolution of 640×480; and a Windows monitor resolution of 1024×768 is equivalent to a Macintosh monitor resolution of 800×600.

You may be wondering what happens when a browser does not support a specific HTML tag (either a later version of HTML that the browser does not support or a proposed extension). If a browser encounters a tag that it does not recognize, it usually ignores it.

THE EVOLUTION OF XHTML

As mentioned earlier, HTML version 4.01 is the final version of HTML because it is being replaced by XHTML. HTML is being replaced because it is useful only for rendering documents in traditional Web browsers. The Web, however, is expanding to other media, called **user agents**, which are devices that are capable of retrieving and processing HTML and XHTML documents. A user agent can be a traditional Web browser or a device such as a mobile phone or PDA, or even an application that simply collects and processes data instead of displaying it.

There are two primary reasons why HTML is not suitable for user agents other than Web browsers. First, even though HTML was originally designed primarily to display data, it has evolved into a markup language that is more concerned with how data appears than with the data itself. Recall that HTML is based on SGML, which defines the data in a document independently of how it will be displayed. Also recall that early in the browser wars, each Web browser began to add extensions (tags and attributes) to HTML to provide functionality for displaying and formatting Web pages. For instance, one extension to the original HTML language is the <font> tag, which allows you to specify the font for data in an HTML document. The <font> tag has nothing to do with the type of data in an HTML document. Instead, it exists solely as a design element for displaying data in a specific typeface within a Web browser. Remember, however, that HTML is based on SGML and should define data independently of the way it displays. Tags like the <font> tag violate this rule. Understand that there is nothing wrong with continuing to author your Web pages using HTML and design elements such as the <font> tag—provided your Web pages will be opened only in a Web browser. Unfortunately, many user agents such as mobile phones and PDAs display only black and white or gray-scale text and are incapable of processing HTML tags that handle the display and formatting of data. User agents such as these require a language that truly defines data (such as a paragraph or heading) independently of the way it displays.

Second, current and older versions of Web browsers allow you to write sloppy HTML code. For instance, earlier you learned that all HTML documents begin with <html> and end with </html>. To be more precise, all HTML documents *should* begin with

1

`<html>` and end with `</html>`. In addition, all HTML documents *should* also include `<head>...</head>` and `<body>...</body>` tag pairs. In practice, however, you can omit any of these tags from an HTML document and a Web browser will still render the page correctly. In fact, although many tags require a closing tag, you can often omit (either intentionally or accidentally) a closing tag and the Web page will usually render properly.

To give you an idea of how lax today's Web browsers are when rendering HTML code, you will create an HTML document that does not include the `<html>`, `<head>`, and `<body>` tags, which are technically required.

To create an HTML document that does not include all of the required tags:

1. Create a new document in your text editor.

2. Without including any `<html>`, `<head>`, or `<body>` tags, type the following statements. Notice that the closing tags are missing for the `<p>` and `<b>` tags.

```
<h1>Chapter 4 -- The Apes</h1>
<p>"...Old Tantor, the elephant, alone of all the wild
savage life, feared him not--and he alone did Kerchak
fear. When Tantor trumpeted, the great ape scurried
with his fellows high among the trees of the second
terrace..."
<p>from <i>Tarzan of the Apes</i><br>
by <b>Edgar Rice Burroughs
```

3. Save the file as **TarzanCh4.html** in the Chapter.01\Chapter folder.

4. Close the **TarzanCh4.html** file and then open it in Internet Explorer or another Web browser. Even though the HTML document does not include all of the required tags, the Web browser displays it properly, as shown in Figure 1-9.

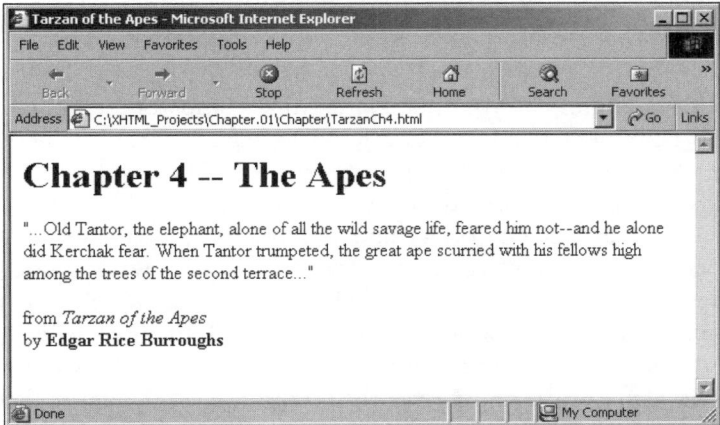

Figure 1-9   TarzanCh4.html file in Internet Explorer

5. Close your Web browser window.

Languages based on SGML use a **Document Type Definition**, or **DTD**, to define the tags and attributes that you can use in a document, and the rules the document must follow when it includes them. When a document conforms to an associated DTD, it is said to be **valid**. When a document does not conform to an associated DTD, it is said to be **invalid**. For example, you may have a DTD that defines tags and elements in a document that will be used by a Human Resources department. The DTD may include tags such as `<employee_name>`, `<position>`, and `<salary>`. The DTD may also define attributes such as an `employeeID` attribute that can be used in the `<employee_name>` tag. Additionally, the Human Resources DTD may define rules about how the tags and attributes can be used in a document. For instance, it may require that the `<employee_name>`, `<position>`, and `<salary>` tags be contained within a `<department>` tag.

You can check whether a document conforms to an associated DTD by using a program called a **validating parser**. You will use a validating parser in Chapter 2.

Some languages that are based on SGML are not required to use DTDs. XML documents, for instance, can be created either with or without a DTD. You will study XML in the next section.

Because HTML is based on SGML, it requires a DTD, and the HTML DTD is built directly into Web browsers. The HTML DTD defines tags such as the `<html>`, `<head>`, and `<body>` tags and defines rules that you must follow when authoring your documents. For instance, one rule that is defined in the HTML DTD states that you must include a `<title>` tag with a `<head>` tag. However, because most Web browsers allow you to write sloppy code, this rule—and almost every other rule defined in the HTML DTD—is usually ignored. Note that you cannot edit the HTML DTD or create your own HTML DTD, although other SGML-based languages do allow you to create your own DTDs.

When a Web browser opens an HTML document, it first compares the document to the DTD. If an HTML document is missing any required tags, the HTML DTD supplies them, allowing the Web browser to render the page correctly. However, if an HTML document uses any tags that are not defined in the HTML DTD, the Web browser ignores them. Because Web browsers operate on a standard computer, they have plenty of processing power to determine the missing required tags in a poorly written document and render the document into a Web page. Additionally, the DTD in a Web browser can be as large as necessary to define the W3C-approved tags and attributes, along with any extensions implemented by the browser. But again, user agents such as mobile phones and PDAs do not have the processing power to interpret sloppy code or the ability to process any extensions that handle the display and formatting of data.

To address these issues and provide a common standard for Web page development, the W3C created XHTML, which combines the tags and attributes of HTML with the structure of a language called XML. In order to be successful with XHTML, you must first understand a little about XML, which you will study for the rest of this chapter. In Chapter 2, you will study how XHTML differs from HTML and how to create XHTML documents.

THE BASICS OF XML

Extensible Markup Language, or **XML**, is used for creating Web pages and defining and transmitting data between applications. Like HTML, XML is based on SGML. Version 1.0 of XML achieved recommendation status by the W3C in 1998 and was still current at the time of this writing. Although XML is a markup language like HTML, it is not a replacement for HTML. XML is primarily a way of defining and organizing data and does not include any of the display capabilities of HTML. It is up to whatever user agent receives the XML document to decide how to display it. In fact, a user agent may not display an XML document at all, but instead may store the information in a database or use it to perform a calculation.

In XML you refer to a tag pair and the data it contains as an **element**. All elements must have an opening and a closing tag. The data contained within an element's opening and closing tags is referred to as its **content**. One concept that can be difficult to grasp is that XML does not specify any elements or attributes. Instead, you define your own elements and attributes to describe the data in your document. The following code is an example of an XML document that defines several elements that describe the data associated with an automobile:

```
<auto>
    <make manufacturer="GM">Chevrolet</make>
    <model>Corvette</model>
    <year>1967</year>
    <color>Red</color>
</auto>
```

The preceding code is the most basic form of an XML document. In order for your XML documents to be properly structured, they must also include an XML declaration and adhere to XML's syntax rules. You will study these requirements in the rest of this section.

The XML Declaration

XML documents should begin with an **XML declaration**, which specifies the version of XML being used. You are not required to include an XML declaration because currently only one version of XML exists, version 1.0. However, it's a good practice to always include the XML declaration because XML will almost certainly evolve into other versions that will contain features not found in version 1.0. Specifying the version with the XML declaration will help ensure that whatever user agent or application is parsing an XML document will know which version to use (assuming that newer versions will be released).

You can use the following three attributes with the XML declaration: version, stand-alone, and encoding. All of the attributes are optional, but you should at least include the version attribute, which designates the XML version number (currently "1.0"). The following statement is an XML declaration that includes only the version attribute:

```
<?xml version="1.0"?>
```

 The XML declaration is not actually a tag, but a processing instruction, which is a special statement that passes information to the user agent or application that is processing the XML document. You can easily recognize processing instructions because they begin with <? and end with ?>.

The encoding attribute of the XML declaration designates the language used by the XML document. Although English is the primary language used on the Web, it is not the only one. As a considerate resident of the international world of the Web, use the encoding attribute of the XML declaration to designate the character set for your XML document. English and many western European languages use the iso-8859-1 character set. Therefore, you should use the following XML declaration in your documents:

```
<?xml version="1.0" encoding="iso-8859-1"?>
```

The `standalone="yes"` attribute indicates that the document does not require a DTD to be rendered correctly. Unlike HTML, XML documents do not require a DTD to be rendered correctly. Because XML does not include predefined elements, it does not need a DTD to define them. However, some XML documents may benefit from a DTD, especially if multiple XML documents share the same elements. If your XML document requires a DTD, then you assign the standalone attribute a value of "no". However, if you are certain that your XML document will not require a DTD, then you assign the standalone attribute value of "yes". For instance, you use the following XML declaration for any XML documents that do not require a DTD:

```
<?xml version="1.0" encoding="iso-8859-1"
standalone="yes"?>
```

Next you create a simple XML document that contains your mailing address.

To create an XML document that contains your mailing address:

1. Start your text editor and create a document.

2. Add the following XML declaration that includes the version, encoding, and standalone attributes:

```
<?xml version="1.0" encoding="iso-8859-1"
standalone="yes"?>
```

3. Type the following opening tag to begin the document:

```
<Mailing_Address>
```

1

4. Next, add the following elements that contain your mailing address. Be sure to replace the text within each tag pair with your own information.

```
<Name>your name</Name><Address>your address</Address>
<City>your city</City><State>your state</State>
<Zip>your zip code</Zip>
```

5. Type the closing mailing address tag, as follows:

```
</Mailing_Address>
```

6. Save the file as **MailingAddress.xml** in the Chapter.01\Chapter folder.

7. Close the **MailingAddress.xml** file in your text editor.

Be sure to type an extension of .xml and not .html or .txt.

Parsing XML Documents

When a Web browser opens an HTML document that is not written properly, such as a document without the closing `</html>` tag, the browser ignores the error and renders the page. In contrast, XML documents must adhere to strict rules. The most important of these rules is that all elements must be closed. When a document adheres to XML's syntax rules, it is said to be **well formed**. You will study XML's rules for writing well-formed documents in the next section.

The W3C uses the term *well formedness*, although grammatically it sounds strange, so this book uses the term *well formed*.

You use a program called a **parser** to check whether an XML document is well formed. There are two types of parsers: non-validating and validating. A non-validating parser simply checks whether an XML document is well formed. A validating parser checks whether an XML document is well formed and if it conforms to an associated DTD. Internet Explorer and other browsers have the capability to act as non-validating parsers. A non-validating parser checks whether a document is well formed, and if it is, displays its XML elements and data. For instance, if you open the automobile XML document in Internet Explorer and the document is well formed, then Internet Explorer will correctly parse and display the document, as shown in Figure 1-10.

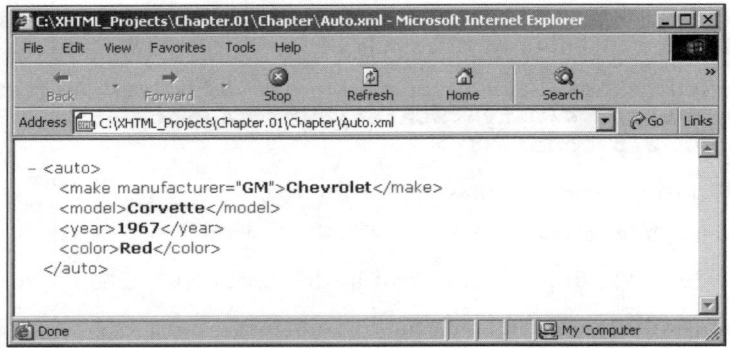

Figure 1-10   Well-formed XML document

If an XML document is not well formed, then the parser displays the error. For example, if the automobile XML document is missing the closing **</auto>** tag, then it is not well formed. In this case Internet Explorer will point to the error, as shown in Figure 1-11.

Figure 1-11   XML document that is not well formed

Internet Explorer uses Extensible Stylesheet Language, or XSL, to format and display XML. The error message in Figure 1-11 explains that Internet Explorer cannot format the XML document using its internal XSL style sheet. A style sheet is a file that defines the layout of a document. XSL is covered in the comprehensive edition of this book.

Next, you will parse the mailing address XML document you created in the last exercise.

To parse the mailing address XML document:

    1. Open the **MailingAddress.xml** file in Internet Explorer or another browser that can be used as a non–validating parser. The easiest way to open an XML document in Internet Explorer is to type the complete path to the file, as

1

shown in Figure 1-12. If you created the document correctly, your Web browser window should appear similar to the figure. If you did not create the document correctly, fix any errors that appear in the browser window and reload the document.

Figure 1-12   MailingAddress.xml file in Internet Explorer

2. Close your Web browser window.

Writing Well-Formed Documents

Well-formed XML documents allow user agents to read the document's data easily. User agents expect XML data to be structured according to specific rules, which allows the user agent to read data quickly without having to decipher the data structure.

In this section, you will study the syntax, or rules, for writing well-formed XML documents. The most important of these rules are:

- All XML documents must have a root element
- XML is case sensitive
- All XML elements must have a closing tag
- XML elements must be properly nested
- Attribute values must appear within quotation marks
- Empty elements must be closed

Next, you will study each of these rules.

All XML Documents Must Have a Root Element

A **root element** contains all the other elements in a document. The `<html>...</html>` element is the root element for HTML documents, although most Web browsers do not require a document to include it. XML documents, however, require a root element that you define yourself. For instance, the root element for the XML automobile data document is the **<auto>** element. If you do not include a root element, then the XML document will not be well formed. The following version of the XML document containing the automobile data is not well formed because it is missing the **<auto>** root element:

```
<?xml version="1.0" encoding="iso-8859-1"
    standalone="yes"?>
<make>Ford</make><model>Mustang</model>
<year>1967</year><color>Red</color>
```

Next, you will start creating an XML document that stores data associated with fiction and nonfiction books. The document is a simple example of an XML document that a bookstore or publisher might use to organize its inventory.

To create an XML document that stores data:

1. Create a new document in your text editor.

2. Type the XML declaration, as follows:

   ```
   <?xml version="1.0" encoding="iso-8859-1"
   standalone="yes"?>
   ```

3. Next, type the opening and closing tags for a root element named **<books>**:

   ```
   <books>
   </books>
   ```

4. Save the file as **Books.xml** in the Chapter.01\Chapter folder, and then open it in Internet Explorer. Your Web browser should look like Figure 1-13.

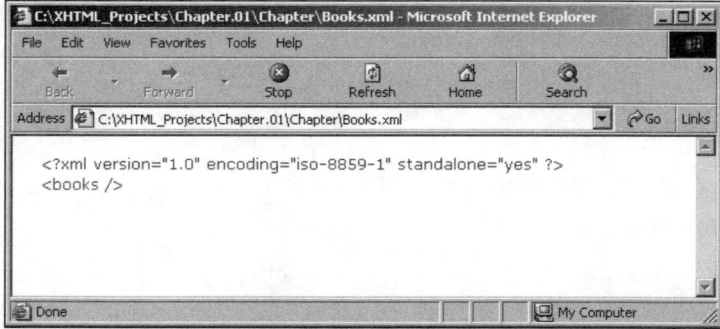

Figure 1-13   Books.xml in Internet Explorer

5. Close your Web browser.

XML is Case Sensitive

Unlike HTML tags, XML tags are case sensitive. For instance, in an HTML document it makes no difference whether the bold tag is uppercase or lowercase. Both of the following HTML statements will be rendered properly in a Web browser:

```
<B>This line is bold.</B>
<b>This line is also bold.</b>
```

You can even mix and match the cases tags in an HTML document, as in the following statements:

```
<B>This line is bold.</b>
<b>This line is also bold.</B>
```

With XML, however, you cannot mix the case of elements. For instance, if you have an opening tag named **<color>** that is all lowercase, you must also use lowercase letters for the closing tag, as follows:

```
<color>Red</color>
```

If you use a different case for an opening and closing tag, they will be treated as completely separate tags, resulting in a document that is not well formed. The following statement, for instance, is incorrect because the case of the closing tag does not match the case of the opening tag:

```
<color>Red</COLOR>
```

For practice, you will introduce a case error into your sample XML document to see the error that displays in your non-validating parser (Internet Explorer).

To introduce a case error into the Books.xml document:

1. Return to the **Books.xml** file in your text editor.

2. Modify the closing **</books>** tag so it is uppercase. Your file should appear as follows:

```
<?xml version="1.0" encoding="iso-8859-1"
standalone="yes"?>
<books>
</BOOKS>
```

3. Save the **Books.xml** file and then open it in Internet Explorer. You should receive an error similar to the error shown in Figure 1-14. As you can see, the BOOKS end tag does not match the books start tag.

4. Return to the Books.xml file in your text editor and change the closing </BOOKS> tag back to lowercase letters, then save the file.

5. Return to the Web browser window that displays the Books.xml file and refresh the window. You can refresh Internet Explorer by clicking the Refresh button. The file should open correctly.

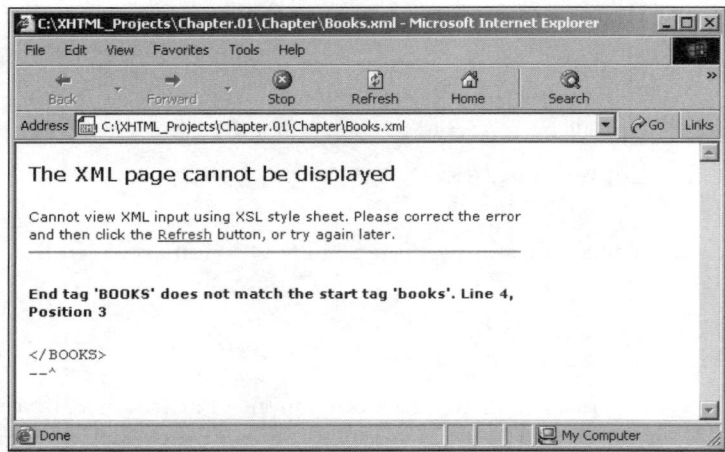

Figure 1-14   Case-sensitivity error in Internet Explorer

6. Close your Web browser.

All XML Elements Must Have Closing Tags

As mentioned earlier, most Web browsers usually ignore errors in an HTML document that is not properly structured and is missing closing tags. One common example is the paragraph element (**<p>**). The **<p>** element should be used to mark a block of text as a single paragraph by enclosing the text within a **<p>...</p>** tag pair, as follows:

```
<p>Sacramento is the capital of California.</p>
```

Many Web authors, however, do not follow this convention and place a **<p>** tag at the end of a block of text to create a new paragraph as follows:

```
Sacramento is the capital of California.<p>
```

One reason it is possible to omit closing tags is that Web browsers usually treat HTML documents as text that contains formatting elements. XML, however, is designed to organize data, not display it. As a result, instead of documents consisting of text that contains elements, as is the case with HTML, XML documents consist of elements that contain text. All elements must have a closing tag or the document will not be well formed. For instance, in the automobile data XML document you saw earlier, each element had a corresponding closing tag. The following version of the document is illegal because there are no corresponding closing tags for the **<make>**, **<model>**, **<year>**, and **<color>** elements:

```
<?xml version="1.0" encoding="iso-8859-1"
     standalone="yes"?>
<auto>
     <make>Ford<model>Mustang
     <year>1967<color>Red
</auto>
```

You may have noticed that the XML declaration does not include a closing tag. This is because the XML declaration is not actually part of the document; it only declares the document as an XML document. For this reason, it does not require a closing tag.

Next, you will add two **<book>** elements to the Books.xml file. Each **<book>** element will contain the title of a book.

To add two **<book>** elements to the Books.xml file:

1. Return to the **Books.xml** file in your text editor.

2. Modify the document as follows to include two **<book>** elements. Be sure to add the elements within the **<books>** root element. For now, do not include the closing **</book>** tag.

```
<?xml version="1.0" encoding="iso-8859-1"
standalone="yes"?>
<books>
        <book>Of Mice and Men
        <book>Diplomacy
</books>
```

3. Save the **Books.xml** file, and then open it in Internet Explorer. You should receive an error similar to the error shown in Figure 1-15. As you can see, the error is raised because Internet Explorer cannot find the ending tag for the **<book>** element.

Figure 1-15   Missing closing tag error raised in Internet Explorer

4. Return to the Books.xml file in your text editor and add the closing **</book>** tags to each of the **<book>** elements, then save the file.

```
<?xml version="1.0" encoding="iso-8859-1"
    standalone="yes"?>
<books>
    <book>Of Mice and Men</book>
    <book>Diplomacy</book>
</books>
```

5. Return to the Web browser window that displays the Books.xml file and refresh the window. Your Web browser should look like Figure 1-16.

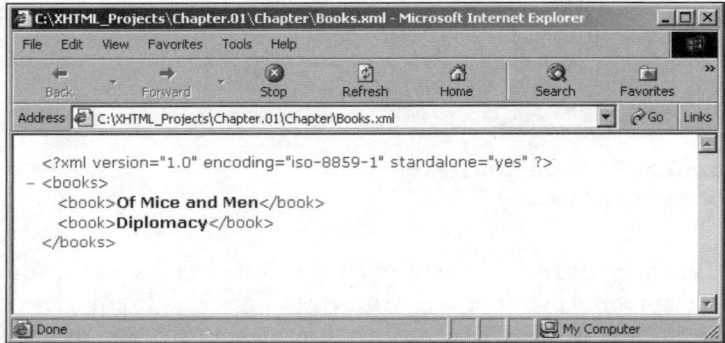

Figure 1-16   Books.xml after adding the <book> elements

6. Close your Web browser.

XML Elements Must Be Properly Nested

Nesting refers to how elements are placed inside other elements. For example, in the following code, the <i> element is nested within the <b> element, while the <b> element is nested within the <p> element.

```
<p><b><i>This paragraph is bold and italicized. </i></b></p>
```

In an HTML document, it makes no difference how the elements are nested. Examine the following HTML statement, which applies bold and italics to the text within a paragraph:

```
<p><b><i>This paragraph is bold and italicized.</b></p></i>
```

In the preceding code, the opening <i> element is nested within the <b> element, which in turn is nested within the <p> element. Notice, however, that the closing </i> element is outside the closing </p> element. This <i> element is the innermost element. In XML, each innermost element must be closed before another element is closed. In the preceding statement, the <b> and <p> elements are closed before the <i> element.

Although the order in which elements are closed makes no difference in HTML, in XML, to be correct the statement must be written as follows:

```
<p><b><i>This paragraph is bold and italicized.</i></b></p>
```

As another example, consider the following version of the automobile data XML document. The code is not well formed because the **<make>** and **<model>** elements are not properly nested.

```
<?xml version="1.0" encoding="iso-8859-1"
    standalone="yes"?>
<auto>
    <make>Ford
            <model>Mustang</make>
     </model>
    <year>1967</year><color>Red</color>
</auto>
```

For the preceding XML code to be well formed, the **<model>** element must be closed before the **<make>** element, as follows:

```
<?xml version="1.0" encoding="iso-8859-1"
    standalone="yes"?>
<auto>
    <make>Ford
            <model>Mustang</model>
     </make>
    <year>1967</year><color>Red</color>
</auto>
```

Next, you will modify the **<book>** elements in the Books.xml file to include nested elements that describe more detailed information about each book.

To modify the Books.xml file to include nested elements:

1. Return to the **Books.xml** file in your text editor.

2. Replace the **<book>** element for *Of Mice and Men* with the following nested elements that contain information on the book's title and author. Notice that the **<title>** and **<author>** elements are nested within the **<book>** element, and that the **<first_name>** and **<last_name>** elements are nested within the **<author>** element.

```
<book>
    <title>Of Mice and Men</title>
    <author>
            <first_name>John</first_name>
            <last_name>Steinbeck</last_name>
    </author>
</book>
```

3. Next, replace the `<book>` element for *Diplomacy* with the following nested elements:

```
<book>
       <title>Diplomacy</title>
       <author>
              <first_name>Henry</first_name>
              <last_name>Kissinger</last_name>
       </author>
</book>
```

4. Save the **Books.xml** file, and then open it in Internet Explorer. Your Web browser should look like Figure 1-17.

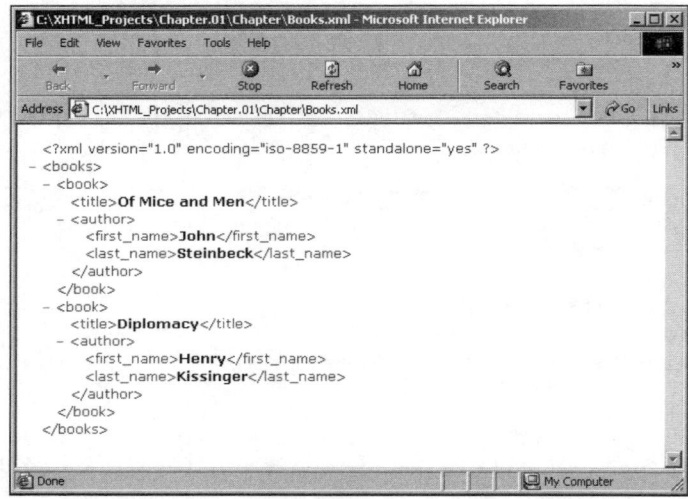

Figure 1-17 Books.xml after adding nested elements

5. Close your Web browser.

Attribute Values Must Appear Within Quotation Marks

The value assigned to an attribute in an HTML document can be either contained in quotation marks or assigned directly to the attribute, provided there are no spaces in the value being assigned. For example, recall that a common HTML attribute is the `src` attribute of the image element (`<img>`). Assign to the `src` attribute the name of an image file that you want to display in your document. The following code shows two `<img>` elements. Even though the first element includes quotation marks around the value assigned to the `src` attribute whereas the second element does not, both statements will function correctly.

```
<img src="dog.gif">Image of a dog</img>
<img src=cat.gif>Image of a cat</img>
```

With XML, you must place quotation marks around the values assigned to an attribute. An example is the `company` attribute of the `<manufacturer>` element you saw earlier in the automobile data XML document. You must include quotation marks around the value assigned to the `company` attribute using a statement similar to `<manufacturer company="General Motors"/>`. Omitting the quotation marks in the statement `<manufacturer company=General Motors/>` results in a document that is not well formed.

> You also cannot include an empty attribute in an element. You must assign a value to an attribute or exclude the attribute from the element. For instance, the statement, `<manufacturer company/>`, is incorrect because no value is being assigned to the `company` attribute.

Next, you will add an attribute named `genre` to each of the `<book>` elements in your example XML document. The `genre` attribute stores a value that describes each book's genre, or literary form.

To add an attribute named `genre` to each of the `<book>` elements:

1. Return to the **Books.xml** file in your text editor.
2. Modify the opening tag for the *Of Mice and Men* `<book>` element so it includes the `genre` attribute, with an assigned value of "fiction":
   `<book genre="fiction">`
3. Modify the opening tag for the *Diplomacy* `<book>` element so it includes the `genre` attribute, with an assigned value of "nonfiction":
   `<book genre="nonfiction">`
4. Save the **Books.xml** file, and then open it in Internet Explorer. Your Web browser should look like Figure 1-18.

Figure 1-18   Books.xml after adding attributes

5. Close your Web browser.

Empty Elements Must Be Closed

Several elements in HTML do not have corresponding ending tags, including the `<hr>` element, which inserts a horizontal rule into the document, and the `<br>` element, which inserts a line break. Elements that do not require an ending tag are called **empty elements** because you cannot use them as a tag pair to enclose text or other elements. You can create an empty element in an XML document by adding a single slash (/) before the tag's closing bracket to close the element. Most often, you use an empty element for an element that does not require content, such as an image. For instance, in the XML document of automobile data, you may create a `<photo>` element with a single attribute that stores the name of an image file. This image file contains a photograph of the automobile. An example of the `<photo>` empty element is shown in the following XML code:

```
<?xml version="1.0" standalone="yes"?>
<auto>
    <photo image_name="mustang.jpg"/>
    <make>Ford</make><model>Mustang</model>
    <year>1967</year><color>Red</color>
</auto>
```

 Remember that the primary purpose of XML is to define and organize data. An empty image element like the one shown in the XML automobile document only provides the name of the associated image file—it does not display it. However, you can display an image from an XML document if you use CSS and XSL.

Next, you will add an empty element named `cover_art` to the **Books.xml** file. This element contains a single attribute that stores the name of an image file containing the cover art for each book.

To add an empty element to the Books XML document:

1. Return to the **Books.xml** file in your text editor.

2. Add a nested empty `cover_art` element to the *Of Mice and Men* `<book>` element, as follows:

```
<book genre="fiction">
    <cover_art filename="mice_and_men.jpg"/>
    <title>Of Mice and Men</title>
    <author>
        <first_name>John</first_name>
        <last_name>Steinbeck</last_name>
    </author>
</book>
```

3. Now add a nested empty `cover_art` element to the *Diplomacy* `<book>` element, as follows:

```
<book genre="nonfiction">
    <cover_art filename="diplomacy.jpg"/>
    <title>Diplomacy</title>
    <author>
        <first_name>Henry</first_name>
        <last_name>Kissinger</last_name>
    </author>
</book>
```

4. Save the **Books.xml** file, and then open it in Internet Explorer. Your Web browser should look like Figure 1-19.

Figure 1-19   Books.xml after adding empty elements

5. Close your Web browser.

COMBINING **XML** AND **HTML**

In this chapter, you spent time studying how XML is used for defining data. Although XML was designed primarily to define data, this does not mean that you cannot use it to create Web pages. You can create formatted Web pages using XML and **Extensible Stylesheet Language**, or **XSL**, which is a specification for formatting XML in a Web browser.

With the growing need to create Web pages that can be easily displayed in *all* user agents, it is clear that an alternative to HTML is needed. For a number of reasons, however, it isn't clear that XML and XSL provide an adequate alternative to HTML at this time. First, getting Web page authors and developers to completely abandon existing HTML techniques is asking a lot. Second, learning XML and XSL is more difficult than learning HTML. Finally, many older browsers simply do not support XML.

 XSL is covered in the comprehensive edition of this book.

To make the transition to XML-based Web pages easier, the W3C combined XML and HTML to create Extensible Hypertext Markup Language. **Extensible Hypertext Markup Language**, or **XHTML**, is a combination of XML and HTML that is used to author Web pages. XHTML is almost identical to HTML, except that it uses strict XML syntax to describe the parts of a document. XHTML is actually considered to be an XML application because it is written in XML, and the XHTML language must adhere to the same requirements as XML. One of XHTML's chief advantages is that XHTML documents are backward-compatible with older browsers, provided you follow several simple rules that you will study in Chapter 2.

Chapter Summary

- ❏ The Internet is a vast network that connects computers all over the world.

- ❏ Tim Berners-Lee created the technology used for the World Wide Web (WWW) at the European Laboratory for Particle Physics (CERN) in Geneva, Switzerland, as a way to easily access cross-referenced documents that existed on the CERN computer network.

- ❏ A hypertext link, or hyperlink, contains a reference to a specific Web page that you can click to quickly open that Web page.

- ❏ A document on the Web is called a Web page and is identified by a unique address called the Uniform Resource Locator, or URL.

- ❏ A Web site refers to the location on the Internet of the Web pages and related files (such as graphic files) that belong to a company, organization, or individual.

- ❏ You display a Web page on your computer screen using a program called a Web browser.

- ❏ A home page is the primary Web page for any given Web site.

- ❏ Hypertext Markup Language, or HTML, is a simple language used to create the Web pages that appear on the World Wide Web.

- ❏ Web pages are commonly referred to as HTML pages or documents.

1

- HTML documents are text documents that contain formatting instructions, called tags, and the text that is to be displayed on a Web page.
- The opening and closing `<html>...</html>` tags are required and contain all the text and other tags that make up the HTML document.
- The `<head>` tag pair and the tags it contains are referred to as the document head.
- The `<body>` tag pair and the text and tags it contains are referred to as the document body.
- Parsing or rendering is a Web browser's process of assembling and formatting an HTML document.
- Because HTML documents are text files, you can create them in any text editor, such as Notepad or WordPad, or any word-processing application capable of creating simple text files.
- Web page design, or Web design, refers to the visual design and creation of the documents that appear on the World Wide Web.
- Web page authoring refers to the creation and assembly of the tags and attributes that make up a Web page.
- User agents are devices capable of retrieving and processing HTML and XHTML documents.
- Languages based on SGML use a Document Type Definition, or DTD, to define the tags and attributes that you can use in a document.
- When a document conforms to an associated DTD, it is said to be valid.
- When a document does not conform to an associated DTD, it is said to be invalid.
- Extensible Markup Language, or XML, is used for creating Web pages and for defining and transmitting data between applications.
- In XML you refer to a tag pair and the data it contains as an element.
- The data contained within an element's opening and closing tags is referred to as its content.
- XML documents should begin with an XML declaration, which specifies the version of XML being used.
- When a document adheres to XML's syntax rules, it is said to be well formed.
- You use a program called a parser to check whether an XML document is well formed.
- User agents expect XML data to be structured according to specific rules, which allows the user agent to read data quickly without having to decipher the data structure.

❑ A root element contains all the other elements in a document.

❑ Nesting refers to how elements are placed inside other elements.

❑ Elements that do not require a closing tag are called empty elements.

❑ Extensible Hypertext Markup Language, or XHTML, is a combination of XML and HTML that is used to author Web pages.

REVIEW QUESTIONS

1. The Internet was first developed by _____.
   a. the Department of Defense
   b. the Department of Agriculture
   c. the Federal Bureau of Investigation
   d. NASA

2. The Internet was originally designed as a communications network capable of surviving a nuclear attack. True or False?

3. Why was the World Wide Web first developed?

4. URL stands for _____.
   a. Unique Resource List
   b. Unnamed Reference Locator
   c. Uniform Resource List
   d. Uniform Resource Locator

5. What is a Web site?

6. A URL is also referred to as a Web address. True or False?

7. HTML is based on _____.
   a. XML
   b. XHTML
   c. SGML
   d. UML

8. HTML 4.01 will be the last version of the HTML language. True or False?

9. A Web browser's process of assembling and formatting an HTML document is called _____. (Choose all that apply.)
   a. parsing
   b. painting
   c. rendering
   d. compiling

1

10. What does the term *Web site programming* refer to?

11. When is it okay to copy another Web author's work and pass it off as your own?

12. Your goal should be to create Web pages that are compatible with as many browser types and versions and possible. True or False?

13. What happens when a browser does not support a specific HTML tag?

    a. The browser attempts to render the tag anyway.

    b. The browser ignores the tag.

    c. The browser contacts the W3C for the correct definition of the tag.

    d. The browser displays an error message.

14. With which tag pair should all HTML documents begin and end?

    a. `<body>...</body>`

    b. `<head>...</head>`

    c. `<html>...</html>`

    d. `<xml>...</xml>`

15. Even though an HTML document may omit the `<html>...</html>`, `<head>...</head>`, and `<body>...</body>` tag pairs, the code will render properly in a browser. True or False?

16. DTD stands for _____.

    a. Data Transfer Display

    b. Digital Technology Definition

    c. Document Test Descriptor

    d. Document Type Definition

17. Which of the following devices can be user agents? (Choose all that apply.)

    a. Mobile phones

    b. Personal digital assistants (PDAs)

    c. Internet Explorer

    d. Netscape

18. What is the correct syntax for an XML declaration that does not require a DTD in order to be rendered correctly?

    a. `<xml version="1.0" standalone="yes">`

    b. `<xml version="1.0" standalone="no">`

    c. `<?xml version="1.0" standalone="yes"?>`

    d. `<?xml version="1.0" standalone="no"?>`

19. Many Web browsers have the capability to act as non-validating parsers for XML documents. True or False?

20. Which of the following syntax rules are required in order for an XML document to be well formed? (Choose all that apply.)

   a. An XML document should not include a root element.

   b. Empty elements must not be closed.

   c. All tags must have a closing tag.

   d. Elements must be properly nested.

21. A _____ element contains other elements on a page.

   a. master

   b. source

   c. base

   d. root

22. Which of the following statements is considered to be well formed?

   a. `<name>Rajesh Singh</name>`

   b. `<name>Rajesh Singh</NAME>`

   c. `<NAME>Rajesh Singh</name>`

   d. `<Name>Rajesh Singh</name>`

23. Which of the following is the correct way to write a well-formed element with an attribute?

   a. `<organization name=General Motors>`

   b. `<organization name="General Motors">`

   c. `<organization "name=General Motors">`

   d. `<"organization name=General Motors">`

24. How do you close the empty element named `<account_number>` in an XML document?

   a. <account_number\>

   b.

   c. </account_number>

   d. <\account_number>

25. XML cannot be used to create Web pages. True or False?

HANDS-ON PROJECTS

Project 1-1

In this exercise, you create an XML document that contains the name and price per pound of different types of coffee beans.

1. Create a new document in your text editor and type the opening XML declaration. Be sure to use all three attributes of the XML declaration.

2. Type the opening and closing tags for a root element named `<coffee_beans>`.

3. Within the `<coffee_beans>` element, create at least three `<coffee>` elements. Each `<coffee>` element should contain nested `<name>` and `<price>` elements. For the content of the `<name>` elements, enter the names of different types of coffees, such as Kona and Columbia. For the content of the `<price>` element, enter the current price per pound for each type of coffee.

4. Save the document as **Coffee.xml** in the Chapter.01\Projects folder.

5. Open the **Coffee.xml** document in Internet Explorer. If you receive any parsing errors, fix them and reopen the document.

Project 1-2

In this exercise, you identify and fix the problems in an XML document that is not well formed.

1. Create a document in your text editor and type the following XML document, but identify and fix each of the errors that prevent it from being well formed.

```
<?xml version="1.0" standalone="yes"?>
<travel>
    <transportation mode=airplane>
        <destination>Paris</destination>
        <depart_date>June 1</depart_date>
        <carrier company=United>
    <transportation mode=train>
        <destination>New Orleans</destination>
        <depart_date>April 15</depart_date>
        <railroad company=Amtrak>
    <transportation mode=automobile>
        <destination>Vancouver</destination>
        <depart_date>August 3</depart_date>
</travel>
```

2. Save the document as **Travel.xml** in the Chapter.01\Projects folder.

3. Open the **Travel.xml** document in Internet Explorer. If you receive any parsing errors, fix them and reopen the document.

Project 1-3

In this exercise, you create an XML document that contains airline flight information.

1. Create a new document in your text editor and type the opening XML declaration. Be sure to use all three attributes of the XML declaration.
2. Create a root element named `<airlines>`.
3. Within the `<airlines>` root element, create three nested `<carrier>` elements for three different airlines. Each `<carrier>` element should include a name attribute that stores the name of the airline. Use the names of whatever airline companies you like.
4. Within each `<carrier>` element, nest at least two `<flight>` elements that contain the following elements: `<departure_city>`, `<destination_city>`, `<flight_number>`, and `<departure_time>`. Use whatever information you like for the content of each element.
5. Save the document as **Airlines.xml** in the Chapter.01\Projects folder.
6. Open the **Airlines.xml** document in Internet Explorer. If you receive any parsing errors, fix them and reopen the document.

Project 1-4

In this exercise, you create an XML document that contains grading information for an elementary school class.

1. Create a new document in your text editor and type the opening XML declaration. Be sure to use all three attributes of the XML declaration.
2. Create a root element named `<report_cards>`.
3. Within the `<report_cards>` root element, create at least three `<student>` elements.
4. Within each `<student>` element, create the following nested elements. Be sure to nest the `<history_grade>`, `<math_grade>`, `<geography_grade>`, and `<english_grade>` elements within the `<grades>` element. Make up some fictitious names and grades for at least three students.

```
<name>content</name>
<grades>
    <history_grade>content</history_grade>
    <math_grade>content</math_grade>
    <geography_grade>content</geography_grade>
    <english_grade>content</english_grade>
</grades>
```

5. Save the document as **ReportCards.xml** in the Chapter.01\Projects folder.
6. Open the **ReportCards.xml** document in Internet Explorer. If you receive any parsing errors, fix them and then reopen the document.

1

CASE PROJECTS

In the following projects, be sure that each XML document includes an XML declaration and is well formed.

Project 1-1

Create an XML document that contains elements you would find in a business letter. Use a root element named `<business_letter>`. Include elements such as company name, logo, company address, subject, salutation, and body. Nest the recipient's name, title, company name, and address within another element named `<to>`. Also, nest the sender's name and title within another element named `<from>`. Save the document as **Letter.xml** in the Chapter.01\Projects folder.

Project 1-2

Create an XML version of your resume. Use a root element named `<resume>`. Include elements such as your name, contact information, and objective. Create an `<employment>` element that includes nested `<employer>` elements for each of your former employers. Each `<employer>` element should include nested elements for the following data: employer name, employer location, position held, employment dates, and responsibilities. Also, create an `<education>` element that includes nested `<school>` elements for your educational experience. Each `<school>` element should include the following nested elements: name of the school, dates attended, and degree obtained. Create any other elements that you deem appropriate, such as `<references>` or `<special_skills>`. Save the document as **Resume.xml** in the Chapter.01\Projects folder.

Project 1-3

Create an XML document that outlines the table of contents for a software reference manual. You can write the table of contents based on any software with which you are proficient. Use a root element named `<reference>`. Within the `<reference>` root element, create a `<manual>` element that contains the name of the manual along with an `<author>` element that contains the author name. Also include elements named `<chapter>` for each chapter of the manual. The `<chapter>` element should include a number attribute that is assigned the chapter number. Within each `<chapter>` element, create an empty `<name>` element that includes a `title` attribute that is assigned the chapter title. Also within each `<chapter>` element create elements for a chapter summary, and for the names of the chapter's major sections. Save the document as **TOC.xml** in the Chapter.01\Projects folder.

2

BUILDING DOCUMENT STRUCTURE

In this chapter, you will:

♦ Learn how to create Extensible Hypertext Markup Language (XHTML) documents
♦ Work with XHTML Document Type Definitions (DTDs)
♦ Study XHTML elements and attributes
♦ Learn about required XHTML elements
♦ Study basic XHTML elements

You use XHTML to define well-formed Web pages, just like the well-formed Extensible Markup Language (XML) documents you created in Chapter 1. This standard is what truly separates XHTML from Hypertext Markup Language (HTML). Writing well-formed XHTML documents prevents you from authoring the sloppy Web pages that are possible with HTML, and allows you to separate a document's content from the way in which it appears in a user agent. To be well formed, an XHTML document must adhere to the same syntax rules as an XML document. However, as you learned in Chapter 1, Web browsers do little to enforce the structure of HTML documents. If most Web browsers simply ignore structural problems on a Web page, how do you know that your XHTML documents are well formed? The answer is to validate your documents against an XHTML DTD.

In order to learn how to build structured documents that are well formed, you study the XHTML DTDs and learn how to validate your Web pages against them. You also study basic structural elements that you use on almost every Web page you build. Although you already learned some of the basic structural elements, such as the <head> and <body> elements, in Chapter 1, in this chapter you study them in greater detail. As you work through this chapter, remember that the goal of XHTML is to write Web pages that are well formed and to separate a document's content from the way in which it appears in a user agent.

CREATING XHTML DOCUMENTS

XHTML version 1.0 was introduced in 2000. It provides a consistent standard for creating Web pages that can function on different user agents, including mobile phones and Personal Digital Assistants (PDAs). This is accomplished though the use of three DTDs: Transitional, Frameset, and Strict. (You learn more about each of these DTDs in the next section.) Recall from Chapter 1 that a DTD defines the elements and attributes that you can use in a document. By writing your Web pages so that they use only the elements and attributes that are defined in one of the XHTML DTDs, you can ensure that your document is well formed.

Even though the XHTML DTDs are an improvement over HTML, they may still be too large for many types of user agents. In fact, many of the elements found in XHTML 1.0, such as graphics, tables, and frames, may not be useable on many user agents, such as PDAs or mobile phones. To display XHTML pages, however, all user agents need to allocate enough space and processing power for the XHTML DTDs, even though they may not support or use many of the elements in the XHTML DTDs. To address these issues, the specifications for XHTML version 1.1 were released in 2001. XHTML 1.1 introduces the concept of modularization. In XHTML 1.1, various features of the language, such as graphics, tables, and frames, are broken into separate modules. This modularization allows Web page authors to write for their Web pages a DTD that utilizes only the modules they need and that are supported on a target user agent. Modularization has enabled the XHTML to become highly adaptable to the many types of user agents that are currently in use or in development.

XHTML 1.1 is covered in the comprehensive edition of this book in the chapter titled *XHTML Modularization*.

One big difference between XML and XHTML is that whereas XML does not contain any predefined elements, XHTML contains almost all the elements that are available in HTML. However, because XHTML is based on XML, you need to follow the XML rules for creating well-formed documents.

Be sure to remember that XHTML is case sensitive and uses lowercase letters for each element name.

Backward Compatibility

To be backward compatible with older browsers, you save XHTML documents with an extension of .html or .htm, just like HTML documents. You must also follow several rules to ensure that the code within your XHTML documents is also backward compatible. Recall that XML requires that empty elements include a slash before the closing bracket to close the element. This rule also applies to XHTML. However, older browsers that do not support XML ignore the element when they see the slash immediately following the element name in an empty element. You can ensure that older browsers are able to read empty elements in a well-formed XHTML document by adding a space between the element name and the closing slash. Older browsers simply ignore the space and the slash and render the element normally. Browsers that support XHTML recognize the slash as closing the empty element. For instance, to properly close the horizontal rule (<hr>) empty element and ensure that it is backward compatible with older browsers, you use the statement <hr />. Be sure to include the space and slash for all empty elements, including the often-used <br> and <img> elements.

The <!DOCTYPE> Declaration

An XHTML document must include a <!DOCTYPE> declaration and the <html>, <head>, and <body> elements. The **<!DOCTYPE> declaration** states the XHTML version of the document and the XHTML DTD (Transitional, Frameset, or Strict) with which the document complies. The syntax for the <!DOCTYPE> declaration is <!DOCTYPE html *type "public identifier" "URL"*>. The html attribute of the <!DOCTYPE> declaration identifies the root element of the document; for XHTML documents this attribute value should always be html. You replace the *type* attribute of the <!DOCTYPE> declaration with PUBLIC or SYSTEM. You use a type of PUBLIC if the DTD is available on the Web or SYSTEM if the DTD is available on the local computer. If you use a type of PUBLIC, then you must also include the public identifier attribute within quotation marks. A public identifier is a text string that is used to identify a DTD on the Web. For instance, the public identifier for one of the XHTML DTDs is "-//W3C//DTD XHTML 1.0 Strict//EN". The final attribute in the <!DOCTYPE> declaration is the Universal Resource Locator (URL) of the DTD. If you use a <!DOCTYPE> declaration of PUBLIC, then the user agent first attempts to use the DTD identified by the public identifier. The public identifiers for XHTML 1.0 are built into current Web browsers and other user agents. However, if the user agent does not recognize the public identifier, it attempts to locate the DTD using the URL.

If an XHTML document is missing the <!DOCTYPE> declaration, it automatically reverts to a standard HTML document.

Figure 2-1 shows an example of a simple XHTML document.

```
<!DOCTYPE html PUBLIC "-//W3C//DTD XHTML 1.0 Strict//EN"
"http://www.w3.org/TR/xhtml1/DTD/xhtml1-strict.dtd">
<html>
<head>
<title>Basic XHTML Document</title>
</head>
<body>
<p>Llamas are from South America.</p>
</body>
</html>
```

Figure 2-1   Basic XHTML document

XHTML DTDs

As you learned earlier, the World Wide Web Consortium (W3C) created XHTML to make the transition to XML-based Web pages easier. To facilitate the transition, the W3C provided three types of XHTML DTDs: Transitional, Frameset, and Strict.

Transitional DTD

One of the goals of XHTML is to separate the way a document is structured from the way it is displayed. To accomplish this, several commonly used HTML formatting and display elements and attributes have been deprecated in XHTML 1.0. Elements and attributes that are considered to be obsolete and that will eventually be eliminated are said to be **deprecated**. The **Transitional DTD** allows you to continue using deprecated elements along with the well-formed document requirements of XML. Table 2-1 lists the elements that are deprecated in XHTML 1.0, but that are still available in the Transitional DTD.

Table 2-1   HTML elements that are deprecated in XHTML 1.0

Element	Description
<applet>	Executes Java applets
<basefont>	Specifies the base font size
<center>	Centers text
<dir>	Defines a directory list
<font>	Specifies a font name, size, and color
<isindex>	Creates automatic document indexing forms
<menu>	Defines a menu list
<s> or <strike>	Formats strikethrough text
<u>	Formats underlined text

The `<basefont>`, `<center>`, `<font>`, `<s>`, `<strike>`, and `<u>` elements are deprecated in favor of Cascading Style Sheets (CSS). The `<applet>` element is deprecated in favor of the `<object>` element; the `<dir>` and `<menu>` elements are deprecated in favor of unordered lists; and the `<isindex>` element is deprecated in favor of the `<input>` element. In later chapters, you will study all of the elements that replace the deprecated elements.

The `<!DOCTYPE>` declaration for the Transitional DTD is as follows:

```
<!DOCTYPE html PUBLIC
"-//W3C//DTD XHTML 1.0 Transitional//EN"
"http://www.w3.org/TR/xhtml1/DTD/xhtml1-transitional.dtd">
```

You should use the Transitional DTD only if you need to create Web pages that use the deprecated elements listed in Table 2-1.

Next, you create a document containing a paragraph from the draft of a fiction novel. You use the Transitional DTD along with the deprecated `<s>` and `<u>` elements. You use the `<s>` element to strike out portions of the paragraph that will be deleted and the `<u>` element to underline new text that will be inserted.

To create a document that uses the Transitional DTD:

1. Start your text editor and create a new document.

2. Type the opening `<!DOCTYPE>` declaration that uses the Transitional DTD, as follows:

```
<!DOCTYPE html PUBLIC "-//W3C//DTD XHTML 1.0 Transitional//EN"
"http://www.w3.org/TR/xhtml1/DTD/xhtml1-transitional.dtd">
```

3. Type the `<html>` element, as follows. Remember that all Web pages must begin and end with the `<html>`...`</html>` tag pair.

```
<html>
</html>
```

4. Within the `<html>` element, add the following `<head>` and `<title>` elements to the document. The title appears in the Web browser's title bar. Remember that the `<head>` element must include a `<title>` element. The `<title>` element cannot exist outside the `<head>` element.

```
<head>
<title>Great American Novel</title>
</head>
```

5. Next, add the following `<body>` element above the closing `</html>` tag:

```
<body>
</body>
```

6. Type the following elements and text between the `<body>`...`</body>` tag pair to create the body of the document.

```
<p>It was a <s>dark and stormy night</s> <u>bright and
sunny day</u>. <s>Lightning streaked the sky, followed by
an angry explosion of thunder.</s> <u>High, soft clouds
accented the sky and a soft wind gently swayed the
trees.</u></p>
```

7. Save the file as **Novel.html** in the Chapter.02\Chapter folder. Be sure your document is saved with an extension of .html.

8. Open the **Novel.html** file in your Web browser. Figure 2-2 displays the Novel.html file as it appears in Internet Explorer.

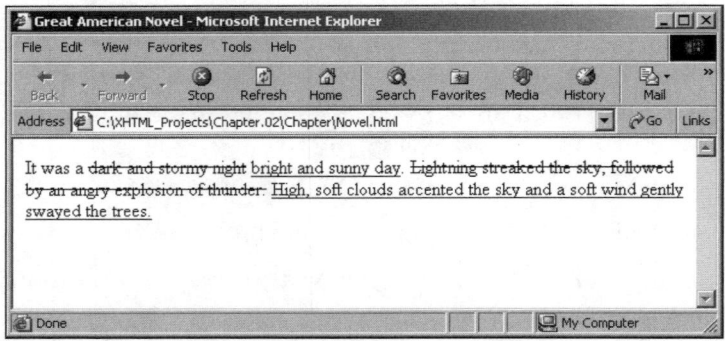

Figure 2-2   Novel.html in Internet Explorer

9. Close your Web browser window.

Frameset DTD

The **Frameset DTD** is identical to the Transitional DTD, except that it includes the `<frameset>` and `<frame>` elements, which allow you to split the browser window into two or more frames, which are independent, scrollable portions of a Web browser window, with each frame capable of displaying a separate URL. The `<!DOCTYPE>` declaration for the Frameset DTD is as follows:

```
<!DOCTYPE html PUBLIC
"-//W3C//DTD XHTML 1.0 Frameset//EN"
"http://www.w3.org/TR/xhtml1/DTD/xhtml1-frameset.dtd">
```

Although you will work with frameset documents in Chapter 5, understand that they have been deprecated in favor of tables. Even though frames have been deprecated, frameset documents are still widely used and you may find them useful. Additionally, you should be able to recognize and work with frameset documents if you need to modify an existing Web page that was created with frames.

Strict DTD

The **Strict DTD** eliminates the elements that were deprecated in the Transitional DTD and Frameset DTD. The <!DOCTYPE> declaration for the Strict DTD is as follows:

```
<!DOCTYPE html PUBLIC
"-//W3C//DTD XHTML 1.0 Strict//EN"
"http://www.w3.org/TR/xhtml1/DTD/xhtml1-strict.dtd">
```

Throughout this book, you primarily use the Strict DTD to learn about the most current Web page authoring techniques.

Validating Web Pages

When you open an XHTML document in a Web browser, the Web browser does not parse the code as it would an XML document. Instead, if the XHTML document is not well formed, the browser simply ignores the errors, as it would with an HTML document, and renders the Web page. To ensure that an XHTML document is well formed and that its elements are valid, you need to use a **validating parser**. **Validation** checks that your XHTML document is well formed, and that the elements in your document are correctly written according to the element definitions in an associated DTD. You are not actually required to validate XHTML documents. If you do not validate an XHTML document and it contains errors, most Web browsers will probably treat it as an HTML document, ignore the errors, and render the page anyway. However, validation can help you spot errors in your code. Even the most experienced Web authors frequently introduce typos or some other error into XHTML documents that prevent the document from being well formed and valid. Remember that if your XHTML document is not well formed, user agents such as mobile phones and PDAs may have trouble rendering it.

Many XHTML validating parsers exist. One of the best available is the W3C MarkUp Validation Service, a free service that validates both HTML and XHTML. The W3C MarkUp Validation Service is located at *http://validator.w3.org*. The main Web page for the service allows you to validate a Web page by entering its Uniform Resource Identifier (URI) and selecting various options in the form shown in Figure 2-3.

 The form shown in Figure 2-3 is located at the bottom of the W3C MarkUp Validation Service Web page, so you may need to scroll down to see it.

To validate a Web page, you enter a URI in the Address box of the W3C MarkUp Validation Service Web page. Once you validate a document, the W3C MarkUp Validation Service displays a results page that lists warnings or errors found in the document.

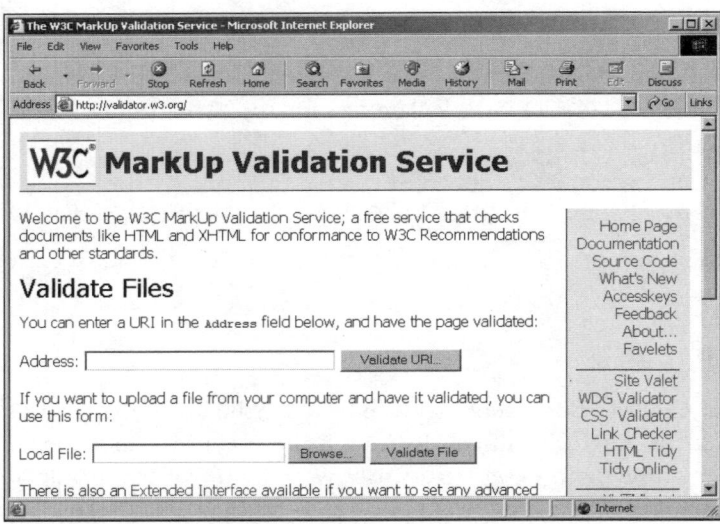

Figure 2-3   W3C Markup Validation Service

The W3C MarkUp Validation Service also includes a separate page that you can use to validate XHTML files by uploading them from your computer. You can open the upload files page of the W3C MarkUp Validation Service by clicking the upload files link at the bottom of the main page or by entering the following URL in your browser's Address box: *http://validator.w3.org/file-upload.html*. Figure 2-4 shows an example of the upload page of the W3C MarkUp Validation Service.

Figure 2-4   Upload page of the W3C Markup Validation Service

Another tool that you can use to validate Web pages is HTML Tidy, a popular stand-alone program that you can download to your computer. In addition to validating HTML and XHTML documents, HTML Tidy also assists in converting HTML documents to XHTML. HTML Tidy is available for numerous platforms and can be downloaded at *http://tidy.sourceforge.net/*.

Next, you validate the Novel.html file using the W3C MarkUp Validation Service.

To validate the Novel.html file:

1. Start your Web browser and enter the URL for the W3C MarkUp Validation Service upload page in the Address box: **http://validator.w3.org/ file-upload.html**.

2. Click the **Browse** button to display the Choose file dialog box.

3. In the Choose file dialog box, navigate to the **Novel.html** file. (You should have stored this file in C:\XHTML_Projects\Chapter.02\Chapter.) Once you locate the file, double-click it or select it and click the **Open** button. The drive, folder path, and filename should appear in the File text box on the upload page.

4. Select **iso-8859-1** in the Encoding box, which specifies that the document uses the character set that is used in English and many Western languages. (You will learn more about how to specify a document's character set in Chapter 3.)

5. Leave the display option check boxes cleared and click the **Validate this file** button. The W3C MarkUp Validation Service validates the document and returns the results displayed in Figure 2-5.

Figure 2-5 Validation results for the Novel.html file

6. Close your Web browser window.

XHTML ELEMENTS AND ATTRIBUTES

In Chapter 1 you learned that in XML you refer to a tag pair and the data it contains as an element. All elements must have an opening tag and a closing tag or the document is not well formed. The data contained within an element's opening and closing tags is referred to as its content. You must close empty elements by adding a space and a slash before the tag's closing bracket. You can think of elements as the basic building blocks of all XHTML pages.

Block-Level and Inline Elements

Two basic types of elements can appear within a document's `<body>` element: block-level and inline. **Block-level elements** are elements that give a Web page its structure. Most Web browsers render block-level elements so they appear on their own line. Block-level elements can contain other block-level elements or inline elements. The `<p>` element and heading elements (`<h1>`, `<h2>`, and so on) are examples of common block-level elements. Table 2-2 lists the block-level elements available in the Strict DTD.

Table 2-2   Block-level elements available in the strict DTD

Element	Description
`<address>`	Address
`<blockquote>`	Block quotation
`<del>`	Deleted text
`<div>`	Generic block-level container
`<dl>`	Definition list
`<fieldset>`	Form control group
`<form>`	Interactive form
`<h1> - <h6>`	Heading elements
`<hr>`	Horizontal rule
`<ins>`	Inserted text
`<noscript>`	Alternate script content
`<ol>`	Ordered list
`<p>`	Paragraph
`<pre>`	Preformatted text
`<table>`	Table
`<ul>`	Unordered list

As you progress through this book, you work with each of the block-level elements listed in Table 2-2.

Inline, or **text–level**, **elements** describe the text that appears on a Web page. Unlike block-level elements, inline elements do not appear on their own lines; they appear within the line of the block-level element that contains them. Examples of inline elements include the **<b>** (bold) and **
** (line break) elements. You study inline elements later in this chapter.

According to the Strict DTD, inline elements must be placed inside a block-level element. If you do not place an inline element inside a block-level element, your document is not well formed. Additionally, any text displayed by your document must also be placed within a block-level element. For instance, if you attempt to validate against the Strict DTD a document that contains the following line, the document will be declared invalid because the text, **<b>** element, and **
** element are not contained within a block-level element:

```
This line contains <b>bold</b> text and <br />
a line break.
```

In order for the preceding code to be well formed, it must be contained within a block-level element, such as the **<p>** element, as follows:

```
<p>This line contains <b>bold</b> text and <br />
a line break.</p>
```

Next, you start creating the home page for the Central Valley Farmers' Market Web site. You create the XHTML document using the Strict DTD. The home page contains information about the farmers' market including contact information, hours of operation, and a featured vendors list. You work on the Central Valley Farmers' Market Web site throughout this chapter in order to learn how to author well-formed XHTML documents.

To start creating the home page for the Central Valley Farmers' Market Web site:

1. Create a new document in your text editor and type the opening **<!DOCTYPE>** declaration that uses the Strict DTD, as follows:

```
<!DOCTYPE html PUBLIC "-//W3C//DTD XHTML 1.0 Strict//EN"
"http://www.w3.org/TR/xhtml1/DTD/xhtml1-strict.dtd">
```

2. Type the **<html>** element, as follows.

```
<html>
</html>
```

3. Within the **<html>** element, add the following **<head>** and **<title>** elements to the document.

```
<head>
<title>Central Valley Farmers' Market Web</title>
</head>
```

4. Next, add the following document **<body>** element within the **<html>** element:

```
<body>
</body>
```

5. Add the following elements to the document body (between the **<body>...</body>** tags). Notice that the text and inline **<b>** element are contained within a block-level **<p>** element.

```
<p>The <b>Central Valley Farmers' Market</b> offers plenty
of fresh picked fruits, vegetables, herbs, and flowers.
Local artisans bring wonderful hand-made arts and crafts.
You will also find lots of baked goods, jams, honey,
cheeses, and other products.</p>
```

6. Save the file as **CentralValley.html** in the Chapter.02\Chapter folder.

7. Open the **CentralValley.html** file in your Web browser. Figure 2-6 displays the CentralValley.html file as it appears in Internet Explorer.

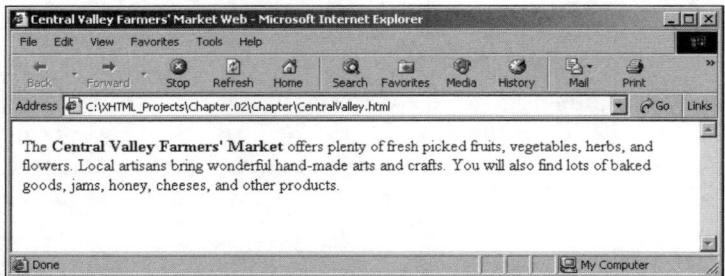

Figure 2-6   The CentralValley.html file in Internet Explorer

8. Close the Web browser window.

Standard Attributes

As you also learned in Chapter 1, you use various parameters, called attributes, to configure many elements. You use an equal sign to assign a value to an attribute, and the attribute must be enclosed within quotation marks. You place attributes before the closing bracket of the starting tag, and you separate them from the tag name or other attributes with a space. Many XHTML attributes are unique to a specific element or can only be used with certain types of elements. For instance, the **src** attribute of the **<img>** element is used for specifying the URL of an image file you want to display. The **src** attribute is available only for two other elements: **<input>** and **<script>**. However, XHTML also includes several **standard**, or **common**, **attributes** that are available to almost every element, with a few exceptions (see the Caution following Table 2-3). The standard XHTML attributes are listed in Table 2-3.

Table 2-3   Standard attributes

Attribute	Description
class	Identifies various elements as part of the same group
dir	Specifies the direction of text
id	Uniquely identifies an individual element in a document
lang / xml:lang	Specifies the language in which the contents of an element were originally written
style	Defines the style information for a specific element
title	Provides descriptive text for an element

The class, id, and title attributes are not valid in the <base>, <head>, <html>, <meta>, <param>, <script>, <style>, and <title> elements; the dir, lang, and xml:lang attributes are not valid in the <base>, <br>, <frame>, <frameset>, <hr>, <iframe>, <param>, and <script> elements; and the style attribute is not valid in the <html>, <head>, <title>, <meta>, <style>, <script>, <param>, and <base> elements.

You learn how to use the class, id, and style attributes when you study CSS in Chapter 8.

Although English is the primary language of the Web, it is certainly not the only language used. In order to be a considerate resident of the international world of the Web, you should designate the language of your elements using the lang and xml:lang attributes. The lang attribute is used in HTML documents, whereas the xml:lang attribute is used in XML-based documents. Because not all browsers support XML, you should include both the lang and the xml:lang attributes in your elements for backward compatibility. Be aware that both attributes simply state the original language in which an element was written; it is up to a user agent that renders the element to decide what to do with the information.

You assign to the lang and xml:lang attributes a two-letter code that represents a language. For instance, the language code for English is en. Therefore, to assign English as the language for a particular element, you add the attributes lang="en" and xml:lang="en" to the element's opening tag. Table 2-4 lists some other examples of two-letter language codes.

Table 2-4   Examples of two-letter language codes

Code	Language
af	Afrikaans
el	Greek
fr	French
it	Italian
ja	Japanese
sa	Sanskrit
zh	Chinese

 If you assign different language codes to the `lang` and `xml:lang` attributes, the value assigned to the `xml:lang` attribute takes precedence, provided the user agent supports XML documents.

The language code assigned to the `lang` and `xml:lang` attributes can be further defined to specify the language spoken in a particular country by adding a hyphen and a two-letter country code to the language code. For instance, the two-letter country code for the United Kingdom is UK. You specify an element's language as English as it is spoken in the United Kingdom using the attributes `lang="en-UK"`and `xml:lang="en-UK"`. Similarly, the two-letter country code for the United State is US. Therefore, you can specify an element's language as English as it is spoken in the United States using the attributes `lang="en-US"` and `xml:lang="en-US"`.

 The language and country-code values you assign to the `lang` and `xml:lang` attributes are not case sensitive. In other words, you can also assign values of en-us or EN-US to both attributes. However, using lowercase letters for the language code and uppercase letters for the country code is a common convention.

 You can find a complete list of language and country codes in the appendix.

Another consideration when specifying the original language in which an element was written is the direction that the language reads. Although you read most Western languages from left to right, people read many world languages, including Arabic and Hebrew, from right to left. For this reason, you should always include the `dir` attribute along with the `lang` and `xml:lang` attributes. You can assign one of two values to the `dir` attribute: `ltr` (for left to right) and `rtl` (for right to left). For Western languages such as English, you assign the `dir` attribute a value of left to right, as follows: `dir="ltr"`.

Like most other XHTML elements, the `<html>` element can include the `lang`, `xml:lang`, and `dir` attributes. Although not required, it is considered good practice to always include these attributes in the `<html>` element to clearly identify the source language and text direction of the original document. Any elements in your document that are written in languages and text directions other than those specified in the `<html>` element should also include the `lang`, `xml:lang`, and `dir` attributes.

The last standard attribute to consider is the `title` attribute, which provides descriptive text for an element similar to the text that appears in a Web browser's title bar. With newer Web browsers, the value assigned to the `title` attribute appears as a ToolTip when you hold your mouse over the element that includes it.

In the simple XHTML document in Figure 2-7, the `<html>` element identifies the document as being written in English with a direction of left to right. However, the `<p>` element in the body includes the `lang` and `xml:lang` attributes to specify UK English as the element's language, along with the `dir` attribute to specify a text direction of left to right. The `title` attribute in the paragraph includes the American translation of the British phrase contained with the `<p>` element. Figure 2-8 shows how the ToolTip appears in Internet Explorer.

```
<!DOCTYPE html PUBLIC
"-//W3C//DTD XHTML 1.0 Strict//EN"
"http://www.w3.org/TR/xhtml1/DTD/xhtml1-strict.dtd">
<html lang="en" xml:lang = "en" dir="ltr">
<head>
<title>ToolTip</title>
<meta http-equiv="content-type"
     content="text/html; charset=iso-8859-1" />
</head>
<body>
<p title="The American translation of this phrase is 'Mama was
hit by a truck after eating a bag of potato chips for dessert.'"
lang="en-UK" xml:lang = "en-UK" dir="ltr">Mum got run over by a
lorry after eating a packet of crisps for afters.</p>
</body>
</html>
```

Figure 2-7   XHTML document demonstrating the `lang`, `xml:lang`, `dir`, and `title` attributes

Next, you modify the `<html>` element for the CentralValley.html file so it includes the `lang`, `xml:lang`, and `dir` attributes. You specify English as the Web page language and a text direction of left to right. You also add a paragraph containing an Italian phrase to the Central Valley Farmer's Market home page. You include in the `<p>` element the `lang` and `xml:lang` attributes to specify Italian as the element's language. You also add a `dir` attribute that specifies a text direction of left to right along with a `title` attribute that includes the English translation of the Italian phrase.

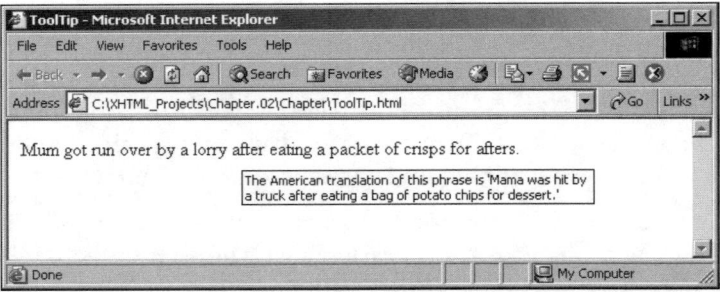

Figure 2-8   Example of a ToolTip created with the title attribute

To add standard attributes to the CentralValley.html file:

1. Return to the **CentralValley.html** file in your text editor.

2. Modify the **<html>** element as follows so it includes **lang**, **xml:lang**, and **dir** attributes:

   ```
   <html lang="en" xml:lang = "en" dir="ltr">
   ```

3. Just above the closing **</body>** tag, add the following **<p>** element that contains the Italian phrase. The **<p>** element also includes the **lang**, **xml:lang**, **dir**, and **title** attributes.

   ```
   <p title="What one puts into a dish, one finds!" lang="it"
   xml:lang = "it" dir="ltr"><i>Quello che ci mette, ci
   trova!</i></p>
   ```

4. Save the **CentralValley.html** file and then open it in your Web browser. Figure 2-9 displays the CentralValley.html file as it appears in Internet Explorer.

5. Close the Web browser window.

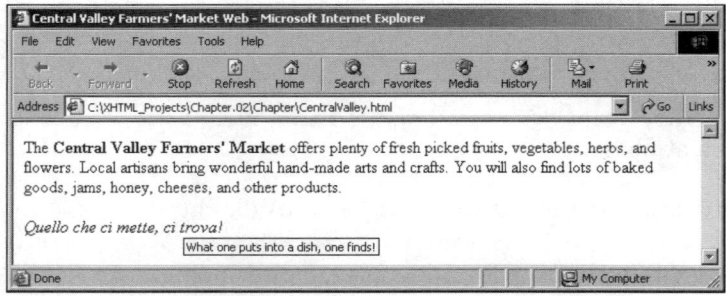

Figure 2-9   The CentralValley.html file after adding the Italian phrase

Boolean Attributes

Several elements in HTML include special attributes called Boolean attributes that do not need a value assigned to them. A **Boolean attribute** specifies one of two values: true or false. The presence of a Boolean attribute in an element's opening tag indicates a value of "true", whereas its absence indicates a value of "false". For example, in Chapter 7 you will learn how to use the empty `<input>` element to create a check box control that can be used on a form. In HTML, you can specify that the check box control is selected, or checked, by default by including the Boolean `checked` attribute within the `<input>` element, as follows:

```
<input type="checked" checked />
```

When a Boolean attribute is not assigned a value, as in the preceding code, it is referred to as having a **minimized form**. However, recall from Chapter 1 that all attribute values must appear within quotation marks. This syntax also means that an attribute must be assigned a value. For this reason, minimized Boolean attributes are illegal in XHTML. You can still use Boolean attributes in XHTML provided you use their full form. You create the **full form** of a Boolean attribute by assigning the name of the attribute itself as the attribute's value. For example, to use the `<input>` element's `checked` Boolean attribute in XHTML, you use the full form of the attribute as follows:

```
<input type="checked" checked="checked" />
```

Remember that to specify a value of false for a Boolean attribute, you simply exclude the attribute from the element. If you do not want a check box control to be selected by default, for instance, you simply exclude the `checked` attribute from the `<input>` element as follows:

```
<input type="checked" />
```

You will work with Boolean attributes in Chapter 7.

REQUIRED ELEMENTS

To better understand how an XHTML document is structured, in this section you study in detail the three elements that must be included in every XHTML document: the `<html>`, `<head>`, and `<body>` elements.

The `<html>` Element

All HTML documents must include an `<html>` element, which tells a Web browser that the instructions between the opening and closing `<html>` tags are to be assembled into an HTML document. The `<html>` element is required and contains all the text and other elements that make up the HTML document. The `<html>` element is also the root element for XHTML documents and is required for XHTML documents to be well formed. To ensure that your XHTML documents are well formed, include the `<html>` element as the root element.

 You may be wondering why XHTML documents do not use a root element of `<xhtml>`. The `<html>` element is necessary for backward compatibility with older browsers that do not recognize the `<!DOCTYPE>` element, which declares the DTD used by an XHTML element.

Next, you learn how to define a default namespace for an XHTML document by using the `xmlns` namespace attribute in the `<html>` element.

The XHTML Namespace

All of the predefined elements in an XHTML document are organized within the **XHTML namespace** that you declare in the `<html>` element. In order to understand what a namespace is, recall from Chapter 1 that you must define your own elements and attributes in an XML document. Because you define your own elements, if an XML document combines multiple XML documents, conflicts among elements can occur. For instance, two separate XML documents may both define an element named `<company>`. If you combine both XML documents into a single document, how does a Web browser know which version of the `<company>` element to use? To address this problem, you identify each `<company>` element by the namespace to which it belongs. A **namespace** organizes the elements and attributes of an XML document into separate groups. You have already used the XML namespace with an attribute. Because the `lang` attribute exists in both HTML and XHTML, you differentiate the two by preceding the XHTML version of the attribute with *xml*, identifying the XML namespace, and a colon using a statement similar to `xml:lang = "en"`.

For elements, you add the namespace and colon before the tag name in both the opening and closing tags. For instance, if one of two versions of the `<company>` element exists in a namespace named *investments*, you would ensure that a Web browser uses the investments namespace version of the element by using a statement similar to the following:

```
<investments:company>AT&T</investments:company>
```

The xml and investments namespaces are examples of **local namespaces** that you specifically apply to individual elements and attributes. In this book, you use local namespaces only when you define a document or element's language using the value `xml:lang`.

A **default namespace** is applied to all of the elements and attributes in an XHTML document, with the exception of elements and attributes to which local namespaces have been applied. With a default namespace, you do not precede element and attribute names with a namespace and colon as you do with local namespaces because the namespace is applied by default to all of the elements and namespaces in the document. You specify a default namespace for an XHTML document by using the **xmlns** namespace attribute in the `<html>` element. Namespaces are identified by a unique URI, which you assign

2

as a value to the `xmlns` attribute. All XHTML documents, regardless of whether they use the Transitional, Frameset, or Strict DTD, use the namespace identified by the following URI: *http://www.w3.org/1999/xhtml*. The following statement shows how to assign the URI to the `xmlns` attribute in the `<html>` element:

```
<html xmlns="http://www.w3.org/1999/xhtml"
lang="en" xml:lang = "en" dir="ltr">
```

According to the W3C XHTML recommendation, the `xmlns` attribute is required in the `<html>` element and must be assigned the *http://www.w3.org/1999/xhtml* URI. To ensure that the elements and attributes in your document are correctly referenced in the XHTML namespace, you should always include in your `<html>` element the `xmlns` attribute, along with the `lang`, `xml:lang`, and `dir` attributes.

 The W3C MarkUp Validation Service seems to ignore the `xmlns` attribute requirement and considers your document to be well formed even if it does not include the `xmlns` attribute.

Next, you modify the `<html>` element for the CentralValley.html file so it includes the `xmlns` attribute:

To modify the `<html>` element for the CentralValley.html file so it includes the `xmlns` attribute:

1. Return to the **CentralValley.html** file in your text editor.

2. Modify the `<html>` element so it includes the `xmlns` attribute, as follows:

```
<html xmlns="http://www.w3.org/1999/xhtml"
lang="en" xml:lang = "en" dir="ltr">
```

3. Save the CentralValley.html file and open it in your Web browser. It should render the same as it did before you modified the `<html>` element.

4. Close the Web browser window.

The Document Head

Web pages consist of two types of information: the content *displayed* by the Web page and information *about* the Web page. The elements within the document body contain the content that the Web page displays. The elements within a document's head section contain information about the Web page itself. The document head does not actually display any information in a browser. Rather, it is a parent element that can contain several child elements. A **parent element** is an element that contains other elements, known as **child elements**. Table 2-5 lists the child elements that can appear in the `<head>` element.

Table 2-5   Child elements of the `<head>` element

Element	Description
`<base>`	Specifies a base URL for all of a document's relative links
`<link>`	Defines the relationship between linked documents
`<meta>`	Defines metadata about a Web page
`<script>`	Contains commands for scripting languages such as JavaScript and VBScript
`<style>`	Defines the style information for a specific element
`<title>`	Contains text that appears in a browser's title bar

Do not confuse the document head with heading elements such as the `<h1>` and `<h2>` elements.

You learn to how to work with most of the child elements of the `<head>` element in later chapters.

The child element of the `<head>` element that you already know is the `<title>` element, which contains text that appears in a browser's title bar. Every Web page in a Web site must have its own title, and you should choose these titles carefully. It may be tempting to use the same title for every Web page in your site. For instance, for the Central Valley Farmers' Market, you may be tempted to use *Central Valley Farmers' Market* as the title for each page on the Web site. Although that title is acceptable for the Web site's home page, good Web authoring practice dictates that you come up with titles that accurately describe each Web page. For the individual Web pages that may make up the farmers' market Web site, better title choices would be text that describes the purpose or content of each page. Some examples of good titles for the farmers' market Web pages might include:

- Central Valley Farmers' Market Produce
- Central Valley Farmers' Market Schedule
- Central Valley Farmers' Market Vendor Directory
- Central Valley Farmers' Market Contact Information

Another important reason to create a good title for each Web page is that the title is the default text that is used when a user adds a bookmark in a Web browser. (In Internet Explorer, bookmarks are called *favorites*.) For instance, Central Valley Farmers' Market is the text that the browser suggests as the description for a bookmark to a page having the title Central Valley Farmers' Market. Although users can change a bookmark description to anything they like, you make users who want to bookmark your Web page a lot happier

2

by using a title that also makes sense as a bookmark name. For instance, if you have a Web site for a shoe repair company, you would not want to use a bare-bones title such as *Shoe Repairs*. Instead, you would want to include the name of the company along with a description of the page, such as *Old World Shoe Repairs Price List*.

In Windows operating systems, the title of a Web page also appears as the title of a taskbar icon when a Web browser window is minimized.

In the <head> element, you can use a single attribute, `profile`, which supplies the URL of a predefined profile containing metadata to use with a document. You will learn about metadata in Chapter 3.

The Document Body

Recall from Chapter 1 that the document body is represented by the **<body>** element and contains other elements that define all of the content a user sees rendered in a browser. Although this book focuses on how to write well-formed XHTML documents, it is worth noting the differences in the use of the **<body>** element in HTML and XHTML.

In Chapter 1 you learned that HTML was designed primarily to display data. With HTML, you can write the content that you want the browser to render, and add to the content any formatting elements you need. XHTML documents consist of elements that contain content, as opposed to HTML documents, which consist of content that contains elements. Understanding this distinction is important because it has a great deal to do with how browsers render content, especially text. In HTML, you can type text within the **<body>** element—or eliminate the **<body>** element entirely—and the browser still renders the text. For instance, the following code is perfectly acceptable for an HTML document:

```
<body>
<b>Llamas</b> are from South America, <br />
<b>kangaroos</b> are from Australia, <br />
and <b>pandas</b> are from China.
</body>
```

In an XHTML document, however, the preceding the code would be invalid because text and inline elements (**<b>** and **
) must be placed within a block element. To make the code valid for XHTML, you must place the text and inline elements inside a block element, such as the **<p> element, as follows:

```
<body>
<p><b>Llamas</b> are from South America, <br />
<b>kangaroos</b> are from Australia, <br />
and <b>pandas</b> are from China.</p>
</body>
```

In HTML, you can also use various attributes in the `<body>` element that affect the appearance of the document, such as the `bgcolor` attribute for setting the background color and the `text` attribute for setting the default color of text. The document formatting attributes of the `<body>` element were deprecated in XHTML Strict and replaced by CSS, although you still see document formatting attributes used frequently on many Web sites. Even though you cannot use document formatting attributes in an XHTML `<body>` element, you can use any of the standard attributes.

BASIC BODY ELEMENTS

In this section, you study the following basic body elements:

- Headings
- Paragraphs and line breaks
- Horizontal rules
- Comments

Basic body elements such as the `<p>` and `<br />` elements are some of the most frequently used elements in Web page authoring. First, let's look at heading elements.

Headings

Heading elements are used for emphasizing a document's headings and subheadings, which helps provide structure by hierarchically organizing a document's content. There are six heading elements, `<h1>` through `<h6>`. The highest level of importance is `<h1>`, and the lowest level of importance is `<h6>`. The following code shows how to create the six heading elements in the document body.

```
<body>
<h1>Heading 1</h1>
<h2>Heading 2</h2>
<h3>Heading 3</h3>
<h4>Heading 4</h4>
<h5>Heading 5</h5>
<h6>Heading 6</h6>
</body>
```

 Each heading element is a block-level element.

Most Web browsers render the heading elements similarly to the output shown in Figure 2-10.

2

Figure 2-10 Heading elements in Internet Explorer

You should choose a heading element based on how the sections of your document fit together, not based on how it appears in a Web browser because different user agents render the output of heading elements differently. Although many Web page authors use heading elements as a formatting tool, the real purpose of heading elements is to provide a way of outlining the content of your document, much as you would create an outline or a table of contents. In an outline format or a table of contents, you should not use a higher-numbered heading unless it is nested in a lower-numbered heading, although this is not a requirement for writing well-formed XHTML documents.

There are some rules of thumb for using headings. Generally, most Web pages should include only a single `<h1>` element as the main heading for a page. You can think of the `<h1>` element as being equivalent to the title of a document. In the same manner that a document should contain only one title, a Web page should contain only one `<h1>` element, which serves as the Web page title. Second-level headings should use the `<h2>` element and additional higher-numbered headings should continue to be nested beneath lower numbered headings. As an example, the following code displays several heading styles that are associated with a Web page that organizes the animal kingdom. The code contains a single `<h1>` element that contains the title of the document, "The Animal Kingdom". Two `<h2>` elements divide the animal kingdom into vertebrates and invertebrates. Within each `<h2>` element, animals are divided in the phylum, or class, of each animal (such as birds or fish) using `<h3>` elements. The order of the heading elements could continue with `<h4>` elements subdividing the animals by subphylum, `<h5>` elements subdividing animals within each subphylum according to species, and so on. Figure 2-11 shows the headings in Internet Explorer.

```
<h1>The Animal Kingdom</h1>
<h2>Vertebrates</h2>
<h3>Fish</h3>
<h3>Birds</h3>
<h3>Mammals</h3>
<h2>Invertebrates</h2>
<h3>Mollusks</h3>
<h3>Anthropods</h3>
<h3>Crustaceans</h3>
```

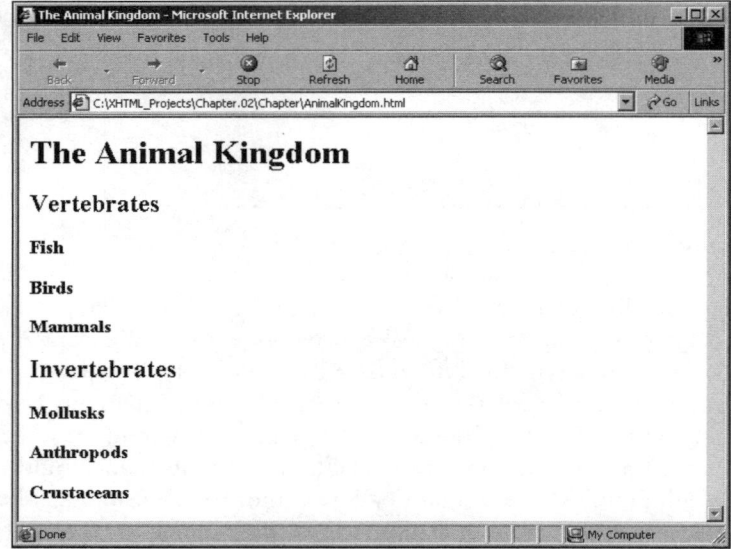

Figure 2-11   Animal kingdom headings

 In practice, few Web page authors make proper use of heading elements as described in the preceding paragraph. However, the proper use of heading elements may grow as well-formed XHTML documents become more popular.

Next, you add heading elements to the CentralValley.html file. The file includes a single <h1> element that contains the Web page title, "Central Valley Farmers' Market". Major sections of the Web page, such as Hours of Operation and a Featured Vendors List, are contained within <h2> elements. The Featured Vendors List <h2> heading also contains <h3> headings containing the name of each featured vendor.

To add heading elements to the CentralValley.html file:

1. Return to the **CentralValley.html** file in your text editor.

2. First, add the following <h1> and <h2> elements as the first elements in the body section, after the opening <body> tag but before the first <p> tag:

```
<h1>Central Valley Farmers' Market</h1>
<h2>About the Market</h2>
```

3. Next, at the end of the body section add the following <h2> element that lists the hours of operation:

```
<h2>Hours of Operation</h2>
<p>The Central Valley Farmers' Market is held every
Tuesday, Thursday, and Saturday from April through October,
then Saturdays only in November until Thanksgiving. The
Market is open from 7 a.m. - 1 p.m. <i>The vendors will be
there rain or shine</i>!</p>
```

4. Finally, to the end of the body section add the following <h2> and <h3> elements that list this week's featured vendors:

```
<h2>Featured Vendor List</h2>
<p>Be sure to visit this week's featured vendors.</p>
<h3>Big Creek Produce</h3>
<p>Offers a diverse selection of produce including
restaurant-quality vegetables and edible flowers. </p>
<h3>Blue Sky Gardens</h3>
<p>Grows a variety of organic vegetables including French
slenderette green beans, spinach, salad greens, squash,
pumpkins, and cherry tomatoes, as well as a vast array of
fresh-cut and dried flowers.</p>
<h3>Maple Ridge Farms</h3>
<p>Specializes in organically grown lettuces, arugula, red
mustard, and other greens.</p>
<h3>Manzi Produce</h3>
<p>Hand picks, hand washes, and hand sorts all of their
products, which include nuts, plants, herbs, perennials,
flowers, wild-gathered items, meat, fruit, and
vegetables.</p>
<h3>Lee Family Farms</h3>
<p>Produces organically grown traditional Asian vegetables
such as bok choy, lemon grass, and hot chili peppers.</p>
```

5. Save the CentralValley.html file and open it in your Web browser. Figure 2-12 shows how some of the new headings appear in Internet Explorer.

Figure 2-12   CentralValley.html file after adding headings

> 6. Close the Web browser window.

Paragraphs and Line Breaks

The paragraph (`<p>`) and line-break (`<br />`) elements provide the simplest way of adding white space to a document. **White space** is an important design element that refers to the empty areas on a page. It makes a page easier to read and is more visually appealing. It is tempting for beginning Web page authors to try and pack each page with as much information as possible, but experienced Web page authors know that the presence of white space is critical to the success of a page, whether you are creating a Web page or a traditional printed page. However, you cannot add white space to a Web page simply by including spaces or carriage returns in a document. As you learned in Chapter 1, most Web browsers ignore multiple, contiguous spaces on a Web page and replace them with a single space. Web browsers also ignore carriage returns. For instance, the following code shows the llamas, kangaroos, and pandas example you saw earlier. Although the document body is properly formed because the content is contained within a `<p>` element, the browser runs the three lines together on the same line because the carriage returns that separate the lines are ignored by Web browsers, as shown in Figure 2-13.

```
<body>
<p><b>Llamas</b> are from South America,
<b>kangaroos</b> are from Australia,
and <b>pandas</b> are from China.</p>
</body>
```

Figure 2-13   ExoticAnimals.html without line breaks

In order for the line breaks to be rendered by the browser, you must add **
** elements as follows. Figure 2-14 shows how a Web browser renders the following code.

```
<body>
<p><b>Llamas</b> are from South America, <br />
<b>kangaroos</b> are from Australia, <br />
and <b>pandas</b> are from China.</p>
</body>
```

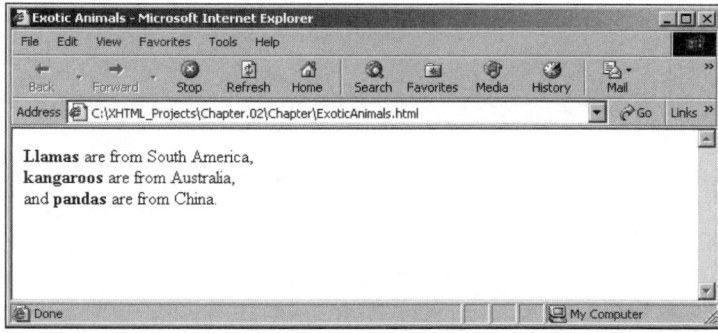

Figure 2-14   ExoticAnimals.html with line breaks

Notice that the **
** element only inserts a line break in an existing paragraph. To create separate paragraphs, the content for each paragraph must exist within its own **<p>** element. The following code shows a modified version of the Exotic Animals page that includes three separate paragraphs. Figure 2-15 shows the output. Notice that there is more white space between the lines when they are enclosed in paragraph elements than when each line ends in a **
** element. The **
** element simply creates a new line within the current paragraph. In comparison, the **<p>** element creates individual paragraphs that are separated by a single line.

```
<body>
<p><b>Llamas</b> are from South America.</p>
<p><b>Kangaroos</b> are from Australia.</p>
<p><b>Pandas</b> are from China.</p>
</body>
```

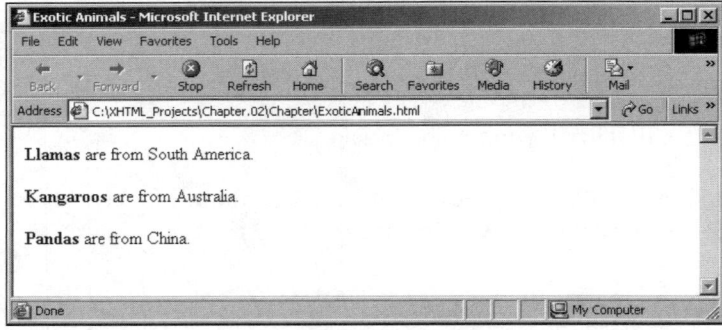

Figure 2-15   ExoticAnimals.html with three separate paragraphs

  Remember that because the <br /> element is an inline element, it must be placed within a block-level element such as the <p> element.

Horizontal Rules

The empty **horizontal-rule (<hr />) element** draws a horizontal rule on a Web page that acts as a section divider. Horizontal rules are useful visual elements for breaking up long documents. Although the <hr /> element is technically a block-level element, it cannot contain any content because it is an empty element. However, because it is a block-level element, it can exist on its own line in the document body without being contained within another block-level element.

  HTML includes several style attributes that you can use to modify the appearance of horizontal rules. However, all of the <hr /> element's style attributes have been deprecated in XHTML in favor of CSS.

The following document body includes an example of a horizontal rule. The output is shown in Figure 2-16.

```
<body>
<p>The following element is a horizontal rule.</p>
<hr />
</body>
```

Figure 2-16   Web page with a horizontal rule

 Remember that because the `<hr>` element is empty, you must close it by adding a space and a slash before its closing bracket, as follows: `<hr />`.

Next, you add horizontal rules to the CentralValley.html file.

To add horizontal rules to the CentralValley.html file:

1. Return to the **CentralValley.html** file in your text editor.

2. Add horizontal rules above each of the `<h2>` elements. You should add three `<hr />` elements in all.

3. Save the CentralValley.html file and open it in your Web browser. Figure 2-17 shows how the horizontal rules appear above the About the Market and Hours of Operation headings.

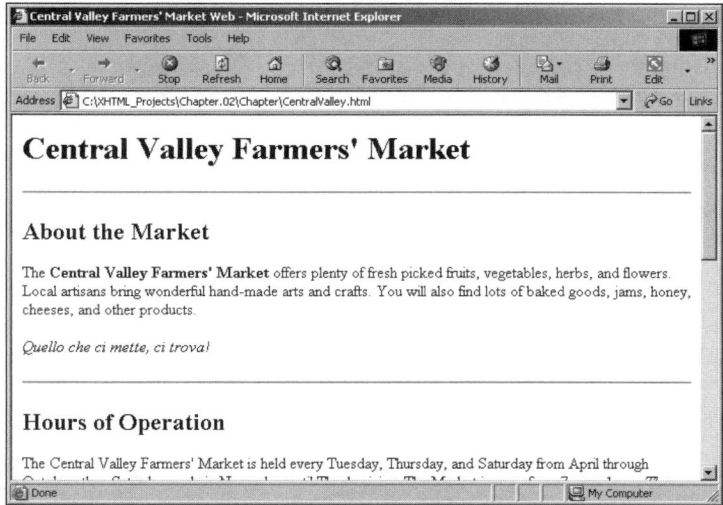

Figure 2-17   CentralValley.html file after adding horizontal rules

4. Close the Web browser window.

Comments

When you work with any type of programming language, whether it is a simple markup language like XHTML or an advanced language like Java or C++, it is considered good practice to add comments to your code. **Comments** are nonprinting lines that you place in your code to contain various types of remarks, including your name and the date you wrote the code, notes to yourself, copyright information, or instructions to future Web page authors and developers who may need to modify your work. When you are working with long documents, comments can make it easier to decipher how the document is structured.

XHTML comments begin with an opening comment tag `<!--` and end with a closing comment tag `-->`. The browser does not render any text located between opening and closing comment tags. Figure 2-18 displays an XHTML document containing comments. Figure 2-19 shows the output in a browser. Notice that the browser does not render any of the text located between the comment tags.

```
<!DOCTYPE html PUBLIC
"-//W3C//DTD XHTML 1.0 Strict//EN"
"http://www.w3.org/TR/xhtml1/DTD/xhtml1-strict.dtd">
<html lang="EN" xml:lang = "EN" dir="ltr">
<head>
<title>Comments</title>
</head>
<body>
<p>The browser renders this line normally because it is located
before the opening comment tag.</p>
<!-- Text on this line does not appear
Text on this line does not appear
This line does not appear either -->
<p>The browser renders this line normally because it is located
after the closing comment tag.</p>
</body>
</html>
```

Figure 2-18   Web page with comments

Figure 2-19   Web page containing comments displayed in a browser

Next, you add comments to the CentralValley.html file.

To add comments to the CentralValley.html file:

1. Return to the **CentralValley.html** file in your text editor.

2. Add to the top of file (above the `<!DOCTYPE>` declaration) the following comments. Be sure to use your name and today's date.

   ```
   <!--
   Home page for the Central Valley Farmers' Market Web site
   your name
   today's date
   -->
   ```

3. Save and close the CentralValley.html file and then open it in your Web browser to confirm that the comments do not appear.

4. Close the Web browser window.

Next, you use the W3C MarkUp Validation Service to validate the CentralValley.html file.

To use the W3C MarkUp Validation Service to validate the CentralValley.html file:

1. Start Internet Explorer and enter the URL for the upload page of the W3C MarkUp Validation Service: **http://validator.w3.org/file-upload.html**.

2. Open and validate the **CentralValley.html** file. If you receive any errors, fix them, and then revalidate the document.

3. Close your Web browser window.

Chapter Summary

□ The `<!DOCTYPE>` declaration states the Extensible Hypertext Markup Language (XHTML) version of the document and the XHTML Document Type Definitions (DTD) with which the document complies.

❐ Elements and attributes that are considered to be obsolete and that will eventually be eliminated are said to be deprecated.

❐ The Transitional DTD allows you to continue using deprecated elements along with the well-formed document requirements of Extensible Markup Language (XML).

❐ The Frameset DTD is identical to the Transitional DTD, except that it includes the `<frameset>` and `<frame>` elements, which allow you to split the browser window into two or more frames.

❐ The Strict DTD eliminates the elements that were deprecated in the Transitional DTD and Frameset DTD.

❐ To ensure that an XHTML document is well formed and that its elements are valid, you need to use a validating parser.

❐ Validation checks that your XHTML document is well formed and that the elements in your document are correctly written according to the element definitions in an associated DTD.

❐ Block-level elements refer to elements that give a Web page its structure.

❐ Inline, or text-level, elements are used for describing the text that appears on a Web page.

❐ XHTML includes several standard, or common, attributes that are available to almost every element.

❐ You should designate the language and text direction of your elements using the `lang`, `xml:lang`, and `dir` attributes.

❐ All XHTML documents, regardless of whether they use the Transitional, Strict, or Frameset DTD, use the namespace identified by the following URI: *http://www.w3.org/1999/xhtml*.

❐ The `<head>` element represents the document head and contains other elements that store information about the Web page or are used by the Web page.

❐ A parent element refers to an element that contains other elements, known as child elements.

❐ The `<body>` element represents the document body and contains other elements that store all of the content a user sees rendered in a browser.

❐ Heading elements, or headings, are used for indicating the importance and structure of a document's headings and subheadings.

❐ White space refers to the empty areas on a page that make the presentation of a page more visually pleasing and easier to read.

❐ The horizontal rule (`<hr />`) element draws a horizontal rule on a Web page that acts as a section divider.

❒ Comments are nonprinting lines that you place in your code that contain various types of remarks, including your name and the date you wrote the code, notes to yourself, copyright information, or instructions to future Web page authors and developers who may need to modify your work.

REVIEW QUESTIONS

1. What is the extension you assign XHTML documents? (Choose all that apply.)

   a. XML

   b. XHTML

   c. html

   d. htm

2. How do you close the empty `<hr>` element in an XHTML document in order for it to be backward compatible with older browsers?

   a. `<hr\>`

   b. `<hr \>`

   c. `<hr/>`

   d. `<hr />`

3. Explain when you should use **PUBLIC** and when you should use **SYSTEM** as the *type* attribute of the `<!DOCTYPE>` declaration.

4. What must you place on the first line of an XHTML document?

   a. an `<html>` tag

   b. an `<xhtml>` tag

   c. a `<title>` tag

   d. a `<!doctype>` declaration

5. Which XHTML DTD(s) allows you to continue using deprecated elements? (Choose all that apply.)

   a. XML

   b. Transitional

   c. Strict

   d. Frameset

6. Explain the use of validation with an XHTML document.

7. You are not required to validate XHTML documents. True or False?

8. _____ elements give a Web page its structure.

    a. XHTML

    b. Block-level

    c. Inline

    d. Meta

9. Inline elements must be placed within block-level elements. True or False?

10. You should designate the language of your elements using the _____ and `xml:lang` attributes.

    a. `country`

    b. `local`

    c. `lang`

    d. `language`

11. Which of the following values can you assign to the `dir` attribute? (Choose all that apply.)

    a. `ltr`

    b. `rtl`

    c. `left`

    d. `right`

12. Which standard attribute can you use to create a ToolTip for an element?

    a. ToolTip

    b. Description

    c. Help

    d. Title

13. Which of the following is the correct full form of a Boolean attribute named selected?

    a. `selected`

    b. `selected="true"`

    c. `selected=""`

    d. `selected="selected"`

14. All of the predefined elements in XHTML are organized within the _____ namespace.

    a. XML

    b. XHTML

    c. HTML

    d. Browser

2

15. The xmlns attribute is required in the `<html>` element in order for an XHTML document to be well formed. True or False?

16. What should you use for a Web page title and why?

17. Explain how you should use heading elements in your documents?

18. Which elements can you use to add white space to a document? (Choose all that apply.)

    a. `<b>`

    b. `<p>`

    c. `<br />`

    d. `<hr />`

19. Horizontal rules are empty elements. True or False?

20. Which is the correct tag pair for an XHTML comment?

    a. `<!-- ... -->`

    b. `<!--> ... <-->`

    c. `<!--> ... </-->`

    d. `<comment>...</comment>`

21. Explain why you use comments in an XHTML document?

HANDS-ON PROJECTS

Project 1-1

In this exercise, you create a Web page that displays an invitation to a graduation party. You create the document so it uses the Transitional DTD.

1. Create a new document in your text editor and type the `<!DOCTYPE>` declaration, `<html>` element, header information, and the `<body>` element. Use the Transitional DTD and "Graduation Party" as the content of the `<title>` element. Your document should appear as follows:

```
<!DOCTYPE html PUBLIC "-//W3C//DTD XHTML 1.0
Transitional//EN"
"http://www.w3.org/TR/xhtml1/DTD/xhtml1-transitional.dtd">
<html lang="en" xml:lang = "en" dir="ltr">
<head>
<title>Graduation Party</title>
</head>
<body>
</body>
</html>
```

2. Next, add the following text and elements to the document body:

```
<center>
<h1>Graduation Party</h1>
<p><i>It's time to celebrate!</i><br />
Join us for a party in honor of</p>
<h2>Monica's Graduation</h2>
<p>Saturday, June 22, 2003<br />
at 2:00 p.m.</p>
<p><b>The Cohen Residence</b><br />
876 Blackbird Road<br />
R.S.V.P. 555-1212</p>
</center>
```

3. Save the file as **Graduation.html** in the Chapter.02\Projects folder.

4. Use the W3C MarkUp Validation Service to validate the Graduation.html file, and then open it in your Web browser and examine how the elements are rendered.

Project 1-2

In this exercise, you create a document that uses five heading elements to organize the cities within Orange County in both California and Florida (both states have counties named Orange).

1. Create a new document in your text editor and type the `<!DOCTYPE>` declaration, `<html>` element, header information, and the `<body>` element. Use the Strict DTD and "Heading Elements" as the content of the `<title>` element. Your document should appear as follows:

```
<!DOCTYPE html PUBLIC "-//W3C//DTD XHTML 1.0 Strict//EN"
"http://www.w3.org/TR/xhtml1/DTD/xhtml1-strict.dtd">
<html lang="en" xml:lang = "en" dir="ltr">
<head>
<title>Heading elements</title>
</head>
<body>
</body>
</html>
```

2. Add to the document body the following `<h1>` and `<h2>` elements for North America and the United States as follows. This document should contain only one `<h1>` element for North America, but may contain additional `<h2>` elements for the other two countries in North America: Canada and Mexico.

```
<h1>North America</h1>
<h2>United States of America</h2>
```

2

3. Next, add the following `<h3>`, `<h4>`, and `<h5>` elements for some of the cities within Orange County in California:

```
<h3>California</h3>
<h4>Orange County</h4>
<h5>Anaheim</h5>
<h5>Huntington Beach</h5>
<h5>Irvine</h5>
<h5>Laguna Beach</h5>
<h5>Newport Beach</h5>
```

4. Next, add the following `<h3>`, `<h4>`, and `<h5>` elements for some of the cities within Orange County in Florida:

```
<h3>Florida</h3>
<h4>Orange County</h4>
<h5>Azalea Park</h5>
<h5>Lake Buena Vista</h5>
<h5>Orlando</h5>
<h5>Winter Garden</h5>
<h5>Winter Park</h5>
```

5. Save the file as **OrangeCounties.html** in the Chapter.02\Projects folder.

6. Use the W3C MarkUp Validation Service to validate the OrangeCounties.html file, and then open it in your Web browser and examine how the elements are rendered.

Project 1-3

In this exercise, you create a Web page that lists baby name choices of expectant parents. You create the girl names and the boy names in separate paragraphs. Each name is separated in the paragraph using line breaks.

1. Create a new document in your text editor and type the `<!DOCTYPE>` declaration, `<html>` element, header information, and the `<body>` element. Use the Strict DTD and "Baby Names" as the content of the `<title>` element.

2. Type the following heading for the Web page:

```
<h1>Baby Names</h1>
```

3. Next, type the following `<h2>` heading along with paragraph and line breaks for the selected girl names:

```
<h2>Girl Names</h2>
<p>Anna<br />
Brenda<br />
Denise<br />
Jessica</p>
```

4. Next, type the following `<h2>` heading along with paragraph and line breaks for the selected boy names:

```
<h2>Boy Names</h2>
<p>Andrew<br />
Colin<br />
George<br />
Stanley</p>
```

5. Save the file as **BabyNames.html** in the Chapter.02\Projects folder.

6. Use the W3C MarkUp Validation Service to validate the BabyNames.html file, and then open it in your Web browser and examine how the elements are rendered.

Project 1-4

In this exercise, you create a Web page that lists five technology companies, separated by horizontal rules. The paragraph containing the company name uses the `title` attribute to store the company's Web address.

1. Create a new document in your text editor and type the `<!DOCTYPE>` declaration, `<html>` element, header information, and the `<body>` element. Use the Strict DTD and "Technology Companies" as the content of the `<title>` element.

2. Type the following text and elements in the document body. Each company's Web address is assigned to the `title` attribute of the `<p>` element that contains the company name. The paragraphs containing each company name are separated by horizontal rules.

```
<p title="www.sun.com">Sun Microsystems</p><hr />
<p title="www.microsoft.com">Microsoft</p><hr />
<p title="www.oracle.com">Oracle</p><hr />
<p title="www.siebel.com">Siebel</p><hr />
<p title="www.bea.com">BEA</p><hr />
```

3. Save the file as **TechCompanies.html** in the Chapter.02\Exercises folder.

4. Use the W3C MarkUp Validation Service to validate the TechCompanies.html file, and then open it in your Web browser and examine how the elements are rendered. Hold your mouse over each company name to see if the Web address assigned to the `title` attribute displays as a ToolTip.

Project 1-5

In this exercise, you create a Web page that lists some foreign language film titles. The film titles are organized by language names defined as `<h2>` elements. You use `lang`, `xml:lang`, and `dir` attributes in the paragraph element that contains each film name to define the element's language and text direction, along with a `title` attribute that lists the film name's English translation.

2

1. Create a new document in your text editor and type the `<!DOCTYPE>` declaration, `<html>` element, header information, and the `<body>` element. Use the Strict DTD and "Foreign Films" as the content of the `<title>` element.

2. Type the following heading for the Web page in the document body:

   ```
   <h1>Foreign Films</h1>
   ```

3. Add the following French language film section:

   ```
   <h2>French</h2>
   <p title="The Beauty of the Day" lang="fr" xml:lang = "fr"
   dir="ltr">Belle de Jour</p>
   <p title="Brotherhood of the Wolf" lang="fr" xml:lang =
   "fr" dir="ltr">Le Pacte des Loup</p>
   ```

4. Add the following Italian language film section:

   ```
   <h2>Italian</h2>
   <p title="The Sweet Life" lang="it" xml:lang = "it"
   dir="ltr">La Dolce Vita</p>
   <p title="Paradise Cinema" lang="it" xml:lang = "it"
   dir="ltr">Cinema Paradiso</p>
   ```

5. Add the following Japanese language film section:

   ```
   <h2>Japanese</h2>
   <p title="Grave of the Fireflies" lang="ja" xml:lang = "ja"
   dir="ltr">Hotaru no Haka</p>
   <p title="Seven Samurai" lang="ja" xml:lang = "ja"
   dir="ltr">Shichinin no Samurai</p>
   ```

6. Save the file as **ForeignFilms.html** in the Chapter.02\Projects folder.

7. Use the W3C MarkUp Validation Service to validate the ForeignFilms.html file, and then open it in your Web browser and examine how the elements are rendered. Hold your mouse over each film name to see if the translation assigned to the `title` attribute displays as a ToolTip.

Project 1-6

In this exercise, you create a Web page that lists online job postings. You include XHTML comments that list the dates that each job posting expires.

1. Create a new document in your text editor and type the `<!DOCTYPE>` declaration, `<html>` element, header information, and the `<body>` element. Use the Strict DTD and "Online Job Postings" as the content of the `<title>` element.

2. Type the following headings for the Web page in the document body. The `<h1>` heading lists the title of the Web page ("Online Job Postings") and the `<h2>` heading lists the current category ("Educational Positions").

   ```
   <h1>Online Job Postings</h1>
   <h2>Educational Positions</h2>
   ```

3. Enter the following job openings and information about each, including comments that list the job posting's expiration date.

```
<h3>Child Day-Care Worker</h3>
<p><b>Description</b>: Organizes and leads activities of pre-
kindergarten children in nursery schools or in
playrooms operated for patrons of theaters, department
stores, hotels, and similar organizations.<br />
<b>Educational requirements</b>: High school diploma or its
equivalent and 2-4 years of experience in the field or in a
related area.</p>
<!-- Job posting expiration date: 10/23/04 -->
<h3>Flight Instructor</h3>
<p><b>Description</b>: Instructs student pilots in flight
procedures and techniques in ground school courses and
flight training.<br />
<b>Educational requirements</b>: Pilot's license and 1000+
hours flight time.</p>
<!-- Job posting expiration date: 7/22/04 -->
```

4. Save the file as **JobPostings.html** in the Chapter.02\Projects folder.

5. Use the W3C MarkUp Validation Service to validate the JobPostings.html file, and then open it in your Web browser and make sure the comments don't appear.

Project 1-7

Many states have "daily number" lottery games in which you can try your luck at guessing certain numbers, depending on the game. For instance, one game may require you to select the correct three winning numbers, whereas another game may require you to select the correct ten winning numbers. In this exercise, you create a Web page that lists the daily winning lottery numbers for "Pick 3", "Pick 5", and "Pick 10" games for the past two days.

1. Create a new document in your text editor and type the `<!DOCTYPE>` declaration, `<html>` element, header information, and the `<body>` element. Use the Strict DTD and "Daily Numbers" as the content of the `<title>` element.

2. Type the following heading for the Web page in the document body:

```
<h1>Daily Numbers</h1>
```

3. Enter the following heading and paragraph elements for the "Pick 3", "Pick 5", and "Pick 10" lottery results for the past two days:

```
<h2>Today</h2>
<h3>Pick 3</h3>
<p>34-3-23</p>
<h3>Pick 5</h3>
<p>4-67-23-3-45</p>
<h3>Pick 10</h3>
```

```
<p>3-24-5-62-87-34-23-67-87-11</p>
<h2>Yesterday</h2>
<h3>Pick 3</h3>
<p>45-68-33</p>
<h3>Pick 5</h3>
<p>98-34-5-78-11</p>
<h3>Pick 10</h3>
<p>2-87-65-23-56-8-7-76-23-99</p>
```

4. Save the file as **DailyNumbers.html** in the Chapter.02\Projects folder.

5. Use the W3C MarkUp Validation Service to validate the DailyNumbers.html file, and then open it in your Web browser.

Project 1-8

In this exercise, you create a Web page that lists prices for toner cartridges.

1. Create a new document in your text editor and type the `<!DOCTYPE>` declaration, `<html>` element, header information, and the `<body>` element. Use the Strict DTD and "Toner Cartridge Sales" as the content of the `<title>` element.

2. Type the following heading for the Web page in the document body:

   ```
   <h1>Toner Cartridge Sales</h1>
   ```

3. Enter the following heading and paragraph elements for selected HP and Lexmark toner cartridges:

   ```
   <hr />
   <h2>HP Toner Cartridges</h2>
   <p><b>Model #</b>: HP C3909A<br />
   <b>Compatibility</b>: LaserJet 5Si/5/5M/5N<br />
   <b>Price</b>: $165.99</p>
   <p><b>Model #</b>:  HP 92275A<br />
   <b>Compatibility</b>: LaserJet 2P/2P+/3P<br />
   <b>Price</b>: $64.45</p>
   <hr />
   <h2>Lexmark Toner Cartridges</h2>
   <p><b>Model #</b>: LEX 1382100<br />
   <b>Compatibility</b>: Optra 4049/3112/3116<br />
   <b>Price</b>: $189.99</p>
   <p><b>Model #</b>:  LEX 1380520<br />
   <b>Compatibility</b>: Lexmark 4019/4028/4029<br />
   <b>Price</b>: $209.00</p>
   ```

4. Save the file as **TonerCartridges.html** in the Chapter.02\Projects folder.

5. Use the W3C MarkUp Validation Service to validate the TonerCartridges.html file, and then open it in your Web browser.

CASE PROJECTS

For the following projects, save the files you create in the Cases folder for Chapter 2. Create the files so they are well formed according to the Strict DTD. To the top of each file add comments that contain your name and today's date. Be sure to validate the files you create with the W3C MarkUp Validation Service.

Project 2-1

Create a Web page for a company that sells and installs satellite TV dishes. Include headings for satellite services such as DirecTV and the Dish Network. Beneath each heading, use a paragraph element that describes the service. Use an Equipment subheading that lists equipment options and costs along with installation costs. Also, include a Programming subheading beneath the heading for each satellite service that lists the programming options and rates that are available for each service. Save the Web page as SatelliteTV.html.

Project 2-2

Create a Web page for a company that sells area rugs. Use <h2> headings to organize the rugs by the following sizes: small, medium, and large. Under each <h2> heading, include the following information about each rug that is for sale: type (such as Navajo or Persian), dimensions, a description of the rug, and price. If the rug is an antique, include the date it was made. Save the Web page as AreaRugs.html.

Project 2-3

Create a Web page for a company that sells mattresses. Use heading elements to organize the mattresses that are for sale by size, such as twin, full, queen, and king. Within the heading element for each mattress size, use additional heading elements for each manufacturer (such as Simmons or Serta). Within each manufacturer's heading, organize the mattresses by degree of support (firm, extra firm, and so on), and include each mattress's price. Save the Web page as Mattresses.html.

Project 2-4

Create a Web page for a company that sells vitamins. Use heading elements to organize the vitamins that are for sale, such as B vitamins and C vitamins. Within the heading element for each vitamin, use additional heading elements for the number of milligrams available for each vitamin (200 mgs, 500 mgs, and so on). Within each milligram heading, organize the vitamins for sale by quantity and price. Save the Web page as Vitamins.html.

3

LINKING AND PUBLISHING BASIC WEB PAGES

In Chapter 1, you learned that hypertext linking is likely the most important aspect of the Web because it allows you to open other Web pages quickly. So far you have studied only the basic structural requirements for creating the elements and attributes within a single Web page. In this chapter, you will begin expanding the capabilities of your Web pages by learning how to create links. You will also study how to publish your completed Web pages so that others can access them on the Web. Finally, you will learn how to use metadata to provide information to search engines and Web servers about the data contained within your Web page.

LINKING WEB PAGES

Almost every Web page contains hypertext links, which are used to open files or navigate to other documents on the Web. You activate a hypertext link by clicking it with your mouse button. A hypertext link in an HTML document is underlined and often displayed in a vivid color. In Internet Explorer, blue is the default color for unvisited links, whereas violet is the default color of previously visited links. A hypertext link uses descriptive text to describe the link; you can click the text displayed by a hyperlink in a Web page to move to the target of the link. The target of a link can be another location on the same Web page, an external Web page, an image, or some other type of document. Other types of elements, such as images, can also be hypertext links to other Web pages, images, or files. The text or image used to represent a link on a Web page is called an **anchor**.

 Different Web browsers use different default colors for visited and unvisited links. You can change the default link colors on a Web page by using Cascading Style Sheets (CSS).

You create a basic hypertext link using the **<a> element** (the *a* stands for anchor). Although you can use a variety of attributes with the <a> element, the one you will use most often is the `href` (for hypertext reference) attribute, which specifies the link's target URL. The following code shows how to use the <a> element to create a link to the W3C MarkUp Validation Service. Figure 3-1 shows the output in Internet Explorer.

```
<p>To validate your XHTML documents, visit the
<a href="http://validator.w3.org/">
W3C MarkUp Validation Service</a>.</p>
```

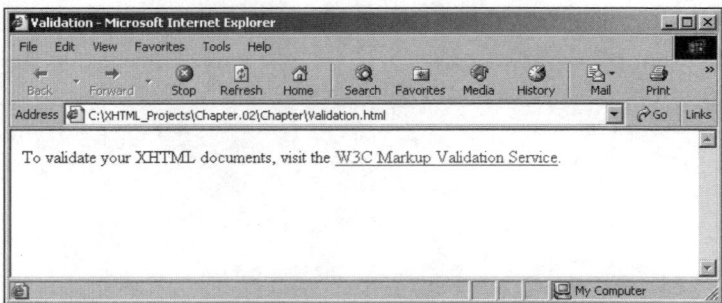

Figure 3-1   Web page with a hypertext link

 Because the <a> element is an inline element, it must be nested within a block-level element in order for your document to be well formed. In the preceding code, for instance, the <a> element is nested within a block-level <p> element.

When you write the descriptive content that will be used as the text for a link, be sure to use something that clearly describes the target of the link. The preceding code, for instance, uses *W3C MarkUp Validation Service* as the descriptive text for a link. It is considered to be very bad form to use text such as *click* or *click here* as the descriptive text for a link. Therefore, you should avoid creating links with descriptive text such as the following:

```
<p>To validate your XHTML documents, <a
href="http://validator.w3.org/">
click here</a> to visit the W3C MarkUp Validation
Service</p>
```

You can easily use an image as a link anchor by replacing the content of an `<a>` element with a nested `<img>` element. For instance, the following code creates the image link shown in Figure 3-2. Notice that the link consists of both descriptive text and an image file. Although descriptive text is not required when you create an image link, it can make it easier for users to identify the image links on your Web page.

```
<p><a href="Noah.html"><img src="Noah.jpg" height="120"
width="120" /><br />Click the image to open Noah's Web
page</a></p>
```

Figure 3-2   Web page with an image link

You may have run across many types of links that use images in the form of buttons to represent hypertext links. For instance, the Mercedes Benz USA Web page that appears in Figure 3-3 uses image links to allow users to find more information about a particular model of automobile by clicking an image of the automobile. The image links for the Mercedes Benz Web page shown in Figure 3-3 are quite effective, and make an extremely well-designed Web page.

Figure 3-3   Mercedes Benz image links

It is not always necessary to use images for links because basic text links, if properly placed on a Web page, can be just as effective. Plus, it takes much less time to create a text-based hyperlink than it does to design an image to use as a hyperlink (assuming, of course, that you possess the necessary design skills and tools to create a professional image). To see just how effective basic text links can be, look at the extremely popular online auction site, eBay, shown in Figure 3-4. eBay constantly changes its links to represent the ever-changing variety of merchandise it sells. To create (or even locate) a new image for the many unique items eBay sells would be incredibly time-consuming and cost inefficient. As shown in Figure 3-4, even the home page contains a large number of text-based hyperlinks that represent various categories or items that are currently offered as specials. Also notice, however, that the page includes images for links that do not change frequently, such as the buying tips, selling tips, and register now buttons at the top of the page, along with representational images for general categories, such as the Gold Necklaces and Great Cruise Deals! links on the right side of the page.

In this chapter you will continue working on the Central Valley Farmers' Market Web site that you created in Chapter 2.

Next, you will add a new contact information page to the Central Valley Farmers' Market Web site that users will access from the home page via a text link.

Figure 3-4   Link examples on eBay

To add a new contact information page to the Central Valley Farmers' Market Web site:

1. Open your text editor and create a new document.

2. Type the `<!DOCTYPE>` declaration, `<html>` element, document head, and the `<body>` element. Use the Strict DTD and "Contact Information for the Central Valley Farmers' Market" as the content of the `<title>` element. Your document should appear as follows:

```
<!DOCTYPE html PUBLIC
"-//W3C//DTD XHTML 1.0 Strict//EN"
"http://www.w3.org/TR/xhtml1/DTD/xhtml1-strict.dtd">
<html xmlns="http://www.w3.org/1999/xhtml" lang="en"
xml:lang = "en" dir="ltr">
<head>
<title>Contact Information for the Central Valley Farmers'
Market</title>
</head>
<body>
</body>
</html>
```

3. Next, add to the document body the following headings and paragraphs that list the contact information for the Central Valley Farmers' Market.

```
<h1>Central Valley Farmers' Market</h1>
<h2>Contact Information</h2>
<p>If you have any questions or concerns about the Central
Valley Farmers' Market, please call (908) 626-3764.</p>
<p>You can also send mail to the Central Valley Farmers'
Market at the following address:</p>
<p>P.O. Box 135<br />
Central Valley, CA 94359</p>
```

4. Add to the end of the body section the following statement that creates a link back to the home page for the Central Valley Farmers' Market:

```
<p><a href="CentralValley.html">Home</a></p>
```

5. Save the file as **Contact.html** in the Chapter.03\Chapter folder for Chapter 3.

Next, you add a link from the CentralValley.html document to the Contact.html document.

To add a link from the CentralValley.html document a link to the Contact.html document:

1. Copy the CentralValley.html file from your Chapter.02\Chapter folder to your Chapter.03\Chapter folder. If you do not have a copy of the CentralValley.html file, you can copy it from the Chapter.03 folder on your Data Disk.

2. Open the **CentralValley.html** file in your text editor.

3. Place the insertion point after the closing `</h1>` tag, press **Enter**, and then type the following elements that create a link to the Contact.html document:

```
<p><a href="Contact.html">Contact Information</a></p>
```

4. Save the **CentralValley.html** file, and then open it in a Web browser. Figure 3-5 shows how the new link appears.

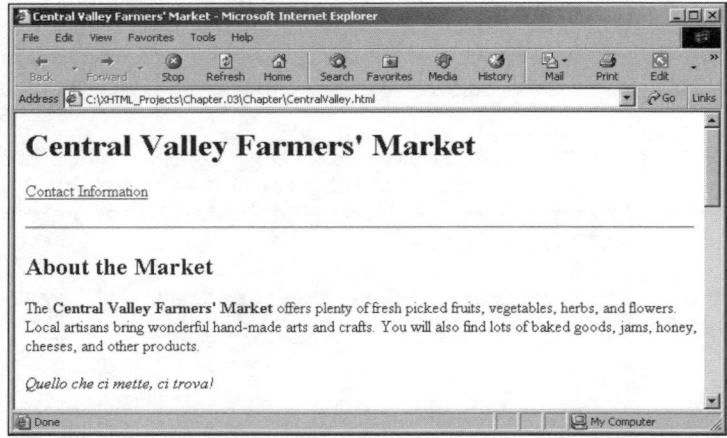

Figure 3-5   CentralValley.html after adding the Contact Information link

5. Click the **Contact Information** link. The Contact.html file should open in your browser window, as shown in Figure 3-6.

6. Click the **Home** link to return to the home page for the Central Valley Farmers' Market.

7. Close the Web browser window.

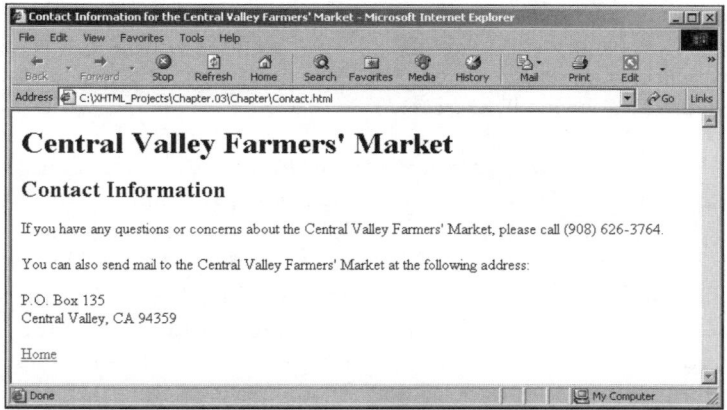

Figure 3-6   Contact.html

To better understand how to work with hypertext links, you need to understand more about URLs, which you will study next.

Uniform Resource Locators

As you learned in Chapter 1, a document on the Web, or a Web page, is identified by a unique address called the Uniform Resource Locator, or URL. A Web page's URL is similar to a telephone number. Each URL consists of two basic parts: a protocol (usually Hypertext Transfer Protocol: HTTP) and either the domain name for a Web server or a Web server's Internet Protocol (IP) address. **Hypertext Transfer Protocol (HTTP)** manages the hypertext links that are used to navigate the Web. HTTP ensures that Web browsers correctly process and display the various types of information contained in Web pages (text, graphics, audio, and so on). The protocol portion of a URL is followed by a colon, two forward slashes, and a host. A **host** refers to a computer system that is being accessed by a remote computer. The host portion of a URL is usually *www* for "World Wide Web." A **domain name** is a unique address used for identifying a computer, often a Web server, on the Internet. The domain name consists of two parts separated by a period. The first part of a domain name is usually text that easily identifies a person or an organization, such as DonGosselin or Course. The last part of a domain name, known as the **domain identifier**, identifies the type of institution or organization. Common domain identifiers include .biz, .com, .edu, .info, .net, .org, .gov, .mil, or .int. Each domain identifier briefly describes the type of business or organization it represents. For instance, .com (for *company*) represents private companies, .gov (for *government*) represents government agencies, and .edu (for *educational*) represents educational institutions. Therefore, the domain name consists of descriptive text for the Web site, combined with the domain identifier. For example, course.com is the domain name for Course Technology. An entire URL would be *http://www.DonGosselin.com* or *http://www.course.com*.

An Internet Protocol, or IP, address is another way to uniquely identify computers or devices connected to the Internet. An IP address consists of a series of four groups of numbers separated by periods. Each Internet domain name is associated with a unique IP address.

In a URL, a specific filename, or a combination of directories and a filename, can follow the domain name or IP address. If the URL does not specify a filename, the requesting Web server looks for a file with one of the following names located in the root or specified directory: index.html, index.shtml, index.htm, default.html, default.shtml, or default.htm. For instance, if you plan to travel and want health information from the Centers for Disease Control and Prevention (CDC) and you enter *http://www.cdc.gov/travel/* in your browser's address box, the Web server automatically opens a file named index.htm. Figure 3-7 identifies the parts of the URL that opens the default file in the travel directory on the CDC's Web site.

 When a URL does not specify a filename, the index.html file or other file that opens automatically may not appear in your Address box after the document renders.

Figure 3-7   Sample URL

Although HTTP is probably the most widely used protocol on the Internet, it is not the only one. Another common protocol is Hypertext Transfer Protocol Secure (HTTPS), which provides secure Internet connections that are used in Web-based financial transactions and other types of communication that require security and privacy. For instance, to use a Web browser to view your account information through Wells Fargo bank, you need to access the following URL:

```
https://banking.wellsfargo.com/
```

Notice that the preceding URL uses the HTTPS protocol. You can either enter this URL in the Address box of your browser window or use it in a link, as follows:

```
<p><a href="https://banking.wellsfargo.com/">
Wells Fargo Online Banking
</a></p>
```

Table 3-1 lists additional protocols that are used with links.

Table 3-1   Common protocols used with links

Protocol	Description
file:///	Accesses a file from a local hard drive
ftp://	Accesses a file from a File Transfer Protocol (FTP) server
gopher://	Accesses a file from a Gopher server
telnet://	Connects a computer to a network server

 Note that the file:/// protocol is followed by three slashes, not just two.

Unlike other protocols, the `mailto` and `news` protocols are followed only by a colon. The `mailto` protocol is most frequently used in links to provide a quick way to send an e-mail message to a specified address. The syntax for using the `mailto` protocol is `mailto:`*`name@domain`*`.com`. Using this syntax with an `<a>` element, you could create a link that sends an e-mail to the President of the United States using the following statement:

```
<p><a href="mailto:president@whitehouse.gov">
Send a message to the president</a></p>
```

Next, you will add a `mailto` link to the contact page for the Central Valley Farmers' Market.

To add a `mailto` link to the contact page for the Central Valley Farmers' Market:

1. Return to the **Contact.html** file in your text editor.

2. Place the insertion point after the closing `</p>` tag in the statement that lists the telephone number, press **Enter**, and then add the following statement that creates a mailto link. Be sure to enter your e-mail address.

```
<p>You can send an e-mail to
<a href="mailto:your_email_address">
Your e-mail address</a>.</p>
```

3. Save and close the **Contact.html** file, then open the **CentralValley.html** file in Internet Explorer. Click the **Contact Information** link, then click the `mailto` link on the Contact.html page and try sending yourself an e-mail message.

4. Close your Web browser window.

ABSOLUTE AND RELATIVE LINKS

An anchor uses the URL to specify the name and location of a Web page. You can use two types of URLs on a Web page: absolute and relative. An **absolute URL** refers to the full Web address of a Web page or to a specific drive and directory. The following elements display an anchor of *My Web Site* and contain an absolute reference to a Web page named index.htm located on a Web site named *www.MyWebSite.com*.

```
<p><a href="http://www.aaai.org/index.html">
American Association for Artificial Intelligence (AAAI)
</a></p>
```

An absolute URL can also refer to a file on a local computer, as in the following code.

```
<p><a href="c:\MyWebPages\HomePage.html">
My Web Site
</a></p>
```

A **relative URL** specifies the location of a file relative to the location of the currently loaded Web page. You use relative URLs to load Web pages located on the same computer as the currently displayed Web page. If the currently displayed Web page is located at *http://www.MyWebSite.com/WebPages*, then the following relative URL looks in the WebPages folder for the AnotherWebPage.html file:

```
<p><a href="AnotherWebPage.html">
Another Web Page
</a></p>
```

You can also use a URL that locates subfolders that are relative to the location of the current Web page folder. For instance, in the following example, the link opens a Web page named YetAnotherWebPage.html from the \MoreWebPages subfolder that exists within the current folder:

```
<p><a href="MoreWebPages/YetAnotherWebPage.html">
Yet Another Web Page
</a></p>
```

When all of your documents reside within the same folder, relative URLs are convenient because you do not have to include the entire location of each file. In addition, if you rename the folder containing the primary document and linked documents or move it to a different computer, you do not have to update the location of relative URLs. For example, suppose you have a primary document that contains 10 links to documents located within the same directory. If you move the primary document and the 10 linked documents to a new location, you do not have to update the relative links. However, if you created each of the 10 links as absolute URLs, you would need to update each URL before the links would function properly.

LINKING WITHIN THE SAME WEB PAGE

The `<a>` element can create either a link to another document or to a bookmark within the current document. **Bookmarks** are internal links within the current document and can be a particularly effective tool for helping users navigate through a long Web page. For instance, examine the Web page shown in Figure 3-8, which contains the W3C's home page for information on HTML and XHTML development. If you visit the Web page and scroll through the document, you will see that it is quite long. In Figure 3-8 at the bottom of the browser window, you can see a group of text links that begins with the "news" link. Many of the links in this group, including the news and recommendations links, do not link to external documents. Instead, they link to other bookmarks (internal links) within the current document. These internal links make it much easier for visitors to navigate through the Web page's contents.

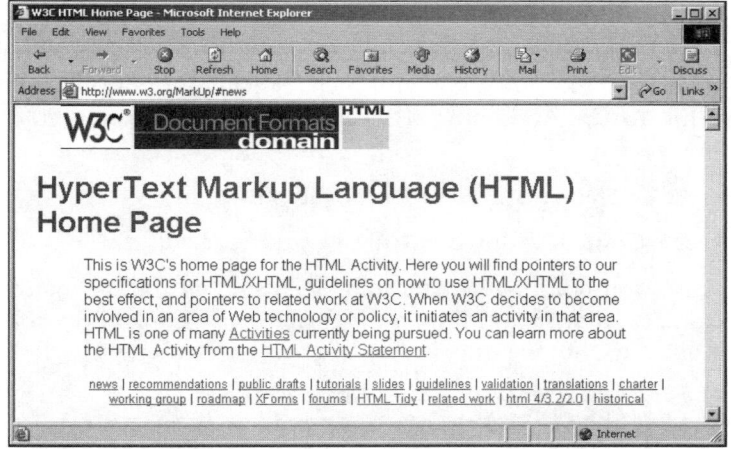

Figure 3-8   The W3C's home page for HTML Activity

You create bookmark links by using the `id` attribute. Recall that the standard `id` attribute uniquely identifies an individual element in a document. Any element that includes an `id` attribute can be the target of a link. For instance, you may have a long Web page with an `<h2>` element near the bottom that reads Summary of Qualifications. To create the element with an `id` attribute of sq1, you use the following statement:

```
<h2 id="sq1">Summary of Qualifications</h2>
```

To create a bookmark, you assign to the `href` attribute of an `<a>` element an `id` value, preceded by the # sign. For instance, to create a bookmark to the `<h2>` element with the `id` of `sq1`, you use the following statement:

```
<p><a href="#sq1">
Read the Summary of Qualifications</a></p>
```

The id attribute replaces the name attribute that is used in HTML. However, many older browsers do not recognize the id attribute. To address this problem the name attribute was not deprecated in the <a> element. To ensure that your links are valid in older browsers, you must use both the id and name attributes inside an <a> element and assign the same value to both attributes.

To create a bookmark to any other element, including heading elements, you nest an <a> element inside another element. If an <a> element does not include an href attribute (it shouldn't when you are creating a bookmark), its contents are treated as normal text and subject to the rules of the parent element. Therefore, the content of an <a> element, without an href attribute, that is nested inside a heading element will be formatted in a browser with the style of the parent heading element. You use the following statement to create the <h2> element with the id of sq1 so it will function in both older and new browsers:

```
<h2><a id="sq1" name="sq1">
Summary of Qualifications</a></h2>
```

Next, you will create bookmarks in the CentralValley.html file by adding links to the <h2> elements. The bookmarks will allow visitors to quickly jump from the top of the CentralValley.html file to the About the Market, Hours of Operation, and Featured Vendor list headings.

To add links to the <h2> elements in the CentralValley.html file:

1. Return to the **CentralValley.html** file in your text editor.

2. Place the insertion point after the closing </p> tag in the statement that creates the Contact Information link, press **Enter**, and then add the following bookmark links to the document's heading level 2 elements:

```
<p><a href="#am1">About the Market</a></p>
<p><a href="#ho1">Hours of Operation</a></p>
<p><a href="#fvl1">Featured Vendor List</a></p>
```

3. Modify the About the Market heading element as follows so it includes an <a> element with the same name and id attributes that you added to the bookmark element:

```
<h2><a id="am1" name="am1">About the Market</a></h2>
```

4. Modify the Hours of Operation heading element as follows so it includes an <a> element with the same name and id attributes that you added to the bookmark element:

```
<h2><a id="ho1" name="ho1">Hours of Operation</a></h2>
```

5. Modify the Featured Vendor List heading element as follows so it includes an <a> element with the same name and id attributes that you added to the bookmark element:

```
<h2><a id="fvl1" name="fvl1">Featured Vendor List</a></h2>
```

6. Save the **CentralValley.html** file, and then open it in a Web browser and test the new links. Figure 3-9 shows how the new bookmark links should appear.

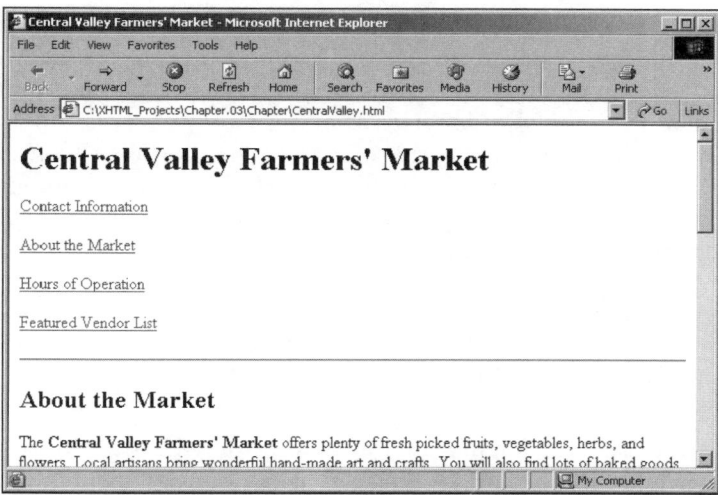

Figure 3-9   Bookmark links in CentralValley.html

7. Close the Web browser window.

PUBLISHING YOUR WEB PAGES

Before you publish your Web pages, you need to make a decision about where the Web site will be hosted, create and register a domain name for the site, and FTP the files to the Web server. How to publish Web pages is often a very confusing issue for new Web authors. **Web hosting** refers to the publication of a Web site for public access. You can use your own computer to host your Web site, provided it is connected to the Internet. However, using your own computer is not usually a good idea for several reasons. First, there are many security and maintenance issues that go with hosting a Web site and that may require skills and time you may not have. Second, the speed of your Internet access is a significant factor. Although broadband Internet access in the form of cable modems, digital subscriber lines (DSL), and satellite systems is growing, many users still access the Internet through slower dial-up modems. If you are using a dial-up modem, your Internet connection will have nowhere near enough speed to allow multiple users to access a Web site hosted on your computer. A final consideration is the speed of your computer. Although you may have a state-of-the-art desktop computer, it will probably still be slower than a professional-strength **Web server**, which is a special type of computer used for hosting Web sites.

Any computer can act as a Web server, although there are special types of computers with extremely large hard drives and memory that are specifically designed for that purpose.

Most people use an Internet Service Provider (ISP) to host their Web sites. An ISP provides access to the Internet along with other types of services including e-mail. Some of the more popular ISPs include America Online, CompuServe, and EarthLink, although many others exist. Almost every ISP offers Web site hosting. Often, an account with an ISP such as America Online automatically includes a limited amount of Web server space (usually 5–10 megabytes) that you can use to host your Web site. Check with your ISP to find out if your account includes Web hosting.

Five to ten megabytes is nowhere near enough storage space for hosting professional Web sites. However, you may find this amount of storage space sufficient to create a personal Web site with a limited number of pages.

There are many advantages to having an ISP host your Web site. Most ISPs have extremely fast Internet connections using advanced fiber-optic connections that are light years more powerful than a dial-up modem. ISPs also have very large and powerful Web servers, along with the expertise and manpower to maintain and manage them. Using a professional Web hosting service allows you to concentrate solely on authoring your Web pages without having to worry about the requirements of hosting.

You can find a comprehensive list of ISPs at *http://www.thelist.com*.

Domain Name Registration

One important decision you need to make is what to use for a domain name. You should pick a domain name that is close to your business name or that describes your Web site. However, you cannot use a domain name that is already in use. For example, you cannot use microsoft.com or harvard.edu. Also, you cannot use a domain name that infringes on another company's trademarked brand name.

To find out the availability of a domain name and register it, you must contact a **domain name registrar**. Domain names are stored in a master database that is maintained by **InterNIC**, the organization responsible for the registration of domain names and IP addresses. Any domain name registrar that is accredited by InterNIC is permitted to access and modify the master domain name database. A domain name registrar's Web site helps you search the master database to find out if the domain name you want to use is available. If your desired domain name is available, for a fee the domain name registrar will assist you in registering the domain name for a specified period of time, usually one to two years.

You can view a list of InterNIC-accredited domain name registrars at *http://www.internic.net/alpha.html*.

A popular domain name registrar is Network Solutions, a division of VeriSign. If you visit the Network Solutions Web site at *http://www.netsol.com*, you can search for the availability of a domain name as shown in Figure 3-10.

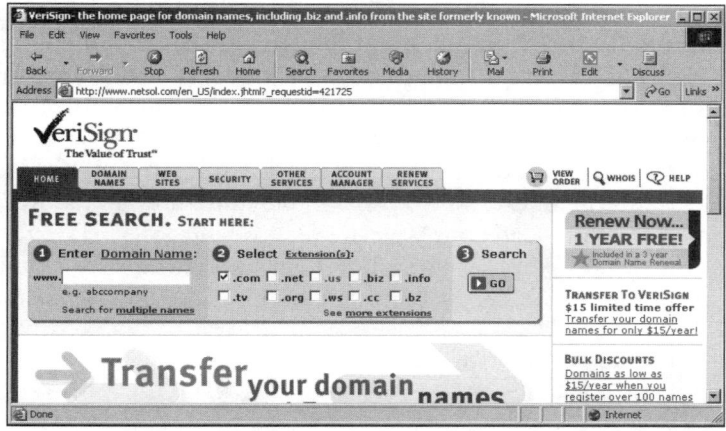

Figure 3-10   Network Solutions Web page

Once you register your domain name, you need to notify your ISP of your domain information. Usually, it is easiest to register your domain name through the ISP you intend to use (assuming they are a domain name registrar) because they can automatically handle the details of setting up the domain for you. However, if you have an existing domain that you want to transfer to another ISP, or if you register your domain name with a different domain name registrar, your ISP usually has a form or some other procedure to assist you in transferring your domain.

File Transfer Protocol

When you are ready to publish your Web site, you usually use FTP to send to the hosting ISP the XHTML documents and other files that make up your Web site. **File Transfer Protocol** (**FTP**) is the protocol used for transferring files across the Internet. A Web browser is not the target for files transferred by FTP. Instead, FTP simply transfers files between an FTP client (your computer) and an FTP server (a server capable of running FTP).

HTTP and FTP are both Internet communication protocols. The biggest difference between HTTP and FTP is that HTTP is primarily used for transmitting Web pages that will be rendered in a browser, whereas FTP is used to transfer any type of file.

To publish your Web site, you must upload your files to your ISP's FTP server. Your ISP will give you a user name and password that you must use to log into the FTP site. Your user name and password should give you permission to upload files to the FTP server. Once you log into an FTP server, you will see a directory structure that looks very similar to Windows Explorer and other types of file-management systems. Your ISP will instruct you where to upload your Web site files.

Various types of commercial and shareware software exist that you can use to access an FTP site. In fact, many HTML Editors such as FrontPage have built-in commands that you can use to log into an FTP server and upload your files. However, most current Web browsers, including Internet Explorer and Netscape, have the capability to act as FTP clients, which means that you can use your browser to log into an FTP server and upload your files. Figure 3-11 shows how the FTP site for Dell Computer appears in Internet Explorer. As you can see in the figure, the FTP site closely resembles Windows Explorer. With this type of interface, to upload your Web site files to your ISP's FTP site, you need only copy the files from your computer using Windows Explorer or My Computer and paste them into the appropriate folder that appears in your Web browser window.

Figure 3-11   Dell Computer FTP site

 Some of the more popular FTP programs include WS_FTP (*http://www.ipswitch.com*) and CuteFTP (*http://www.globalscape.com*) for Windows, and Fetch (*http://www.fetchsoftworks.com*) for Macintosh.

If you do not have a login account, many FTP sites allow you to access the site anonymously. When you access an FTP site anonymously, you can download files from the site, but you cannot upload files. The Dell Computer FTP site shown in Figure 3-11 is an example of an anonymous FTP site. Although many anonymous FTP sites exist, in order to protect the privacy of their clients, the majority of ISPs do not allow anonymous logins to Web hosting FTP sites. When you use Internet Explorer to log into your ISP's Web hosting FTP site, you will be presented with a login dialog box similar to Figure 3-12.

Figure 3-12   FTP login dialog box

The process of uploading files is very similar to the process of downloading files. Next, you will practice downloading files from the NASA FTP site. You will need to experiment with uploading files to your ISP's FTP site on your own.

To practice downloading files from the NASA FTP site:

1. Open Internet Explorer, enter the following URL in the Address box, and then press **Enter**. The URL accesses the NASA FTP site and opens the saturn directory, which is located several directories deep in the FTP site's directory structure. You should see a list of the images that are located within the saturn directory. Although you can display an image simply by clicking its filename, you will download one of the files and use it on a Web page.

   ```
   ftp://nssdcftp.gsfc.nasa.gov/photo_gallery/image/
   planetary/saturn/
   ```

2. Right-click the **saturn.jpg** file and select **Copy** from the **Shortcut** menu.

3. Use Windows Explorer or My Computer to paste the file in the Chapter.03\ **Chapter** folder.

4. Next, create a new document in your text editor and type the following code that creates a simple Web page to display the saturn.jpg file:

   ```
   <!DOCTYPE html PUBLIC
   "-//W3C//DTD XHTML 1.0 Strict//EN"
   "http://www.w3.org/TR/xhtml1/DTD/xhtml1-strict.dtd">
   <html xmlns="http://www.w3.org/1999/xhtml" lang="en"
   xml:lang = "en" dir="ltr">
   ```

```
<head>
<title>Image of Saturn</title>
</head>
<body>
<p><img src="saturn.jpg" /></p>
</body>
</html>
```

5. Save the file as **Saturn.html** in the **Chapter.03\Chapter** folder for Chapter 3.

6. Open **Saturn.html** in a Web browser. Figure 3-13 displays the Saturn.html file as it appears in Internet Explorer.

Figure 3-13   Saturn.html

7. Close the Web browser window.

Advertising Your Web Site

You are undoubtedly familiar with Web sites such as Yahoo! and AltaVisa that help you locate Web sites that match search criteria. To draw visitors to your Web site, your best bet is to get listed on sites such as these. There are two types of sites that users can use to search for Web pages: Web directories and search engines. **Web directories** are listings of Web sites that have been compiled by humans. **Search engines** use software to "crawl" or "spider" their way through the Web and automatically compile an index of Web sites. Yahoo! is an example of a Web directory that is compiled by humans, whereas HotBot is an example of a search engine that finds Web sites automatically.

3

If you publish your Web site and do nothing else, most search engines will eventually find it. Directories may also find your site, although it may take some time. Waiting for search engines and directories to come to you, however, is not the best way of advertising your site. Your best bet is to submit your site to a search engine or Web directory when you first publish it or whenever you make major changes to it. Most search engines and directories have a button that allows you to submit a site. For instance, AltaVista includes a Submit A Site link at the bottom of its home page that you can use to submit your site.

 Another option is to go through a commercial service that automatically submits your site to multiple search engines for a fee. One service promises to submit your Web site to over 1000 search engines. But, most people would probably find it difficult to name 10 search engines. Rather than spending money, you may want to submit your site to the most popular search engines yourself.

 A Web site with which you may want to familiarize yourself is Search Engine Watch at *http://www.searchenginewatch.com*. Search Engine Watch is devoted to monitoring and providing information about search engines and directories, and lists the major search engines in various categories.

Directories such as Yahoo! that are compiled by humans require that you include a description of your Web site when you submit it. In comparison, to find information about a Web site, a search engine's "spider" (also called a "crawler" or "robot") will visit a page on the site, record information about the page in an index, and then follow any links to other pages within the site and index their information. The spider will then revisit the site on a regular basis to see if its information has changed. The search engine then relies on special software to sort through the information indexed by the spider and return a set of results to a user. The information that a spider indexes about a Web page varies by search engine. Some search engines index the entire page or only the first few lines of a page. Other search engines, however, rely on a Web page's metadata.

METADATA

The term **metadata** means information about information. In a Web page, you use the <meta> element to provide information to search engines and Web servers about the information in your Web page. You must place the <meta> element within the <head> element. You can use three primary attributes with the <meta> element: name, content, and http-equiv. You use the content attribute to provide information that is required by both the name and http-equiv attributes. Therefore, the only required attribute in the <meta> element is the content attribute.

The name Attribute

You use the name attribute to define the name of the information you want to provide about the Web page. You can use any text you like as the value of the name attribute. For instance, you may want to include a <meta> element that contains the author of and copyright information about a document. To do this, you create two <meta> elements in a document's head. You would assign a value of "author" to the name attribute in the first <meta> element and a value of "copyright" to the name attribute in the second <meta> element. Both elements must include a content attribute that contains the associated value for each name attribute. The following statements illustrate this use of the <meta> element:

```
<html lang="EN" xml:lang = "EN" dir="ltr">
<head>
<title>Publishing Information</title>
<meta name="author" content="Don Gosselin" />
<meta name="copyright" content ="(c) 2003, Course Technology" />
</head>
```

Two values that are used by some search engines are *description* and *keyword*. Many search engines create a description of a Web page based on the first 200 characters following the opening <body> tag, unless the Web page includes a description <meta> element. You can think of this description <meta> element as equivalent to the description you might submit for a particular Web page to a directory such as Yahoo!. Keywords are the words that describe the type of Web page a user is looking for and will likely type into a Web directory or search engine. You can create a keyword <meta> element that lists the keywords you want a search engine to associate with your Web page. You separate the keywords you assign to the content attributes with commas.

```
<html lang="EN" xml:lang = "EN" dir="ltr">
<head><title>Publishing Information</title>
<meta name="description" content="Frank's Fishery offers a
large selection of fishing gear at low prices." />
<meta name="keywords" content ="fishing tackle, fishing
equipment, fishing rods, fishing poles, ocean fishing,
fresh water, tackle box, fishing lures, tackle shops, sport
fishing, angler, fishing, tackle, bait, hooks, lures" />
<meta http-equiv="content-type"
     content="text/html; charset=iso-8859-1" />
</head>
```

In an attempt to trick search engines into returning their Web pages more often during searches, some Web page authors pack their keywords list with repetitious or unrelated words. Some search engines will not index a document that contains too many repetitious words, whereas other search engines will ban altogether a site that lists keywords that are unrelated to its site. Most spiders will ignore the entire keyword list if it repeats the same keyword more than seven times. Additionally, most search engines will truncate a description that is longer than 200 characters and will only process the first 1000 characters in a keywords list.

Next, you will add keyword and description `<meta>` elements to the home page for the Central Valley Farmers' Market.

To add keywords and description meta elements to the home page for the Central Valley Farmers' Market:

1. Return to the **CentralValley.html** file in your text editor.

2. Above the closing `</head>` tag, add the following `<meta>` element that creates the description meta element:

   ```
   <meta name="description" content="The Central Valley
   Farmers' Market sells fresh produce, hand-made crafts,
   baked goods, and a variety of other products." />
   ```

3. After the description `<meta>` element, add the following keyword `<meta>` element:

   ```
   <meta name="keywords" content ="market, farmers' market,
   organic produce, fresh produce, vegetables, fruit, herbs,
   crafts, baked goods" />
   ```

4. Save the **CentralValley.html** file.

Hiding Web Pages from Search Engines

Recall that a search engine's spider will visit a Web page, index its information, follow any links to other pages within the site, and index the resulting information. However, your Web site may include pages that you do not want to be included in any search engine indexes. For instance, you may have a page that stores personal information or private data that, although not private enough to encrypt using special security software or a protocol such as HTTPS, should not be returned to a user who performs a search in a search engine. Or, your site may include test pages or pages that are under construction that do not need to be posted in search engine indexes. You can inform search engine spiders that you do not want certain pages on your site to be indexed by placing a file named robots.txt in the root directory of the Web server that hosts your Web site. This technique is called the Robots Exclusion Protocol (recall that spiders are also called "robots"). You place statements in the robots.txt file that inform search engine spiders of the directories and files you do not want indexed, similar to the following:

```
User-agent: *
Disallow:/personal/
Disallow:/development/
```

The first statement in the preceding code specifies that the instructions in the file apply to all spiders that access the Web site. The second two statements specify the names of folders that the spiders should skip when indexing the Web site.

Although the robots.txt file is very effective in preventing spiders from indexing certain pages on your Web site, it is not very useful for the average Web page author. The average Web page author does not have access to the root directory of the hosting ISP's Web server. Only an ISP's webmaster or someone with administrative rights would have access to the Web server's root directory. An alternate method for preventing spiders from indexing certain pages on your Web site is to create a robots `<meta>` element for each Web page. You create a robots `<meta>` element by assigning a value of *robots* to the `<meta>` element's `name` attribute. You then assign to the `content` attribute one or more of the following values: *index*, *noindex*, *nofollow*, or *none*. The index value instructs a spider to index the page, the noindex value instructs a spider not to index the page, and the nofollow value instructs a spider not to follow any links on the page. For instance, the following `<meta>` element instructs a robot to index the page, but not to follow any links on the page.

```
<meta name="robots" content="index, nofollow" />
```

Assigning a value of none to the `content` attribute is the equivalent of assigning both the `noindex` and `nofollow` attributes, as shown in the following example:

```
<meta name="robots" content="none" />
```

Next, you will add to the home page for the Central Valley Farmers' Market a robots `<meta>` element that allows spiders to index the page, but not to follow any links on the page.

To add a robots `<meta>` element to the home page for the Central Valley Farmers' Market that allows spiders to index the page, but not to follow any links on the page:

1. Return to the **CentralValley.html** file in your text editor.

2. Above the closing `</head>` tag, add the following `<meta>` element to create a robot `<meta>` element that allows spiders to index the page, but not to follow any links on the page:

```
<meta name="robots" content="index, nofollow" />
```

3. Save the **CentralValley.html** file.

The `http-equiv` Attribute

When a user wants to access a Web page, either by entering its URL in a browser's Address box or by clicking a link, the user's Web browser asks the Web server for the Web page in what is referred to as a **request**. What the Web server returns to the user is called the **response**. One part of the response is the requested Web page. Another important part of the response is the **response header**, which is sent to the Web browser before the Web page is sent in order to provide information that the browser needs to render the page. One of the most important pieces of information in the response header is the type of data, or content-type, that the server is sending. For Web pages, you create a content-type <meta> element to specify a content type that the document uses.

One important use of the <meta> element is to specify a document's character encoding. Although you can specify a document's character encoding when you validate it with the W3C Markup Validation Service, it is important that you specify the character encoding within the document in order to allow a Web server to construct a response header. You use the http-equiv attribute to create a content-type <meta> element, which a Web server will use to construct a response header. A requesting browser will use the content type in the response header to properly render the Web page. To create a content-type <meta> element, you assign a value of *content-type* to the http-equiv attribute in a <meta> element. You then assign to the content attribute a value of *text/html; charset=iso-8859-1*, which specifies that the document's MIME type is "text/html" and that the document uses the iso-8859-1 character set. The following statement shows how to construct the same content-type meta elements that you have created since Chapter 2:

```
<meta http-equiv="content-type"
      content="text/html; charset=iso-8859-1" />
```

Multipurpose Internet Mail Extensions (MIME) is a protocol that was originally developed to allow different file types to be transmitted as attachments to e-mail messages. Now MIME has become a standard method of exchanging files over the Internet, although the technology is still evolving. You specify MIME types with two-part codes separated by a forward slash (/). The first part specifies the MIME type, and the second part specifies the MIME subtype.

The W3C strongly encourages the use of content-type <meta> elements to specify an XHTML document's character set. However, a content-type <meta> element is not required because most current Web browsers can figure out the character set of an XHTML document. For XHTML documents you create in this book, you will include the content-type <meta> elements.

The content-type <meta> element is just one of many response-header meta elements that you can construct with the http-equiv attribute. You can find a complete listing of other response-header <meta> elements to use with the http-equiv attribute at *http://www.vancouver-webpages.com/META/*.

Next, you add the content-type `<meta>` element to the documents you created in this chapter and validate them with the W3C MarkUp Validation Service:

To add the content-type `<meta>` element to the documents you created in this chapter and validate them with the W3C MarkUp Validation Service:

1. Return to the CentralValley.html file and, above the closing `</head>` tag, add the following `<meta>` element to create a content-type meta tag that specifies a MIME type of text/html and a character set of *iso-8859-1*:

```
<meta http-equiv="content-type"
      content="text/html; charset=iso-8859-1" />
```

2. Save and close the **Central Valley.html** file.

3. Return to the Contact.html file and add a content-type `<meta>` element above its closing `</head>` tag.

4. Save and close the **Contact.html** file.

5. Return to the Saturn.html file and add a content-type `<meta>` element above its closing `</head>` tag.

6. Save and close the **Saturn.html** file.

7. Start your Web browser and enter the URL for the upload page of the W3C MarkUp Validation Service: **www.validator.w3org/file-upload.html**. Open and validate the **CentralValley.html**, **Contact.html**, and **Saturn.html** files. If you receive any warnings or errors, fix them, and then revalidate the documents.

8. Close your Web browser.

CHAPTER SUMMARY

❐ The text or image used to represent a link on a Web page is called an anchor.

❐ You create a basic hypertext link using the `<a>` element.

❐ Hypertext Transfer Protocol (HTTP) manages the hypertext links that are used to navigate the Web.

❐ A host refers to a computer system that is being accessed by a remote computer.

❐ The last part of a domain name, known as the domain identifier, identifies the type of institution or organization.

❐ An absolute Uniform Resource Locator (URL) refers to the full Web address of a Web page or to a specific drive and directory.

❐ A relative URL specifies the location of a file relative to the location of the currently loaded Web page.

❑ Bookmarks are internal links within the current document.

❑ Web hosting refers to the publication of a Web site for public access.

❑ To find out the availability of a domain name and register it, you must contact a domain name registrar.

❑ Domain names are stored in a master database that is maintained by InterNIC, the organization responsible for the registration of domain names and Internet Protocol (IP) addresses.

❑ File Transfer Protocol (FTP) is the protocol used for transferring files across the Internet.

❑ Web directories are listings of Web sites that have been compiled by humans.

❑ Search engines use software to "crawl" or "spider" their way through the Web and automatically compile an index of Web sites.

❑ You use the `<meta>` element to provide information to search engines and Web servers about the information in your Web page.

❑ When a user wants to access a Web page, either by entering its URL in a browser's Address box or by clicking a link, the user's Web browser asks the Web server for the Web page in what is referred to as a request.

❑ What the Web server returns to the user is called the response.

❑ The response header is sent to the Web browser before the Web page is sent in order to provide information that the browser needs to render the page.

REVIEW QUESTIONS

1. What is the default color in Internet Explorer of an unvisited link?

   a. blue

   b. purple

   c. magenta

   d. green

2. The host portion of a URL is usually _____.

   a. web

   b. ftp

   c. http

   d. www

3. The last part of a domain name, known as the _____, identifies the type of institution or organization.

   a. domain

   b. domain identifier

   c. protocol

   d. IP address

4. If a URL does not specify a filename, the requesting Web server looks for a file with which of the following names? (Choose all that apply.)

   a. index.html

   b. index.htm

   c. default.html

   d. default.htm

5. What protocol do you use to automatically send an e-mail message to a specified address?

   a. `ftp://`

   b. `mail:`

   c. `mailto:`

   d. `telnet://`

6. Explain the difference between absolute and relative URLs.

7. What is the correct syntax for creating a bookmark that is compatible with both older and newer browsers?

   a. `<h3 name="mt1">Management Team</h3>`

   b. `<h3 id="mt1" name="mt1">Management Team</h3>`

   c. `<h3><a name="mt1">Management Team</a></h3>`

   d. `<h3><a id="mt1" name="mt1">Management Team</a></h3>`

8. Explain why you should use an ISP to host a Web site.

9. Domain names are stored in a master database that is maintained by _____.

   a. Microsoft

   b. Netscape

   c. the W3C

   d. InterNIC

10. You can register a domain name yourself. True or False?

11. Most current Web browsers, including Internet Explorer and Netscape, have the capability to act as FTP clients. True or False?

3

12. What is FTP used for? (Choose all that apply.)

    a. Uploading files

    b. Downloading files

    c. Installing Web applications

    d. Indexing a Web site's content

13. Yahoo! is a search engine. True or False?

14. Explain the differences between search engines and Web directories.

15. Which attribute of the `<meta>` element is required in all `<meta>` elements?

    a. `description`

    b. `content`

    c. `name`

    d. `http-equiv`

16. How many characters are you limited to in a description `<meta>` element?

    a. 50

    b. 100

    c. 200

    d. 300

17. How many characters are you limited to in a keyword `<meta>` element?

    a. 250

    b. 500

    c. 1000

    d. You can use as many characters as you like.

18. To get search engines to return your Web pages more often during searches, you should pack the keyword list with repetitious or unrelated words. True or False?

19. Explain why you would use a robots `<meta>` element instead of the robots.txt file to inform search engine spiders of the directories and files you do not want indexed.

20. Which of the following values can you assign to the `content` attribute in a robots `<meta>` element? (Choose all that apply.)

    a. index

    b. noindex

    c. nofollow

    d. none

HANDS-ON PROJECTS

Project 3-1

In this exercise, you create the home page for a shoe repair service.

1. Create a new document in your text editor, and type the opening `<!DOCTYPE>` declaration, `<html>` element, `<head>` element, content-type `<meta>` element, and `<body>` element. Use the Strict DTD and "Olde World Shoe Repair" as the content of the `<title>` element. Your document should appear as follows:

```
<!DOCTYPE html PUBLIC
"-//W3C//DTD XHTML 1.0 Strict//EN"
"http://www.w3.org/TR/xhtml1/DTD/xhtml1-strict.dtd">
<html xmlns="http://www.w3.org/1999/xhtml" lang="en"
xml:lang = "en" dir="ltr">
<head>
<title>Olde World Shoe Repair</title>
<meta http-equiv="content-type" content="text/html;
charset=iso-8859-1" />
</head>
<body>
</body>
</html>
```

2. Create the document body shown in Figure 3-14. Be sure to add internal links to the Shoe Repair and Leather Repair headings.

3. Save the document as **OldeWorldShoeRepair.html** in the Chapter.03\ Projects folder.

Project 3-2

In this exercise, you add a new Web page to the Olde World Shoe Repair Web site.

1. Return to the OldeWorldShoeRepair.html file in your text editor and add the following `<a>` element after the Leather Repair link but above the horizontal rule:

```
<p><a href="ContactUs.html">Contact Information</a></p>
```

2. Create a new document in your text editor and type the opening `<!DOCTYPE>` declaration, header information, and opening `<body>` tag. Use the Strict DTD and "Contact Information" as the content of the `<title>` element. (You will find it easiest to copy the existing elements in the OldeWorldShoeRepair.html file and paste them into the new file, then simply change the contents of the `<title>` element.)

Figure 3-14 Olde World Shoe Repair

3. Add to the document body an **<h1>** element that reads "Olde World Shoe Repair" and an **<h2>** element that reads "Contact Information", as follows:

```
<h1>Olde World Shoe Repair</h1>
<h2>Contact Information</h2>
```

4. Add the following contact information to the document:

```
<p>123 Main Street<br />
Anywhere, USA 12345<br />
Phone: (565) 555-1212</p>
<p>You can send us an e-mail at
<a href=mailto:info@oldworldshoes.com>info@oldworld
    shoes.com</a>.</p>
```

5. Type the following link that returns to the Olde World Shoe Repair home page:

```
<p><a href="OldeWorldShoeRepair.html">Home</a></p>
```

6. Save the file as **ContactUs.html** in the Chapter.03\Projects folder.

7. Use the W3C MarkUp Validation Service to validate the OldeWorldShoeRepair.html and ContactUs.html files, and then open the OldeWorldShoeRepair.html file in your Web browser and test the links. Note that because the OldeWorldShoeRepair.html file does not contain much text, it will not be obvious that the links to the bookmark elements work unless your browser window is sized to be fairly small.

Project 3-3

In this exercise, you create a page for an employment Web site that includes a `mailto` link that job seekers can use to receive new job postings via e-mail.

1. Create a new document in your text editor, and type the opening `<!DOCTYPE>` declaration, `<html>` element, `<head>` element, content-type `<meta>` element, and `<body>` element. Use the Strict DTD and "Job Postings" as the content of the `<title>` element.

2. Type the following header elements and `mailto` link:

   ```
   <h1>Coast City Employment Opportunities</h1>
   <h2>Job Postings</h2>
   <p><a href="mailto:jobpostings@coastcity.gov">
   Send us a message to receive new job postings via
   e-mail.</a></p>
   ```

3. Save the file as **JobPostings.html** in the Chapter.03\Projects folder.

4. Use the W3C MarkUp Validation Service to validate the JobPostings.html file, and then open it in your Web browser and test the mailto link.

Project 3-4

Although the bookmark links you created in this chapter jumped only to elements on the current page, you can also create bookmark links to specific elements on other pages. You create a link to a bookmark on another page by appending the # sign to the page's URL followed by the value assigned to the `id` and `name` attributes of the element that is the target of the link. For example, to jump to an element with an `id` and `name` attribute of "mh2" on a Web page named MedicalHistory.html, you use the following `<a>` element: `<a href="MedicalHistory.html#mh2">Serious Illnesses</a>`. In this exercise, you create a main Web page that lists some hiking destinations in the San Francisco Bay area. Each hiking destination includes a link that jumps to a heading on another Web page that describes information about the hike.

1. Create a new document in your text editor, and type the opening `<!DOCTYPE>` declaration, `<html>` element, `<head>` element, content-type `<meta>` element, and `<body>` element. Use the Strict DTD and "San Francisco Bay Area Hiking Guide" as the content of the `<title>` element.

2. Add to the document body the following heading elements and hiking destination links that link to bookmarks on a Web page named HikingDestinations.html.

   ```
   <h1>San Francisco Bay Area</h1>
   <h2>Hiking Guide</h2>
   <p><a href="HikingDestinations.html#hd1">
       Fort Funston</a></p>
   <p><a href="HikingDestinations.html#hd2">
       Rodeo Beach</a></p>
   <p><a href="HikingDestinations.html#hd3">
       Mission Peak</a></p>
   ```

3. Save the file as **HikingGuide.html** in the Chapter.03\Projects folder.

4. Create another document in your text editor, and type the opening `<!DOCTYPE>` declaration, `<html>` element, `<head>` element, content-type `<meta>` element, and `<body>` element. Use the Strict DTD and "San Francisco Bay Area Hiking Destinations" as the content of the `<title>` element.

5. Add to the document body the following heading and paragraph elements that list information about each hiking destination. Notice that the `<h3>` elements include `id` and `name` attributes.

```
<h1>San Francisco Bay Area</h1>
<h2>Hiking Destinations</h2>
<h3><a id="hd1" name="hd1">Fort Funston</a></h3>
<p>Distance: 1.5 Miles<br />
Elev. (low/high): 0/183 ft.<br />
Difficulty: Easy</p>
<h3><a id="hd2" name="hd2">Rodeo Beach</a></h3>
<p>Distance: 4.3 Miles<br />
Elev. (low/high): 20/850 ft.<br />
Difficulty: Easy</p>
<h3><a id="hd3" name="hd3">Mission Peak</a></h3>
<p>Distance: 5.6 Miles<br />
Elev. (low/high): 425/2453 ft.<br />
Difficulty: Moderate</p>
```

6. Type the following link that returns to the San Francisco Bay Area Hiking Guide home page:

```
<p><a href="HikingGuide.html">Hiking Guide</a></p>
```

7. Save the file as **HikingDestinations.html** in the Chapter.03\Projects folder.

8. Use the W3C MarkUp Validation Service to validate the HikingGuide.html and HikingDestinations.html files, and then open the HikingGuide.html file in your Web browser and test the links. Because the HikingDestination.html file does not contain much text, it will not be obvious that the links to the bookmark elements work unless your browser window is sized to be fairly small.

Project 3-5

In this exercise, you create a simple Web page for a ballroom dancing studio that includes description and keyword `<meta>` elements.

1. Create a new document in your text editor, and type the opening `<!DOCTYPE>` declaration, `<html>` element, `<head>` element, content-type `<meta>` element, and `<body>` element. Use the Strict DTD and "Ballroom Dancing" as the content of the `<title>` element.

2. Add the following description and keyword `<meta>` elements above the closing `</head>` tag:

```
<meta name="description" content="San Francisco Bay Area's
best place to learn to dance. Private lessons and group
classes available in Swing, Salsa, Tango, Lindy Hop, Cha
Cha, Rumba, Samba, Waltz, Foxtrot, Tango, Hip Hop, Hustle,
Two-Step, and many others." />

<meta name="keywords" content="dance, dancing, ballroom,
ballroom dance, ballroom dancing, dance lessons, swing,
salsa, tango, lindy hop, cha cha, rumba, samba, waltz,
foxtrot, tango, hip hop, hustle, two-step" />
```

3. Add to the document body the following heading and paragraph elements:

```
<h1>Coast City</h1>
<h2>Ballroom Dancing</h2>
<p>Private lessons and group classes available in Swing,
Salsa, Tango, Lindy Hop, Cha Cha, Rumba, Samba, Waltz,
Foxtrot, Tango, Hip Hop, Hustle, Two-Step, and many
others.</p>
```

4. Save the file as **BallroomDancing.html** in the Chapter.03\Projects folder.

5. Use the W3C MarkUp Validation Service to validate the BallroomDancing.html file.

Project 3-6

In this exercise, you create a family's Web page that contains a robots `<meta>` element to prevent spiders from indexing its content.

1. Create a new document in your text editor, and type the opening `<!DOCTYPE>` declaration, `<html>` element, `<head>` element, content-type `<meta>` element, and `<body>` element. Use the Strict DTD and "The Tanaka Family Web Page" as the content of the `<title>` element.

2. Add the following robots `<meta>` element above the closing `</head>` tag. The content attribute is assigned a value of "none" to instruct spiders not to index the page and not to follow any links on the page.

```
<meta name="robots" content="none" />
```

3. Add to the document body the following heading and paragraph elements:

```
<h1>The Tanaka Family </h1>
<h2>Welcome to Our Web Page</h2>
<p>This page is dedicated to keeping our friends and family
 up to speed on what's going on in our busy lives!</p>
<p>Feel free to <a href="mailto:tanakas@coastcity.com">
send us a message</a>.</p>
```

4. Save the file as **TanakaFamily.html** in the Chapter.03\Projects folder.

5. Use the W3C MarkUp Validation Service to validate the TanakaFamily.html file.

CASE PROJECTS

For the following projects, save the files you create in the Chapter.03\Cases folder. Create the files so they are well formed according to the Strict DTD. Be sure to validate the files you create with the W3C MarkUp Validation Service.

Project 3-1

Create a Book of the Month Club Web site. The home page should describe the current month's selection, including book title, author, publisher, ISBN number, number of pages, and so on. Create separate Web pages for the book selections for the last three months. Add links to the home page that open each of the three Web pages. Save the home page as BookClub.html and the Web pages for previous months using the name of the month.

Project 3-2

Create a Web site for a boat rental company. On the home page, describe the company and the types of boats it rents. Create separate Web pages for rental rates and reservations. On the rental rates page, list the types of boats available and their rental rates according to the length of the boat. Include rates for one day, 3-6 days, and 7 or more days. On the reservations page, include a `mailto` link that visitors can use to send a message to reserve a boat. Instruct the visitor on the type of information to include in their message, including the boat length, rental dates, and contact information. Save the home page as BoatRentals.html, the rental rates page as Rates.html, and the reservations page as Reservations.html.

Project 3-3

Create a Web site for the Central Valley Pottery Studio. On the home page, describe the studio and explain what it teaches and the different types of classes it offers. Create separate Web pages for the following: Adult Classes, Kids' Classes, and Workshops. Within each Web page, include the following information about each class: day, time, dates, instructor, and cost. Save the home page as PotteryStudio.html. Save the Adult Classes Web page as Adults.html, the Kids Classes Web page as Kids.html, and the Workshops Web page as Workshops.html.

Project 3-4

Create a Web site for a bug extermination company. On the home page, describe the company's general services and include links to other pages that contain detailed information on the company's procedures for exterminating different types of bugs. Include pages for cockroaches, fleas, and ticks. Also, include a page that contains information on ordering an inspection. Add links from the inspection Web page to the home page, cockroaches page, fleas page, and ticks page. Save the home page as Exterminator.html. Save the cockroaches page as Cockroaches.html, the fleas page as Fleas.html, the ticks page as Ticks.html, and the inspection page as Inspection.html.

4

TEXT AND IMAGES

In this chapter, you will:

♦ Learn how to work with text-formatting elements
♦ Study phrase elements
♦ Study block-level text elements
♦ Work with quotations
♦ Add special characters to your Web pages
♦ Add images to your Web pages
♦ Create image maps

In Chapter 3, you learned about some of the most basic structural elements common to all XHTML documents. However, the most important part of a Web page is the text it displays. The text and images on the page represent the information that a visitor to your Web page is interested in. That information may include a schedule of classes, a price list, information about a company, or directions to a particular location. Although the visual display of text is important to today's Web browsers, the *type of information* represented by the text will likely be more important as the Web evolves to other types of user agents. For this reason, XHTML includes numerous elements for working with text, along with several elements and techniques for working with images. In this chapter, you study how to work with text and image elements and how to create an image map, which allows users to navigate to different Web pages by clicking an image.

TEXT-FORMATTING ELEMENTS

Recall that early in the browser wars, Web browser makers began to add their own extensions to HTML, such as the bold and font elements, in order to provide functionality for displaying and formatting Web pages. These extensions did nothing to describe the type of data being presented, but served only to instruct a Web browser how to display and format the date. Consider the bold element. Although it works fine for visually displaying text in boldface type, how should a user agent for the visually impaired that verbally reads the contents of a Web page handle the bold element? Should the user agent shout the content contained within the bold element? To address these types of issues, XHTML uses two types of inline elements for managing the formatting of text in an XHTML document: formatting elements and phrase elements. **Formatting elements** provide specific instructions about how their contents should be displayed. For instance, the <b> element instructs user agents to display its contents as boldface text. **Phrase elements**, however, primarily identify or describe their contents. For instance, the <em> element is an emphasized piece of data, similar to a quotation. How the <em> element is rendered is decided by each user agent, although most current Web browsers display the contents of the <em> element using italics. However, a user agent for the visually impaired may use the <em> element to pronounce the text it contains with more emphasis, in order to get the meaning across to the visually impaired Web site visitor.

Generally, you should strive to use only Cascading Style Sheets (CSS) to manage the display of elements on your Web pages. However, because several of the basic formatting elements are so commonly used, they are not deprecated in XHTML Strict.

The text-formatting elements that are available in XHTML Strict are listed in Table 4-1.

Table 4-1   Text-formatting elements

Element	Description
<b>	Formats text in boldface type
<big>	Formats text in a larger font
<i>	Formats text in italic type
<small>	Formats text in a smaller font
<sub>	Formats enclosed text as a subscript
<sup>	Formats enclosed text as a superscript
<tt>	Formats enclosed text as teletype or monospaced text

 As discussed in Chapter 1, several elements that were popular in HTML, including the <basefont>, <center>, <font>, <s>, <strike>, and <u> elements, are deprecated in XHTML Strict in favor of CSS.

You are probably already familiar with the elements listed in Table 4-1. However, to be sure you understand the formatting each element produces, Figure 4-1 contains the code for a simple Web page that uses each element. Figure 4-2 shows the output in a Web browser.

```
<!DOCTYPE html PUBLIC
"-//W3C//DTD XHTML 1.0 Strict//EN"
"http://www.w3.org/TR/xhtml1/DTD/xhtml1-strict.dtd">
<html xmlns="http://www.w3.org/1999/xhtml" lang="en" xml:lang = "en" dir="ltr">
<head>
<title>Text Formatting Elements</title>
<meta http-equiv="content-type"
    content="text/html; charset=iso-8859-1" />
</head>
<body>
<p><b>Bold text</b></p>
<p><big>Big text</big></p>
<p><i>Italicized text</i></p>
<p><small>Small text</small></p>
<p><sub>Subscripted</sub> text</p>
<p><sup>Superscripted</sup> text</p>
<p><tt>Teletype text</tt></p>
</body>
</html>
```

Figure 4-1   Web page with text-formatting elements

Figure 4-2   Output of a Web page with text-formatting elements

Most of the text-formatting elements in Figure 4-2 are self-explanatory. The **<bold>** element produces about the equivalent of applying bold to a word in a program such as Microsoft Word. The **<big>** element renders its content in a slightly larger font than that used for the other elements on a page. Similarly, the **<small>** element renders its content in a slightly smaller font than that used for the other elements on the page.

Next, you start creating a Web site for the New Millennium Health Club & Fitness Center Web site. The Web site contains health tips, exercise suggestions, and contact information. You work on the Web site throughout this chapter. First you create the home page using text-formatting elements.

To create a home page using text-formatting elements:

1. Start your text editor and create a new document.

2. Type the `<!DOCTYPE>` declaration, `<html>` element, document head, and the `<body>` element. Use the Strict DTD and "New Millennium Health Club Home Page" as the content of the `<title>` element. Your document should appear as follows:

```
<!DOCTYPE html PUBLIC
"-//W3C//DTD XHTML 1.0 Strict//EN"
"http://www.w3.org/TR/xhtml1/DTD/xhtml1-strict.dtd">
<html xmlns="http://www.w3.org/1999/xhtml" lang="en"
xml:lang = "en" dir="ltr">
<head>
<title>New Millennium Health Club Home Page</title>
<meta http-equiv="content-type"
content="text/html; charset=iso-8859-1" />
</head>
<body>
</body>
</html>
```

3. Add to the document body the following elements that contain the company's name and motto. The motto uses text-formatting elements to create boldface and italicized text. The motto is a French phrase that translates to "to your health." The statement is missing two French characters that you add later in this chapter when you learn how to add special characters to your Web pages. The last statement inserts a horizontal rule.

```
<h1>New Millennium</h1>
<h2>Health Club & Fitness Center</h2>
<p><b>Our motto is <i>A votre sante!</i></b></p>
<hr />
```

4. After the horizontal rule, type the following anchor elements that link to headings within the current document, along with another horizontal rule:

```
<p><a href="#ht1">Today's Health Tip</a><br />
<a href="#ot1">Online Trainer</a><br />
<a href="#cu1">Contact Us</a></p>
<hr />
```

5. Next, add the following elements to create the Today's Health Tips heading and section. Instead of typing the elements and content, you can copy them from the HealthTips.txt file, located in the Chapter.04\Chapter folder.

```
<h2><a id="ht1" name="ht1">Today's Health Tip</a></h2>
<p>Caryn Honig wrote in the online edition of <i>Health &
 Fitness Sports Magazine</i> the following advice about
energy bars:</p>

<p>Energy bars can contain high amounts of calories and
fat. Many contain palm kernel oil, which is saturated
enough to stay solid at room temperature, preventing
the coating from melting. Palm kernel oil is twice as
saturated as lard. Try to avoid the bars that are high
in saturated fat. When looking for an energy bar, read
the labels. Stay away from bars with ma huang, ephedra,
large amounts of caffeine and large amounts of ginseng.
Stick to the natural ingredients, such as oats, fruit
juice, and nuts. Often times, you are better off with
an apple, a handful of nuts, or some other type of
snack that fills you up with less calories, fat and
artificial additives.</p>
<hr />
```

6. Now add the following elements to create the Online Trainer heading and section. The section contains three anchors that link to other Web pages.

```
<h2><a id="ot1" name="ot1">Online Trainer</a></h2>
<p>What muscle group do you want to work on?</p>
<p><a href="Chest.html">Chest</a><br />
<a href="Arms.html">Arms</a><br />
<a href="Legs.html">Legs</a></p>
<hr />
```

7. Finally, add the following elements to create the Contact Us heading and section.

```
<h2><a id="cu1" name="cu1">Contact Us</a></h2>
<p>NMHCFC<br />
100 Kent Street<br />
Coast City, CA<br />
Phone: (912) 543-4563<br />
Fax: (912) 452-3452<br />
Email: <a href="mailto:info@nmhcfc.com">
info@nmhcfc.com</a><br /></p>
<hr />
```

8. Save the file as **HealthClub.html** in the Chapter.04\Chapter folder.

9. Open the **HealthClub.html** file in your Web browser. Figure 4-3 displays the HealthClub.html file as it appears in Internet Explorer. Do not click any of the links beneath the Online Trainer heading because you still need to create the target Web pages.

10. Close your Web browser window.

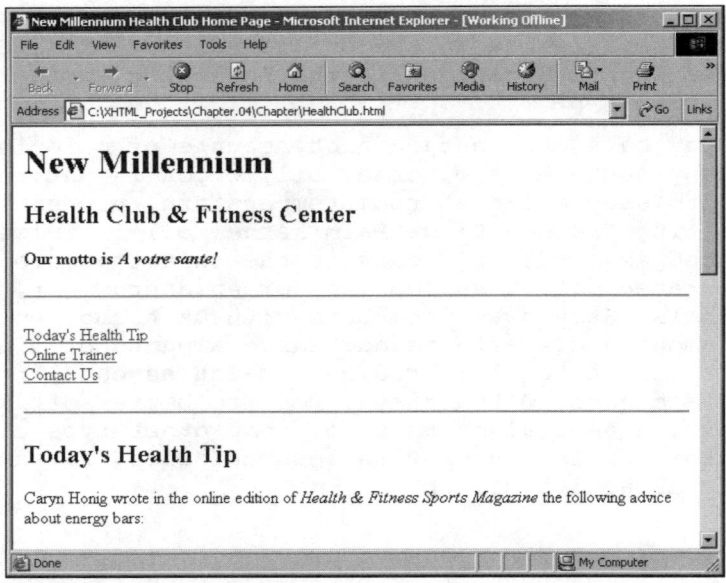

Figure 4-3   HealthClub.html

PHRASE ELEMENTS

Although text–formatting elements are commonly used and work perfectly well for displaying text with a specific style of formatting, it is a much better choice to format the text on your Web pages using a phrase element that more adequately describes its content. Using phrase elements helps ensure that your Web pages are compatible with user agents that may not be capable of handling formatting elements. Table 4-2 lists the phrase elements that are available in XHTML, along with how each element is rendered by most Web browsers.

Current Web browsers use similar conventions for displaying the content of phrase elements. For instance, most Web browsers render the **<em>** element in italics.

 Phrase elements are preferred over text-formatting elements for handling simple types of formatting (such as bold and italics) on a Web page. However, CSS is preferable for managing the display of elements on your Web pages.

Table 4-2   Phrase elements

Element	Description	Renders As
`<abbr>`	Specifies abbreviated text	Default text
`<acronym>`	Identifies an acronym	Default text
`<cite>`	Defines a citation	Italics
`<code>`	Identifies computer code	Monospace font
`<dfn>`	Marks a definition	Italics
`<em>`	Defines emphasized text	Italics
`<kbd>`	Indicates text that is to be entered by a visitor to a Web site	Monospace font
`<samp>`	Identifies sample computer code	Monospace font
`<strong>`	Defines strongly emphasized text	Bold
`<var>`	Defines a variable	Italics

4

Figure 4-4 contains the code for a simple Web page that uses each phrase element. Figure 4-5 shows the output in a Web browser.

```
<!DOCTYPE html PUBLIC
"-//W3C//DTD XHTML 1.0 Strict//EN"
"http://www.w3.org/TR/xhtml1/DTD/xhtml1-strict.dtd">
<html xmlns="http://www.w3.org/1999/xhtml" lang="en" xml:lang = "en" dir="ltr">
<head>
<title>Phrase Elements</title>
<meta http-equiv="content-type"
content="text/html; charset=iso-8859-1" />
</head>
<body>
<p><abbr>Abbreviation</abbr></p>
<p><acronym>Acronym</acronym></p>
<p><cite>Citation</cite></p>
<p><code>Code</code></p>
<p><dfn>Definition</dfn></p>
<p><em>Emphasis</em></p>
<p><kbd>Keyboard</kbd></p>
<p><samp>Sample</samp></p>
<p><strong>Strong</strong></p>
<p><var>Variable</var></p>
</body>
</html>
```

Figure 4-4   Web page with phrase elements

Figure 4-5   Output of Web page with phrase elements

The two most common text-formatting elements are the `<b>` and `<i>` elements. You should use the `<strong>` phrase element in place of the `<b>` text-formatting element, and the `<em>` phrase element in place of the `<i>` text-formatting element. This allows user agents other than Web browsers to better understand the meaning of each element, although current Web browsers still render the `<strong>` element as boldface and the `<em>` element in italics. Consider the following code written with the `<b>` and `<i>` elements:

```
<p><b>Yogi Berra said</b><br />
<i>When you come to a fork in the road, take it.</i></p>
```

Now consider the following version of the code that uses the `<strong>` and `<em>` elements instead of the `<b>` and `<i>` elements:

```
<p><strong>Yogi Berra said</strong><br />
<em>When you come to a fork in the road, take it.</em></p>
```

Both versions render identically in a Web browser. The version using the phrase elements, however, is the preferred method, as shown in Figure 4-6, because each phrase element more clearly describes its contents, rather than simply determining how text should appear in a browser, as is the case of text-formatting elements such as the `<i>` and `<b>` elements. Recall the earlier example of a user agent for the visually impaired that verbally reads the contents of a Web page. This type of user agent may have difficulty rendering the bold element, whose primary purpose is to visually make text appear boldface. However, the same user agent may be able to more easily handle the <strong> element by speaking its content with a louder intonation. In other words, the <strong> element specifies that the user agent should speak the text in a stronger voice. Similarly, the user agent may speak the contents of an <em> element with greater inflection in order to provide more emphasis.

Figure 4-6   Identical output of text-formatting elements and phrase elements

Next, you modify the paragraph in the HealthClub.html file that contains the motto so it uses the <strong> and <em> phrase elements instead of the <b> and <i> text-formatting elements.

To use the <strong> and <em> phrase elements instead of the <b> and <i> text-formatting elements:

1. Return to the **HealthClub.html** file in your text editor.

2. Modify the paragraph containing the motto so it uses the <strong> and <em> phrase elements instead of the <b> and <i> text-formatting elements. The modified statement should read as follows:

   ```
   <p><strong>Our motto is <em>A votre
   sante!</em></strong></p>
   ```

3. Save the **HealthClub.html** file and then open it in your Web browser. The paragraph containing the motto should appear the same as it did before you changed the text-formatting elements to phrase elements.

4. Close your Web browser window.

You use the remainder of the phrase elements to clearly identify specific types of content in your XHTML documents. Several of the phrase elements, such as the <cite> and <dfn> elements, are designed for formal or more technical types of documents. However, you should use phrase elements for any type of content that is best described by a phrase element. For instance, if one of your Web pages includes a formal definition of a term, you should use the <dfn> element to mark the first instance of the term in your document. Similarly, all citations within your documents should be marked with the <cite> element.

In the Today's Health Tip heading, the text within the paragraph that lists the author's name and the date of publication should be contained in a `<cite>` element. You now modify the paragraph so that it contains a `<cite>` element.

To modify the paragraph so that it contains a `<cite>` element:

1. Return to the **HealthClub.html** file in your text editor.

2. Modify the paragraph that lists the author's name and publication so that it contains a citation that lists the author's name and the publication date within a `<cite>` element. Also change the `<i>` elements around the magazine name to `<em>` elements. The modified paragraph should read as follows:

   ```
   <p>Caryn Honig wrote in the July, 2002 online edition
   of <em> Health & Fitness Sports Magazine </em> the
   following advice about energy bars <cite>(Honig 2002)
   </cite>:</p>
   ```

3. Save the **HealthClub.html** file and then open it in your Web browser. The portion of the paragraph within the `<cite>` element should appear in italics, as shown in Figure 4-7.

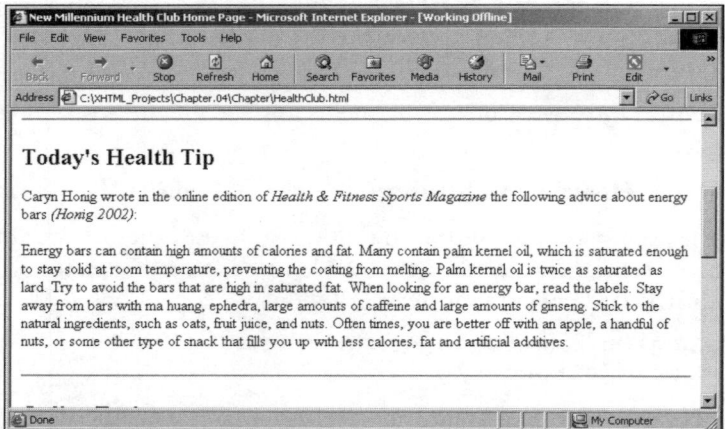

Figure 4-7   HealthClub.html after adding a `<cite>` element

4. Close your Web browser window.

Next, you create the three Web pages that are the target of the links in the Online Trainer heading: Chest.html, Arms.html, and Legs.html. Each Web page contains definitions of various weight-lifting exercises. You use the `<dfn>` element to identify each definition along with the `<strong>` element to make each defined term appear in boldface.

To create the Chest.html document:

1. Create a new document in your text editor.

2. Type the `<!DOCTYPE>` declaration, `<html>` element, document head, and the `<body>` element. Use the Strict DTD and "New Millennium Health Club Chest Exercises" as the content of the `<title>` element.

3. Add to the document body the following two heading elements to start the page:

```
<h1>New Millennium Health Club</h1>
<h2>Chest Exercises</h2>
```

4. After the `<h2>` element, add the following `<h3>` elements that contain definitions for each of the chest exercises. Notice that each term is contained within `<dfn>` and `<strong>` elements. Instead of typing the elements and content, you can copy them from the ChestExercises.txt file, located in the Chapter.04\Chapter folder.

```
<h3>Bench Press</h3>

<p>To perform the <dfn><strong>bench press</strong>
</dfn>, lie on a horizontal bench and hold a barbell
over your chest with your arms extended to form a right
angle with your chest. Lower the barbell to your chest
and then push upwards until your arms are completely
extended again.</p>

<h3>Incline Press</h3>

<p>To perform the <dfn><strong>incline press</strong>
</dfn>, lie on a bench with an inclined back and hold a
barbell out from your chest with your arms extended to
form a right angle with your chest. Lower the barbell
to your chest and then push upwards until your arms are
completely extended.</p>

<h3>Decline Press</h3>

<p>To perform the <dfn><strong>decline press</strong>
</dfn>, lie on a bench with a declined back and hold a
barbell out from your chest with your arms extended to
form a right angle with your chest. Lower the barbell
to your chest and then push upwards until your arms are
completely extended.</p>
```

5. Finally, add the following anchor that returns the visitor to the health club's home page:

```
<p><a href="HealthClub.html">Home</a></p>
```

6. Save the file as **Chest.html** in the Chapter.04\Chapter folder.

4

To create the Arms.html document:

1. Create a new document in your text editor.

2. Type the `<!DOCTYPE>` declaration, `<html>` element, document head, and the `<body>` element. Use the Strict DTD and "New Millennium Health Club Arm Exercises" as the content of the `<title>` element.

3. Add to the document body the following two heading elements to start the page:

   ```
   <h1>New Millennium Health Club</h1>

   <h2>Arm Exercises</h2>
   ```

4. After the `<h2>` element, add the following `<h3>` elements that contain definitions for each of the arm exercises. Instead of typing the elements and content, you can copy them from the ArmExercises.txt file, located in the Chapter.04\Chapter folder.

   ```
   <h3>Bicep Curls</h3>

   <p>Perform <dfn><strong>bicep curls</strong></dfn> with
   a barbell in the standing position by contracting your
   biceps to raise the barbell to the level of your chest
   and then lowering the barbell until your arms are
   completely extended.</p>

   <h3>Dumbbell Curls</h3>

   <p>Perform <dfn><strong>dumbbell curls</strong></dfn>
   by holding a dumbbell in each hand, either in the seated
   or standing position, contracting your biceps one at a
   time to raise the dumbbell to the level of your chest,
   and then lowering the dumbbell until your arm is
   completely extended.</p>

   <h3>Tricep Extensions</h3>

   <p>Perform <dfn><strong>tricep extensions</strong></dfn>
   using an overhead tricep bar in the standing position.
   Holding the tricep bar overhead with your arms extended,
   bend your elbows until the bar touches the back of your
   neck, and then extend your arms again.</p>
   ```

5. Finally, add the following anchor that returns the visitor to the health club's home page:

   ```
   <p><a href="HealthClub.html">Home</a></p>
   ```

6. Save the file as **Arms.html** in the Chapter.04/Chapter folder.

To create the Legs.html document:

1. Create a new document in your text editor.

2. Type the `<!DOCTYPE>` declaration, `<html>` element, document head, and the `<body>` element. Use the Strict DTD and "New Millennium Health Club Leg Exercises" as the content of the `<title>` element.

3. Add to the document body the following two heading elements to start the page:

```
<h1>New Millennium Health Club</h1>
<h2>Leg Exercises</h2>
```

4. After the `<h2>` element, add the following `<h3>` elements that contain definitions for each of the leg exercises. Instead of typing the elements and content, you can copy them from the LegExercises.txt file, located in the Chapter.04\Chapter folder.

```
<h3>Leg Curls</h3>

<p>Perform <dfn><strong>leg curls</strong></dfn> using a
leg curl machine by extending your legs until they are
parallel with the floor and then lowering them.</p>

<h3>Squats</h3>

<p>Perform <dfn><strong>squats</strong></dfn> by placing a
barbell on your shoulders, squatting until your thighs are
parallel with the floor, and then returning to the standing
position.</p>

<h3>Calf Raises</h3>

<p>Perform <dfn><strong>calf raises</strong></dfn> by
placing a barbell on your shoulders, standing on your toes
as high as you can, and then returning your foot to a flat
position.</p>
```

5. Finally, add the following anchor that returns the visitor to the health club's home page:

```
<p><a href="HealthClub.html">Home</a></p>
```

6. Save the file as **Legs.html** in the **Chapter 4/Chapter** folder.

7. Open the **HealthClub.html** file in your Web browser and test the links in the Online Trainer heading. Figure 4-8 shows the Chest.html file in Internet Explorer.

8. Close your Web browser window.

4

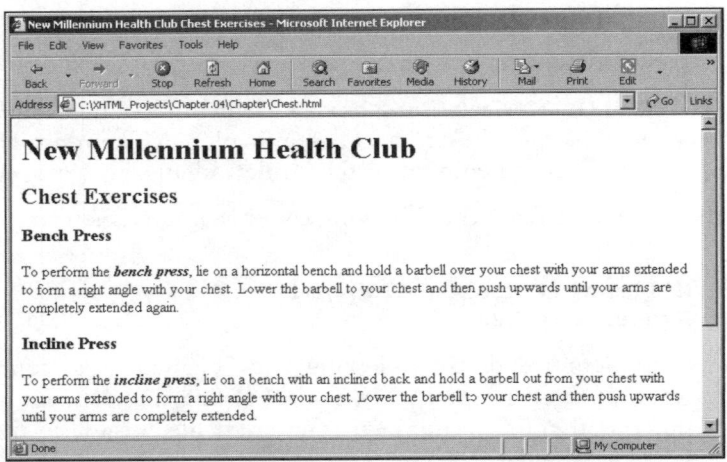

Figure 4-8   Chest.html

Recall that you use the `<abbr>` phrase element to specify abbreviated text and the `<acronym>` phrase element to identify what an acronym stands for. Most Web browsers render the `<abbr>` and `<acronym>` elements using default text. You can use the `title` attribute in conjunction with both of these phrase elements to provide Web site visitors with the long form of each element's content. The `title` attribute displays the long form of each element's content in a ToolTip. The following code includes both `<abbr>` and `<acronym>` elements. Figure 4-9 shows the output and the ToolTip that appears when you hold your mouse over the `<acronym>` element.

```
<p>The <acronym title="Aquatic Ecosystem Health and
Management Society">AEHMS</acronym> was established in 1989
to promote holistic, ecosystemic, and integrated
initiatives for the conservation and management of global
aquatic resources. This year's annual conference will take
place in Chicago, <abbr title="Illinois">IL</abbr>.</p>
```

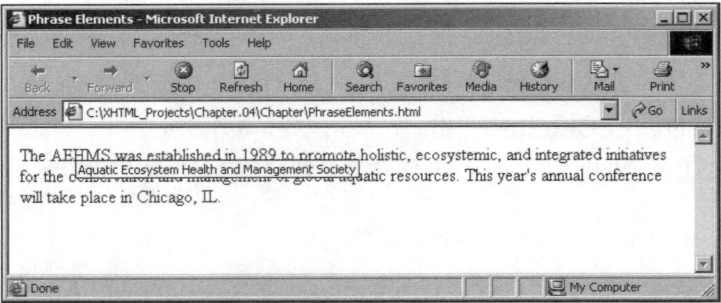

Figure 4-9   ToolTip for an `<acronym>` element

Next, you modify the contact information in HealthClub.html so that the acronym for Millennium Health Club & Fitness Center is identified as an acronym and the state (California) is identified as an abbreviation. You use the `title` attribute to provide the long form of each element in a ToolTip.

To add `<acronym>` and `<abbr>` elements to HealthClub.html:

1. Return to the **HealthClub.html** file in your text editor.

2. In the Contact Us heading, modify the paragraph containing the contact information so that the acronym for Millennium Health Club & Fitness Center is tagged as an acronym and the state (California) is tagged as an abbreviation. The modified paragraph should look as follows:

```
<p><acronym title="New Millennium Health Club & Fitness
Center">NMHCFC</acronym><br />
100 Kent Street<br />
Coast City, <abbr title="California">CA</abbr><br />
Phone: (912) 543-4563<br />
Fax: (912) 452-3452<br />
Email: <a href="mailto:info@nmhcfc.com">
info@nmhcfc.com</a><br /></p>
```

3. Save the **HealthClub.html** file and then open it in your Web browser. The contact information should render the same as it did before you added the `<acronym>` and `<abbr>` elements. Hold your mouse over the NMHCFC acronym to see whether the long form of the acronym appears.

4. Close your Web browser window.

BLOCK-LEVEL TEXT ELEMENTS

In Chapter 3 you learned about the various types of block-level elements that are available in the Strict DTD, including the two most basic block-level text elements: the paragraph and heading elements. In this section, you study the following additional block-level text elements:

- `<address>`
- `<del>`
- `<ins>`
- `<pre>`

The `<address>` Element

You use the **`<address>` element** to supply contact information for a Web page. Usually, you place the `<address>` element either at the beginning or the end of the Web page. Within the `<address>` element, you place any data, including paragraphs and links, that is part of the contact information for the Web page. Most Web browsers render the contents of the `<address>` element in italics.

 It is considered good Web page authoring practice to always include on a Web page contact information that visitors can use to provide comments about the Web site, even if you only include the e-mail address of the site's webmaster.

If you scroll to the bottom of the home page for the Saint John String Quartet in New Brunswick, Canada, at *http://flay.hil.unb.ca/sjsq/*, you will see contact information in italics, as shown in Figure 4-10.

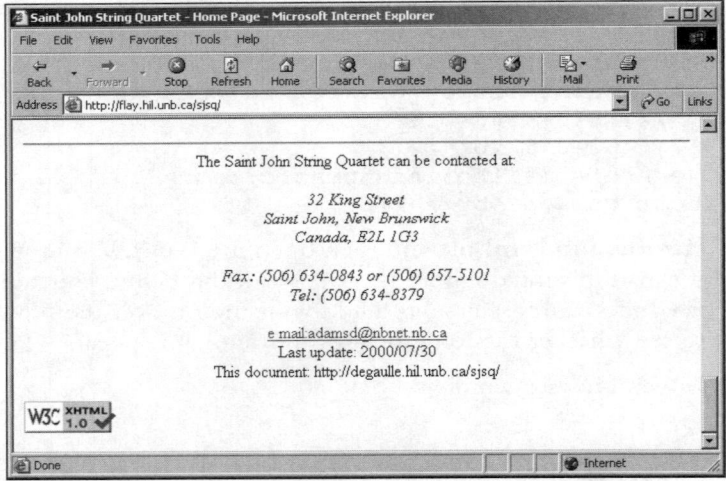

Figure 4-10   Contact information for the Saint John String Quartet

The contact information shown in Figure 4-10 is created using the following `<address>` element:

```
<address>32 King Street<br />
Saint John, New Brunswick<br />
Canada, E2L 1G3<br /><br />
Fax: (506) 634-0843 or (506) 657-5101<br />
Tel: (506) 634-8379<br /></address>
```

 Remember that, by default, Web browsers render the contents of an `<address>` element in italics. However, you can change the default appearance of block-level elements (as well as inline elements) using CSS, which you will study in Chapter 6.

Next, you modify the contact information in HealthClub.html so that it is described by the **<address>** element.

To modify the contact information in HealthClub.html so that it is defined by the **<address>** element:

1. Return to the **HealthClub.html** file in your text editor.

2. In the Contact Us heading, replace the **<p>** element surrounding the contact information with an **<address>** element, as follows:

```
<address><acronym title="New Millennium Health Club &
Fitness Center">NMHCFC</acronym><br />
100 Kent Street<br />
Coast City, <abbr title="California">CA</abbr><br />
Phone: (912) 543-4563<br />
Fax: (912) 452-3452<br />
Email: <a href="mailto:info@nmhcfc.com">
info@nmhcfc.com</a><br /></address>
```

3. Save the **HealthClub.html** file and then open it in your Web browser. The contact information should now appear in italics.

4. Close your Web browser window.

The <del> and <ins> Elements

The **<del>** and **<ins>** elements are used for marking changes to a document. The **<del>** element marks text to be deleted from a document, whereas the **<ins>** element marks text to be inserted into a document. You most often see these elements used in drafts of legal documents or other types of formal documents. Most Web browsers render the contents of **<del>** elements with strikeout text and the contents of **<ins>** elements as underlined text. The following code shows how to use the **<del>** and **<ins>** elements to mark up a paragraph in a legal document. Figure 4-11 shows how the code renders in Internet Explorer.

```
<h2>ARTICLE V: STRUCTURE OF THE BOARD OF DIRECTORS</h2>
<h3>Section 1. INITIAL BOARD</h3>
<p>The initial Board of Directors of the Corporation
("Initial Board") shall <del>consist of nine At Large
members, the President (when appointed) and those</del>
<ins>be the Board that exists prior to the time of the
seating of</ins> Directors that have been selected in
accordance with these bylaws by any Supporting
Organization(s) that exists under Section 3(a) of Article
VI <del>during the term of any of such</del>, <ins>and
shall consist of nine</ins> At Large members<ins> and the
President</ins>.</p>
```

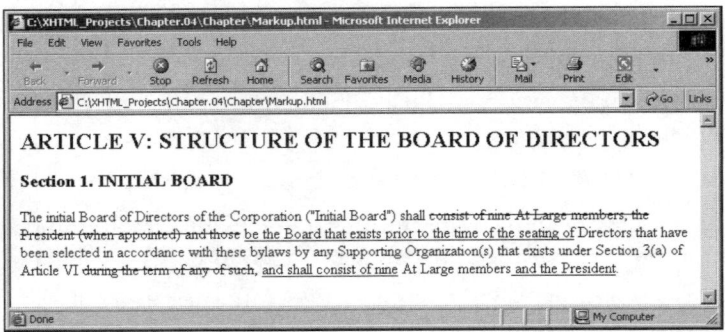

Figure 4-11   Marked-up paragraph of a legal document

When using the `<del>` and `<ins>` elements to mark up documents, especially with legal and other types of formal documents, it is important to know why a change was made and when it was made. For this reason, the `<del>` and `<ins>` elements include two optional attributes: `cite` and `datetime`. You assign to the `cite` attribute the URL of a Web page containing an explanation for the change. The `datetime` attribute specifies the date and time a change was made.

The only purpose of these attributes is to identify the location of a URL containing an explanation for a change and the date and time the change was made; they are not rendered by a browser or visible in a ToolTip.

The value you assign to the `datetime` attribute must be in the following format:

   *YYYY-MM-DD*T*hh:mm:ss*TZD

In the preceding format, *YYYY* represents the year, *MM* represents the month, and *DD* represents the day of the month, from 1 to 31. *T* is a required character that represents the beginning of the time portion of the attribute. In the time portion of the attribute, *hh* is the hour, *mm* represents the minutes, and *ss* represents the seconds. *TZD* represents the time zone, and it can be one of three values: Z, which indicates that the time is in Coordinated Universal Time (UTC); the number of hours and minutes ahead of UTC in the format +*hh:mm*; or the number of hours and minutes behind UTC in the format –*hh:mm*. If you use the Z value, it must be uppercase.

The following time value is in UTC format and represents July 27, 2002, at 9:30:45 P.M. Pacific Standard Time:

   `2002-07-27T21:30:45Z`

The preceding value represents any time in the world. The example just uses Pacific Standard Time for reference. You can also use the following format to create a more localized time value. Because the West Coast of the United States is eight hours earlier than UTC format, the following time value subtracts eight hours from the UTC time:

```
2002-07-27T21:30:45-08:00
```

The following code shows an example of an `<ins>` element that includes the `cite` attribute (assigned a fictitious URL) and the `datetime` attribute:

```
<p><ins cite="http://draftrevisions.newcorporation.com"
datetime="2002-11-05T14:30:32Z">The authorized number of
Directors shall be no less than nine (9) and no more than
nineteen (19).</ins></p>
```

Instead of using the `cite` attribute, you can provide a brief explanation of why a change was made using the `title` attribute, allowing readers of the document to view the reason for the change through an element's ToolTip.

Unlike most XHTML elements, the `<ins>` and `<del>` elements can act as both inline and block-level elements. However, when used as block-level elements, the `<ins>` and `<del>` elements do not appear on their own line, as do most other block-level elements. You must separate block-level `<del>` and `<ins>` elements using `<p>` or `<br>` elements. For instance, the following block-level `<ins>` and `<del>` elements are separated by an empty `<p>` element. Figure 4-12 shows the output.

```
<ins>The Board of Directors shall elect the Chairman
annually.</ins>

<p></p>

<del>The regular term of office of a Director of the Board
shall be three (3) years.</del>
```

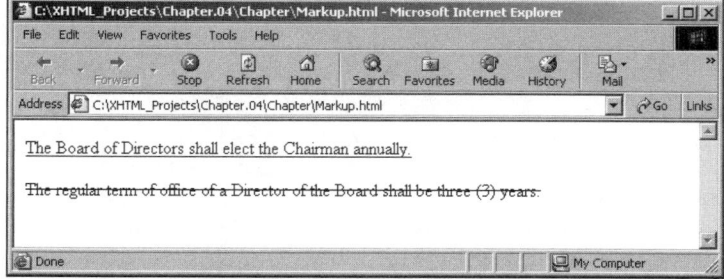

Figure 4-12   Block-level `<del>` and `<ins>` elements

When used as block-level elements, the `<del>` and `<ins>` elements cannot contain other block-level elements.

The <pre> Element

The **<pre> element** (short for preformatted text) tells a Web browser that any text and line breaks contained between the opening and closing tag are to be rendered exactly as they appear. The user agent should display the contents of a **<pre>** element in a monospace font, leave any white space intact, and should not wrap long lines of text. Current Web browsers follow these rules, although some types of non-visual user agents do not recognize white space.

The **<pre>** element was originally designed as a way of preserving column alignment and line spacing. In current browsers, you will find it is much easier to use tables to manage column alignment. However, the **<pre>** element is still typically used to contain computer output or programming code that needs to be rendered in a monospace font and that needs to retain its original line breaks, spaces, and white space. The following code uses a **<pre>** element to manage some JavaScript code. Notice that the **<p>** elements also use the **<strong>**, **<dfn>**, **<var>**, and **<code>** phrase elements. Figure 4-13 shows the output.

```
<p>An <dfn><strong>infinite loop</strong></dfn> is a
situation in which a loop statement never ends because its
conditional expression is never updated or is never
<var>false</var>. Consider the following <code>while</code>
statement:</p>

<pre>

var count = 1;

while (count <= 10) {

    alert("The number is " + count);

}

</pre>

<p>Although the <code>while</code> statement in the
preceding example includes a conditional expression that
checks the value of a count variable, there is no code
within the <code>while</code> statement body that changes
the count variable value.</p>
```

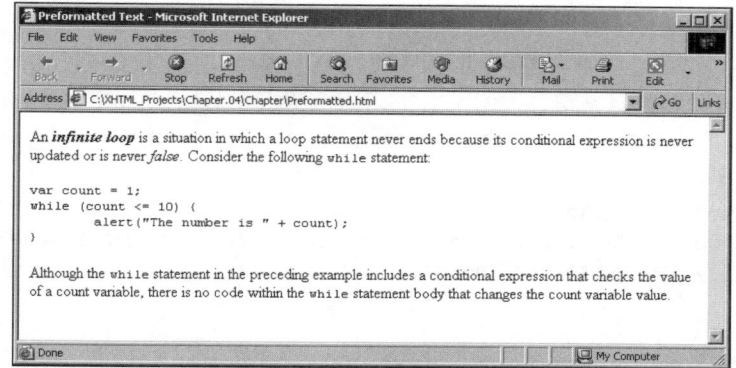

Figure 4-13   Web page with a `<pre>` element

 Because the `<pre>` element is primarily designed as a way of providing constant formatting in a monospace font, the W3C strongly discourages using CSS to modify the display of `<pre>` elements.

Next, you add `<pre>` elements to the Chest.html, Arms.html, and Legs.html files that contain exercise routines for each of the muscle groups.

To add a `<pre>` element to the Chest.html file that contains an exercise routine:

1. Return to the **Chest.html** file in your text editor.

2. Above the anchor element that links to HealthClub.html, add the following `<h3>` and `<pre>` element that contains an exercise routine for the chest muscle group. You can create the spacing using spaces or tabs.

   ```
   <h3>Routine</h3>
   ```

   ```
   <p>Perform the following routine three times a week using
   80% of your maximum weight:</p>
   ```

   ```
   <pre>
   ```

   ```
   EXERCISE               SETS                 REPETITIONS
   Bench press            3                    12
   Incline press          2                    8
   Decline press          2                    8
   ```

   ```
   </pre>
   ```

3. Save and close the **Chest.html** file.

To add a `<pre>` element to the Arms.html file that contains an exercise routine:

1. Return to the **Arms.html** file in your text editor.

2. Above the anchor element that links to HealthClub.html, add the following `<h3>` and `<pre>` element that contains an exercise routine for the arms muscle group.

```
<h3>Routine</h3>
<p>Perform the following routine three times a week using
80% of your maximum weight:</p>

<pre>

EXERCISE                SETS          REPETITIONS
Bicep curls             3             12
Dumbbell curls          2             8
Tricep extensions       3             12

</pre>
```

3. Save and close the **Arms.html** file.

To add a `<pre>` element to the Legs.html file that contains an exercise routine:

1. Return to the **Legs.html** file in your text editor.

2. Above the anchor element that links to HealthClub.html, add the following `<h3>` and `<pre>` element that contains an exercise routine for the legs muscle group.

```
<h3>Routine</h3>

<p>Perform the following routine three times a week using
80% of your maximum weight:</p>

<pre>

EXERCISE                SETS          REPETITIONS
Leg curls               3             12
Squats                  3             12
Calf raises             3             18

</pre>
```

3. Save and close the **Legs.html** file, and then open HealthClub.html in your Web browser. Open the links in the Online Trainer section and see how the `<pre>` elements appear. Figure 4-14 shows an example of the Chest.html file in Internet Explorer.

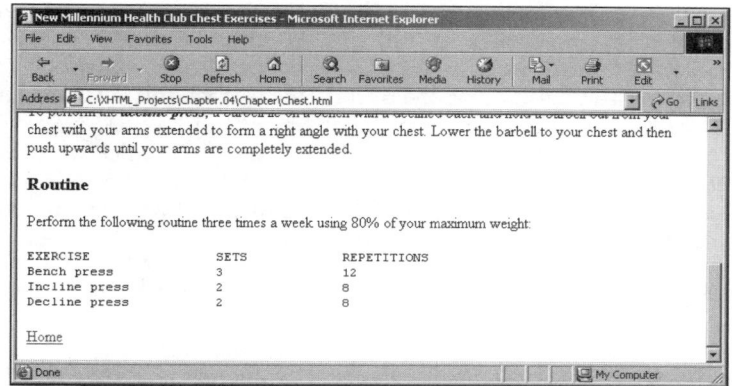

Figure 4-14   Chest.html after adding a `<pre>` element

4. Close your Web browser window.

QUOTATIONS

Quotations represent another type of data commonly found on Web pages. In this section, you study the two elements used for describing quotations: `<blockquote>` and `<q>`. Quotations are no more or less important than other types of data you find on Web pages, but because the `<blockquote>` element is a block-level element and the `<q>` element is an inline element, it is easier to discuss both elements in the same section. First you will learn about the `<blockquote>` element.

The `<blockquote>` Element

The **`<blockquote>` element** is a block-level element that defines long quotations on Web pages. The `<blockquote>` element includes an optional `cite` attribute to which you can assign a URL that cites the quotation, provided you found it on the Web. The only purpose of the `cite` attribute is to identify the location of a URL that is the original source of a quotation; the value assigned to it is not rendered by a browser or visible in a ToolTip. In order for users to see the value assigned to the `cite` attribute, they must view the Web page's HTML code.

The following code uses the `<blockquote>` element to define a quotation from Abraham Lincoln. Readers can find the quotation at the URL for The Quotations Page that is assigned to the `cite` attribute.

```
<p>Abraham Lincoln once wrote:</p>

<blockquote cite="http://www.quotationspage.com/quotes/
Abraham_Lincoln"><p>When the conduct of men is designed to
be influenced, persuasion, kind unassuming persuasion,
```

```
should ever be adopted. It is an old and true maxim that
'a drop of honey catches more flies than a gallon of gall.'
So with men. If you would win a man to your cause, first
convince him that you are his sincere friend. Therein is
a drop of honey that catches his heart, which, say what he
will, is the great highroad to his reason, and which, once
gained, you will find but little trouble in convincing him
of the justice of your cause, if indeed that cause is
really a good one.</p></blockquote>
```

Most Web browsers indent `<blockquote>` elements on both sides, as shown in Figure 4-15.

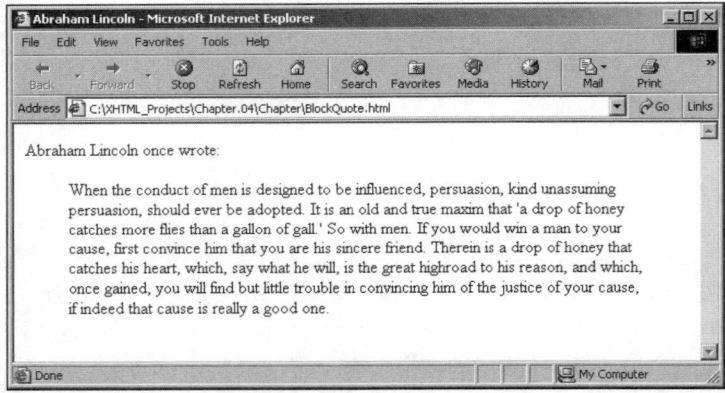

Figure 4-15   A `<blockquote>` element displayed in a Web browser

Next, you modify the long quotation in the Today's Health Tip section in HealthClub.html so that it is defined by a `<blockquote>` element.

To modify the long quotation in the Today's Health Tip section in HealthClub.html so that it is defined by a `<blockquote>` element:

1. Return to the **HealthClub.html** file in your text editor.

2. Add a `<blockquote>` element to the long quotation in the Today's Health Tip heading. Within the opening `<blockquote>` tag, include the `cite` attribute and assign to it a value of `http://www.healthandfitnessmag.com/ hw_col1.htm`, which is the URL where the quotation can be found on the Web. The modified quotation should appear as follows:

```
<blockquote
cite="http://www.healthandfitnessmag.com/
hw_col1.htm">
<p>Energy bars can contain ... and artificial
additives.</p></blockquote>
```

3. Save the **HealthClub.html** file and then open it in your Web browser. Figure 4-16 shows how the modified quotation appears in Internet Explorer.

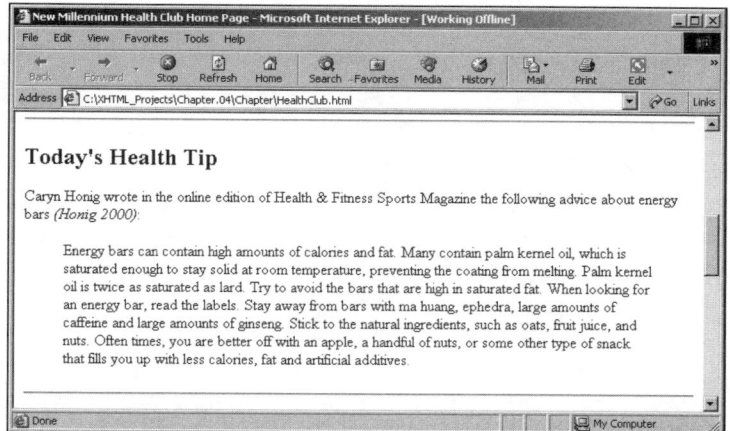

Figure 4-16   HealthClub.html after adding a `<blockquote>` element

4. Close your Web browser window.

The `<q>` Element

The **`<q>` element** is an inline element that you use to specify short quotations on your Web page. You can also include the `cite` attribute with the `<q>` element. Recall that you can assign to the `cite` attribute the URL where you found the quotation. For instance, the following code uses the `<q>` element to define a shorter quotation, also by Abraham Lincoln, that can be found at the same URL for The Quotations Page Web site:

```
<p>Abraham Lincoln once said, <q
cite="http://www.quotationspage.com/quotes/Abraham_Lincoln"
>Whatever you are, be a good one.</q></p>
```

The preceding code renders on one line if you run it in a Web browser. However, current Web browsers are not consistent in the way that they display `<q>` elements. Unlike the `<blockquote>` element, the W3C recommends that user agents place quotation marks around the contents of a `<q>` element. Netscape and other browsers follow this convention and add the quotation marks, as follows:

```
Abraham Lincoln once said, "Whatever you are, be a good one".
```

Internet Explorer and some other browsers, however, render the contents of a `<q>` element without quotation marks, as follows:

```
Abraham Lincoln once said, Whatever you are, be a good one.
```

You could manually add quotation marks, but in browsers that automatically add their own quotation marks (such as Netscape), the content of your **<q>** elements would be surrounded by two sets of quotation marks, like this:

```
Abraham Lincoln once said, ""Whatever you are, be a good
one"".
```

An alternative is to use an **<em>** element with the **<q>** element, as follows. With this technique, the content of any **<q>** elements appears in italics, which is sufficient in most cases to mark the content as a quotation.

```
<p>Abraham Lincoln once said, <em><q
cite="http://www.quotationspage.com/quotes/
Abraham_Lincoln">Whatever you are, be a good
one.</q></em></p>
```

Figure 4-17 shows how the preceding code renders in Internet Explorer.

Figure 4-17   A quote identified with the <q> and <em> elements

Next, you modify the motto at the top of the HealthClub.html file so that it is defined by a **<q>** element.

To modify the motto at the top of the HealthClub.html file so that it is defined by a **<q>** element:

1. Return to the **HealthClub.html** file in your text editor.

2. Add a **<q>** element to the motto at the top of the page. Within the opening **<q>** element, include the **cite** attribute and assign to it a value of *http://babelfish.altavista.com/*, which is the URL to Alta Vista's Babel Fish Web site, where you can translate words and phrases to and from multiple languages. Also include a **title** attribute containing the English translation of the phrase. The modified paragraph should read as follows:

```
<p><strong>Our motto is <em><q
cite="http://babelfish.altavista.com/" title="The English
translation of this phrase, provided by Babel Fish at
babelfish.altavista.com, is 'To your health'.">A votre
sante!</q></em></strong></p>
```

3. Save the **HealthClub.html** file and then open it in your Web browser. The motto should appear the same as it did before you added the <q> element.

4. Close your Web browser window.

SPECIAL CHARACTERS

4

You will often find it necessary to add special characters to your XHTML documents, such as a copyright symbol (©) or a foreign character such as the Latin capital letter E with a circumflex (Ê). You add special characters to an XHTML document using numeric character references or character entity references.

Numeric Character References

A **numeric character reference** inserts a special character using its numeric position in the Unicode character set. **Unicode** is a standardized set of characters from many of the world's languages.

The character set that is most commonly used today is the American Standard Code for Information Interchange, or ASCII, which is a standardized set of numeric representations for English characters. The Unicode character set contains the ASCII character set as a subset. In fact, Unicode will eventually replace ASCII entirely because of ASCII's limitation to English characters.

A number represents each character in the Unicode character set. To display a character using a numeric character reference, place an ampersand (&) and the number sign (#) before the character's Unicode number and a semicolon after the Unicode number. For instance, the Unicode numbers for the uppercase letters A, B, and C, are 65, 66, and 67, respectively. You could display these letters using the following numeric character references:

```
<p>&#65;</p>
<p>&#66;</p>
<p>&#67;</p>
```

The preceding numeric character references would render in Web browsers as A, B, and C.

Clearly, you do not need to use numeric character references for letters or numbers. However, you use the same syntax to display special characters in the Unicode character set. For instance, the Unicode number for a copyright symbol is 169. Therefore, you can display the copyright symbol on a Web page using a numeric character reference of ©.

You can find a complete list of numeric character references at *http://www.macchiato.com/unicode/charts.html*.

Numeric character references and character entity references (which you study in the next section) are both defined using an ampersand. For this reason, a Web browser may be confused if it encounters an ampersand within the text of a Web page. Therefore, you should use a numeric character reference of & in place of any ampersands in your document. The home page for the Millennium Health Club & Fitness Center contains two instances of an ampersand: one in the name of the club itself and another in the title of Health & Fitness Sports Magazine, found in the Today's Health Tip section. The French phrase should be written as À votre santé. The numeric character reference for the À character is À, and the numeric character reference for the é character is é. You now add each numeric character reference to the HealthClub.html file.

To add numeric character references to the HealthClub.html file:

1. Return to the **HealthClub.html** file in your text editor.

2. First, add the numeric character reference for the ampersand in the <h2> element so it reads as follows:

   ```
   <h2>Health Club &#038; Fitness Center</h2>
   ```

3. Next, modify the motto contained within the <q> element so it includes the numeric character references for the two foreign letters. The modified paragraph should read as follows:

   ```
   <p><strong>Our motto is <em><q
   cite="http://babelfish.altavista.com/" title="The English
   translation of this phrase, provided by Babel Fish at
   babelfish.altavista.com, is 'To your health'.">&#192; votre
   sant&#233;</q></em></strong>!</p>
   ```

4. Finally, add the numeric character reference for the ampersand to *Health & Fitness Sports Magazine* in the first paragraph in the Today's Health Tip section so it reads as follows:

   ```
   <p>Caryn Honig wrote in the online edition of <em>Health
   &#038; Fitness Sports Magazine</em> the following advice
   about energy bars: <cite>(Honig 2002)</cite></p>
   ```

5. Save the **HealthClub.html** file and then open it in your Web browser. Although the ampersands will appear the same, you should now see the foreign characters in the French phrase, as shown in Figure 4-18.

6. Close your Web browser window.

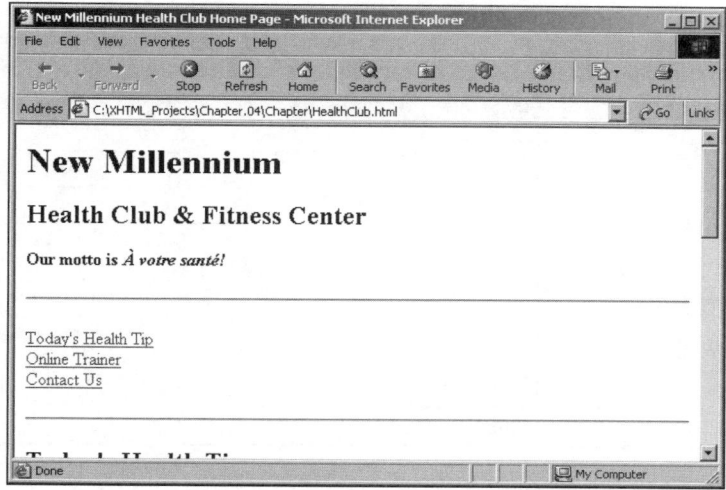

Figure 4-18   HealthClub.html after adding numeric character references

Character Entities

Using numeric character references can be difficult because you must know a character's exact number within the Unicode character. This can be challenging considering that the Unicode character set is capable of representing more than 65,000 characters. Therefore, you may find it easier to use a **character entity reference**, or **character entity**, which uses a descriptive name for a special character instead of its Unicode number. For instance, the descriptive name for the copyright symbol is *copy*. Therefore, you can display the copyright symbol on a Web page using a character entity of ©. Note that you do not include the number sign (#) after the ampersand as you do with numeric character references. Also note that character entities are case-sensitive. For instance, if you use an uppercase *C* in the copyright character entity, a Web browser will not recognize it as a character entity and will display the text *&Copy;* instead of the copyright symbol.

Table 4-3 lists the numeric character references and character entities for some of the more commonly used special characters.

Character entities do not exist for all of the characters in Unicode. You can find a complete list of the available character entities, along with their corresponding numeric character reference, in the appendix.

Table 4-3   Commonly used special characters

Character	Description	Numeric Character Reference	Character Entity
	Non-breaking space		
¢	Cent	&#162;	&cent;
£	Pound	&#163;	&pound;
¥	Yen	&#165;	&yen;
©	Copyright	&#169;	&copy;
®	Registered trademark	&#174;	&reg;
<	Less than	&#60;	&lt;
>	Greater than	&#62;	&gt;
&	Ampersand	&#38;	&amp;
"	Quotation	&#34;	&quot;

The non-breaking space, less than, greater than, ampersand, and quotation symbols listed in Table 4–3 require a little further explanation. Most Web browsers ignore multiple, contiguous spaces on a Web page and replace them with a single space. For instance, if you include two spaces between the abbreviation for a state and the zip code in a mailing address, most Web browsers will automatically render the two spaces as a single space. To force Web browsers to render multiple spaces, you must add a non-breaking space using the   character entity. The following code shows how to use two   character entities to force two spaces between the state and zip code in a mailing address:

```
<p>Elvis Presley<br />
Graceland Mansion<br />
3734 Elvis Presley Blvd.<br />
Memphis, TN  38116</p>
```

As you know, the less than and greater than symbols mark the beginning and end of XHTML tags. However, if you add either symbol to the text within your Web page as part of a mathematical equation or for some other purpose, a Web browser will interpret them as the beginning or ending bracket of an XHTML tag, which will cause problems in how your page renders. The solution is to use the appropriate character entity.

Earlier you saw an example of a `<pre>` element with some JavaScript code that contained a less than symbol. If you were to validate the code using the W3C Markup Validation Service, the code would be declared invalid because the service assumes that the less than symbol is the starting bracket of a tag that does not include a closing bracket. In order for the code to be valid, you can use the character entity for the less than symbol (`&lt;`), as follows:

```
<pre>
var count = 1;
while (count &lt;= 10) {
    alert("The number is " + count);
}
</pre>
```

The purpose of the elements and text in the preceding code is only to correctly render the JavaScript code in a browser—not to actually execute the code. The JavaScript code would not execute properly with a character entity replacing the less than symbol.

You should use character entities for any quotations you want to include in your Web pages. Because quotation marks are used for assigning values to element attributes, a Web browser may be confused if it encounters quotations within the text of a Web page. For example, the following code displays a heading element for a construction company's Web page, along with the company's motto. For the motto to appear within quotation marks, it is enclosed within " character entities.

```
<h1>Sanders &amp; Sons Construction, Inc.</h2>
<h2>Our motto is &quot;Pride before profit&quot;</h2>
```

Next, you replace the numeric character references in the French phrase in the HealthClub.html file with character entities. The character entity for the ampersand is &, the character entity for the uppercase *A* with a grave accent is À, and the character entity for the lowercase *e* with an acute accent is é.

To replace the numeric character entities in the French phrase in the HealthClub.html file with character entities:

1. Return to the **HealthClub.html** file in your text editor.

2. Modify the numeric character references in the motto so they read as follows:

```
<p><strong>Our motto is <em><q
cite="http://babelfish.altavista.com/" title="The English
translation of this phrase, provided by Babel Fish at
babelfish.altavista.com, is 'To your health'.">&Agrave;
votre sant&eacute;</q>
</em>!</strong></p>
```

3. Save the **HealthClub.html** file and then open it in your Web browser. The foreign characters in the motto should appear the same as they did before you replaced the numeric character references with the character entities.

4. Close your Web browser window.

THE <img> ELEMENT

One of the more visually pleasing parts of a Web page is its images. Web pages today include images in the form of company logos, photographs of products and works of art, drawings, animation, image maps, and other types of graphics. Commerce-oriented Web pages that do not include images would be hard pressed to attract—and keep—visitors.

Many commercial services on the Web offer images that you can purchase for use on your Web pages. Many public-domain images also exist that you can use freely. You can find images by searching for "images" or "clipart". One particularly useful place to search for images is the Images tab on the Google search engine's Web page at *http://www.google.com*. Once you find an image you want to use on your Web page, you can download it to your computer by right clicking the image and selecting the Save command from the shortcut menu that appears. Be sure to observe any copyright or licensing requirements before using any images you find.

From Chapter 2, you already know the basics of how to include images on Web pages, including how to use images as links. Recall that the `src` attribute specifies the filename of an image file. To include the `src` attribute within the `<img>` element, you type `img src="mygraphic.gif">`. The `<img>` element also includes other attributes, as listed in Table 4-4.

Table 4-4   Attributes of the `<img>` element

Attribute	Description
`src`	Specifies the filename of the image file
`alt`	Specifies alternate text to display in place of the image file
`longdesc`	Identifies the URL of a Web page containing a long description of an image
`width`	Defines the width of an image
`height`	Defines the height of an image
`usemap`	Identifies an image to be used as a client-side image map
`ismap`	Identifies an image to be used as a server-side image map

The `alt` Attribute

For an XHTML document to be well formed, the `<img>` element must include the `src` and `alt` attributes. The `alt` attribute, which specifies alternate text to display in place of the image file, is very important for user agents that do not display images, such as the text-based Lynx Web browser and Web browsers that are designed for users of Braille and speech devices. Additionally, alternate text will display if an image has not yet downloaded, if the user has turned off the display of images in their Web browsers, if for some reason the image is not available. The following `<img>` element displays a photo of a father teaching his son how to fly a kite, and the element's `alt` attribute is assigned an appropriate value, *Photo of a father teaching his son how to fly a kite*. If the image has not yet been downloaded or if users have turned off the display of images in their Web browsers, they will see the alternate text shown in Figure 4-19.

```
<img src="kite.jpg" alt="Photo of a father teaching his son
how to fly a kite." />
```

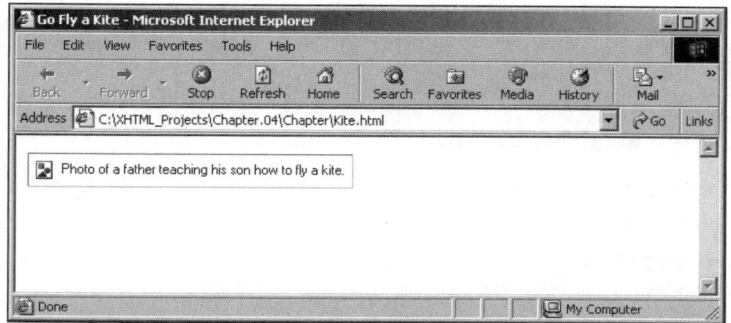

Figure 4-19   Alternate text displayed in a Web browser

The `alt` attribute also serves another purpose: For any `<img>` elements that do not include a `title` attribute, the value assigned to the `alt` attribute appears as a ToolTip in Internet Explorer and other browsers when you hold your mouse over the image. However, if an `<image>` element includes a `title` attribute, the value assigned to the `title` attribute will appear as a ToolTip instead of the value assigned to the `alt` attribute. For instance, if you visit the Branch Libraries page of the New York Public Library (*http://www.nypl.org/branch/*), you will see the New York Public Library logo in the upper-left corner of the page. If you view the source code for the page, you will find the following `<img>` element that displays the logo:

```
<img src="/branch/navbars/images/titlecap2.gif"
class="nsixfix" width="251" height="38" alt="The New York
PublicLibrary" />
```

Notice that the `alt` attribute is assigned a value of *The New York Public Library*. If you hold your mouse over the logo image on the Web page, the value assigned to the `alt` attribute appears as the ToolTip, as shown in Figure 4-20.

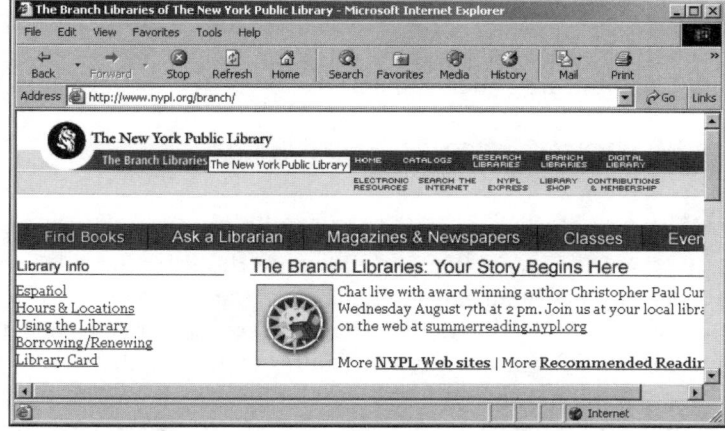

Figure 4-20   The Branch Libraries page of the New York Public Library

The Chapter.04\Chapter folder contains an image file named curls.jpg. You now add this image, along with some alternate text, to the HealthClub.html file.

To add an image with alternate text to the HealthClub.html file:

1. Return to the **HealthClub.html** file in your text editor.

2. Add the following **<img>** element above the **<h2>** element that reads *Health Club & Fitness Center*.

   ```
   <p><img src="curls.jpg" alt="Photo of a man and a woman
   using dumbbells to perform bicep curls." /></p>
   ```

3. Save the **HealthClub.html** file and then open it in your Web browser. Figure 4-21 shows how the image appears in Internet Explorer, along with the alternate text that appears as a ToolTip.

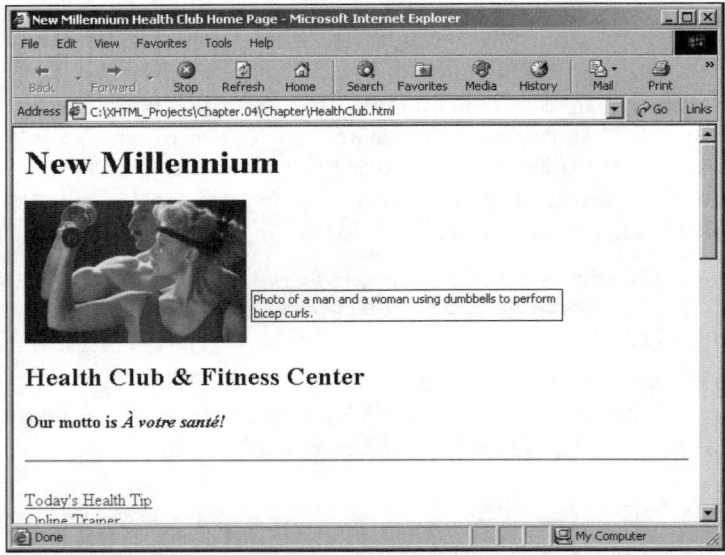

Figure 4-21   HealthClub.html after adding an image

4. Close your Web browser window.

Height and Width

When you create an **<img>** element that includes only the **src** and **alt** attributes, a Web browser needs to examine the image and determine the number of pixels to reserve for it. This can significantly slow down the time it takes for a Web page to render. However, if you use the **height** and **width** attributes to specify the size of an image, the Web browser will use their values to reserve enough space on the page for each image. This allows the Web browser to render all of the text on the page and then go back and render each image after it finishes downloading. Each image placeholder displays the image's alternative text until the image itself is rendered.

In Figure 4-19, you saw the placeholder for the kite.jpg image displaying its alternative text. Because the `<img>` element did not include `height` and `width` attributes, the Web browser reserved only enough space to display the alternative text. The image itself is actually 353 pixels in height and 533 pixels in width. The following code shows a modified version of the `<img>` element for the kite.jpg image, but this time it includes `height` and `width` attributes. Figure 4-22 shows the placeholder that the Web browser now reserves for the image.

```
<img src="kite.jpg" alt="Photo of a father teaching his son
how to fly a kite." height="353" width="533" />
```

Figure 4-22   Placeholder for the kite.jpg image

 You can find the height and width of an image using almost any graphics program such as Adobe Photoshop, Macromedia Fireworks, and PaintShop Pro. You can also quickly determine the height and width of an image by opening the image in Internet Explorer or Netscape, right-clicking the image, and then selecting Properties from the shortcut menu. Both browsers display a Properties dialog box that shows the selected image's height and width in pixels.

It is very important to always assign `height` and `width` attribute values that are the exact dimensions of the original image. Do not use the `height` and `width` attributes to resize an image on your Web page. If you want an image of a different size, use an image-editing program to create a new, smaller version of the image. (Most image-editing programs include commands that automatically reduce the size of an image by a specified percentage or number of pixels.) Using the `height` and `width` attributes to change the size of an image on a Web page results in a poor quality image. One reason for this has to do with how you calculate the new dimensions of the image. Unless you correctly calculate the proportions of the number of pixels for both the `height` and `width` attributes that represent the image's new size, the image will appear stretched or squished and of poor quality. Figure 4-23 shows how the kite.jpg image appears using the height and width of the original image. Figure 4-24, however, shows the image resized to a height of 150 pixels and a width of 400 pixels. As you can see, the image in Figure 4-24 is significantly out of proportion from the original.

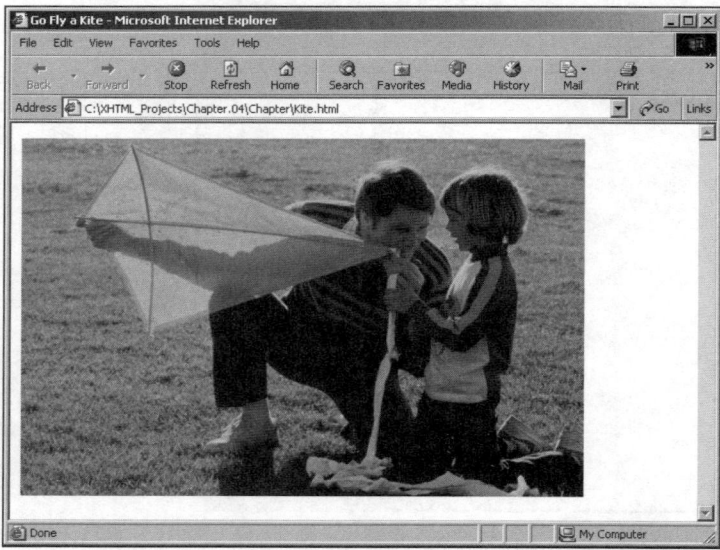

Figure 4-23   Kite.jpg scaled to its original size

Figure 4-24   Kite.jpg scaled to 150 pixels high by 400 pixels wide

Another reason not to use the `height` and `width` attributes to modify the size of an image is that although you may reduce how the image appears in a browser, the browser still needs to download the original image in its original size, which may result in the page rendering more slowly than necessary. This can be especially problematic for slow dial-up modem connections. One solution that many Web developers use for image-intensive Web sites is to create small "thumbnail" versions of an image that visitors to a Web site can view to get a rough idea of what the image looks like. If visitors want to see the image in a larger size, they can click the thumbnail version of the image, which is usually contained in an `<a>` element. The link will then open a larger-sized version of the image or another Web page that displays the larger image along with more information. The important thing to understand is that the thumbnail version of the image is not the original image reduced using the `height` and `width` attributes of the `<img>` element. Rather, the thumbnail images are entirely separate images that have been resized using image-editing software.

Real estate agents commonly use thumbnails on their Web sites to display pictures of homes and other types of property. If visitors are interested in a particular piece of real estate, they can click a thumbnail image of the property to view the image in a larger size, along with information about the property. Figure 4-25 shows a Web page from REALTOR.com that displays thumbnail images of homes for sale in Madison, Wisconsin. Each thumbnail image is fairly small—only about 5 kilobytes, 110 pixels in height, and 165 pixels in width. Clicking a thumbnail displays a much larger version of the image. For instance, clicking the first thumbnail opens the Web page shown in Figure 4-26, which displays a larger version of the image. In this case, the larger image is about 15 kilobytes, 300 pixels in width, and 200 pixels in height—about three times the size of the thumbnail version of the image.

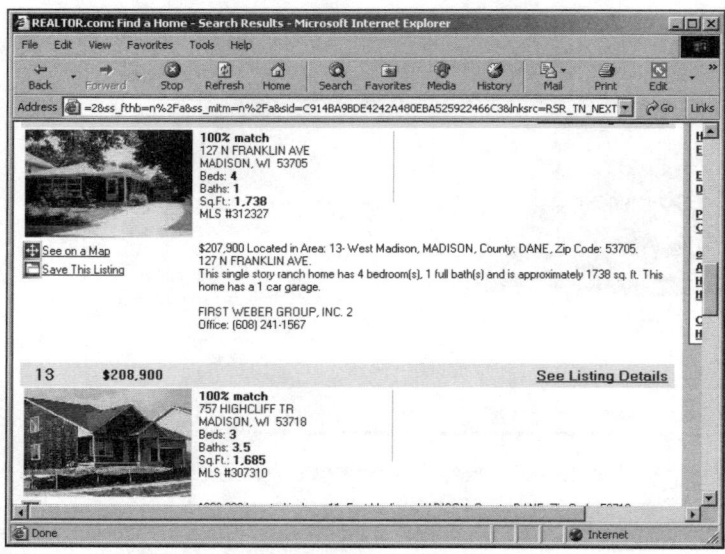

Figure 4-25   Web page with thumbnail images

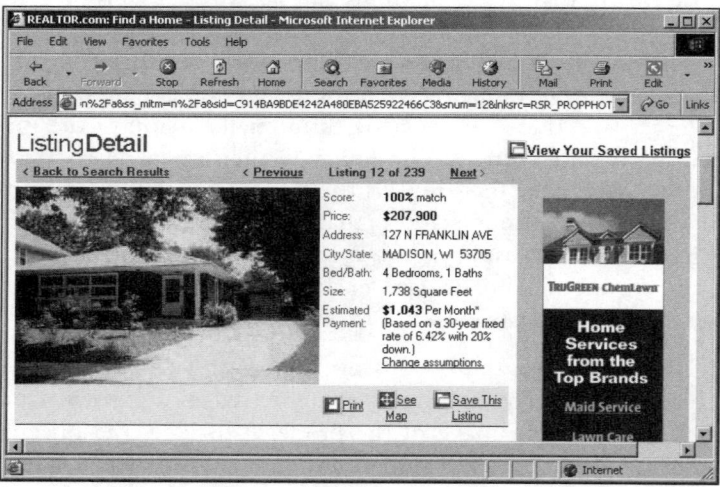

Figure 4-26   Larger version of thumbnail image

Next, you add the height and width properties to the curls.jpg image in the HealthClub.html file. The height of curls.jpg is 133 pixels and its width is 200 pixels.

To add the height and width properties to the curls.jpg image:

1. Return to the **HealthClub.html** file in your text editor.

2. Add the height and width properties to the <img> element as follows.

```
<img src="curls.jpg" alt="Photo of a man and a woman using
dumbbells to perform bicep curls." height="133" width="200"
/>
```

3. Save the **HealthClub.html** file and then open it in your Web browser. The image should appear the same as it did before you added the height and width properties.

4. Close your Web browser window.

Using Images from Other Locations

All of the image files you have used so far have been relative in that they are located on the same computer as the currently displayed document. For instance, the `src` attribute of the following <img> element is relative because it assumes that the kite.jpg file exists within the same folder as the Web page.

```
<img src="kite.jpg" alt="Photo of a father teaching his son
how to fly a kite." height="353" width="533" />
```

You can also place images in subfolders that are *relative* to the location of the current Web page folder. For instance, the following <img> element assumes that the kite.jpg file is located in a subfolder named graphics.

```
<img src="graphics/kite.jpg" alt="Photo of a father
teaching his son how to fly a kite." height="353"
width="533" />
```

You can link to images at other locations on the Web by assigning an absolute URL to the `src` attribute of the <img> element. You can see one example of linking to an image on the Web at the W3C Web page for validating XHTML documents. After you successfully validate a Web page using the W3C Markup Validation Service, you can add the W3C XHTML image to your Web page to show that your document is valid. At the bottom of the W3C Markup Validation Service Web page are instructions for adding the W3C XHTML image to your Web page. You can download the image, place it in a folder on your Web site, and use it as a relative file, or, you can link directly to the image at the W3C site. The validation page of the W3C Markup Validation Service includes the following code that you can use to add the image to your Web page by accessing the image directly from the W3C Web site. Figure 4-27 shows how the image appears at the bottom of the Branch Libraries page of the New York Public Library.

```
<p>
  <a href="http://validator.w3.org/check/referer">
  <img src="http://www.w3.org/Icons/valid-xhtml10"
    alt="Valid XHTML 1.0!" height="31" width="88" /></a>
</p>
```

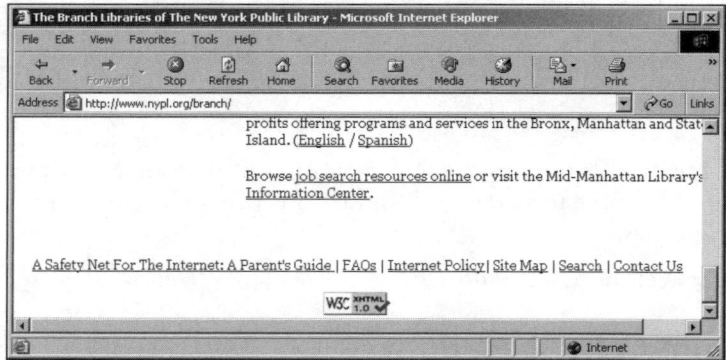

Figure 4-27   W3C XHTML-compliant image added to the Branch Libraries page of the New York Public Library

You will add the W3C XHTML logo to the New Millennium Health Club & Fitness Center Web site after you validate it at the end of this chapter.

IMAGE MAPS

Images maps allow users to navigate to different Web pages by clicking an image. An image map consists of an image that is divided into regions. Each region is then associated with a URL; these regions are called **hot zones**. You can open the URL associated with each region by clicking the hot zone with your mouse. One of the most common uses of image maps is to create graphical menus that you can use for navigation. Using an image to create links to other Web pages gives you more flexibility than you would have using hypertext links, and allows for a great deal more creativity. For instance, Figure 4-28 displays the home page for the Congressional Internet Caucus Advisory Committee. The page contains two image maps: one at the top of the page that includes the Home, Search, and About buttons, and another on the left side of the page that begins with the Issues button. These types of navigational elements would be almost impossible to create without image maps.

The buttons you see on the Web page in Figure 4-28 are not really buttons. Rather, they are simply part of a larger image. For instance, the image map at the top of the page is created using the image shown in Figure 4-29.

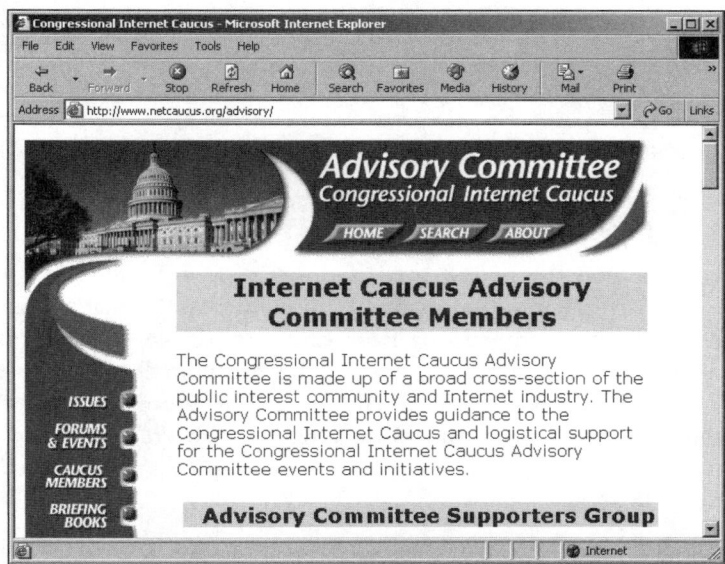

Figure 4-28   Web page with image maps

Figure 4-29   Navigational image map

To create an image map, you must include the following elements on your Web page:

- An `<img>` element that contains an `src` attribute specifying the name of the image file and a `usemap` attribute specifying the value assigned to the `id` and `name` attributes of the `<map>` element.

- A `<map>` element that specifies mapping coordinates and includes `id` and `name` attributes that have the same values as used in the `<img>` element `usemap` attribute.

- `<area>` elements nested within the `<map>` element that identify the coordinates within the image that will be recognized as hot zones.

There are two types of image maps: server-side image maps created with the `ismap` attribute of the `<img>` element and client-side image maps created with the `usemap` attribute of the `<img>` element. With server-side image maps, the code that maps each region of an image is located on a server. In comparison, with client-side image maps, the code that maps each region of an image is part of an HTML document that renders in a browser. This chapter covers client-side image maps.

You precede the value you assign to the `usemap` attribute (which is the value assigned to the `id` and `name` attributes of the `<map>` element) in the `<img>` element by a number sign (#). For instance, the image map at the top of the Congressional Internet Caucus Advisory Committee home page uses an `<img>` element similar to the following to load an image name upright.gif that references a `<map>` element name BUTTMAP1":

```
<img usemap="#BUTTMAP1" src="/images/upprght.gif" alt=""
width="492" height="120">
```

The **`<map>` element** defines the coordinates used to create an image map's hot zones. In addition to the standard attributes available to all elements, the `<map>` element also includes the `name` attribute in order to be backward compatible with older browsers. (Recall that in XHTML the `id` attribute replaces the `name` attribute that was used in HTML.) The values of the `id` and `name` attributes specify the name of the map, and you assign the same values to the `id` and `name` attributes. To create a `<map>` element with a name of navigationMap, you use the statement `map  id="navigationMap" name="navigationMap">`.

The **`<area>` element** defines a region within an image map and is nested within a `<map>` element. The `<area>` element is empty, so you must include a space and a slash (/) at the end of the `<area>` tag. Table 4-5 lists attributes of the `<area>` element.

Table 4-5   Common `<area>` element attributes

Attribute	Description
`coords`	The coordinates of the shape in pixels. The coordinates you enter depend on the shape you specify with the `shape` attribute.
`href`	The URL associated with the area.
`nohref`	A placeholder for areas that are not to be associated with a URL.
`shape`	The shape of the defined region.
`alt`	Alternate text to display in place of the area.

As with the `<img>` element, the `alt` attribute is required with the `<area>` element in order to provide alternative text in the event that the image map cannot be displayed.

When you use the `<area>` element to define a region as a hot zone on an image map, you use the `shape` attribute to specify the shape of the region and the `coords` attribute to specify the coordinates of the shape's pixels. The `shape` attribute can be set to circle, rect (for rectangle), or poly (for polygon). The coordinates you specify will depend on the value you assign to the `shape` attribute. For example, the following code shows the syntax for assigning coordinates for each type of shape. You assign four coordinates for the rect shape, one for each corner of the rectangle. For the circle shape, you include the x and y coordinates that identify where the center of the circle should be placed, along with the radius to determine how large the circle should be. Because a polygon can be any type of shape, you can use as many x, y pairs as necessary to define the shape of the object.

```
shape="rect" coords="upper-left x, upper-left y,
    lower-right x, lower-right y"

shape="circle" coords="center-x, center-y, radius"

shape="poly" coords="x1,y1, x2,y2, x3,y3,..."
```

The image map at the top of the Congressional Internet Caucus Advisory Committee home page contains hot zones for the Home, Search, and About buttons. The three hot zones are created using a **shape** attribute of "rect", similar to the following code:

```
<map id="BUTTMAP1" name="BUTTMAP1">

<area shape="rect" coords="172,80,243,99"alt="Home page" />

<area shape="rect" coords="259,82,330,99" alt="Search" />

<area shape="rect" coords="341,81,401,98"

    alt="About Net Caucus" />

</map>
```

Figure 4-30 shows another example of an image map, this one created with an image of a pie chart. The code uses polygon **shape** attributes to create hot zones associated with each wedge of the pie chart. Figure 4-31 shows the resulting image map in a Web browser.

```
<!DOCTYPE html PUBLIC
"-//W3C//DTD XHTML 1.0 Strict//EN"
"http://www.w3.org/TR/xhtml1/DTD/xhtml1-strict.dtd">
<html xmlns="http://www.w3.org/1999/xhtml" lang="en" xml:lang =
"en" dir="ltr">
<head><title>Sources of Income</title>
<meta http-equiv="content-type"
content="text/html; charset=iso-8859-1" /></head>
<body>
<p>Click a piece of the pie to learn more about each source of income.</p>
<p><img usemap="#income_chart" src="income.jpg" alt="Pie chart of
income broken down by category" width="468" height="321" />
<map id="income_chart" name="income_chart">
<area shape="poly" coords="253,160,252,22,355,69,381,118,384,195,318,278"
href="tuition.html" alt="Tuition fees" />
<area shape="poly" coords="253,160,318,278,217,291,147,246"
href="Endowments.html" alt="Endowments" />
<area shape="poly" coords="253,160,147,245,117,185,120,126"
href="Investments.html" alt="Investment income" />
<area shape="poly" coords="253,160,119,125,141,80,185,40"
href="Research.html" alt="Research grants" />
<area shape="poly" coords="253,160,185,40,253,22" href="Other.html" alt=
"Other income" /></map>
</body>
</html>
```

Figure 4-30   Pie chart image-map code

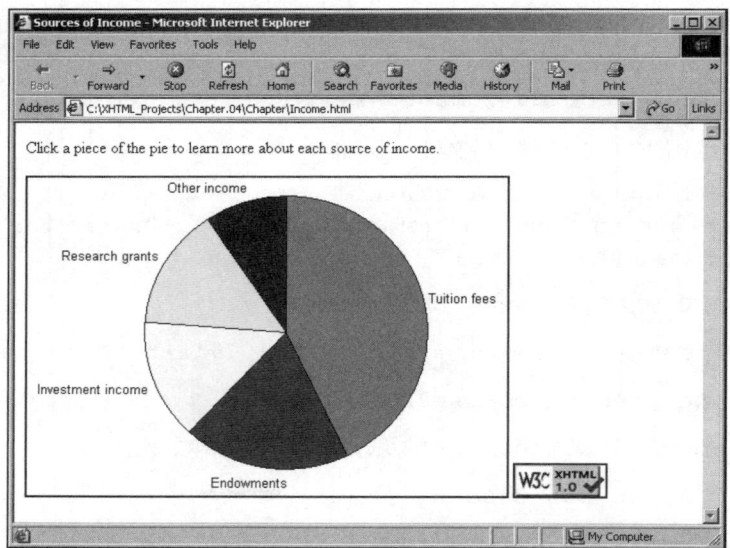

Figure 4-31   Pie chart image map in a Web browser

Next, you will add an image map to the Online Trainer section of the New Millennium Health Club & Fitness Center's home page. The image is a picture of Leonardo da Vinci's Vitruvian Man that is contained in the Chapter.04\Chapter folder. Clicking an area of the body in the image (chest, arms, or legs) will open the associated Web page.

To add an image map to HealthClub.html:

1. Return to the **HealthClub.html** file in your text editor.

2. Replace the first paragraph following the Online Trainer heading with the following paragraph:

   ```
   <p>Click the muscle group that you want to work on.</p>
   ```

3. Next, replace the `<p>` element that contains the links to the other Web pages with the following `<p>` element that displays the image, named DaVinci.jpg, that is used as an image map. The image map's name is "vitruvian_man".

   ```
   <p><img usemap="#vitruvian_man" src="DaVinci.jpg"
   alt="Image of Leonardo da Vinci's Vitruvian Man."
   width="205" height="205" /></p>
   ```

4. After the `<img>` element, add the following `<map>` element, which uses `shape` attributes of "rect" to map each of the muscle groups:

   ```
   <p><map id="vitruvian_man" name="vitruvian_man">

   <area shape="rect" coords="0, 0, 78, 49" href="Arms.html"
   alt="Right arm" />
   ```

```
<area shape="rect" coords="128, 0, 205,49" href="Arms.html"
alt="Left arm" />

<area shape="rect" coords="76, 33,128, 55"
href="Chest.html"alt="Chest" />

<area shape="rect" coords="40, 100, 175, 205"
href="Legs.html" alt="Legs" />

</map></p>
```

5. Save and close the **HealthClub.html** file, and then open it in your Web browser. Test the image map to see if all of the links work. Figure 4-32 shows how the map appears in Internet Explorer.

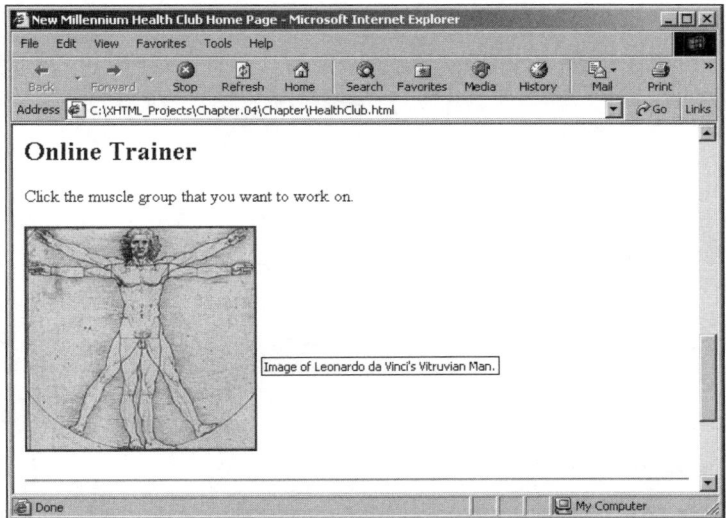

Figure 4-32   HealthClub.html after adding an image map

6. Close your Web browser window.

Your final task is to use the W3C Markup Validation Service to validate the New Millennium Health Club & Fitness Center's Web site and add the W3C XHTML logo to its Web pages.

To validate the New Millennium Health Club & Fitness Center's Web site and add the W3C XHTML logo to its Web pages:

1. Start your Web browser and enter the URL for the upload page of the W3C Markup Validation Service: **http://validator.w3.org/file-upload.html**.

2. Open and validate the **HealthClub.html** file. If you receive any errors, fix them, and then revalidate the document. Once the document is valid, add the following code above the closing **</body>** tag to display the W3C XHTML logo:

```
<p><a href="http://validator.w3.org/check/referer">
<img src="http://www.w3.org/Icons/valid-xhtml10"
alt="Valid XHTML 1.0!" height="31" width="88" /></a></p>
```

3. Repeat the validation process for the **Chest.html**, **Arms.html**, and **Legs.html** files. Once the documents are valid, add the code for the W3C XHTML logo above each file's closing **</body>** tag. Then, open the **HealthClub.html** file in your Web browser and examine how the logo appears.

Your computer must be connected to the Internet in order for you to see the W3C XHTML logo on your Web pages.

4. Close your text editor and your Web browser.

CHAPTER SUMMARY

❑ Formatting elements provide specific instructions as to how their contents should be displayed.

❑ Phrase elements primarily describe their contents.

❑ You use the **<address>** element to supply contact information for a Web page.

❑ The **<del>** and **<ins>** elements are used for marking changes to a document.

❑ The **<pre>** element (short for preformatted text) tells a Web browser that any text and line breaks contained between the opening and closing tags are to be rendered exactly as they appear.

❑ The **<blockquote>** element is a block-level element that you use to define long quotations on your Web pages.

❑ The **<q>** element is an inline element that you use to define short quotations on your Web pages.

❑ A numeric character reference inserts a special character using its numeric position in the Unicode character set.

❑ Unicode is a standardized set of characters from many of the world's languages.

❑ Character entity references, or character entities, use a descriptive name for a special character instead of its Unicode number.

❑ The `<img>` element must include an `src` attribute and the `alt` attribute in order for a Web page to be well formed.

❑ When you use the height and width attributes with the `<img>` element to specify the size of your images, the Web browser will use their values to reserve enough space on the page for each image.

❑ The values you assign to the height and width attributes of the `<img>` element should always be the exact dimensions of the original image.

❑ Images maps allow users to navigate to different Web pages by clicking an image. An image map consists of an image that is divided into regions. Each region is then associated with a URL; these regions are called hot zones.

❑ The `<map>` element defines the coordinates used to create an image map's hot zones.

❑ The `<area>` element defines a region within an image map and is nested within a `<map>` element.

REVIEW QUESTIONS

1. What is the difference between text-formatting elements and phrase elements?

2. You should use text-formatting elements over phrase elements. True or False?

3. Which of the following elements are text-formatting elements? (Choose all that apply.)

    a. `<b>`

    b. `<small>`

    c. `<sup>`

    d. `<tt>`

4. Which of the following elements are phrase elements? (Choose all that apply.)

    a. `<big>`

    b. `<i>`

    c. `<code>`

    d. `<dfn>`

5. Which element should be used in place of the `<b>` element?

    a. `<big>`

    b. `<strong>`

    c. `<bold>`

    d. `<cite>`

6. Which element should be used in place of the `<i>` element?

   a. `<var>`

   b. `<samp>`

   c. `<em>`

   d. `<dfn>`

7. How do most Web browsers render the `<abbr>` and `<acronym>` elements?

   a. As default text

   b. As boldface

   c. In italics

   d. In a slightly larger font

8. Which of the following elements should you define with the `<address>` element? (Choose all that apply.)

   a. Mailing address

   b. E-mail address

   c. Telephone number

   d. Fax number

9. Which of the following elements are used in the Strict DTD for marking changes to a document? (Choose all that apply.)

   a. `<strike>`

   b. `<ins>`

   c. `<del>`

   d. `<u>`

10. When you are marking up the draft of a legal document, when should you use the `cite` and `datetime` attributes?

11. What is the correct format for the value you assign to the `datetime` attribute?

    a. *YYYY-MM-DDhh:mm:ssTZD*

    b. *YY-MM-DDThh:mm:ssTZD*

    c. *YY-MM-DDThh:mm:ss*

    d. *YYYY-MM-DDThh:mm:ssTZD*

12. The `<ins>` and `<del>` elements can act as both inline and block-level elements. True or False?

13. Why would you use the `<pre>` element and how does a user agent display its contents?

14. How are the contents of the `<blockquote>` element displayed in a Web browser?

    a. As default text

    b. Indented on both sides

    c. As italicized text

    d. In quotation marks

15. User agents should render the contents of the `<q>` element in quotation marks. True or False?

16. What is the numeric character reference for an ampersand?

    a. `&#036;`

    b. `&#037;`

    c. `&#038;`

    d. `&#039;`

17. What is the character entity for a quotation mark?

    a. `&q;`

    b. `&quot;`

    c. `&quotation;`

    d. `&qt;`

18. Most Web browsers will ignore multiple, contiguous spaces on a Web page and replace them with a single space. True or False?

19. Which of the following attributes of the `<img>` element are required in order for an XHTML document to be well formed? (Choose all that apply.)

    a. alt

    b. longdesc

    c. usemap

    d. width

20. Why should you use the height and width attributes with the `<img>` element?

21. The `height` and `width` attributes should always be the exact dimensions of the original image. True or False?

22. How do you create thumbnail images?

23. Which attribute do you include with the `<img>` element to create a client-side image map?

    a. `ismap`

    b. `usemap`

    c. `map`

    d. `getmap`

24. Which of the following values can you apply to the **<area>** element's **shape** attribute? (Choose all that apply.)

a. circle

b. square

c. poly

d. rect

HANDS-ON PROJECTS

Project 4-1

In this exercise, you create a document that uses text-formatting elements for a mobile oil change company named "Grease and Go".

1. Create a new document in your text editor.

2. Type the **<!DOCTYPE>** declaration, **<html>** element, document head, and the **<body>** element. Use the Strict DTD and "Grease and Go" as the content of the **<title>** element.

3. Add the following heading elements to the document body.

```
<h1>Grease and Go</h1>
<h2>Mobile Oil Change Service</h2>
```

4. Use text-formatting elements to create the paragraphs shown in Figure 4-33.

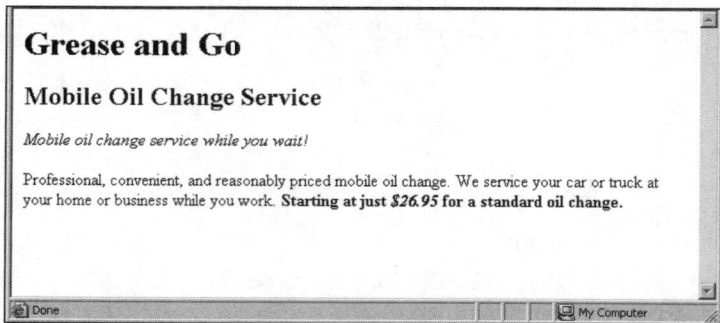

Figure 4-33   Exercise 4-1

5. Save the file as MobileOilChange.html in the Chapter.04\Projects folder.

6. Close the MobileOilChange.html file in your text editor and then use the W3C Markup Validation Service to validate it. Once the file is valid, open it in your Web browser.

7. Close your Web browser window.

Project 4-2

In this exercise, you create a document that uses phrase elements for a stunt-training school named "Freefall Stunt School".

1. Create a new document in your text editor.

2. Type the `<!DOCTYPE>` declaration, `<html>` element, document head, and the `<body>` element. Use the Strict DTD and "Freefall Stunt School" as the content of the `<title>` element.

3. Add the following heading elements to the document body.

   `<h1>Freefall Stunt School</h1>`

   `<h2>General Information</h2>`

4. Use phrase elements to create the paragraph shown in Figure 4–34.

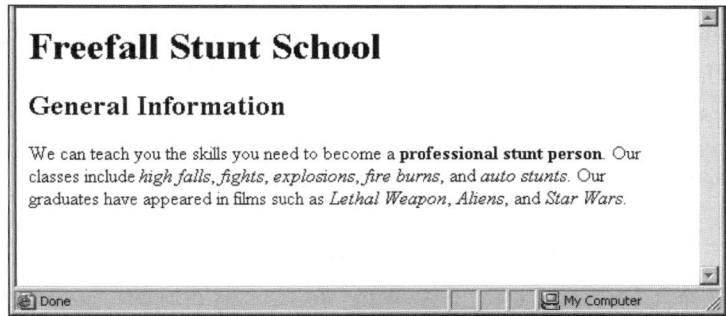

Figure 4-34   Project 4-2

5. Save the file as StuntSchool.html in the Chapter.04\Projects folder.

6. Close the StuntSchool.html file in your text editor and then use the W3C Markup Validation Service to validate it. Once the file is valid, open it in your Web browser.

7. Close your Web browser window.

Project 4-3

In this exercise, you create a document that uses a `<pre>` element to contain a phrase from the Robot in the 1960s television series, *Lost in Space*.

1. Create a new document in your text editor.

2. Type the `<!DOCTYPE>` declaration, `<html>` element, document head, and the `<body>` element. Use the Strict DTD and "Lost in Space" as the content of the `<title>` element.

3. Add the following elements and text to the document body.

```
<pre>Danger, danger Will Robinson!
My sensors indicate an intruder present.</pre>
<p>Robot, from the 1960's television series, <cite>Lost in
Space</cite>.</p>
```

4. Save the file as Robot.html in the Chapter.04\Projects folder.

5. Close the Robot.html file in your text editor and then use the W3C Markup Validation Service to validate it. Once the file is valid, open it in your Web browser.

6. Close your Web browser window.

Project 4-4

In this exercise, you create a document that lists the month and year that the *New York Times Book Review* gave its review of Victor Villaseñor's novel, *Children of Another Revolution*. You will use the <cite> element for *New York Times Book Review* and *Children of Another Revolution*. For the ñ character, use the ñ character entity.

1. Create a new document in your text editor.

2. Type the <!DOCTYPE> declaration, <html> element, document head, and the <body> element. Use the Strict DTD and "New York Times Book Review" as the content of the <title> element.

3. Add the following elements and text to the document body.

```
<p>In September, 1991, the <cite>New York Times Book
Review</cite> gave its review of Victor Villase&ntilde;or's
<cite>Children of Another Revolution</cite>.</p>
```

4. Save the file as BookReview.html in the Chapter.04\Projects folder.

5. Close the BookReview.html file in your text editor and then use the W3C Markup Validation Service to validate it. Once the file is valid, open it in your Web browser.

6. Close your Web browser window.

Project 4-5

In this exercise, you create a document that quotes the first paragraph from Chapter 1 of John Jakes' novel *Heaven and Hell*.

1. Create a new document in your text editor.

2. Type the <!DOCTYPE> declaration, <html> element, document head, and the <body> element. Use the Strict DTD and "Heaven and Hell" as the content of the <title> element.

3. Add the following elements and text to the document body.

```
<p>The first chapter in John Jakes' novel <cite>Heaven and
Hell</cite> begins as follows:</p>

<blockquote><p>All around him, pillars of fire shot
skyward. The fighting had ignited the dry underbrush, then
the trees. Smoke brought tears to his eyes and made it hard
to see the enemy skirmishers.</p></blockquote>
```

4. Save the file as JohnJakes.html in the Chapter.04\Projects folder.

5. Close the JohnJakes.html file in your text editor and then use the W3C Markup Validation Service to validate it. Once the file is valid, open it in your Web browser.

6. Close your Web browser window.

Project 4-6

In this exercise, you create a document that uses character entities to provide the Greek spelling of *Prometheus*.

1. Create a new document in your text editor.

2. Type the `<!DOCTYPE>` declaration, `<html>` element, document head, and the `<body>` element. Use the Strict DTD and "Prometheus" as the content of the `<title>` element.

3. Add the following elements and text to the document body. Notice that the name Prometheus is described using the `<em>` element. Also notice that the attributes in the `<p>` element identify the element as being written in the Greek language (the Greek language code is "el") with a direction of left to right.

```
<p>In Greek, <em>Prometheus</em> is spelled</p>
<p lang="el" xml:lang = "el"
dir="ltr">&Pi;&rho;&omicron;&mu;&eta;&theta;&epsilon;
&alpha;&sigma;</p>
```

4. Save the file as Prometheus.html in the Chapter.04\Projects folder.

5. Close the Prometheus.html file in your text editor and then use the W3C Markup Validation Service to validate it. Once the file is valid, open it in your Web browser.

6. Close your Web browser window.

Project 4-7

In this exercise, you create a document that contains an image of a professor. The Chapter.04\Exercises folder contains an image file named professor.jpg that you can use for this exercise.

1. Create a new document in your text editor.

2. Type the `<!DOCTYPE>` declaration, `<html>` element, document head, and the `<body>` element. Use the Strict DTD and "Professor" as the content of the `<title>` element.

3. Add the `<img>` element to the document body.

   ```
   <p><img src="professor.jpg" /></p>
   ```

4. Modify the `<img>` element so it includes alternate text along with the `height` and `width` attributes. Use a Web browser or an image-editing program to find the height and width of the image.

5. Save the file as Professor.html in the Chapter.04\Projects folder.

6. Close the Professor.html file in your text editor and then use the W3C Markup Validation Service to validate it. Once the file is valid, open it in your Web browser.

7. Close your Web browser window.

Project 4-8

In this exercise, you create a document that includes an image map of a person's head. Clicking each part of the head, such as an eye, ear, or nose, will open another Web page that contains a photo and definition of the selected body part.

1. Search the Internet for an image of a head that you can use as an image map, along with images of different parts of the head such as an image of an eye, an image of an ear, and so on.

2. Create a new document in your text editor.

3. Type the `<!DOCTYPE>` declaration, `<html>` element, document head, and the `<body>` element. Use the Strict DTD and "Head Map" as the content of the `<title>` element.

4. Add to the document body a map of the head image you found. Use the appropriate shape type for each hot zone. For example, use rect shapes for the ears and circle shapes for the eyes.

5. Save the file as HeadMap.html in the Chapter.04\Projects folder.

6. Next, create Web pages for each of the hot zones you added to the head image. Include in each hot zone's Web page the image you found of the associated body part, along with a formal definition of it. (You can find a formal definition of each body part on *http://dictionary.reference.com*.) Be sure to cite the source of each definition. Add links to each Web page to return to the HeadMap.html document. Save each Web page you create using the name of the body part, such as Ear.html or Eye.html.

7. Use the W3C Markup Validation Service to validate the files you created. Once the files are valid, open the HeadMap.html file in your Web browser and test the image map.

8. Close your Web browser window.

CASE PROJECTS

For the following projects, save the files you create in the Chapter.04\Cases folder. Create the files so they are well formed according to the Strict DTD. Be sure to validate the files you create with the W3C Markup Validation Service.

Project 4-1

Create a Web site for a pet photography service named Central Valley Pet Photography. On the home page, include a description of the service and contact information. Create the contact information using appropriate phrase elements. Use an acronym in the address of CVPP for the company name. Include a Samples page and a Pricing page. Search the Internet for images of pets that you can include on the Samples page. Save the home page as PetPhotos.html, the Samples page as Samples.html, and the Pricing page as Pricing.html.

Project 4-2

Create a Web site that contains photos and biographical information of your favorite actors. Place thumbnail images of each actor along with his or her name on the site's home page. Then, use the thumbnail image and actor names to create links to separate pages for each actor. Each actor's page should display a larger version of the same photo along with biographical information, including film and television credits. You can find thumbnail and full-sized versions of photos, along with biographical information for many actors by searching *http://movies.yahoo.com/*. Save the home page as ActorBios.html and save each individual actor's Web page using his or her first and last name. For instance, Robert DeNiro's Web page should be named RobertDeNiro.html.

Project 4-3

Create a Web site that sells natural rocks, gems, minerals, and crystals. Include links on the home page for different categories such as amethyst, geodes, quartz, and fossils. Search the Internet for image files of different types of rocks, gems, minerals, and crystals. The Web page for each category should include a picture and name of the item, along with price, weight, size, and a description. Save the home page as RocksAndGems.html and the Web page for each category using the category name.

Project 4-4

Search the Internet for an image of a sports team photo. Use the image to create an image map that uses each player as a hot zone. Clicking a hot zone should open a separate Web page that displays the player's statistics for the associated sport. For instance, with a photo of a baseball team, clicking a player should open a page that displays the player's batting average, number of errors, and so on. You can make up any statistical information you like. Save the home page as SportsTeam.html and save each individual team member's Web page using his or her first and last name. Make up whatever names you like for each team member.

5

FRAMES

In this chapter, you will:

♦ Work with the Frameset Document Type Definition (DTD)
♦ Create frames
♦ Use the `target` and `base` attributes
♦ Create nested frames
♦ Format frames
♦ Use the `<noframes>` element
♦ Create inline frames

In this chapter, you learn how to create Web pages using frames, which are independent, scrollable portions of a Web browser window, with each frame capable of displaying a separate document. Since Netscape first introduced frames into its browsers, they have been both a useful tool and a source of complaint among Web page authors and users. In fact, frames have been deprecated in XHTML. However, because they are still widely used, you learn how to create and work with them in this chapter.

THE FRAMESET DTD

Frames must be defined in a separate document from other HTML code. This has always been a source of irritation to Web page authors who prefer to keep all of a Web page's code within one document. Additionally, although correctly authored frames are quite useful in creating an easily navigable Web page, they come with a price. One problem is that frames divide an already small computer screen into much smaller regions that, if not authored properly, can be confusing to a visitor. Another problem is that Web pages that use frames consume considerably more bandwidth than Web pages that do not use frames because frame-based Web pages consist of multiple documents that the browser must download and render. Although this is becoming less of a problem thanks to the growing availability of broadband Internet access, you must still consider the future when the Web becomes available to user agents such as mobile phones and Personal Digital Assistants (PDAs). Imagine how difficult it would be to read and navigate through a frame-based Web page on a mobile phone's tiny screen. Frames are also incompatible with some older browses, can be difficult for some search engines to index, and can be difficult to translate to Web browsers for the visually impaired.

Because of the many problems and complaints associated with frames, they are deprecated in XHTML in favor of tables, which you will study in Chapter 6. If frames are deprecated, then why study them at all? You study frames primarily because they are so widely used and will more than likely continue to be widely used for some time. Because frames are so common, the W3C created the Frameset DTD to allow Web page authors to create frames in well-formed documents until the Web completely switches to XML-based Web sites using the Strict DTD. As you learned in Chapter 1, the Frameset DTD is identical to the Transitional DTD, except that it includes the `<frameset>` and `<frame>` elements, which allow you to split the browser window into two or more frames. Although you use the Frameset DTD in this chapter, you will continue to write the rest of your XHTML code so it conforms to the Strict DTD and conforms to the most current Web page authoring techniques.

Next, you start creating a frame-based Employee Directory Web page. The Web page lists the first few names in a company's employment directory as hyperlinks in the left frame. Clicking an employee name displays the employee's photo in the right frame. The use of frames makes it much easier for a visitor to the Web site to navigate through the employee directory.

To start creating a frame-based Employee Directory Web page:

1. Start your text editor and create a new document.

2. Type the `<!DOCTYPE>` declaration, `<html>` element, and the document head. Use the Frameset DTD and "Employee Directory" as the content of the

`<title>` element. Be sure not to add a `<body>` element; they are not required in frameset documents. Your document should appear as follows:

```
<!DOCTYPE html PUBLIC
"-//W3C//DTD XHTML 1.0 Frameset//EN"
"http://www.w3.org/TR/xhtml1/DTD/xhtml1-frameset.dtd">
<html xmlns="http://www.w3.org/1999/xhtml" lang="en" xml:lang = "en"
dir="ltr">
<head>
<title>Employee Directory</title>
<meta http-equiv="content-type"
content="text/html; charset=iso-8859-1" />
</head>
</html>
```

3. Save the file as **EmployeeDirectory.html** in the **Chapter.05\Chapter** folder.

CREATING FRAMES

The documents you have created so far have consisted of a single Web browser window that can display only one document at a time. Using frames, you can split a single Web browser window into multiple windows, each of which can open a different document. **Frames** are independent, scrollable portions of a Web browser window, with each frame capable of displaying a different document. Figure 5-1 shows an example of the Bibliomania Web site, which contains free online versions of classic literature, articles, poetry, interviews, and various study guides and reference material. Bibliomania makes extensive use of frames to display the content of the material it offers. Figure 5-1 uses frames to display a page from Jules Verne's *Around the World in 80 Days.*

Figure 5-1   Frames in Bibliomania

You divide a document into frames using the **<frameset>** element. The <frame> element and other <frameset> elements are the only items that you can place inside a <frameset> element. The Web browser ignores any other text or elements. The <frameset> element replaces the <body> element that is used in non-frame documents. Do not place <body> elements at the beginning of a document containing <frameset> elements. If you do, the browser ignores the <frameset> element and displays only the data contained within the <body> element.

You can create frames in a document in horizontal rows, vertical columns, or both. Two attributes of the <frameset> element, rows and cols, determine whether frames are created as rows or columns. The **rows attribute** determines the number of horizontal frames to create. The **cols attribute** determines the number of vertical frames to create. To set the dimensions of the frame, you assign a string to the rows or cols attribute containing the percentage of space or the number of pixels each row or column should take up on the screen, separated by commas. For example, <frameset rows="50%, 50%" cols="50% , 50%"> creates two rows, which each take up 50% of the height of the screen, and two columns, which each take up 50% of the width of the screen. You must define more than one row or more than one column, or the Web browser will ignore your frames. Figure 5-2 shows an example of the frames created using <frameset rows="50%, 50%" cols="50%, 50%">.

Figure 5-2   Frames created with <frameset rows="50%, 50%" cols="50%, 50%">

You can create frames using just rows or just columns. For example, Figure 5-3 shows the frames created with <frameset rows="50%, 50%">, and Figure 5-4 shows the frames created with <frameset cols="50%, 50%">.

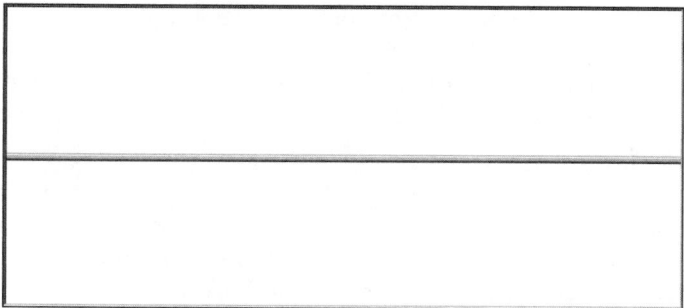

Figure 5-3   Frames created with `<frameset rows="50%, 50%">`

5

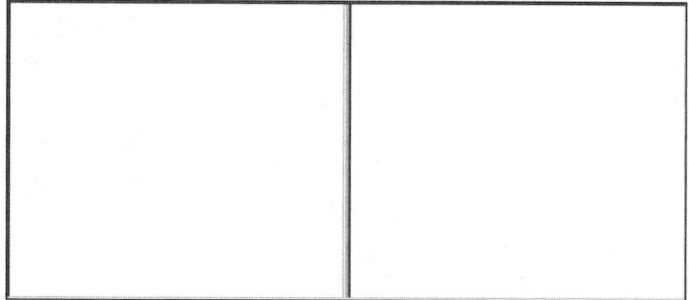

Figure 5-4   Frames created with `<frameset cols="50%, 50%">`

When you use percentages to specify the dimensions of a frame, the percentages are relative to the size of the window; that is, they adjust for the size of the window. In contrast, pixels represent exact or absolute sizes. They do not adjust for the size of the window. Users can set different default dimensions for their Web browser windows or resize their Web browser windows. Relative percentages can take these variations into account, whereas exact pixels cannot. For example, if you create two frames, each 100 pixels wide, they will not adjust for the actual dimensions of users' Web browser windows. If a user's screen is too small, your frames may be cut off. If a user's screen is a larger size, your frames might look strangely small. These size problems do not occur when you use percentages, because with percentages, the dimensions of the frame are calculated on the basis of the visible window.

It is helpful to use an asterisk (*) in your document to represent the size of frames that do not require an exact number of pixels or exact window percentage. The asterisk allocates any remaining screen space to an individual frame. If more than one frame is sized using an asterisk, then the remaining screen space is divided evenly. For example, `<frameset cols="100, *">` creates two frames in a column, using pixels to represent one column and an asterisk to represent the other. The left column will always remain 100 pixels wide, but the right column will be sized according to the visible screen space. If you examine the underlying document for the Bibliomania page shown in Figure 5-1, you will find a statement similar to `<frameset rows="60,*">`, which creates a row at the top of the page (containing the Bibliomania logo and the navigation buttons for the currently displayed content) that is sized to 60 pixels. The asterisk allows the second row on the page to use the remainder of the screen space.

You can use combinations of pixels, percentages, and the asterisk to create frames. For example, the tag `<frameset rows="100, 50%, *">` creates three rows: the first row is 100 pixels high, the second row takes up 50% of the visible window, and the asterisk allocates the remainder of the visible window to the third row.

The `<frameset>` element creates the initial frames within a document. You use the empty **`<frame>` element** to specify options for individual frames. The `src` attribute of the `<frame>` element specifies the document to be opened in an individual frame. You place `<frame>` elements within the `<frameset>` element. You can assign a name to a frame using the `name` attribute, and you can then use the name as a target for a hyperlink. You need a separate frame element for each frame in your window.

The browser opens the URLs of frames in the order in which it encounters each `<frame>` element, on a left-to-right, top-to-bottom basis. For example, the following code creates four frames, in two columns and two rows.

```
<frameset rows="50%, 50%" cols="50%, 50%">
      <frame src="frame1.html" />
      <frame src="frame2.html" />
      <frame src="frame3.html" />
      <frame src="frame4.html" />
</frameset>
```

Figure 5-5 shows the order in which the URL specified by a `<frame>` element loads into each frame.

Figure 5-5   URL load order

Next you add `<frameset>` and `<frame>` elements to the EmployeeDirectory.html file. The frame elements create a narrow column on the left frame that contains the list of employee names. The right frame, which displays an employee's photo, is a larger column that takes up the remainder of the screen width.

To add `<frameset>` and `<frame>` elements to the EmployeeDirectory.html file:

1. Return to the **EmployeeDirectory.html** file in your text editor.

2. After the closing `</head>` tag, add `<frameset cols="20%, *">` to start the frame set. The 20% in the code creates the narrow column on the left; the asterisk creates the wide column on the right.

3. Add the following two `<frame>` elements after the opening `<frameset>` tag. The first `<frame>` element opens a Web page named EmployeeList.html, which contains a list of employee names. The second frame opens a Web page named Start.html, which contains an opening message to display in the right frame.

   ```
   <frame src="EmployeeList.html" name="list" />
   <frame src="Start.html" name="display" />
   ```

4. Type the closing `</frameset>` tag above the closing `</html>` tag:

   ```
   </frameset>
   ```

5. Save the EmployeeDirectory.html file. Before you can open the EmployeeDirectory.html file in a browser, you need to create the Start.html and EmployeeList.html files. If you attempt to open the EmployeeDirectory.html file, you browser will display an error that it could not find the files.

Next you create the Start.html file. You create the EmployeeList.html file later. Note that because the Start.html and EmployeeList.html files are not frames, you create them using the Strict DTD.

To create the Start.html file:

1. Create a new document in your text editor.

2. Type the `<!DOCTYPE>` declaration, `<html>` element, document head, and the `<body>` element. Use the Strict DTD and "Welcome" as the content of the `<title>` element.

3. Add to the document body the following line to instruct the user to click an employee name in the list:

   ```
   <p>Click an employee name in the list to display his or her
   picture and employment information.</p>
   ```

4. Save the file as **Start.html** in the **Chapter.05\Chapter** folder and then close it in your text editor.

5

USING THE `target` AND `base` ATTRIBUTES

One popular use of frames creates a table of contents frame on the left side of a Web browser window with a display frame on the right side. The display frame shows the contents of a URL selected from a link in the table of contents frame, similar to the Bibliomania page you saw in Figure 5-1. This type of design eliminates the need to open a separate Web browser window when you want to display another document. In other words, it allows you to display a table of contents that users can use to navigate to other documents on a Web site. Figure 5-6 shows a document that is split into two frames. Each frame displays a different document associated with a different URL. The left frame contains a document that lists some of the architectural wonders of the world, and the right frame contains a document instructing the user to select the name of an architectural structure from the left frame. When you click the name of an architectural structure, a new document containing its picture and description opens in the right frame, as shown in Figure 5-7.

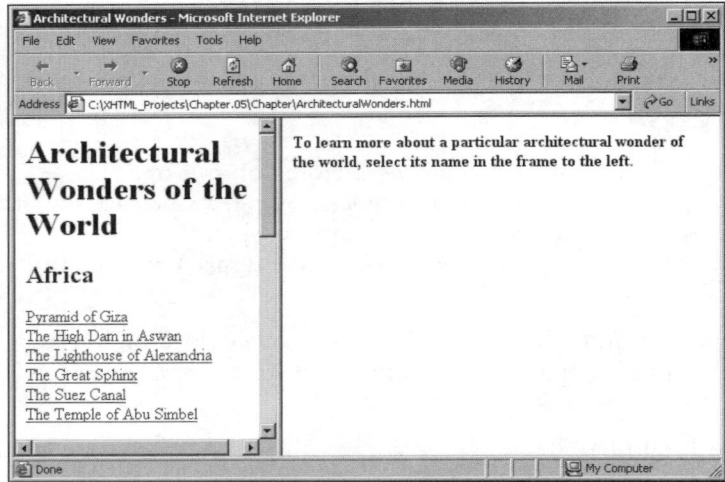

Figure 5-6   Architectural Wonders document

The Architectural Wonders page of Allwonders.com at *http://www.allwonders.com/architectural.htm* inspired the Architectural Wonders frame example you see in this chapter. Allwonders.com is a creative Indian company that specializes in Web consulting and development services.

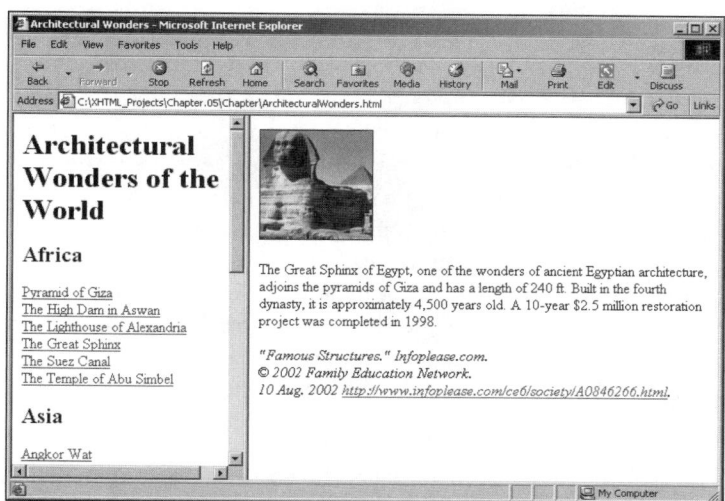

Figure 5-7 Architectural Wonders document after selecting a structure

The following code shows the `<frameset>` and `<frame>` elements used to create the Architectural Wonders document.

```
<frameset cols="250,*">
    <frame src="StructuresList.html" name="list" />
    <frame src="Welcome.html" name="display" />
</frameset>
```

The Architectural Wonders document creates two column frames. The first column is 250 pixels wide, and the second column takes up the remainder of the window. Two `<frame>` elements open documents in each individual frame. The document in the left frame contains hyperlinks for each structure name. You use the `target` attribute of the `<a>` element to get the document for each hyperlink to open in the right frame. The **target attribute** determines in which frame or Web browser window a document opens. For example, the name assigned to the right frame in the Architectural Wonders document is *display*. When you click *The Great Sphinx* hyperlink in the left frame (named *list*), the sphinx.html file opens in the display frame. The syntax for the `<a>` element to open the sphinx.html file in the display frame is `<a href="sphinx.html" target="display">The Great Sphinx</a>`. The following is an example of the code that appears in the document displayed in the left frame. Notice that it uses the `target` attribute repeatedly:

```
...
<h2>Asia</h2>
<p><a href="angkor_wat.html" target="display">Angkor Wat</a><br />
<a href="borobudur.html" target="display">Borobudur Temple</a><br />
<a href="great_wall.html" target="display">Great Wall of China</a><br />
```

```
<a href="taj_mahal.html" target="display">Taj Mahal, India</a><br />
<a href="halicarnassus.html" target="display">The Mausoleum at
Halicarnassus</a><br />
...additional structures
```

When you are using the same target window or frame for a long list of hyperlinks, it is easier to use the **target** attribute in the **<base>** element instead of repeating the **target** attribute within each hyperlink. You use the **target** attribute with the **<base> element** to specify a default target for all links in a document, using the assigned name of a window or frame. Although the **<base>** element is available in the Strict DTD, the **target** attribute is deprecated, so in order to specify a default target link using the **<base>** element and the **target** attribute, you must use the Transitional DTD. The **<base>** element must be placed within the document head, not within the document body. The following code shows how you can write the preceding statements more efficiently using the **<base>** element.

```
<!DOCTYPE html PUBLIC
"-//W3C//DTD XHTML 1.0 Transitional//EN"
"http://www.w3.org/TR/xhtml1/DTD/xhtml1-transitional.dtd">
<html xmlns="http://www.w3.org/1999/xhtml" lang="en" xml:lang = "en"
dir="ltr">
<head>
<title>Structures List</title>
<meta http-equiv="content-type"
content="text/html; charset=iso-8859-1" />
<base target="display" />
</head>
<body>
...
<h2>Asia</h2>
<p><a href="angkor_wat.html">Angkor Wat</a><br />
<a href="borobudur.html">Borobudur Temple</a><br />
<a href="great_wall.html">Great Wall of China</a><br />
<a href="taj_mahal.html">Taj Mahal, India</a><br />
<a href="halicarnassus.html">The Mausoleum at Halicarnassus</a><br />
...additional structures
```

You can also assign one of four optional values to a <base> element's target attribute: _blank, _parent, _self, or _top. The _blank value opens all links in a new window. The _parent value opens all links in the parent frameset. The _self value opens all links within the current frame. The _top value opens all links in the main browser window.

Next you create the EmployeeList.html file, which contains a list of the employee names in the Employee Directory Web page. Clicking an employee name in the left frame will open his or her photo in the right frame. The .jpg files for the employees are located in your Chapter.05\Chapter folder.

To create the EmployeeList.html file:

1. Create a new document in your text editor.

2. Type the `<!DOCTYPE>` declaration, `<html>` element, document head, and the `<body>` element. Use the Transitional DTD and "Employees" as the content of the `<title>` element. Because each employee's photo will always open in the right frame, include in the head section the `<base target="display">` element to specify the right frame (named display) as the default target. Your document should appear as follows:

```
<!DOCTYPE html PUBLIC
"-//W3C//DTD XHTML 1.0 Transitional//EN"
"http://www.w3.org/TR/xhtml1/DTD/xhtml1-transitional.dtd">
<html xmlns="http://www.w3.org/1999/xhtml" lang="en" xml:lang = "en"
dir="ltr">
<head>
<title>Employees</title>
<meta http-equiv="content-type"
content="text/html; charset=iso-8859-1" />
<base target="display" />
</head>
<body>
</body>
</html>
```

3. Add to the document body the list of links for each employee. Each link opens a simple Web page that displays a .jpg graphic file containing each employee's photo. The employee Web pages have already been created for you and are located in your Chapter.05\Chapter folder.

```
<p><a href="Akahoshi.html">Akahoshi, Lee</a><br />
<a href="Alansi.html">Alansi, Paul</a><br />
<a href="Alland.html">Alland, Gary</a><br />
<a href="Armstrong.html">Armstrong, Bruce</a><br />
<a href="Asuncion.html">Asuncion, Linda</a><br />
<a href="Avery.html">Avery, Janice</a></p>
```

You can open an image file, such as a .jpg file, directly in a Web browser. For instance, the preceding link for Janice Avery could open her associated .jpg file instead of a Web page as follows: `<a href="Avery.jpg">Avery, Janice</a></p>`. However, it is considered bad practice to open an image file or other type of multimedia file directly in a frame primarily because there is no way of specifying alternate text with the `alt` attribute. For this reason, any images or other multimedia files should be displayed in a frame through a Web page.

4. Save the file as **EmployeeList.html** in the **Chapter.05\Chapter** folder and then close it in your text editor.

5. Now that you have created the EmployeeList.html file and the Start.html file, you can open the **EmployeeDirectory.html** file in your Web browser. Click each employee's name to see if the links work correctly. Figure 5-8 shows an example of the file displaying Linda Asuncion in Internet Explorer.

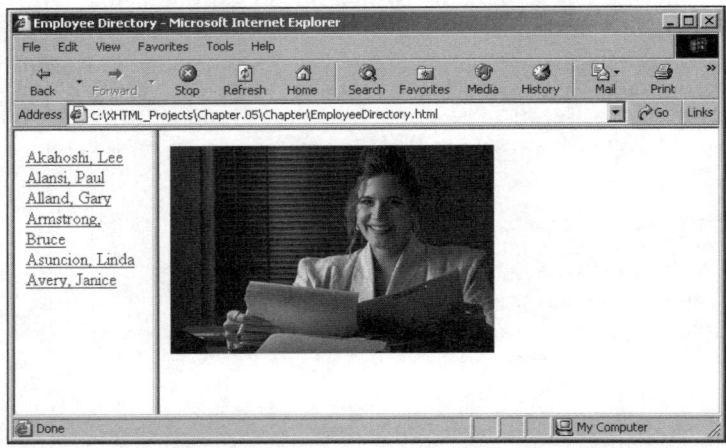

Figure 5-8   Employee Directory.html frameset document

6. Close the Web browser window.

NESTING FRAMES

Each individual frame within a window can contain its own set of frames. You accomplish this nesting by including a `<frameset>` element *inside* another `<frameset>` element. Frames that are contained within other frames are called **nested frames**.

As a Web browser starts creating frames, the browser loads the URLs of frames in the order in which it encounters each `<frame>` element. The following code creates a parent frameset consisting of two rows and two columns. The second frame contains a nested frameset that also consists of two rows and two columns. The text displayed in each frame is contained within the file specified by each frame's `src` attribute. Figure 5-9 shows how the frames would appear.

```
<!-- The following line creates the main frame set -->
<frameset rows="50%, 50%" cols="50%, 50%">
    <!-- The following line assigns frame1.html as the
    URL of the first frame in the main frame set -->
    <frame src="frame1.html" />
    <!-- The following line creates a nested frame set
```

```
        inside the second frame in the main frame set -->
    <frameset rows="50%, 50%" cols="50%, 50%">
        <!-- The following lines assign URLs
    to the nested frames -->
        <frame src="frame1.html" />
        <frame src="frame2.html" />
        <frame src="frame3.html" />
        <frame src="frame4.html" />
    </frameset>
    <!-- The following lines assign URLs to the
      third and fourth frames in the main frame set -->
    <frame src="frame3.html" />
    <frame src="frame4.html" />
</frameset>
```

5

Figure 5-9   Nested frames

In Figure 5-9, the first **<frameset>** element creates the four parent frames in the window. The first **<frame>** element assigns the URL frame1.html to the first frame in the parent frame set. The second **<frameset>** element is nested inside the second frame in the parent frame set. Each nested frame is then assigned a URL. The nested frames appearing in Figure 5-9 are more complicated and cumbersome than frames you would normally find on the Web.

The following code shows a more typical example, using the Architectural Wonders Web page. The right column of the parent frame contains a nested frameset consisting of two rows. The first row displays a picture of the structure and the second row displays the description. The frameset has also been modified to open by default the first structure in the list, the Pyramids of Giza. Figure 5-10 shows how the Architectural Wonders Web page with nested frames appears in Internet Explorer.

```
<frameset cols="250,*">
    <frame src="StructuresList.html" name="list" />
    <frameset rows="40%,*">
        <frame src="giza.jpg" name="picture" />
        <frame src="giza.html" name="description" />
    </frameset>
</frameset>
```

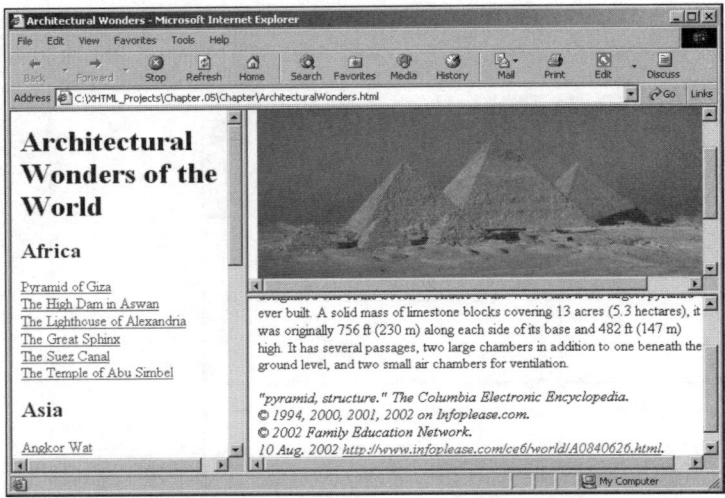

Figure 5-10   Architectural Wonders Web page with nested frames

Next you modify the Employee Directory Web page so that it includes a nested frame. The parent frameset consists of two rows: the first row displays a title for the Employee Directory, and the second row contains a nested frameset, consisting of the employee list and the frame that displays the employee's photo.

To add a nested frame to the Employee Directory Web page:

1. Return to the **EmployeeDirectory.html** file in your text editor.

2. Add **<frameset rows="20%,*">** above the existing **<frameset>** element. The existing frameset will be nested inside a new frameset.

3. After the opening tag for the new frameset, add **<frame src="Title.html" name="title" />** to specify that a document named Title.html will open in the first frame.

4. Create a closing **</frameset>** tag before the document's closing **</html>** tag to end the new frameset.

5. Save and close the file.

Next you need to create the Title.html file that opens in the first frame of the Employee Directory Web page.

To create the Title.html file:

1. Create a new document in your text editor.

2. Type the **<!DOCTYPE>** declaration, **<html>** element, document head, and the **<body>** element. Use the Strict DTD and "Title Page" as the content of the **<title>** element.

3. Add the following heading element to the document body:

   <h1>Employee Directory</h1>

4. Save the file as **Title.html** in the **Chapter.05\Chapter** folder, close it, and then reopen the **EmployeeDirectory.html** file in your Web browser. Figure 5-11 shows an example of the file with Paul Alansi selected.

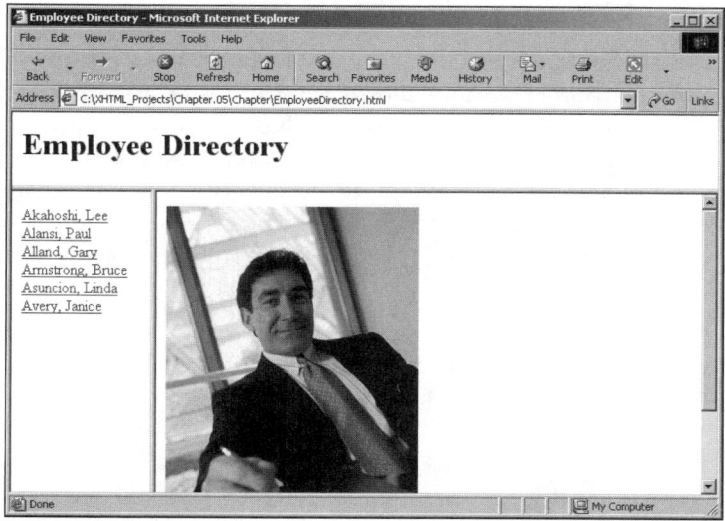

Figure 5-11 EmployeeDirectory.html with nested frames

5. Close the Web browser window.

FRAME FORMATTING

You can use a variety of attributes with the `<frame>` element to specify a frame's appearance and behavior. Table 5-1 lists some of the attributes of the `<frame>` element.

Table 5-1   `<frame>` element attributes

Attribute	Description
frameborder	Specifies whether to display a border around the frame
framespacing	Determines the amount of space between frames in Internet Explorer
longdesc	Identifies the URL of a Web page containing a long description of a frame
marginheight	Specifies the top and bottom margins of the frame in pixels
marginwidth	Specifies the left and right margins of the frame in pixels
name	Assigns a name to an individual frame
noresize	Disables the user's ability to resize an individual frame
scrolling	Determines whether a frame includes scroll bars
src	Specifies the URL to be opened in a frame

The `frameborder` Attribute

One other attribute you should understand is the **frameborder attribute**, which specifies whether to display a border around the frame. You assign to the `frameborder` attribute a value of "1" to display a border and a value of "0" to suppress the border. Even though you may suppress the border for one frame, a border may still appear if neighboring frames have their `frameborder` attributes turned on. For instance, the following frameset code suppresses the border for the header frame in the Beowulf document. However, because the middle frame does not suppress its border, you still see a border between the two frames.

```
<frameset rows="20%, *, 20%">
    <frame src="header.html" frameborder="0" />
    <frame src="body.html" name="body" />
    <frame src="navigationbar.html" />
</frameset>
```

Even if you suppress the border on a neighboring frame, you still see a small border between two frames in Internet Explorer. You would not see any border in Netscape.) For instance, even though the following code suppresses the border for both the header frame and middle frame, you can still see a small border in Internet Explorer, as shown in Figure 5-12:

```
<frameset rows="20%, *, 20%">
    <frame src="header.html" frameborder="0" />
    <frame src="body.html" name="body" frameborder="0" />
    <frame src="navigationbar.html" />
</frameset>
```

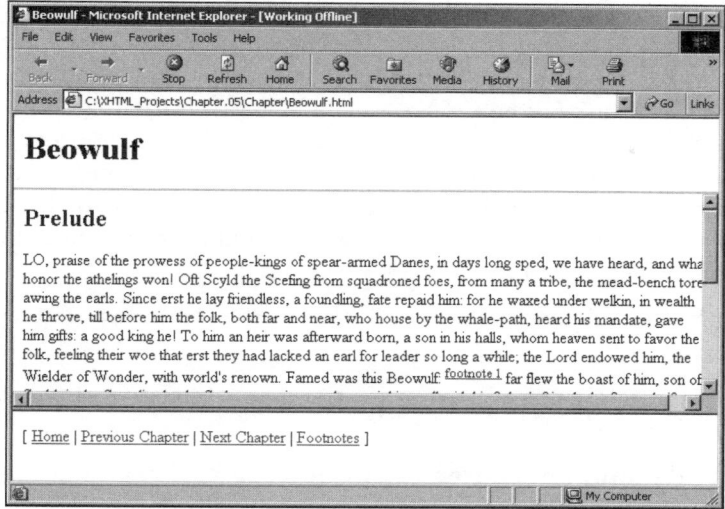

Figure 5-12 Beowulf document with frame borders suppressed between the header and body frames

To completely suppress a border between two frames in Internet Explorer, you must include the **framespacing** attribute and assign to it a value of zero. The **framespacing** attribute determines the amount of space between frames in Internet Explorer. The following frameset suppresses the border between the header and body frames because it includes the **framespacing** attribute for both **<frame>** elements:

```
<frameset rows="20%, *, 20%">
    <frame src="header.html" frameborder="0" framespacing="0" />
    <frame src="body.html" name="body" frameborder="0"
        framespacing="0" />
    <frame src="navigationbar.html" />
</frameset>
```

The **framespacing** attribute is proprietary to Internet Explorer. Although other Web browsers will ignore the **framespacing** attribute, remember that if you use it in your documents, they will not be well formed. If you must suppress the frame borders in your documents, use the **framespacing** attribute. However, remember that the goal of this book is (and your goal as a Web page author should be) to write well-formed documents. Therefore, you will not use the **framespacing** attribute in this book.

The **longdesc** Attribute

In Chapter 2, you learned how to use the common **title** attribute to provide descriptive text for an element. You should include the **title** attribute in your **<frame>** elements to describe the content of a frame. However, the **title** attribute should contain only a short description of the contents of the frame, which is insufficient for user agents that do not support frames, particularly user agents for the visually impaired. In order for your frame documents to be more accessible to non-visual user agents, you should include the **longdesc** attribute in your **<frame>** elements and assign to it the URL of a Web page containing a long description of the frame. The inclusion of the **longdesc** attribute is especially important for a frame that displays image, video, or other type of multimedia as its contents. A non-visual user agent can access the URL assigned to the **longdesc** attribute and read its content to a user. Note that you should use the **longdesc** attribute in a **<frame>** element in addition to a **title** attribute.

Next, you add **title** and **longdesc** attributes to the **<frame>** elements in the EmployeeDirectory.html file.

To add **title** and **longdesc** attributes to the **<frame>** elements in the EmployeeDirectory.html file:

1. Return to the **EmployeeDirectory.html** file in your text editor.

2. Add **title** and **longdesc** attributes to each **<frame>** element, as follows:

```
...
<frame src="Title.html" name="title"
    title="Employee List Title Frame" longdesc="EmployeeListTitle_
    Content.html" />
<frameset cols="20%, *">
    <frame src="EmployeeList.html" name="list"
    title="Employee List Frame" longdesc=" EmployeeList_Content.html" />
    <frame src="Start.html" name="display"
    title="Employee Photo Frame" longdesc="EmployeeFrame_Content.html"
/>
</frameset>
...
```

3. Save the **EmployeeDirectory.html** file.

Next, you create the long description files for the Employee Directory frames. You will not be able to navigate to these files using a standard Web browser. However, you should create them in the event that a non-visual browser accesses the Employee Directory Web site.

To create the long description files for the Employee Directory frames:

1. Create a new document in your text editor.

2. Type the **<!DOCTYPE>** declaration, **<html>** element, document head, and the **<body>** element. Use the Strict DTD and "Title Frame" as the content of the **<title>** element.

3. Add to the document body the following elements and long description text:

```
<p>The Employee List Title Frame includes a single
heading that reads <em>Employee Directory</em>.</p>
```

4. Save the file as **EmployeeListTitle_Content.html** in the **Chapter.05\Chapter** folder and then close it in your text editor.

5. Create a new document in your text editor.

6. Type the `<!DOCTYPE>` declaration, `<html>` element, document head, and the `<body>` element. Use the Strict DTD and "Employee List" as the content of the `<title>` element.

7. Add to the document body the following elements and long description text:

```
<p>The Employee List Frame contains a list of hyperlinked
employee names. Clicking an employee name displays a
Web page with the employee's photo in the Employee Photo
Frame.</p>
```

8. Save the file as **EmployeeList_Content.html** in the **Chapter.05\Chapter** folder and then close it in your text editor.

9. Create a new document in your text editor.

10. Type the `<!DOCTYPE>` declaration, `<html>` element, document head, and the `<body>` element. Use the Strict DTD and "Employee Photo" as the content of the `<title>` element.

11. Add to the document body the following elements and long description text:

```
<p>The Employee Photo Frame displays a Web page with the
photo of an employee whose name has been clicked in the
Employee List Frame.</p>
```

12. Save the file as **EmployeeFrame_Content.html** in the **Chapter.05\Chapter** folder and then close it in your text editor.

The `marginheight` and `marginwidth` Attributes

The **marginheight** and **marginwidth** attributes determine the margins of the frame in pixels. Figure 5-13 shows the Beowulf Web page from Figure 5-12 after the attributes `marginheight="50"` and `marginwidth="50"` have been added to the `<frame>` element for the middle frame. Notice how much larger the top and left margins appear in the bottom frame. The new element for the middle frame reads `<frame src="body.html" marginheight="50" marginwidth="50" />`.

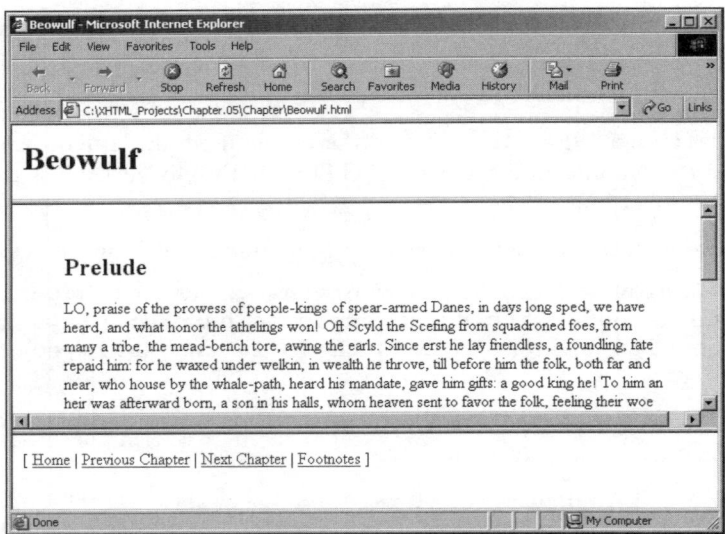

Figure 5-13   Frame with `marginheight` and `marginwidth` attributes

The `noresize` Attribute

You have already used the `src` attribute to specify a URL for a frame. You have also used the `name` attribute to specify a frame as a target for a hypertext link. The Boolean **noresize attribute** disables the user's ability to resize an individual frame. Normally, users can adjust the size of frames to suit their own purposes. You use the `noresize` attribute when, for example, you want to add a title that should always be visible in a frame or on a Web page. Or, you may want to create a list of hyperlinks at the bottom of a Web page to help users navigate through your site. To disable resizing of a frame, add the `noresize` attribute to the `<frame>` element and assign to it a value of "noresize" using the following statement: `noresize="noresize"`.

The `scrolling` Attribute

By default, a Web browser automatically adds scroll bars to a frame when the contents of the frame are larger than the visible area. You can disable a frame's scroll bars using the **scrolling attribute**. The `scrolling` attribute can take one of three values: yes, no, and auto. A value of *yes* always turns on the scroll bars, even when the contents of a frame fit within the visible area. A value of *no* completely disables a frame's scroll bars, even when the contents of a frame do not fit within the visible area. *Auto* turns the scroll bars on and off, depending on the visibility of the contents within a frame. In other words, if the content of a frame is too large to be displayed, then the scroll bars appear when a value of *auto* is assigned to the `scrolling` attribute. However, if the content of a frame will completely fit within the frame, then the scroll bars do not appear when a value of auto is assigned to the **scrolling** attribute. Selecting a value of *auto* is equivalent to not including the **scrolling** attribute in the **<frame>** element.

The following code shows an example of a Web page that includes both the **noresize** and **scrolling** attributes. Figure 5-14 shows how the code renders in a Web browser. The Web page contains three frames. The top frame provides a title for the Web page, and the bottom frame contains navigation buttons and hyperlinks. The middle frame contains the main content of the Web page. Because we do not want the user to resize the top and bottom frames, the **<frame>** elements for the top and bottom frames include the **noresize** attribute. The **scrolling** attribute has also been set to no for the top and bottom frames, because the user does not need to scroll through them.

```
<frameset rows="20%, *, 20%">
    <frame src="header.html" noresize="noresize" scrolling="no" />
    <frame src="body.html" name="body" />
    <frame src="navigationbar.html" noresize="noresize" scrolling="no" />
</frameset>
```

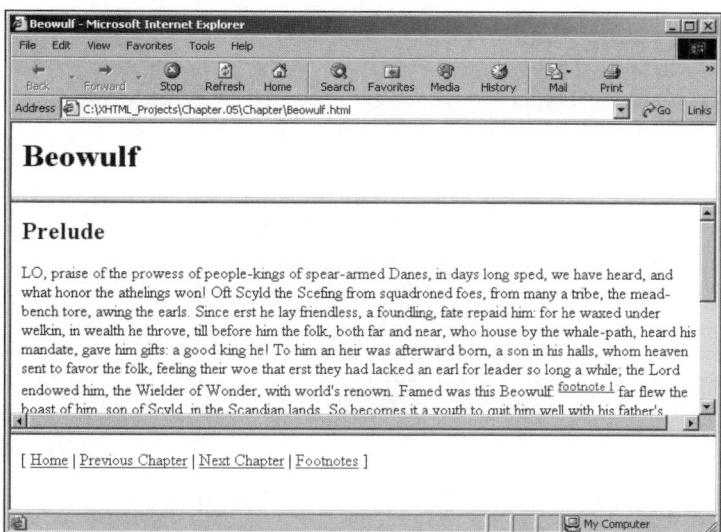

Figure 5-14   Web page that includes noresize and scrolling attributes

 In the Web page in Figure 5-14, the **noresize** attributes in the top and bottom frames essentially eliminate resizing in the middle frame.

Next, you add **noresize** and **scrolling** attributes to the title frame of the Employee Directory document.

To add `noresize` and `scrolling` attributes to the title frame of the Employee Directory document:

1. Return to the **EmployeeDirectory.html** file in your text editor.

2. Add **noresize="noresize"** and **scrolling="no"** just before the slash and closing bracket in the first **<frame>** element. The modified element should appear as follows:

```
<frame src="Title.html" name="title"
    title="Employee List Title Frame"
    longdesc="EmployeeListTitle_Content.html"
    noresize="noresize" scrolling="no" />
```

3. Save the file, and then open the **EmployeeDirectory.html** file in your Web browser. You should no longer be able to resize the title frame. You should not be able to see the scrollbar.

4. Close your Web browser window.

THE <noframes> ELEMENT

The **<noframes>** element displays a message to users of Web browsers that are not capable of displaying frames. For your frameset document to be well formed, you must place the **<noframes>** element within a **<frameset>** element. The **<noframes>** element must also include a **<body>** element in order to be well formed. The **<noframes>** element usually precedes the last **<frameset>** element. The following code shows an example of the **<noframes>** element.

```
<frameset rows="20%, *, 20%">
    <frame src="header.html" noresize="noresize" scrolling=no>
    <frame src="body.html">
    <frame src="navigationbar.html"
            noresize="noresize" scrolling=no>
<noframes>
<body>
<p>You cannot view this Web page because your Web browser
does not support frames. You can view a no frames version of this
Web page at <a href="no_frames.html">no_frames.html</a>.</p>
</body>
</noframes>
</frameset>
```

 Web browsers that are capable of displaying frames ignore the <noframes> element.

Next you add a **<noframes>** element to the Employee Directory document.

To add a `<noframes>` element to the Employee Directory document:

1. Return to the **EmployeeDirectory.html** file in your text editor.

2. Just before the last closing `</frameset>` tag, add the following `<noframes>` element to warn users of frame-incompatible browsers that they cannot view this Web page.

```
<noframes><body>

<p>You cannot view this Web page because your Web browser
does not support frames.</p>

</body></noframes>
```

3. Save and close the file. Now, if someone opens the EmployeeDirectory.html file in a frame-incompatible browser, they will see the no frames message.

Next, you validate the Employee Directory Web page. Because of the multiple frames that make up this Web page, you do not add the W3C XHTML logo.

To validate the Employee Directory Web page:

1. Start Internet Explorer and enter the URL for the upload page of the W3C Markup Validation Service: **http://validator.w3.org/file-upload.html**.

2. Open and validate the **EmployeeDirectory.html** file. If you receive any errors, fix them, and then revalidate the document.

3. Repeat the validation process for the **Title.html, EmployeeList.html, Start.html, Title_Content.html, EmployeeList_Content.html,** and **EmployeeFrame_Content.html** files.

4. Close your Web browser.

INLINE FRAMES

Instead of using `<frameset>` and `<frame>` elements, you can insert an inline frame into a non-frame document using the `<iframe>` element. The `<iframe>` element creates an **inline frame** that displays another document within the body of the current document. You use an inline frame when you want to display another document within the current document, but you do not need to divide the Web browser into multiple frames. Like frames that you create with the `<frameset>` and `<frame>` elements, inline frames are deprecated, so you cannot use them with documents that conform to the Strict DTD. Therefore, to write well-formed documents that include inline frames, you must use the Transitional DTD or the Frameset DTD.

The `<iframe>` element contains many of the same attributes as the `<frame>` element. Table 5-2 lists the `<iframe>` element attributes.

Table 5-2 `<iframe>` element attributes

Attribute	Description
align	Specifies how the inline frame will be aligned according to the content on the left and right sides
frameborder	Specifies whether to display a border around the inline frame
height	Specifies the height of an inline frame
longdesc	Identifies the URL of a Web page containing a long description of an inline frame
marginheight	Specifies the top and bottom margins of the inline frame in pixels
marginwidth	Specifies the left and right margins of the inline frame in pixels
name	Assigns a name to an individual inline frame
scrolling	Determines whether an inline frame includes scroll bars
src	Specifies the URL to be opened in an inline frame
width	Specifies the width of an inline frame

The only inline frame attributes in Table 5-2 that differ from `<frame>` element attributes are the `align`, `height`, and `width` attributes. The `align` attribute specifies how the inline frame will be aligned according to the content on its left and right sides. You assign one of five values to the align attribute: `left`, `right`, `top`, `middle`, and `bottom`. The `height` and `width` attributes determine the size of the inline frame. The remaining attributes function in the same manner as they do for `<frame>` elements.

You can create inline frames using either an empty `<iframes>` element or by using an `<iframes>...</iframes>` tag pair. If you use an `<iframes>...</iframes>` tag pair, then you should include as its content a message to users of Web browsers that are not capable of displaying frames, the same as with the `<noframes>` element. For example, the following code shows an inline frames version of the Architectural Wonders document you saw earlier. Notice that the code uses the `<base>` element to set the default target to the `<iframe>` element, using the assigned name of *display*.

Figure 5-15 shows how the document appears in Internet Explorer.

```
...
<base target="display" />
</head>
<body>
<h1>Architectural Wonders of the World</h1>
<h2>Africa</h2>
<p><a href="giza.html">Pyramid of Giza</a><br />
<a href="aswan.html">The High Dam in Aswan</a><br />
<a href="alexandria.html">The Lighthouse of Alexandria</a><br />
<a href="sphinx.html">The Great Sphinx</a><br />
<a href="suezcanal.html">The Suez Canal</a><br />
<a href="abu_simbel.html">The Temple of Abu Simbel</a></p>
<iframe src="Welcome.html" name="display" height="250" width="600"
scrolling="yes" align="middle" marginheight="20" marginwidth="20"
title="Architectural Wonders Frame"
longdesc="WondersFrame_Content.html">
```

```
<p>You cannot view this Web page because your Web browser
does not support inline frames.</p>
</iframe>
</body>
```

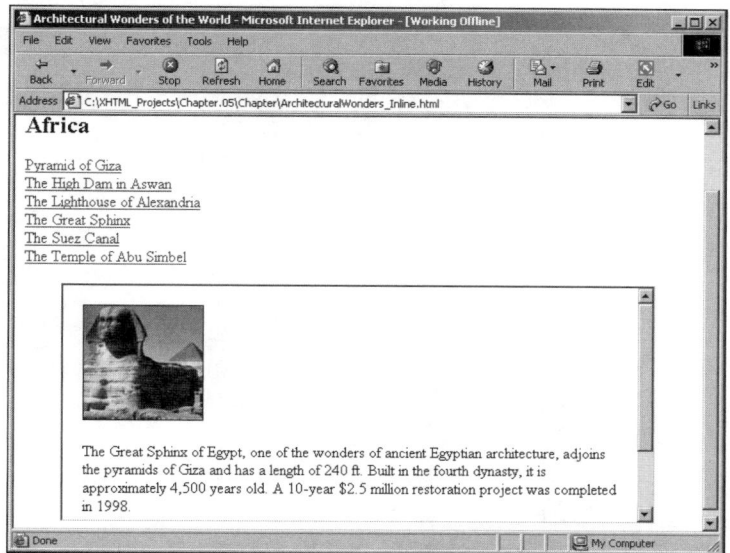

Figure 5-15   Inline frames version of the Architectural Wonders document

Next, you create an inline frames version of the Employee Directory document.

To create an inline frames version of the Employee Directory document:

1. Open the **EmployeeList.html** file in your text editor and immediately save it as **EmployeeList_Inline.html** in your Chapter.05\Chapter folder.

2. Add the following **<h1>** element immediately after the opening **<body>** tag:

   <h1>Employee Directory</h1>

3. Add the following **<iframe>** element immediately above the closing **</body>** tag. Notice that the frame opens the Start.html file by default and that it assigns a value of EmployeeFrame_Content.html, the same as with the frameset version of the document.

   ```
   <iframe src="Start.html" name="display" height="450" width="450"
   align="middle" marginheight="20" marginwidth="20"
   title="Employee Directory" longdesc="EmployeeFrame_Content.html">
   <p>You cannot view this Web page because your Web browser
   does not support inline frames.</p>
   </iframe>
   ```

4. Save and close the file in your text editor and then use the W3C Markup Validation Service to validate it.

5. Open the **EmployeeList_Inline.html** file in your Web browser. Test the links to see if they open properly in the inline frame. Figure 5-16 shows an example of the file displaying Gary Alland.

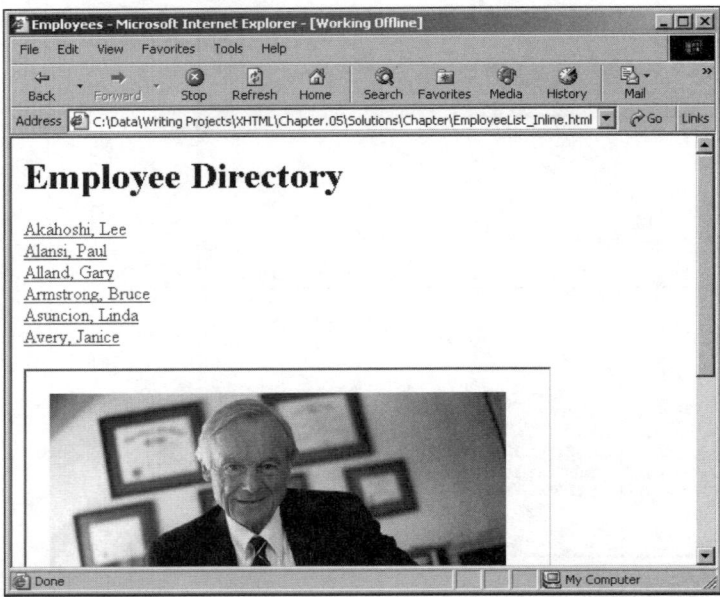

Figure 5-16   Inline frames version of the Employee Directory document

6. Close your text editor and Web browser window.

Chapter Summary

❑ Frames are independent, scrollable portions of a Web browser window, with each frame capable of displaying its own URL.

❑ A document is divided into frames using the `<frameset>` element.

❑ The `<frame>` element and other `<frameset>` elements are the only items that can be placed inside a `<frameset>` element.

❑ The `rows` attribute determines the number of horizontal frames to create.

❑ The `cols` attribute determines the number of vertical frames to create.

❑ The empty `<frame>` element is used to specify options for individual frames, including a frame's URL.

❑ The `target` attribute determines in which frame or Web browser window a URL opens.

❑ The `<base>` element is used to specify a default target for all links in a document, using the assigned name of a window or frame.

❑ Frames that are contained within other frames are called nested frames.

❑ As a Web browser starts creating frames, it loads the URLs of frames in the order in which it encounters each `<frame>` element.

❑ The `frameborder` attribute specifies whether to display a border around the frame.

❑ The `longdesc` attribute specifies the URL of a Web page containing a long description of the frame.

❑ The `noresize` attribute disables the user's ability to resize an individual frame.

❑ The `marginheight` and `marginwidth` attributes determine the margins of the frame in pixels.

❑ You can disable a frame's scroll bars using the `scrolling` attribute.

❑ To completely suppress a border between two frames in Internet Explorer, you must include the proprietary `framespacing` attribute and assign to it a value of zero.

❑ If you use the `framespacing` attribute, your documents will not be well formed.

❑ The `<noframes>` element displays an alternate message to users of Web browsers that are not capable of displaying frames.

❑ For your frameset document to be well formed, you must place the `<noframes>` element within a `<frameset>` element.

❑ The `<iframe>` element creates an inline frame that displays another document within the body of the current document.

REVIEW QUESTIONS

1. Explain why frames are deprecated in XHTML.
2. Which of the following tag pairs is used to create frames?
   a. `<begin frame>...</end frame>`
   b. `<frameset>...</frameset>`
   c. `<new frame>...</new frame>`
   d. `<framebuild>...</framebuild>`

5

3. The `<frame>` element and other `<frameset>` elements are the only items that can be placed inside a `<frameset>` element. True or False?

4. The size of rows and columns in a frame can be set using a percentage of the screen size or by using _____.

   a. inches

   b. picas

   c. pixels

   d. a Web browser's internal sizing capability

5. Which symbol can be used to allocate any remaining screen space to an individual frame?

   a. *

   b. &

   c. %

   d. #

6. The URLs of frames are loaded in the order in which each `<frame>` element is encountered _____.

   a. alphabetically

   b. top to bottom and left to right

   c. left to right and top to bottom

   d. according to each `<frame>` element's order attribute

7. Which is the correct syntax for a `<frame>` element that loads a URL of MyHomePage.html?

   a. `<frame href="MyHomePage.html">`

   b. `<frame url="MyHomePage.html">`

   c. `<frame html="MyHomePage.html">`

   d. `<frame src="MyHomePage.html">`

8. The _____ attribute of the `<a>` element determines into which frame or window a URL opens.

   a. `openinwin`

   b. `select`

   c. `goal`

   d. `target`

9. The _____ element is used for specifying a default target for all links in a document using the assigned name of a window or frame.

   a. `<base>`

   b. `<source>`

   c. `<target>`

   d. `<default>`

10. A frame set contained within another frame set is called a(n) _____ frame.

    a. controlling

    b. relative

    c. nested

    d. integral

11. Which values can you assign to the `frameborder` attribute to suppress the display of a border around a frame? (Choose all that apply.)

    a. 0

    b. false

    c. off

    d. no

12. The `framespacing` attribute can be used to write well-formed documents. True or False?

13. Explain why frames are deprecated in XHTML.

14. Which attribute(s) of the `<frame>` element is/are used to determine a frame's left and right margins?

    a. `sidemargins`

    b. `inside` and `outside`

    c. `marginleft` and `marginright`

    d. `marginwidth`

15. To prevent a user from resizing a frame, you include the _____ attribute within the `<frame>` element.

    a. `noresize`

    b. `noresize="1"`

    c. `noresize="true"`

    d. `noresize="noresize"`

16. Which of the following attributes of the `<frame>` element turns off scroll bars for an individual frame?

    a. `verticalscroll="0"`, `horizontalscroll="0"`

    b. `showScrollbars="off"`

    c. `scrolling="no"`

    d. `scrollbars="no"`

17. Which element is used to display an alternate message to users of Web browsers that are unable to display frames?

    a. `<noframes>`

    b. `<noscript>`

    c. `<alternate>`

    d. `<missingframes>`

18. Well-formed frameset documents do not need to include a `<noframes>` element. True or False?

19. Which element is used to create inline frames?

    a. `<frames>`

    b. `<iframe>`

    c. `<iframes>`

    d. `<inline>`

20. Explain the type of content you should include in an inline frame's tag pair.

HANDS-ON PROJECTS

Project 5-1

In this exercise, you create a frame-based Web page with two column frames. The left frame displays some stock symbols as links. Clicking a stock symbol displays in the right frame the name of the company represented by the stock symbol, along with the closing price on its most recent day of trading.

1. Create a new document in your text editor, and type the opening `<!DOCTYPE>` declaration, `<html>` element, and header information. Do not include an opening `<body>` tag. Use the Frameset DTD and "Stock Prices" as the content of the `<title>` element.

2. Add to the document the following `<frameset>` and `<frame>` elements. The document that opens by default in the stock frame is for the first stock in the list.

```
<frameset cols="20%,*">
    <frame src="Stocks.html" />
    <frame src="Cisco.html" name="stock" />
</frameset>
```

3. Save the file as **StockPrices.html** in the Chapter.05\Projects folder, and validate it with the W3C Markup Validation Service.

4. Create another document in your text editor, and type the opening `<!DOCTYPE>` declaration, `<html>` element, header information, and the `<body>` element. Use the Transitional DTD and "Stocks" as the content of the `<title>` element. Then, add to the document body the following list of links that will display in the right frame:

```
<p><a href="Cisco.html">CSCO</a><br />
<a href="Intel.html">INTC</a><br />
<a href="Oracle.html">ORCL</a><br />
<a href="Sun.html">SUNW</a><br />
<a href="Microsoft.html">MSFT</a><br /></p>
```

5. Save the file as **Stocks.html** in the Chapter.05\Projects folder and validate it with the W3C Markup Validation Service.

6. Create a Web page for each stock symbol in the list of links you created for the Stocks.html document. Use the company name for the title of each Web page. For instance, the full company name for the CSCO stock symbol is Cisco. Include on each company's Web page its name and the date and closing price on the stock's most recent day of trading. You can search for a stock's closing price on its most recent day of trading at *http://finance.yahoo.com* or on another search engine. Use the Strict DTD and the name of the company as the content of each Web page's `<title>` element. Save each file in the Chapter.05\Projects folder, and validate it with the W3C Markup Validation Service.

7. Open **StockPrices.html** in your Web browser and test the links.

8. Close your Web browser window.

Project 5-2

In this exercise, you create a frame-based Web page with two column frames. The left frame displays some animal names as links. Clicking an animal name displays its picture in the right frame. The image files you need for the exercise are located in the Chapter.05\Projects folder.

1. Create a new document in your text editor, and type the opening `<!DOCTYPE>` declaration, `<html>` element, and header information. Do not include an opening `<body>` tag. Use the Frameset DTD and "Animals" as the content of the `<title>` element.

2. Add to the document the following `<frameset>` and `<frame>` elements. The document that opens by default in the animal_picture frame is for the first animal in the list.

```
<frameset cols="20%,*">
    <frame src="Animals.html" />
    <frame src="Elephant.html" name="animal_picture" />
</frameset>
```

3. Save the file as **Animals.html** in the Chapter.05\Exercises folder, and validate it with the W3C Markup Validation Service.

4. Create another document in your text editor, and type the opening `<!DOCTYPE>` declaration, `<html>` element, header information, and the `<body>` element. Use the Transitional DTD and "Animals" as the content of the `<title>` element. Then, add to the document body the following list of links that displays in the right frame:

```
<p><a href="Elephant.html">Elephant</a><br />
<a href="Gazelle.html">Gazelle</a><br />
<a href="Giraffe.html">Giraffe</a><br />
<a href="Lion.html">Lion</a><br />
<a href="PolarBear.html">Polar bear</a><br />
<a href="Rhino.html">Rhino</a><br />
<a href="Tiger.html">Tiger</a><br />
<a href="Zebra.html">Zebra</a></p>
```

5. Save the file as **AnimalList.html** in the Chapter.05\Projects folder, and validate it with the W3C Markup Validation Service.

6. Create a Web page for each document in the list of links you created for the AnimalList.html document. Use the Strict DTD and the name of each of the animals for each Web page's `<title>` element. Save each file in the Chapter.05\Projects folder, and validate it with the W3C Markup Validation Service.

7. Open **Animals.html** in your Web browser and test the links.

8. Close your Web browser window.

Project 5-3

In this exercise, you create a nested frame-based Web page that lists prices for a tool rental company. The top frame contains a heading element, and the left frame contains a list of tool categories as links. Clicking a tool category displays descriptive information and rental prices for the category's tools in the right frame.

1. Create a new document in your text editor, and type the opening `<!DOCTYPE>` declaration, `<html>` element, and header information. Do not include an opening `<body>` tag. Use the Frameset DTD and "Rental Tools" as the content of the `<title>` element.

2. Add to the document the following `<frameset>` and `<frame>` elements. The document that opens by default in the description frame is for the first tool category.

```
<frameset rows="20%,*">
    <frame src="ToolsTitle.html" />
    <frameset cols="20%,*">
        <frame src="Tools.html" name="list" />
        <frame src="Drills.html" name="description" />
    </frameset>
</frameset>
```

3. Save the file as **RentalTools.html** in the Chapter.05\Projects folder, and validate it with the W3C Markup Validation Service.

4. Create another document in your text editor for the first row in the frameset, and type the opening `<!DOCTYPE>` declaration, `<html>` element, header information, and the `<body>` element. Use the Strict DTD and "Rental Tools Title Frame" as the content of the `<title>` element. Then, add to the document body a single `<h1>` element that reads "Rental Tools".

5. Save the file as **ToolsTitle.html** in the Chapter.05\Projects folder, and validate it with the W3C Markup Validation Service.

6. Create another document in your text editor, and type the opening `<!DOCTYPE>` declaration, `<html>` element, header information, and the `<body>` element. Use the Transitional DTD and "Tool Categories" as the content of the `<title>` element. Then, add to the document body the following list of links that displays in the right frame:

```
<p><a href="Drills.html">Drills</a><br />
<a href="Ladders.html">Ladders</a><br />
<a href="Saws.html">Saws</a></p>
```

7. Save the file as **Tools.html** in the Chapter.05\Projects folder, and validate it with the W3C Markup Validation Service.

8. Create Web pages using the Strict DTD for each of the tool category links in the Tools.html file. For each Web page, include a heading element that lists the tool category. Use the name of each category for the content of the `<title>` element. Also, search the Internet for rental information on tools for each category that you can use in the document body for each Web page. Save each document in the Chapter.05\Projects folder using the name of the appropriate link in the Tools.html file as the filename. Be sure to validate each document with the W3C Markup Validation Service.

9. Open **RentalTools.html** in your Web browser and test the links.

10. Close your Web browser window.

Project 5-4

In this exercise, you add a `<noframes>` element to the frameset Web page you created in Exercise 5-3.

1. Open the **RentalTools.html** file in your text editor.

2. Add the following `<noframes>` element above the last closing `<frameset>` tag:

```
<noframes><body>
<p>You cannot view this Web page because your Web browser
does not support frames.</p>
</body></noframes>
```

3. Save the **RentalTools.html file**, and validate it with the W3C Markup Validation Service.

4. Open it in your Web browser and confirm that the content of the `<noframes>` element is not visible.

5. Close your Web browser window.

Project 5-5

In this exercise, you create a nested frame-based Web page that lists descriptive information about each of the Hawaiian Islands. The top frame contains a heading element and the left frame contains the Hawaiian island names as links. Clicking an island name displays descriptive information about the island in the right frame.

1. Create a new document in your text editor, and type the opening `<!DOCTYPE>` declaration, `<html>` element, and header information. Do not include an opening `<body>` tag. Use the Frameset DTD and "Hawaiian Islands" as the content of the `<title>` element.

2. Add to the document the following `<frameset>` and `<frame>` elements. The document that opens by default in the description frame is for the first island in the list.

```
<frameset rows="15%,*">
    <frame src="IslandsTitle.html" />
    <frameset cols="20%,*">
        <frame src="Islands.html" name="list" />
        <frame src="Hawaii.html" name="description" />
    </frameset>
</frameset>
```

3. Save the file as **HawaiianIslands.html** in the Chapter.05\Projects folder, and validate it with the W3C Markup Validation Service.

4. Create another document in your text editor for the first row in the frameset, and type the opening `<!DOCTYPE>` declaration, `<html>` element, header information, and the `<body>` element. Use the Strict DTD and "Hawaiian Islands Title Frame" as the content of the `<title>` element. Then, add to the document body a single `<h1>` element that reads "Hawaiian Islands".

5. Save the file as **IslandsTitle.html** in the Chapter.05\Projects folder, and validate it with the W3C Markup Validation Service.

6. Create another document in your text editor, and type the opening `<!DOCTYPE>` declaration, `<html>` element, header information, and the `<body>` element. Use the Transitional DTD and "Islands" as the content of the `<title>` element. Then, add to the document body the following list of links that displays in the right frame:

```
<p><a href="Hawaii.html">Hawaii</a><br />
<a href="Kahoolawe.html">Kahoolawe</a><br />
<a href="Kauai.html">Kauai</a><br />
<a href="Lanai.html">Lanai</a><br />
```

```
<a href="Maui.html">Maui</a><br />
<a href="Molokai.html">Molokai</a><br />
<a href="Niihau.html">Niihau</a><br />
<a href="Oahu.html">Oahu</a></p>
```

7. Save the file as **Islands.html** in the Chapter.05\Projects folder, and validate it with the W3C Markup Validation Service.

8. Create Web pages using the Strict DTD for each of the links in the Islands.html file. For each Web page, include a heading element that lists the name of the island. Use the name of each island for the content of the `<title>` element. Also, search the Internet for descriptive information about each of the Hawaiian Islands that you can use in the document body for each Web page. Save each document in the Chapter.05\Projects folder using the name of the appropriate link in the Islands.html file as the filename. Be sure to validate each document with the W3C Markup Validation Service.

9. Open **HawaiianIslands.html** in your Web browser and test the links.

10. Close your Web browser window.

Project 5-6

In this exercise, you add frame formatting to the frameset Web page you created in Exercise 5-5. You also create long description files for each of the frames in the frameset.

1. Open **HawaiianIslands.html** in your text editor.

2. Add `title`, `longdesc`, `noresize`, and `scrolling` attributes to the first `<frame>` element that displays the IslandsTitle.html file. Also, add `title` and `longdesc` attributes to the `<frame>` elements in the nested frameset. Your modified code should appear as follows:

```
<frameset rows="15%,*">
    <frame src="IslandsTitle.html"
        title="Hawaiian Islands Title Frame" longdesc="IslandsTitle_
        Content.html"
        noresize="noresize" scrolling="no" / >
    <frameset cols="20%,*">
        <frame src="Islands.html" name="list"
            title="Hawaiian Islands List Frame"
            longdesc="IslandsList_Content.html" />
        <frame src="Hawaii.html" name="description"
            title="Hawaiian Islands Description Frame"
            longdesc="IslandsFrame_Content.html" />
    </frameset>
</frameset>
```

3. Save the **HawaiianIslands.html** file, and validate it with the W3C Markup Validation Service.

4. Create the long description files for each of the frames. Save each file in the Chapter.05\Projects folder, and validate it with the W3C Markup Validation Service.

5. Open **HawaiianIslands.html** in your Web browser. You should no longer be able to resize the top frame and its scroll bars should not be visible.

6. Close your Web browser window.

Project 5-7

In this exercise, you create a Web page that contains three inline frames. Each inline frame displays the home page of a major news Web site.

1. Create a new document in your text editor.

2. Type the `<!DOCTYPE>` declaration, `<html>` element, document head, and the `<body>` element. Use the Transitional DTD and "Top Stories" as the content of the `<title>` element.

3. Add to the document body the following heading element:

   ```
   <h1>Top Stories</h1>
   ```

4. Add to the end of the document body the following heading element and inline frame, which links to the ABC News Web site at *http://abcnews.go.com/*:

   ```
   <h2>ABC News</h2>
   <iframe src="http://abcnews.go.com/" height="250" width="600"
   name="abc" scrolling="yes" align="middle" title="ABC News"
   longdesc="ABC_Content.html">
   <p>You cannot view this Web page because your Web browser
   does not support inline frames.</p>
   </iframe>
   ```

5. Next, add to the end of the document body the following heading element and inline frame, which links to the CNN Headline News Web site at *http://www.cnn.com/HLN/*:

   ```
   <h2>CNN Headline News</h2>
   <iframe src="http://www.cnn.com/HLN/" height="250" width="600"
   name="cnn" scrolling="yes" align="middle" title="CNN Headline News"
   longdesc="CNN_Content.html">
   <p>You cannot view this Web page because your Web browser
   does not support inline frames.</p>
   </iframe>
   ```

6. Finally, add to the end of the document body the following heading element and inline frame, which links to the MSNBC News Web site at *http://www.msnbc.com/*:

   ```
   <h2>MSNBC News</h2>
   <iframe src="http://www.msnbc.com/" height="250" width="600"
   name="msnbc" scrolling="yes" align="middle" title="MSNBC News"
   longdesc="MSNBC_Content.html">
   <p>You cannot view this Web page because your Web browser
   does not support inline frames.</p>
   </iframe>
   ```

7. Save the file as **TopStories.html** in the Chapter.05\Projects folder, and validate it with the W3C Markup Validation Service.

8. Create the long description files for each of the inline frames. Save each file in the Chapter.05\Projects folder, and validate it with the W3C Markup Validation Service.

9. Open **TopStories.html** in your Web browser and see if the Web pages open correctly in each inline frame.

10. Close your Web browser window.

CASE PROJECTS

5

For the following projects, save the files you create in the Chapter.05\Cases folder. Be sure to validate the files you create with the W3C Markup Validation Service.

Project 5-1

Create a frame-based Web site that sells vending machines. Search the Internet for "vending machines" to find information and images that you can use. The Web site should sell different types of vending machines, such as snacks and beverages. Create links in one frame for each type of vending machine. Clicking the vending machine name should open in another frame a picture of the vending machine along with features, specifications, and pricing. Save the frameset document as VendingMachines.html. Use whatever names you like for the other documents you create.

Project 5-2

Create a frame-based Web site that lists information on houseplants. Search the Internet for "houseplants" to find information and images that you can use. Create links in one frame for various types of houseplants. Clicking a plant name should open in another frame a picture of the plant along with information about the plant and growing tips. Save the frameset document as Houseplants.html. Use whatever names you like for the other documents you create.

Project 5-3

Create a Web site for a vacation destination that sells time-share properties. Create a list of property links using resort names and locations. Clicking a property name should open a Web page for the property in an inline frame. Include in each property's Web page the resort name, location of the property, number of bedrooms, number of bathrooms, price, and the number of weeks per year that the time-share includes. Save the main Web page as Timeshares.html and the Web page for each property using the name of the resort.

6

TABLES AND LISTS

In this chapter, you will:

♦ Create basic tables
♦ Structure tables
♦ Format tables
♦ Create lists

When HTML was first introduced, it provided no way to create tables, which are essentially rows and columns of tabular data. Tables were introduced in HTML 3.2 and Web authors quickly realized how useful they were. Tables provide an effective way of structuring and displaying data in an organized format that is difficult to achieve using standard text formatting elements such as the <p> element. Additionally, tables are replacing frames that are used for designing effective navigation systems and laying out pages.

Another way of structuring and displaying data in an organized format is through the use of lists, which you study at the end of this chapter.

CREATING BASIC TABLES

Tables are collections of rows and columns that you use to organize and display data. In a table, the intersection of any given row and column is called a **cell**. You are probably familiar with traditional tables that organize data in columns and rows. Tables are widely used for displaying data on Web pages. However, Web page tables are not limited to displaying simple text. Tables are also commonly used for displaying images. Figure 6-1, for instance, shows a page from the Minneapolis Institute of Arts Web site that uses a table to display thumbnail images of selected works from their paintings collection along with basic information about each painting. Each thumbnail image is also a hypertext link that opens a larger version of the image.

Figure 6-1   Images displayed in a table

Although the most common use of tables is to create rows and columns of data like the page from the Minneapolis Institute of Arts Web site, they are also used to lay out Web pages, much like frames have been used. Recall from Chapter 5 that frames are deprecated in XHTML. Even though frames are deprecated, the navigation, document layout possibilities, and functionality they provide are still very useful. For instance, Figure 6-2 shows the home page for a company called House of Fans. Although the home page looks as if it were created with frames, it is actually created using tables.

Although tables are quite useful for all types of document layout, the W3C discourages using tables for document layout because tables can be difficult for non-visual user agents, such as Braille and speech devices, to interpret. Additionally, user agents with small monitors, such as Personal Digital Assistants (PDAs), and browsers that use large fonts may have difficulty rendering a Web page that is laid out using tables. Instead, the W3C encourages the use of Cascading Style Sheets (CSS) for document layout. (You will study CSS in more detail in Chapter 8.) However, using CSS for document layout can be a difficult and time-consuming task, so most Web page authors continue to use tables for this purpose. Nevertheless, if you anticipate that users with disabilities will frequently visit your Web site, then you should seriously consider avoiding the use of tables for document layout.

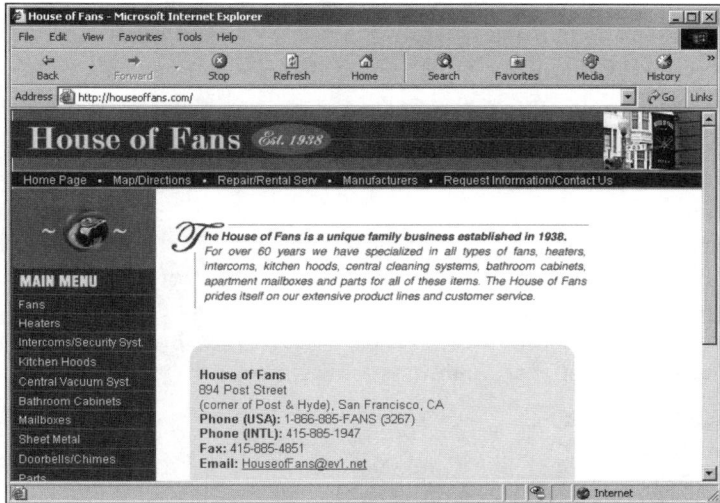

Figure 6-2   House of Fans home page

Basic `<table>` Elements

You create tables using the **`<table>` element**. Within the `<table>` element you can nest a number of other elements that specify the content of each cell along with the structure and appearance of the table. The elements you use for building a table are listed in Table 6-1:

Table 6-1   Table elements

Element	Defines
`<caption>`	A table caption
`<col>`	A table column
`<colgroup>`	A table column group
`<tbody>`	A table body
`<td>`	Table data
`<tfoot>`	A table footer
`<th>`	A table heading
`<thead>`	A table header
`<tr>`	A table row

The `<table>` element also includes several attributes that affect the appearance and structure of a table. You will learn about each of these elements and attributes as you progress through this chapter.

To help ensure that your Web pages are well formed, you should always type the opening `<table>` tag and the closing `</table>` tag at the same time, and then go back and fill in the elements and content that you want to appear in the table.

The `<td>` Element

Cells are the most basic parts of a table. You create a cell within the `<table>` element using the **`<td>` element**. The `<td>` element stands for "table data". The content of each `<td>` element is the data that will appear in the table cell. Each **`<td>`** element essentially represents a column in the table. You declare table cells within table row elements that you create with the **`<tr>` element**. Each `<tr>` element you include within a `<table>` element creates a separate row. The following code shows the basic syntax for creating a table that consists of three columns and two rows:

```
<table border="1">
    <!-- Row 1 -->
    <tr>
        <td>column 1</td>
        <td>column 2</td>
        <td>column 3</td>
    </tr>
    <!-- Row 2 -->
    <tr>
        <td>column 1</td>
        <td>column 2</td>
        <td>column 3</td>
    </tr>
</table>
```

By default, tables are displayed without borders. The `<table>` element in the preceding code includes a `border` attribute that creates a 1-pixel border around the table so you can see the table more clearly in a Web browser. You will learn more about borders later in this chapter.

Figure 6-3 shows how the preceding table appears in a Web browser.

The `<td>` element includes four attributes, `headers`, `abbr`, `scope`, and `axis` that allow non-visual browsers to render the heading information of a cell. You can find information on each of these attributes on the W3C Web site at the following URL: *http://www.w3.org/TR/html4/struct/tables.html*.

Figure 6-3   Simple table

As another example, consider Table 6-2, which lists the days of the week in English, French, and German.

Table 6-2   Days of the week in English, French, and German

Sunday	Dimanche	Sonntag
Monday	Lundi	Montag
Tuesday	Mardi	Dienstag
Wednesday	Mercredi	Mittwoch
Thursday	Jeudi	Donnerstag
Friday	Vendredi	Freitag
Saturday	Samedi	Samstag

To display Table 6-2 as a table on a Web page, you use the following table elements. Figure 6-4 shows how the table appears in a Web browser.

```
<table border="1">
  <tr><td>Sunday</td><td>Dimanche</td><td>Sonntag</td></tr>
  <tr><td>Monday</td><td>Lundi</td><td>Montag</td></tr>
  <tr><td>Tuesday</td><td>Mardi</td><td>Dienstag</td></tr>
  <tr><td>Wednesday</td><td>Mercredi</td><td>Mittwoch</td></tr>
  <tr><td>Thursday</td><td>Jeudi</td><td>Donnerstag</td></tr>
  <tr><td>Friday</td><td>Vendredi</td><td>Freitag</td></tr>
  <tr><td>Saturday</td><td>Samedi</td><td>Samstag</td></tr>
</table>
```

Table cells are not limited to displaying text. You can include almost any type of element as the content of the `<td>` element, including `<img>` elements. For example, the following code consists of a single row with three cells that display the flags for the United States, Canada, and Mexico. Each cell contains a paragraph element, an image element, and some text. Figure 6-5 shows how the table appears in a Web browser.

Figure 6-4   Days of the week table

```
<table border="1">
  <tr>
    <td>
      <p>American Flag<br />
      <img src="america.gif" alt="Image of the American Flag"
      height="76" width="132" /></p>
    </td>
    <td>
      <p>Canadian Flag<br />
      <img src="canada.gif" alt="Image of the Canadian Flag"
      height="76" width="132" /></p>
    </td>
    <td>
      <p>Mexican Flag<br />
      <img src="mexico.gif" alt="Image of the Mexican Flag"
      height="76" width="132" /></p>
    </td>
  </tr>
</table>
```

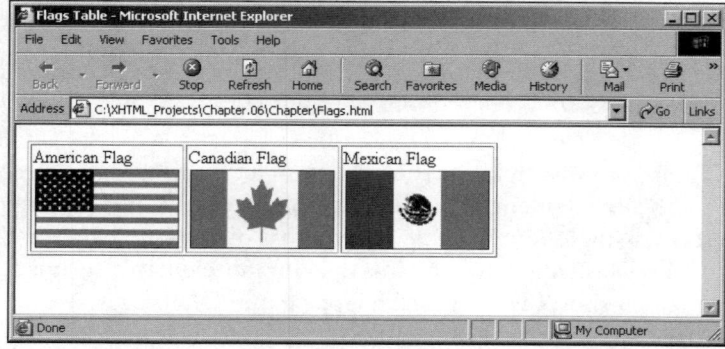

Figure 6-5   Flags table

Next, you start creating the weekly schedule for a commuter railroad. Because a schedule's data is tabular in nature, it makes sense to create it in a table instead of using heading and text elements.

To start creating the weekly schedule for a commuter railroad:

1. Start your text editor and create a new document.

2. Type the `<!DOCTYPE>` declaration, `<html>` element, document head, and `<body>` element. Use the Strict DTD and "Metropolitan Commuter Railroad" as the content of the `<title>` element. Your document should appear as follows:

```
<!DOCTYPE html PUBLIC
"-//W3C//DTD XHTML 1.0 Strict//EN"
"http://www.w3.org/TR/xhtml1/DTD/xhtml1-strict.dtd">
<html xmlns="http://www.w3.org/1999/xhtml" lang="en" xml:lang =
"en" dir="ltr">
<head>
<title>Metropolitan Commuter Railroad</title>
<meta http-equiv="content-type"
content="text/html; charset=iso-8859-1" />
</head>
<body>
</body>
</html>
```

3. Add to the document body the following heading element:

```
<h2>Pleasantville to Coast City</h2>
```

4. Next, add to the end of the document body the following simple table, which includes the railroad's departure and arrival times from Pleasantville to Coast City:

```
<table border="1">
    <tr><td>6:00 a.m.</td>
        <td>7:00 a.m.</td></tr>
    <tr><td>7:00 a.m.</td>
        <td>8:00 a.m.</td></tr>
    <tr><td>8:00 a.m.</td>
        <td>9:00 a.m.</td></tr>
    <tr><td>4:00 p.m.</td>
        <td>5:00 p.m.</td></tr>
    <tr><td>5:00 p.m.</td>
        <td>6:00 p.m.</td></tr>
    <tr><td>6:00 p.m.</td>
        <td>7:00 p.m.</td></tr>
</table>
```

5. Save the file as **Schedule.html** in the Chapter.06/Chapter folder.

6

6. Open the **Schedule.html** file in your Web browser. Figure 6-6 shows how the file should appear in your Web browser.

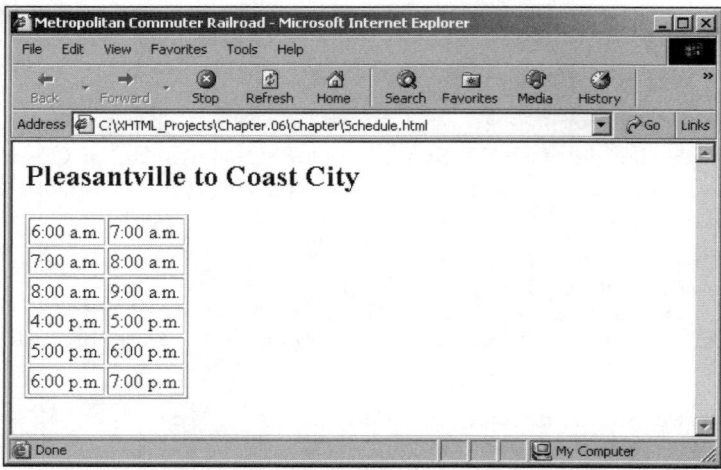

Figure 6-6 Schedule table

7. Close your Web browser window.

The <th> Element

Table cells can contain two types of information: data that you define with the <td> element and heading information that you define with the **<th> element**. Heading information usually describes the contents of a single column or multiple columns within a table. The content of a <th> element will appear as the heading for a single column or multiple columns. User agents render the content of a <th> element in a distinct manner; most Web browsers display heading information in a bold typeface and align it in the center of the column.

 Like the <td> element, the <th> element can contain plain text and almost any type of XHTML element.

Consider the days of the week table you saw earlier. It would be more useful if it included heading information that listed each column's language, as shown in Table 6-3.

Table 6-3   Days of the week with heading information

English	French	German
Sunday	Dimanche	Sonntag
Monday	Lundi	Montag
Tuesday	Mardi	Dienstag
Wednesday	Mercredi	Mittwoch
Thursday	Jeudi	Donnerstag
Friday	Vendredi	Freitag
Saturday	Samedi	Samstag

6

You place the data you want to use as a column's heading information within the beginning and ending `<th>` tags. The following code shows how to add the heading information in Table 6-3 to the XHTML code for the table. Figure 6-7 shows the output.

```
<table border="1">
  <tr><th>English</th><th>French</th><th>German</th></tr>
  <tr><td>Sunday</td><td>Dimanche</td><td>Sonntag</td></tr>
  <tr><td>Monday</td><td>Lundi</td><td>Montag</td></tr>
  <tr><td>Tuesday</td><td>Mardi</td><td>Dienstag</td></tr>
  <tr><td>Wednesday</td><td>Mercredi</td><td>Mittwoch</td></tr>
  <tr><td>Thursday</td><td>Jeudi</td><td>Donnerstag</td></tr>
  <tr><td>Friday</td><td>Vendredi</td><td>Freitag</td></tr>
  <tr><td>Saturday</td><td>Samedi</td><td>Samstag</td></tr>
</table>
```

Figure 6-7   Days of the week table after adding table heading information

Next, you will add heading information to the Schedule.html file.

To add heading information to the Schedule.html file:

1. Return to the **Schedule.html** file in your text editor.

2. Add the following heading information elements immediately after the opening `<table>` tag:

```
<tr><th>Depart Pleasantville</th><th>Arrive Coast City</th></tr>
```

3. Save the **Schedule.html** file and then open it in your Web browser. The heading information you entered should appear as the first row in the table, in a bold typeface and centered.

4. Close your Web browser window.

Captions and Summaries

Most tables include a caption that describes the data in the table. You create a caption for a Web page table using the **<caption> element**. The <caption> element must be the first element following the <table> element, and you can include only a single <caption> element per table. A caption should provide a short phrase or title that clearly describes the contents of the table. Most Web browsers center the <caption> above the table. The following code creates a table that lists baseball players who have ten or more runs batted in (RBIs) in a baseball game. The table includes a caption and headings. Figure 6-8 shows how the table appears in a Web browser.

```
<table border="1">
<caption>10+ RBI in a Game</caption>
<tr><th>Player</th><th>Team</th><th>Date</th><th>RBI</th></tr>
<tr><td>Jim Bottomley</td><td>Cardinals</td>
     <td>9/24/1924</td><td>12</td></tr>
<tr><td>Mark Whiten</td><td>Cardinals</td>
     <td>9/7/1993</td><td>12</td></tr>
<tr><td>Wilbert Robinson</td><td>Orioles</td>
     <td>6/10/1892</td><td>11</td></tr>
<tr><td>Tony Lazzeri</td><td>Yankees</td>
     <td>5/24/1936</td><td>11</td></tr>
<tr><td>Phil Weintraub</td><td>Giants</td>
     <td>4/30/1944</td><td>11</td></tr>
<tr><td>Rudy York</td><td>Red Sox</td>
     <td>7/27/1946</td><td>10</td></tr>
<tr><td>Walker Cooper</td><td>Reds</td>
     <td>7/6/1949</td><td>10</td></tr>
<tr><td>Norm Zauchin</td><td>Red Sox</td>
     <td>5/27/1955</td><td>10</td></tr>
<tr><td>Reggie Jackson</td><td>A's</td>
     <td>6/14/1969</td><td>10</td></tr>
<tr><td>Fred Lynn</td><td>Red Sox</td>
     <td>6/18/1975</td><td>10</td></tr>
<tr><td>Nomar Garciaparra</td><td>Red Sox</td>
     <td>5/10/1999</td><td>10</td></tr>
</table>
```

Figure 6-8   RBI table with caption

You may be tempted to provide a caption for tables simply by using heading elements instead of the `<caption>` element. However, the `<caption>` element is important because it allows non-visual user agents to understand the purpose of a table. Because heading elements are not directly associated with a table, a user agent has no way of knowing whether one is used for a table caption. If you want to change the visual appearance of a table caption, you can include elements such as the `<strong>` element within the `<caption>` element, or use CSS.

For short or simple tables, the `<caption>` element is usually sufficient for describing the purpose of the table. For long or complex tables, however, you should also include the **summary attribute** of the `<table>` element, which allows you to provide a more detailed summary of a table's structure and content for use in non-visual user agents. For instance, the following code shows a modified version of the 10+ RBI table with a **summary** attribute included in the `<table>` element:

```
<table border="1" summary="This table lists the Major League
Baseball Players who have batted in ten or more runners in a
single game, along with their team, the date of the game, and the
RBI number for each player.">
<caption><b>10+ RBI in a Game</b></caption>
<tr><th>Player</th><th>Team</th><th>Date</th><th>RBI</th></tr>
<tr><td>Jim Bottomley</td><td>Cardinals</td>
     <td>9/24/1924</td><td>12</td></tr>
<tr><td>Mark Whiten</td><td>Cardinals</td>
```

```
<td>9/7/1993</td><td>12</td></tr>
...
</table>
```

Next, you add a table caption and summary to the Schedule.html file.

To add a caption and summary to the Schedule.html file:

1. Return to the **Schedule.html** file in your text editor.

2. Modify the table so it includes the caption element and **summary** attribute shown below in boldface:

```
<table border="1" summary="This table lists the departure and
arrival times from Pleasantville to Coast City.">
    <caption>Weekday Schedule</caption>
    <tr><th>Depart Pleasantville</th>
        <th>Arrive Coast City</th></tr>
    <tr><td>6:00 a.m.</td><td>7:00 a.m.</td></tr>
...
```

3. Save the **Schedule.html** file and then open it in your Web browser. Figure 6-9 shows how the file should appear in your Web browser.

Figure 6-9   Schedule.html after adding heading information, a `<caption>` element, and a `summary` attribute

4. Close your Web browser window.

Table Widths

Even though a Web author creates a table and determines its content, it is the user agent that determines how wide the table should be. Web browsers size each column to be as wide as the widest item in each cell, up to the width of the browser window. However, for design purposes you may want to specify that your table take up a certain number of pixels in width or a percentage of the Web browser window. You use the **width attribute** of the `<table>` element to specify the size of a table. You can assign a fixed value in pixels or a percentage representing the visible width of a Web browser window. For instance, the following table includes a `width` attribute that specifies that the RBI table should take up 100% of the visible Web browser window. Figure 6-10 shows the output.

```
<table border="1" width="100%">
<caption>10+ RBI in a Game</caption>
<tr><th>Player</th><th>Team</th><th>Date</th><th>RBI</th></tr>
<tr><td>Jim Bottomley</td><td>Cardinals</td>
<td>9/24/1924</td><td>12</td></tr>
<tr><td>Mark Whiten</td><td>Cardinals</td>
<td>9/7/1993</td><td>12</td></tr>
...
```

Figure 6-10   Table that take up 100% of the visible Web browser window

You cannot adjust the widths of individual cells in a table. However, you can adjust the width of columns in the table using the `<colgroup>` or `<col>` elements, which you will study later in this chapter.

Next, you modify the Schedule.html file so the table takes up 100% of the Web browser window.

To modify the Schedule.html file so the table takes up 100% of the Web browser window:

1. Return to the **Schedule.html** file in your text editor.

2. Add the `width` attribute to the opening `<table>` tag, as follows:

```
<table border="1" width="100%" summary="This table lists the
departure and arrival times from Pleasantville to Coast City.">
    <caption>Weekday Schedule</caption>
    <tr><th>Depart Pleasantville</th>
        <th>Arrive Coast City</th></tr>
    <tr><td>6:00 a.m.</td><td>7:00 a.m.</td></tr>
...
```

3. Save the **Schedule.html** file and then open it in your Web browser. Your table should take up 100% of the visible Web browser window.

4. Close your Web browser window.

Horizontal Alignment

You can use the **align attribute** to adjust the horizontal alignment of the contents of all table elements with the exception of the `<table>` and `<caption>` elements. The values you can assign to the `align` attribute are left, center, right, and justify. As an example of the `align` attribute, the following code shows the RBI table with the heading information row alignment changed to left by placing an `align="left"` attribute in the row's opening `<tr>` element. (Recall that heading information is aligned center by default.) Figure 6-11 shows the output.

```
<table border="1" width="100%">
<caption>10+ RBI in a Game</caption>
<tr align="left"><th>Player</th><th>Team</th>
    <th>Date</th><th>RBI</th></tr>
<tr><td>Jim Bottomley</td><td>Cardinals</td>
<td>9/24/1924</td><td>12</td></tr>
<tr><td>Mark Whiten</td><td>Cardinals</td>
<td>9/7/1993</td><td>12</td></tr>
...
```

Figure 6-11   Table that includes an `align` attribute in the heading information row

You can align individual `<td>` or `<th>` elements, although if you want an entire row to have exactly the same alignment, it is easier to place the `align` attribute in the row's opening `<tr>` tag.

Next, you modify the Schedule.html file so the data in the table cells are centered. To modify the Schedule.html file so the data in the table cells are centered:

1. Return to the **Schedule.html** file in your text editor.
2. Add `align="center"` attributes to each of the `<td>` elements, as follows:

```
<table border="1" width="100%" summary="This table lists the
departure and arrival times from Pleasantville to Coast City.">
     <caption>Weekday Schedule</caption>
     <tr><th>Depart Pleasantville</th>
          <th>Arrive Coast City</th></tr>
     <tr><td align="center">6:00 a.m.</td>
          <td align="center">7:00 a.m.</td></tr>
     <tr><td align="center">7:00 a.m.</td>
          <td align="center">8:00 a.m.</td></tr>
     <tr><td align="center">8:00 a.m.</td>
          <td align="center">9:00 a.m.</td></tr>
     <tr><td align="center">4:00 p.m.</td>
          <td align="center">5:00 p.m.</td></tr>
     <tr><td align="center">5:00 p.m.</td>
          <td align="center">6:00 p.m.</td></tr>
     <tr><td align="center">6:00 p.m.</td>
          <td align="center">7:00 p.m.</td></tr>
</table>
```

3. Save the **Schedule.html** file and then open it in your Web browser. Figure 6-12 shows how the file should appear in your Web browser.

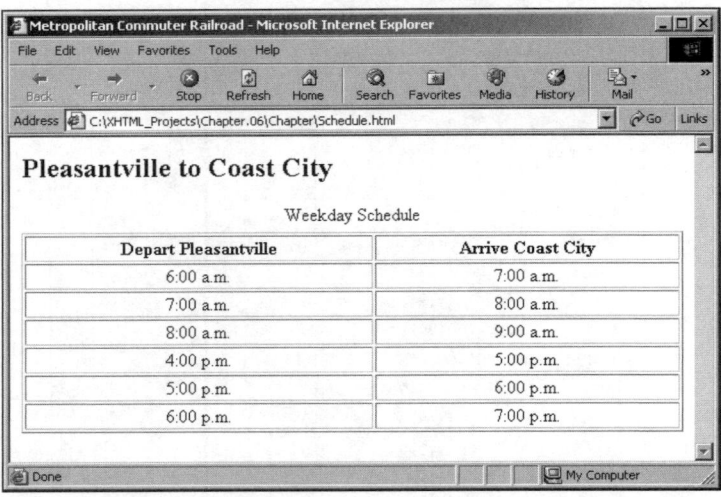

Figure 6-12   Schedule.html after adjusting the table width to 100% and centering the contents of each cell

4. Close your Web browser window.

STRUCTURING TABLES

In the last section you studied the basic table elements that are necessary for a document to be well formed. However, there are cases when you may want to have more control over individual parts of a table or entire sections, such as the columns, to make it easier to apply formatting. In this section you study elements that give a table its structure and give you more control over your tables. Although table structure elements are not required in order for your documents to be well formed, it is a good idea to include them to clearly identify the different parts of your tables. Table structure elements also allow you to apply default alignment and CSS styles to entire sections of a table and to adjust the width of individual columns.

Row Groups

You can create table **row group elements** that consist of a table header, table body, and table footer. A table header refers to the rows of `<th>` elements that make up the table headings. The table body refers to the rows of data that make up the body of a table. The table footer refers to information that should be placed at the bottom of a table. To define a table header, you use the `<thead>` **element**; to define the table body, you use the `<tbody>` element; and to define the table footer, you use the `<tfoot>` element. These elements allow user agents to scroll through the body of a table independent of its header and footer. At the time of this writing, however, most Web browsers do not support table scrolling, although that is expected to change as new browser versions are released that provide greater support for XHTML. Nevertheless, it is a good practice to include row group elements in order to provide a clear structure for your tables. Additionally, you can set the alignment for all the elements in a row group because each row group element supports the `align` attribute.

 Each row group must contain at least one `<tr>` element.

The next section discusses the specific syntax for each row group element.

Table Header

You must place the `<thead>` element after any `<caption>`, `<colgroup>`, and `<col>` elements and before the `<tbody>` and `<tfoot>` elements. Typically, you place table heading information (created with the `<th>` element) within the `<thead>` element, as follows. Notice that the `align` attribute is now included in the `<thead>` element instead of the `<tr>` element that defines the table header information.

```
<table border="1" width="100%">
<caption>10+ RBI in a Game</caption>
<thead align="left">
<tr><th>Player</th><th>Team</th>
    <th>Date</th><th>RBI</th></tr>
</thead>
<tr><td>Jim Bottomley</td><td>Cardinals</td>
<td>9/24/1924</td><td>12</td></tr>
<tr><td>Mark Whiten</td><td>Cardinals</td>
<td>9/7/1993</td><td>12</td></tr>
...
```

Next, you modify the Schedule.html file so it includes a `<thead>` element.

To modify the Schedule.html file so it includes a `<thead>` element:

1. Return to the **Schedule.html** file in your text editor.

2. Add a `<thead>` element so it encloses the heading information row, as follows:

```
<table border="1" width="100%" summary="This table lists the
departure and arrival times from Pleasantville to Coast City.">
    <caption>Weekday Schedule</caption>
    <thead>
        <tr><th>Depart Pleasantville</th>
            <th>Arrive Coast City</th></tr>
    </thead>
...
```

3. Save the **Schedule.html** file.

Table Body

The <tbody> element should contain the rows of data that make up the body of a table. Although most browsers do not yet support scrolling a table body independent of its header and footer, you can use the <tbody> element to align a table body and to apply CSS formatting to the table body. You can also include multiple <tbody> elements to control different parts of the table body. Even though you won't study CSS in detail until Chapter 8, the following version of the RBI table includes three <tbody> elements, each of which includes a style attribute that specifies the color of the text within each element. Each <tbody> element is assigned a different color that distinguishes which players hit 10, 11, or 12 RBIs. (Parts of the table are excluded to save space.)

```
<table border="1" width="100%">
<caption>10+ RBI in a Game</caption>
<thead align="left">
<tr><th>Player</th><th>Team</th><th>Date</th><th>RBI</th></tr>
</thead>
<tbody style="color:blue">
<tr><td>Jim Bottomley</td><td>Cardinals</td>
<td>9/24/1924</td><td>12</td></tr>
...
</tbody>
<tbody style="color:red">
<tr><td>Tony Lazzeri</td><td>Yankees</td>
<td>5/24/1936</td><td>11</td></tr>
...
</tbody>
<tbody style="color:green">
<tr><td>Walker Cooper</td><td>Reds</td>
<td>7/6/1949</td><td>10</td></tr>
...
</tbody>
</table>
```

Next, you modify the Schedule.html file so it includes a <tbody> element that center aligns the cells in the table body.

To add a <tbody> element in the Schedule.html file:

1. Return to the **Schedule.html** file in your text editor.

2. Add the following <tbody> element immediately after the closing </thead> tag. Notice that the element's align attribute is assigned a value of "center".

   <tbody align="center">

3. Delete the align="center" attributes in each of the <td> elements. You should delete 12 attributes.

4. Add a closing **</tbody>** tag immediately above the closing **</table>** tag.

5. Save the **Schedule.html** file and then open it in your Web browser. Your file should appear the same as it did with the align attributes in the <td> elements.

6. Close your Web browser window.

Table Footers

The `<tfoot>` element defines information that should be placed at the bottom of a table. You use the `<tfoot>` element to provide additional information about the columns or about the table itself. The `<tfoot>` element must be placed before the `<tbody>` element in order to allow a user agent to render the structure of the table before it receives the potentially large amount of data that may appear in the table body. The following code shows the RBI table with a `<tfoot>` element. Figure 6-13 shows the table in a Web browser.

```
<table border="1" width="100%">
<caption>10+ RBI in a Game</caption>
<thead align="left">
<tr><th>Player</th><th>Team</th><th>Date</th><th>RBI</th></tr>
</thead>
<tfoot>
<tr align="center"><td>Statistics provided by
<a href="http://www.baseballimmortals.net/">
Baseball Immortals</a></td></tr>
</tfoot>
<tbody  style="color:blue">
<tr><td>Jim Bottomley</td><td>Cardinals</td>
<td>9/24/1924</td><td>12</td></tr>
...
```

Figure 6-13   RBI table with `<thead>`, `<tbody>`, and `<tfoot>` elements in a Web browser

Next, you add to the Schedule.html file a `<tfoot>` element.

To add to the Schedule.html file a `<tfoot>` element:

1. Return to the **Schedule.html** file in your text editor.

2. Add the following `<tfoot>` element immediately after the closing `</thead>` tag.

```
<tfoot align="center">
   <tr><td>Please board at least 5 minutes prior to departure.</td>
   <td>Arrival times are approximate.</td></tr>
</tfoot>
```

3. Save the **Schedule.html** file and then open it in your Web browser. Figure 6-14 shows how the file should appear in your Web browser.

Figure 6-14   Schedule.html after adding a table footer

4. Close your Web browser window.

Columns

There are times when you may want to format the columns in your tables, either individually or as a group. In this section you study **column groups**, which are used for applying default alignment, width, and CSS styles to groups of columns within a table.

Column Groups

You use the `<colgroup>` **element** to create a column group in a table. You must place a `<colgroup>` element after a table's `<caption>` element and before its `<thead>` element. The `<colgroup>` element can be created either as an empty element or as a tag pair that contains `<col>` elements as its content. (You will study `<col>` elements shortly.) The `<colgroup>` element includes the `align` attribute and a `span` attribute that you use to specify the number of columns in the group. For example, consider the following modified version of the RBI table. The table now includes two column groups: one for each player's name and another for the player statistics columns. The default value of the `span` attribute is "1", so the first column group does not include the `span` attribute because it applies only to the player name column. The second column group, however, includes a `span` attribute that is assigned a value of "3" so that it applies to the remaining columns in the table. The second column group also includes an `align` attribute that is assigned a value of "center" so the contents of the three statistics columns are center aligned. Notice that each `<colgroup>` element is created as an empty element. Figure 6-15 shows how the figure appears in a Web browser.

6

```
<table border="1" width="100%">
<caption>10+ RBI in a Game</caption>
<colgroup />
<colgroup span="3" align="center" />
<thead align="left">
...
```

Figure 6-15   RBI table with column groups

The empty **<col> element** allows you to apply formatting to an individual column in a column group. You can also use the `span` attribute to format multiple columns in a column group. For instance, the second `<colgroup>` element in the following modified version of the RBI table now contains two `<col>` elements, one for each of the columns in the column group. The first `<col>` element center aligns the Team column, and the second `<col>` element uses the **span** attribute to right align both the Date and RBI columns. Figure 6-16 shows how the table appears in a Web browser.

```
<table border="1" width="100%">
<caption>10+ RBI in a Game</caption>
<colgroup />
<colgroup span="3">
     <col align="center" />
     <col span="2" align="right" />
</colgroup>
<thead align="left">
. . .
```

 The attributes of the `<col>` element override the attributes of the `<colgroup>` element.

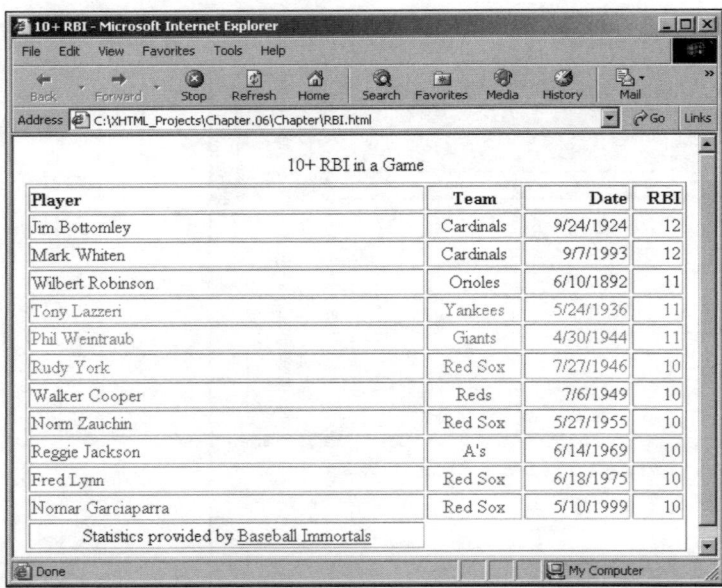

Figure 6-16   RBI table with column groups and `<col>` elements

Column Widths

As you learned earlier, you use the **width** attribute of the `<table>` element to determine the width of a table. However, you cannot use the `<table>` element's **width** attribute to adjust the size of cells or columns in a table, which are determined automatically by each user agent. In addition, you cannot adjust the widths of individual table cells with the `<td>` and `<th>` elements. However, you can adjust the widths of columns using the **width** attribute of the `<colgroup>` or `<col>` elements.

You specify the width of a `<colgroup>` or `<col>` element by assigning to the `width` attribute a fixed value in pixels or a percentage representing a portion of the space that is available for the table (which is the visible width of a Web browser window). In the following code, the first `<colgroup>` element specifies that the Player column of the RBI table must occupy 40% of the table width, and the second `<colgroup>` element specifies that the remainder of the columns must each occupy 100 pixels. Notice that the `<table>` element does not include the `width` attribute. If you include the `width` attribute in a `<table>` element, it will override the `width` attributes of any `<colspan>` or `<col>` elements defined within the table. Figure 6-17 shows how the table appears in a Web browser.

```
<table border="1">
<caption>10+ RBI in a Game</caption>
<colgroup width="40%" />
<colgroup span="3" align="left" width="100">
     <col align="center">
     <col span="2" align="right">
</colgroup>
<thead align="left">
<tr><th>Player</th><th>Team</th><th>Date</th><th>RBI</th></tr>
...
```

Figure 6-17   RBI table with column groups that include `width` attributes in a Web browser

Next, you add to the Schedule.html file a column group that includes the `span` and `width` attributes to specify the size of the columns in the table.

To add to the Schedule.html file a column group that specifies the size of the columns in the table:

1. Return to the **Schedule.html** file in your text editor.

2. Delete the **width="100%"** attribute from the opening **<table>** tag.

3. Above the **<thead>** element, add the following column group that spans both the arrival and departure columns and sets both columns to 200 pixels in width:

   ```
   <colgroup span="2" width="200" />
   ```

4. Save the **Schedule.html** file and then open it in your Web browser. Figure 6-18 shows how the file should appear in your Web browser.

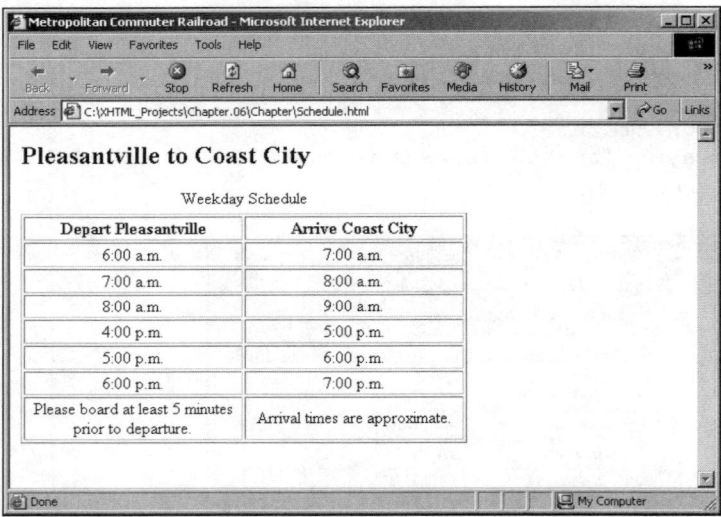

Figure 6-18　Schedule.html after adding a column group

5. Close your Web browser window.

Using Tables to Simulate Frames

If you want to use tables to simulate frames, you create a table with the same number of cells as the number of frames you want. For instance, if you want to create two horizontal frames (one at the top of a page and one on bottom), you create a table with two rows, with each row containing a single `<td>` element. Similarly, if you want to create two vertical frames, you create a table with a single row containing two `<td>` elements. You can place almost any content you like within a cell, so to create a navigation menu on the left and a content pane on the right, you would place a list of hyperlinks in the left cell and display each link's associated content in the right cell. However, one of the big differences between frames and tables that simulate frames is that when you click a link in a table, the link opens an entirely new page in the same browser window—it does not display a new URL in a different area of the same page as occurs with frames. Therefore, to get the same document layout effect with a two-column table in which the left column contains a list of links, each document that is a target of the links must duplicate the table that simulates the frameset.

To help you understand how to use tables to simulate frames, consider the following document, which uses a table to simulate the Architectural Wonders of the World frame-based Web page you saw in Chapter 5. The table consists of a single row with two cells. The tags for the single row and two cells appear in boldface. The left cell contains a list of the links to each Architectural Wonder of the World, and the right cell displays the information associated with the selected link, including an `<img>` element that displays an image of the structure. Notice that each of the links in the left cell opens a new Web page—clicking a link doesn't simply replace the contents of the right cell. The following document is for the Great Sphinx of Egypt. Figure 6-19 shows how the document appears in a Web browser. Although it does not look precisely like the page you created with frames in the last chapter, the functionality is similar.

```
<!DOCTYPE html PUBLIC
"-//W3C//DTD XHTML 1.0 Transitional//EN"
"http://www.w3.org/TR/xhtml1/DTD/xhtml1-transitional.dtd">
<html xmlns="http://www.w3.org/1999/xhtml" lang="en"
xml:lang="en" dir="ltr">
<head>
<title>Architectural Wonders of the World</title>
<meta http-equiv="content-type" content="text/html;
    charset=iso-8859-1" />
</head>
<body>
<h1>Architectural Wonders of the World</h1>
<table border="1">
<colgroup width="30%" />
<colgroup width="70%" />
<tr>
<td>
```

6

```
<h2>Africa</h2>
<a href="sphinx.html">Pyramid of Giza</a><br />
<a href="aswan.html">The High Dam in Aswan</a><br />
<a href="alexandria.html">The Lighthouse of
    Alexandria</a><br />
<a href="sphinx.html">The Great Sphinx</a><br />
<a href="suezcanal.html">The Suez Canal</a><br />
<a href="abu_simbel.html">The Temple of Abu Simbel</a>
</td>
<td><img src="sphinx.jpg" alt="Photo of the Sphinx"
    width="122" height="122" />
<p>The Great Sphinx of Egypt, one of the wonders of ancient
Egyptian architecture, adjoins the pyramids of Giza and has a
length of 240 ft. Built in the fourth dynasty, it is
approximately 4,500 years old. A 10-year $2.5 million restoration
project was completed in 1998.</p>
<p><cite>&quot;Famous Structures.&quot; Infoplease.com.<br/>
© 2002 Family Education Network.<br />
10 Aug. 2002 <a
href="http://www.infoplease.com/ce6/society/A0846266.html">http:/
/www.infoplease.com/ce6/society/A0846266.html</a>.</cite></p>
</td>
</tr>
</table>
</body>
</html>
```

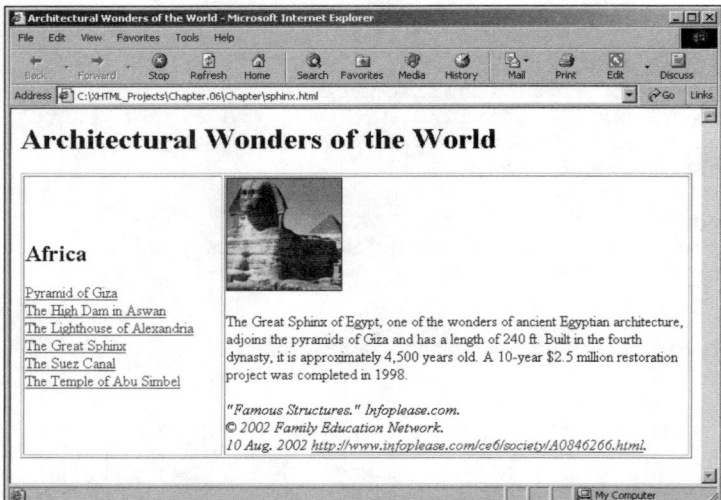

Figure 6-19   Table-based version of the Architectural Wonders of the World Web page

Suppose you want one of the cells within a frame–simulation table to contain another table. Because table cells can include almost any content, you can nest a table within a table cell. There is nothing particularly complicated about nesting a table within a table cell. All you need to do is place a **<table>** element and the text and child elements it contains within a `<td>`...`</td>` tag pair in another table. For example, the following code contains a parent table consisting of one row with two cells. Each cell contains its own table that lists snow depth for this year and last year for some areas of the Sierra Mountains in California. Figure 6-20 shows how the tables render in a browser. Because the parent table does not include a **border** attribute, the two nested tables appear to float next to each other.

```
<h1>Snow Depth</h1>
<table width="100%">
<tr>
<td>
<table border="1" width="100%">
<tr><th>Location</th><th>This Year</th><th>Last Year</th></tr>
<tr><td>Bear Valley</td><td>17</td><td>28</td></tr>
<tr><td>Carson Pass</td><td>10</td><td>29</td></tr>
<tr><td>Donner Pass</td><td>10</td><td>46</td></tr>
</table>
</td>
<td>
<table border="1" width="100%">
<tr><th>Location</th><th>This Year</th><th>Last Year</th></tr>
<tr><td>Echo Summit</td><td>7</td><td>21</td></tr>
<tr><td>Mammoth</td><td>24</td><td>14</td></tr>
<tr><td>Pinecrest</td><td>13</td><td>12</td></tr>
</table>
</td>
</tr>
</table>
```

Figure 6-20   Nested tables

You now modify the Schedule.html file so it includes a one-row, two-cell table that simulates a frameset. The left table cell contains hyperlinks, and the right cell displays each link's associated content.

To modify the Schedule.html file so it includes a one-row, two-cell table that simulates a frameset:

1. Return to the **Schedule.html** file in your text editor.

2. Add the following <h1> element above the <h2> element:

```
<h1>Metropolitan Commuter Railroad</h1>
```

3. Immediately above the <table> tag, add the following elements for the parent table that simulates a frameset. The first <td> element includes two hyperlinks: one for Schedule.html and another for a file named Fares.html that you create shortly. Notice that only two <td> elements are defined. The first <td> element contains the links. The second opening <td> tag includes the schedule table as its content.

```
<table width="100%" border="1">
<colgroup span="1" width="100" />
<tr>
    <td><a href="schedule.html">Schedule</a><br />
    <a href="fares.html">Fares</a></td>
<td>
```

4. To complete the new parent table, add the following closing </td>, </tr>, and </table> tags immediately above the closing </body> tag.

```
</td></tr>
</table>
```

5. Save the **Schedule.html** file and then immediately save it as **Fares.html** in the Chapter.06\Chapter folder.

6. In the Fares.html file, replace the schedule table with the following fares table. Do not delete any of the tags for the parent table.

```
<table border="1">
    <caption>One-Way Fares</caption>
    <colgroup span="3" width="200" />
    <thead>
        <tr><th>Passenger</th><th>Weekdays</th>
        <th>Weekends/Holidays</th></tr>
    </thead>
    <tbody align="center">
        <tr><td>Adult (13-64)</td>
            <td>$3.25</td>
            <td>$5.60</td></tr>
        <tr><td>Youth (6-12)</td>
            <td>$2.45</td>
            <td>$4.20</td></tr>
        <tr><td>Senior (65+)</td>
            <td>$1.60</td>
            <td>$2.80</td></tr>
```

```
<tr><td>Disabled</td>
      <td>$1.25</td>
      <td>$2.30</td></tr>
<tr><td>Child (0-5)</td>
      <td>FREE</td>
      <td>FREE</td></tr>
  </tbody>
</table>
```

7. Save the **Fares.html** file, and then open it in your Web browser. Figure 6-21 shows how the file should appear in your Web browser. Test the links to be sure that both files open correctly.

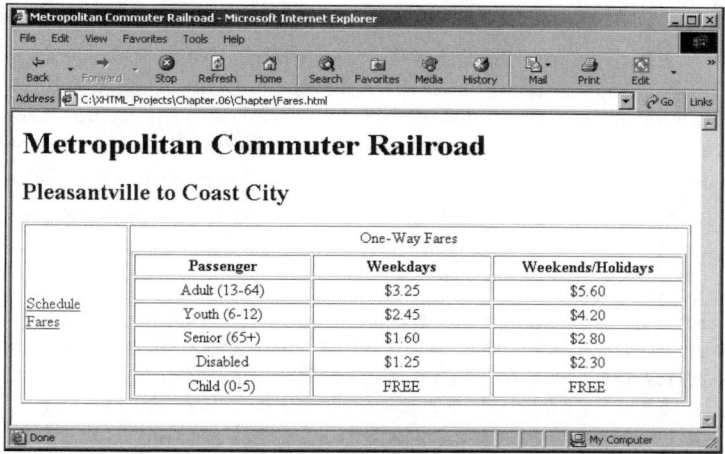

Figure 6-21   Fares.html in a Web browser

8. Close your Web browser window.

FORMATTING TABLES

As you learned in Chapter 1, you should handle the visual display of content with CSS. Nevertheless, you can use several types of built-in table formatting options without CSS, even when using the Strict DTD. You study the following types of table formatting in this section:

- Table borders
- Table frames
- Table rules
- Empty cells
- Cell margins

- Cells that span multiple rows or columns
- Vertical alignment

Web page authors still use two deprecated attributes of the <table> element, align and bgcolor. The align attribute sets a table's horizontal alignment, whereas the bgcolor attribute sets a table's background color. In fact, the bgcolor attribute was also available for use with the <td>, <tr>, and <th> elements. The <td>, <tr>, and <th> elements also included several other formatting attributes that are now deprecated. In order for your XHTML documents to be well formed with the Strict DTD, be sure to use CSS for any table formatting that was formerly accomplished with deprecated attributes.

Borders

As you learned earlier, tables are created without borders. You use the <table> element's **border attribute** to add a border to a table. The value you assign to the border attribute determines the thickness of the border in pixels. For instance, the following code shows a 5-pixel border around a table that lists American life expectancy. Figure 6-22 shows the output of the table in a Web browser.

```
<table border="5">
<caption><b>American Life Expectancy</b></caption>
<tr><th>Group</th><th>At Birth</th><th>At Age 65</th></tr>
<tr><td>Males</td><td>74.1</td><td>16.3</td></tr>
<tr><td>Females</td><td>79.5</td><td>19.2</td></tr>
<tr><td>All Americans</td><td>76.9</td><td>17.9</td></tr>
</table>
```

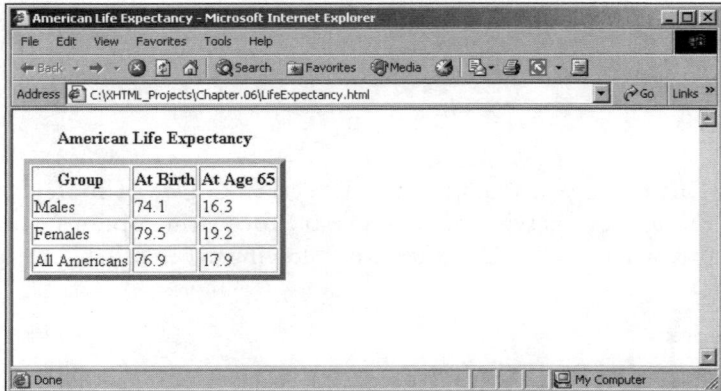

Figure 6-22 Table with a 5-pixel border in a Web browser

The `frame` Attribute

In addition to the `border` attribute, you can include the **frame attribute** in the `<table>` element to specify which sides of the table should display a border. Table 6-4 lists the values that you can assign to the `frame` attribute.

Table 6-4   `frame` attribute values

Value	Description
above	The frame appears on the top side only.
below	The frame appears on the bottom side only.
box or border	The frame appears around all four sides.
hsides	The frame appears on the top and bottom sides only.
lhs	The frame appears on the left side only.
rhs	The frame appears on the right side only.
void	The frame does not appear.
vsides	The frame appears on the left and right sides only.

The default value of the `frame` attribute is "void", unless the `border` attribute is assigned a positive value, and then the default value of the `frame` attribute is "box" or "border".

The following code shows another example of the American life expectancy table. In this version the `<table>` element includes a `frame` attribute that is assigned a value of "above". Figure 6-23 shows the table in a Web browser.

```
<table border="3" frame="above">
<caption><b>American Life Expectancy</b></caption>
<tr><th>Group</th><th>At Birth</th><th>At Age 65</th></tr>
<tr><td>Males</td><td>74.1</td><td>16.3</td></tr>
<tr><td>Females</td><td>79.5</td><td>19.2</td></tr>
<tr><td>All Americans</td><td>76.9</td><td>17.9</td></tr>
</table>
```

Next, you modify the parent table in the Schedule.html and Fares.html files so that the border is visible only on the top and bottom of the table.

To modify the parent table so the table border is visible only on the top and bottom:

1. Return to the **Schedule.html** file in your text editor.

2. Add the `frames="hsides"` attribute to the parent table's opening `<table>` tag (the first `<table>` tag in the document), as follows:

```
<table width="100%" border="1" frame="hsides">
. . .
```

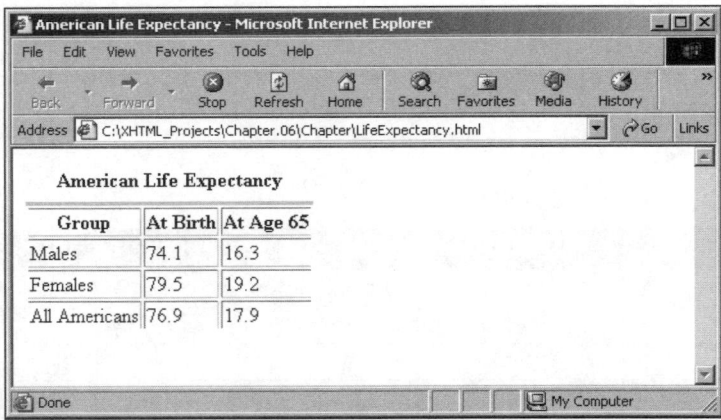

Figure 6-23   Table with a `frame` attribute value of `"above"`

3. Save the **Schedule.html** file, and return to the **Fares.html** file in your text editor.

4. Make the same change to the Fares.html file by adding the `frame="hsides"` attribute to the parent table's opening `<table>` tag, as follows:

```
<table width="100%" border="1" frame="hsides">
. . .
```

5. Save the **Fares.html** file and then open it in your Web browser. As you can see, the document is starting to look a little more like a frameset document. Open the **Schedule.html** document by clicking the **Schedule** link and make sure that the parent table looks the same as it does in the Fares.html file.

6. Close your Web browser window.

Rules

When you use the `border` or `frame` attributes, rules (or lines) that separate the rows and columns appear by default. However, you can include the **rules attribute** in the `<table>` element to specify which rules should appear in a table. Table 6-5 lists the values that you can assign to the `rules` attribute.

Table 6-5   `rules` attribute values

Value	Description
none	Rules do not appear.
groups	Rules appear between row and column groups only. (You will study row and column groups later in this chapter.)
rows	Rules appear between rows only.
cols	Rules appear between columns only.
all	Rules appear between rows and columns.

When you include a `border` or `frame` attribute, the default value of the `rules` attribute is "`all`".

The following figure shows another example of the American life expectancy table, but this time the `<table>` element includes a `rules` attribute that is assigned a value of "`rows`". As you can see in Figure 6-24, rules appear between the rows, but not between the columns.

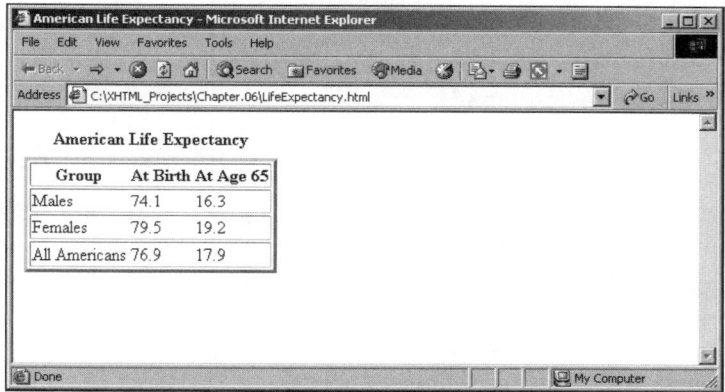

Figure 6-24   Table with a `rules` attribute value of "`rows`"

Next, you modify the Fares.html and Schedule.html files so that the parent tables use a `rules` attribute with a value of "`cols`". You also modify the nested table in Fares.html so it uses a `rules` attribute with a value of "`rows`".

To add a `rules` attribute with a value of "`cols`" to the fares and schedules tables and to add a `rules` attribute with a value of "`rows`" to the nested table:

1. Return to the **Schedule.html** file in your text editor.

2. Add the "`rules`="`cols`" attribute to the parent table's opening `<table>` tag, as follows:

   ```
   <table width="100%" border="1" frame="hsides" rules="cols">
   ```

3. Save the **Schedule.html** file, and return to the **Fares.html** file in your text editor.

4. Make the same change to the Fares.html file by adding the `rules`="`cols`" attribute to the parent table's opening `<table>` tag, as follows:

   ```
   <table width="100%" border="1" frame="hsides" rules="cols">
   ```

5. Add the `rules="rows"` attribute to the nested fare table's opening `<table>` tag (the second `<table>` tag in the document), as follows:

```
<table border="1" rules="rows">
...
```

6. Save the **Fares.html** file and then open it in your Web browser. Figure 6-25 shows how the file should appear in your Web browser.

Figure 6-25   Fares.html after adding the `frames` attribute to the parent table and the `rules` attribute to the fares table

7. Close your Web browser window.

Displaying Empty Cells

It is often necessary to include empty cells in tables. For instance, the following code shows a table that tracks the retail cost of diesel fuel and gasoline for each week in August and September 2002. Let's assume that you do not yet have the data for September, but you still want to include rows in the table for September. Therefore, the following code does not include cells (`<td>` elements) for the gas and diesel prices in September, but it does include cells containing the weeks.

```
<table border="1">
<caption>Retail Diesel and Gasoline Prices</caption>
<tr><th>Week Ending</th><th>Diesel</th><th>Gasoline</th></tr>
<tr><td>8/5/2002</td><td>130.4</td><td>143.7</td></tr>
<tr><td>8/12/2002</td><td>130.3</td><td>143.5</td></tr>
<tr><td>8/19/2002</td><td>133.3</td><td>143.4</td></tr>
<tr><td>8/26/2002</td><td>137.0</td><td>144.4</td></tr>
<tr><td>9/2/2002</td></tr>
<tr><td>9/9/2002</td></tr>
<tr><td>9/16/2002</td></tr>
```

```
<tr><td>9/23/2002</td></tr>
<tr><td>9/30/2002</td></tr>
</table>
```

Unfortunately, most Web browsers do not render the borders around empty cells. For example, Figure 6-26 shows that the borders around the empty cells in the preceding code are missing.

Figure 6-26   Missing borders around empty cells

To fix this problem, you need to add a `<td>` element for each empty cell, and include a non-breaking space character entity (` `) as each cell's content. For instance, the following code shows a version of the retail diesel and gasoline prices table with empty cells created with non-breaking space character entities. Figure 6-27 shows the output in a Web browser.

```
<table border="1">
<caption>Retail Diesel and Gasoline Prices</caption>
<tr><th>Week Ending</th><th>Diesel</th><th>Gasoline</th></tr>
<tr><td>8/5/2002</td><td>130.4</td><td>143.7</td></tr>
<tr><td>8/12/2002</td><td>130.3</td><td>143.5</td></tr>
<tr><td>8/19/2002</td><td>133.3</td><td>143.4</td></tr>
<tr><td>8/26/2002</td><td>137.0</td><td>144.4</td></tr>
<tr><td>9/2/2002</td><td> </td><td> </td></tr>
<tr><td>9/9/2002</td><td> </td><td> </td></tr>
<tr><td>9/16/2002</td><td> </td><td> </td></tr>
<tr><td>9/23/2002</td><td> </td><td> </td></tr>
<tr><td>9/30/2002</td><td> </td><td> </td></tr>
</table>
```

Figure 6-27   Table with empty cells created with non-breaking space character entities

Next, you add a new column to the schedule table for stops in the city of Central Valley, which lies between Pleasantville and Coast City. However, only some trains stop in Central Valley. Therefore, you add empty cells for the times that the trains do not stop at the Central Valley station.

To add empty cells for the times that the trains do not stop at the Central Valley station:

1. Return to the **Schedule.html** file in your text editor.

2. As shown in the following code, change the value assigned to the **span** attribute in the nested schedule table's **<colgroup>** element from "2" to **"3"**. Add the bold statements in the following code to the nested schedule table with the following code. Notice that the empty cells include the non-breaking space character entity.

```
<table border="1" summary="This table lists the departure and
arrival times from Pleasantville to Coast City.">
  <caption>Weekday Schedule</caption>
  <colgroup span="3" width="200" />
  <thead>
     <tr><th>Depart Pleasantville</th>
     <th>Central Valley</th>
     <th>Arrive Coast City</th></tr>
  </thead>
  <tfoot align="center">
     <tr><td>Please board at least 5 minutes prior to
departure.</td>
<td> </td>
<td>Arrival times are approximate.</td></tr>
```

```
      </tfoot>
      <tbody align="center">
      <tr><td>6:00 a.m.</td>
        <td>6:30 a.m.</td>
        <td>7:00 a.m.</td></tr>
      <tr><td>7:00 a.m.</td>
        <td> </td>
        <td>8:00 a.m.</td></tr>
      <tr><td>8:00 a.m.</td>
        <td>8:30 a.m.</td>
        <td>9:00 a.m.</td></tr>
      <tr><td>4:00 p.m.</td>
        <td> </td>
        <td>5:00 p.m.</td></tr>
      <tr><td>5:00 p.m.</td>
        <td>5:30 p.m.</td>
        <td>6:00 p.m.</td></tr>
      <tr><td>6:00 p.m.</td>
        <td> </td>
        <td>7:00 p.m.</td></tr>
      </tbody>
    </table>
```

3. Save the **Schedule.html** file and then open it in your Web browser. Figure 6-28 shows how the file should appear in your Web browser.

Figure 6-28   Schedule.html after adding a new column with empty cells

4. Close your Web browser window.

Cell Margins

You can adjust the margins of the cells in a table by using the `<table>` element's `cellspacing` and `cellpadding` attributes. The **cellspacing attribute** specifies the amount of horizontal and vertical space between table cells. You assign to the `cellspacing` attribute a value representing the number of pixels that you want between table cells. For instance, the following code shows the American life expectancy table with a `cellspacing` attribute that specifies 10 pixels between the table cells. Figure 6-29 shows how the table appears in a Web browser.

```
<table border="1" cellspacing="10">
<caption><b>American Life Expectancy</b></caption>
<tr><th>Group</th><th>At Birth</th><th>At Age 65</th></tr>
<tr><td>Males</td><td>74.1</td><td>16.3</td></tr>
<tr><td>Females</td><td>79.5</td><td>19.2</td></tr>
<tr><td>All Americans</td><td>76.9</td><td>17.9</td></tr>
</table>
```

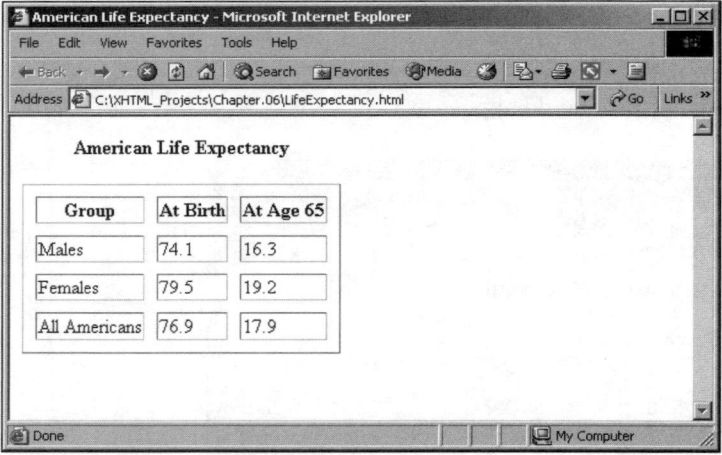

Figure 6-29 Table with 10 pixels between the table cells

In comparison, the **cellpadding attribute** specifies the amount of horizontal and vertical space between each cell's border and the contents of the cell. For instance, the following code shows the American life expectancy table with a `cellpadding` attribute that specifies 20 pixels between each cell's border and content. Figure 6-30 shows how the table appears in a Web browser.

```
<table border="1" cellpadding="20">
<caption><b>American Life Expectancy</b></caption>
<tr><th>Group</th><th>At Birth</th><th>At Age 65</th></tr>
<tr><td>Males</td><td>74.1</td><td>16.3</td></tr>
<tr><td>Females</td><td>79.5</td><td>19.2</td></tr>
<tr><td>All Americans</td><td>76.9</td><td>17.9</td></tr>
</table>
```

Figure 6-30   Table with 20 pixels between each cell's border and content

 The cellspacing and cellpadding attributes apply to all of the cells within a table; you cannot specify either of these attributes for individual cells within the table.

You can use both the cellspacing and cellpadding attributes together to create different combinations of spacing and padding within your tables. For instance, Figure 6-31 shows the output of the American life expectancy table after assigning a cellspacing value of "5" and a cellpadding value of "10" within the opening <table> tag.

Figure 6-31   Table with 5 pixels between the table cells and 10 pixels between each cell's border and content

Cells that Span Multiple Rows or Columns

You can cause cells to span multiple rows or columns by including the **rowspan** or **colspan attributes** in the <td> or <th> elements. As an example of the **colspan** attribute, the following table shows a breakdown of the animal kingdom into phylum and class. Figure 6–32 shows the table in a Web browser.

```
<table border="1" width="100%">
  <tr><th width="25%">Kingdom</th>
    <th width="25%">Phylum</th>
    <th width="25%">Class</th></tr>
  <tr><td width="25%" rowspan="4">Animalia</td>
    <td width="25%" rowspan="2">Chordata</td>
    <td width="25%">Mammalia</td></tr>
  <tr><td width="25%">Amphibia</td></tr>
  <tr><td width="25%" rowspan="2">Arthropoda</td>
    <td width="25%">Insecta</td></tr>
  <tr><td width="25%">Arachnida</td></tr>
</table>
```

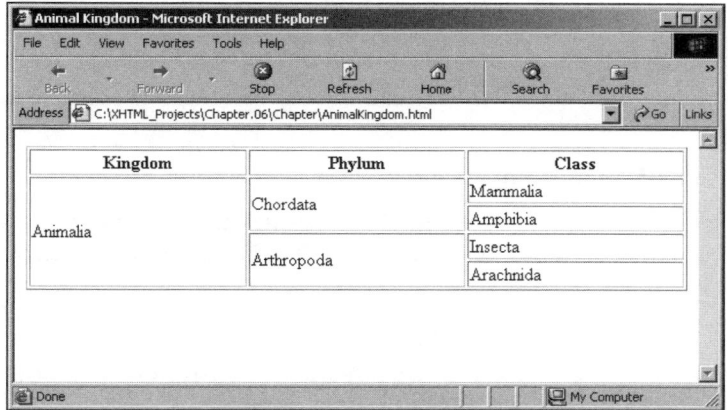

Figure 6-32   Table with cells that span multiple rows

The following table shows an alternate version of the animal kingdom table, but this time with cells that span multiple columns. Figure 6-33 shows the table in a Web browser.

```
<table border="1" width="94%">
  <tr><td width="23%"><b>Kingdom</b></td>
    <td width="102%" colspan="4" align="center">
     Animalia</td></tr>
  <tr><td width="23%"><b>Phylum</b></td>
    <td width="52%" colspan="2" align="center">Chordata</td>
    <td width="50%" colspan="2"
align="center">Arthropoda</td></tr>
  <tr><td width="23%"><b>Class</b></td>
    <td width="27%" align="center">Mammalia</td>
    <td width="25%" align="center">Amphibia</td>
    <td width="25%" align="center">Insecta</td>
    <td width="25%" align="center">Arachnida</td></tr>
</table>
```

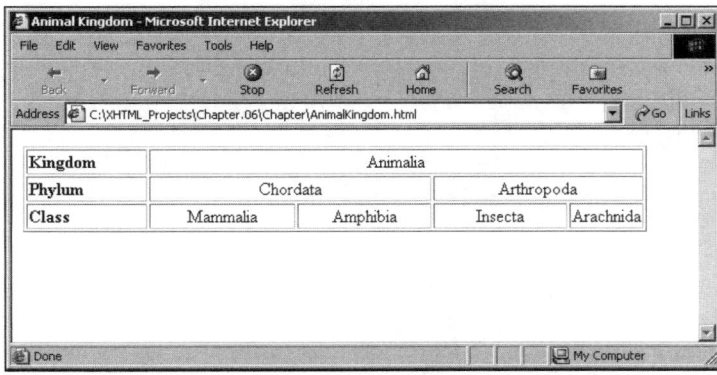

Figure 6-33   Table with cells that span multiple columns

Next, you modify the Schedule.html file so the schedule table includes cells that span multiple rows and columns.

To modify the Schedule.html file so the schedule table includes cells that span multiple rows and columns:

1. Return to the **Schedule.html** file in your text editor.

2. First, modify the `span` attribute in the schedule table's `<colspan>` element so it is assigned a value of `"4"` instead of "3". The modified element should appear as follows:

```
<colgroup span="4" width="200" />
```

3. Modify the `<thead>` section in the schedule table, as follows, so the heading information includes a new "Rush Hour" column:

```
<thead>
    <tr><th>Rush Hour</th><th>Depart Pleasantville</th>
    <th>Central Valley</th><th>Arrive Coast City</th></tr>
</thead>
```

4. Next, add to the table body the following `<td>` elements, highlighted in boldface, which create two new cells that span several rows:

```
<tbody align="center">
    <tr><td rowspan="3">Morning</td>
    <td>6:00 a.m.</td>
    <td>6:30 a.m.</td>
    <td>7:00 a.m.</td></tr>
    <tr><td>7:00 a.m.</td>
    <td> </td>
    <td>8:00 a.m.</td></tr>
    <tr><td>8:00 a.m.</td>
    <td>8:30 a.m.</td>
    <td>9:00 a.m.</td></tr>
    <tr><td rowspan="3">Evening</td>
    <td>4:00 p.m.</td>
...
```

5. Finally, edit the `<tfoot>` element to create the following statements, which create a single footer cell that spans the other columns in the table:

```
<tfoot align="center">
    <tr><td colspan="4">Please board at least 5 minutes
        prior to departure. Arrival times are approximate.
    </td></tr>
</tfoot>
```

6. Save the **Schedule.html** file and then open it in your Web browser. Figure 6-34 shows how the file should appear in your Web browser.

7. Close your Web browser window.

Figure 6-34   Schedule.html after adding cells that span multiple rows and columns

Vertical Alignment

In addition to the `align` attribute for horizontally aligning columns, you can use the **valign attribute**, which adjusts the vertical alignment of the contents of all table elements with the exception of the `<table>` and `<caption>` elements. The values you can assign to the `valign` attribute are `top`, `middle`, `bottom`, and `baseline`. The default `valign` attribute is "`middle`". If you examine the animal kingdom table in Figure 6-32, which included cells that spanned multiple rows, you will see that by default the contents of the cells are aligned in the middle of each cell. The following code shows the animal kingdom table with cells that span multiple rows. However this time, the `<td>` elements include a `valign` attribute that aligns the cell contents at the top of the cells. Figure 6-35 shows the table in a Web browser.

```
<table border="1" width="100%">
  <tr><th width="25%">Kingdom</th>
    <th width="25%">Phylum</th>
    <th width="25%">Class</th></tr>
  <tr><td width="25%" rowspan="4" valign="top">Animalia</td>
    <td width="25%" rowspan="2" valign="top">Chordata</td>
    <td width="25%">Mammalia</td></tr>
  <tr><td width="25%">Amphibia</td></tr>
  <tr><td width="25%" rowspan="2" valign="top">Arthropoda</td>
    <td width="25%">Insecta</td></tr>
  <tr><td width="25%">Arachnida</td></tr>
</table>
```

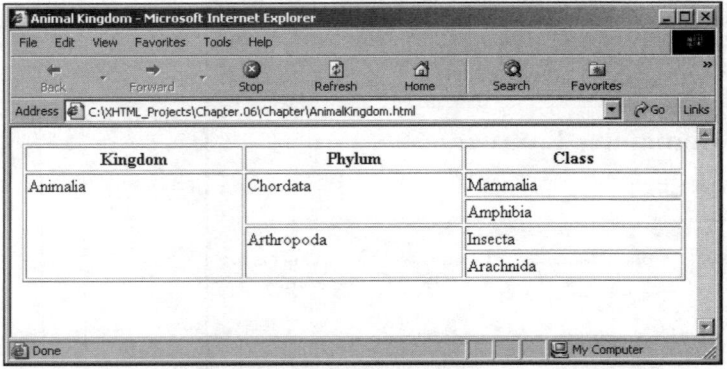

Figure 6-35   Table with data vertically aligned at the tops of each cell

Next, you modify the Schedule.html and Fares.html files so the links in the left cell of the parent table are vertically aligned at the top instead of the default middle.

To modify the Schedule.html and Fares.html files so the links in the left cell of the parent table are vertically aligned at the top:

1. Return to the **Schedule.html** file in your text editor.

2. Add **valign="top"** to the first **<td>** element in the parent table, as follows:

```
<table width="100%" border="1" frame="hsides rules="cols">
<colgroup span="1" width="100%"/>
<tr>
    <td valign="top"><a href="schedule.html">Schedule</a><br />
```

3. Save the **Schedule.html** file.

4. Open the **Fares.html** file and add the same **valign="top"** attribute to the first **<td>** element in the parent table.

5. Save the **Fares.html** file.

6. Open **Schedule.html** in a Web browser and examine the vertical alignment of its cell contents. Click the **Fares** link and examine the vertical alignment of its cell contents. Figure 6-36 shows how the Fares.html file should appear in your Web browser.

7. Close your Web browser window.

Finally, you validate the Schedule.html and Fares.html files.

To validate the Schedule.html and Fares.html files:

1. Start your Web browser and enter the URL for the upload page of the W3C Markup Validation Service: **validator.w3.org/file-upload.html**.

2. Open and validate the **Schedule.html** file. If you receive any errors, fix them, and then revalidate the document.

Figure 6-36   Fares.html after adding the `valign` attribute to the first cell in the parent table

3. Repeat the validation process for the **Fares.html** file.

4. Close your Web browser.

CREATING LISTS

Lists are a very important tool in proper Web page authoring because they provide a way of logically ordering a series of words or numbers. They also provide a simple, yet effective design technique for making it easier for Web site visitors to locate information. You can add three types of lists to a Web page: unordered lists, ordered lists, and definition lists. Table 6-6 lists the elements used to create these lists.

Table 6-6   List elements

Element	Description
`<ul>`	Block-level element that creates an unordered list
`<ol>`	Block-level element that creates an ordered list
`<li>`	Inline element that defines a list item
`<dl>`	Block-level element that creates a definition list
`<dt>`	Inline element that defines a definition list term
`<dd>`	Inline element that defines a definition list item

This section presents the most basic information regarding working with lists. To change the formatting and appearance of lists, you must use CSS. See Chapter 8 for detailed information on working with CSS.

Unordered Lists

An **unordered list** is a series of bulleted items. To define the items you want to appear in the bulleted list, you nest `<li>` elements within a `<ul>` element. The following code creates the unordered list shown in Figure 6-37.

```
<h1>Justice Society Of America</h1>
<h2>Founding Members</h2>
<ul>
    <li>The Flash</li>
    <li>The Green Lantern</li>
    <li>The Spectre</li>
    <li>The Hawkman</li>
    <li>Dr. Fate</li>
    <li>The Hour-Man</li>
    <li>The Sandman</li>
    <li>The Atom</li>
    <li>Johnny Thunder</li>
</ul>
```

Figure 6-37   Unordered list of superheroes

Next, you add a Courtesy Rules page with unordered lists to the Metropolitan Commuter Railroad Web site.

To add a Courtesy Rules page with unordered lists to the Metropolitan Commuter Railroad Web site:

1. Return to the **Schedule.html** file in your text editor and modify the first cell in the parent table as follows so it includes a new link to a page named Rules.html:

   ```
   <td valign="top"><a href="schedule.html">Schedule</a><br />
   <br/><a href="fares.html">Fares</a><br />
   <a href="rules.html">Courtesy Rules</a></td>
   ```

2. Save and close the **Schedule.html** file.

3. Return to the **Fares.html** file in your text editor and modify the first cell in the parent table as follows so it includes the new link to the Rules.html file, as follows:

   ```
   <td valign="top"><a href="schedule.html">Schedule</a><br />
   <a href="fares.html">Fares</a><br />
   <a href="rules.html">Courtesy Rules</a></td>
   ```

4. Save the **Fares.html** file and immediately save it as **Rules.html** in your Chapter.06\Chapter folder.

5. Replace the nested fares table with the following unordered rules list:

   ```
   <ul>
   <li>Smoking is not permitted on Metropolitan Commuter Railroad
   trains.</li>
   <li>No seats are reserved. Please do not inconvenience other
   customers by holding seats or blocking seats with parcels or
   wraps.</li>
   <li>Please refrain from placing feet on seats or upper deck
   railings.</li>
   <li>Please do not block the doors, making it difficult for
   passengers to detrain or entrain at their stations.</li>
   <li>Please be considerate of others and keep volume on head sets
   low.</li>
   <li>Help us to maintain a clean environment by not leaving litter
   on trains, in stations, or in stairwells and walkways.</li>
   <li>Passengers whose conduct is disorderly or unsafe will not be
   allowed on the train.</li>
   <li>Obscene language, or that which is disturbing to other
   passengers, is prohibited.</li>
   </ul>
   ```

6. Save the file as **Rules.html** and validate it with the W3C Markup Validation Service.

7. Open the **Rules.html** file in your Web browser. Figure 6-38 displays the document in a Web browser.

8. Close your Web browser window.

6

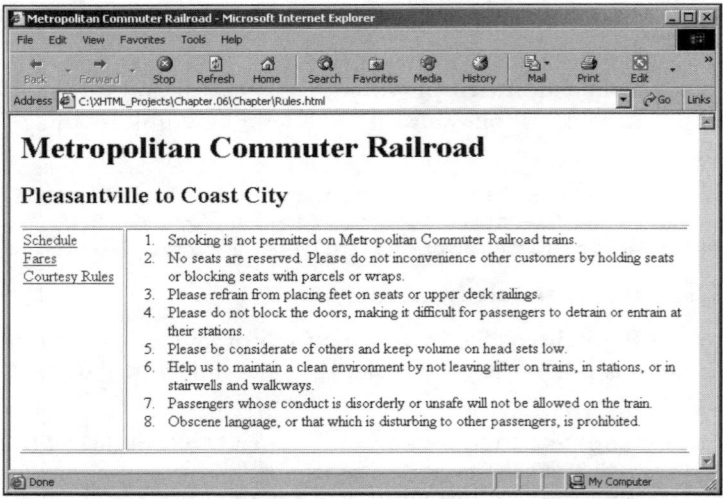

Figure 6-38 Unordered courtesy rules list

Ordered Lists

An **ordered list** is a series of numbered items. To define the items you want to appear in the numbered list, you nest **<li>** elements within an **<ol>** element. The following code creates the ordered list shown in Figure 6-39.

```
<p>The following actors, from first to most recent, have played
James Bond:</p>
<ol>
    <li>Sean Connery</li>
    <li>George Lazenby</li>
    <li>Roger Moore</li>
    <li>Timothy Dalton</li>
    <li>Pierce Brosnan</li>
</ol>
```

Figure 6-39 Ordered list of James Bond actors

Next, you modify the unordered courtesy rules list for the Metropolitan Commuter Railroad you created in the last exercise so that it becomes an ordered list.

To change the unordered courtesy rules list to an ordered list:

1. Return to the **Rules.html** file in your text editor.

2. Change the `<ul>` and `</ul>` tags to `<ol>` and `</ol>` tags, as follows:

```
<ol>
<li>Smoking is not permitted on Metropolitan Commuter Railroad
trains.</li>
<li>No seats are reserved. Please do not inconvenience other
customers
...
</ol>
```

3. Save the **Rules.html** file and validate it with the W3C Markup Validation Service.

4. Open **Rules.html** in your Web browser. Figure 6-40 displays the document in a Web browser.

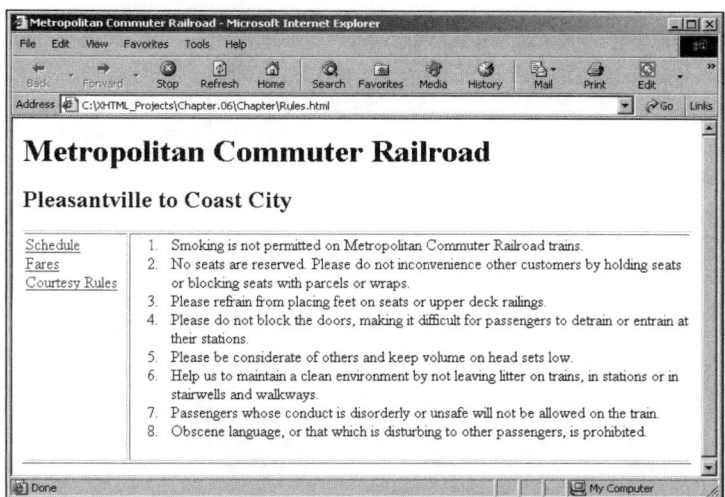

Figure 6-40   Ordered courtesy rules list

5. Close your text editor and Web browser window.

Definition Lists

A **definition list** is a series of terms and their definitions. Web browsers render each term and its definition on separate lines with an indented left margin. You create a definition list by using the `<dl>` element. Within the `<dl>` element, you nest `<dt>` elements for term names and `<dd>` elements for term definitions. The following code creates the definition list shown in Figure 6-41.

```
<h1>Electrical Terms</h1>
<h2>Beginning with the Letter <em>'O'</em></h2>
<dl>
    <dt><b>Ohm</b></dt>
    <dd>Measurement unit for electrical resistance
    or impedance.</dd>
    <dt><b>Ohmmeter</b></dt>
    <dd>An instrument used for measuring resistance
    in Ohms.</dd>
    <dt><b>Overcurrent</b></dt>
    <dd>An electrical current that is in excess of an
    appliance's rated current or the ampacity of a
    conductor.</dd>
    <dt><b>Overload</b></dt>
    <dd>A load that exceeds the rating of a system
    or mechanism.</dd>
</dl>
```

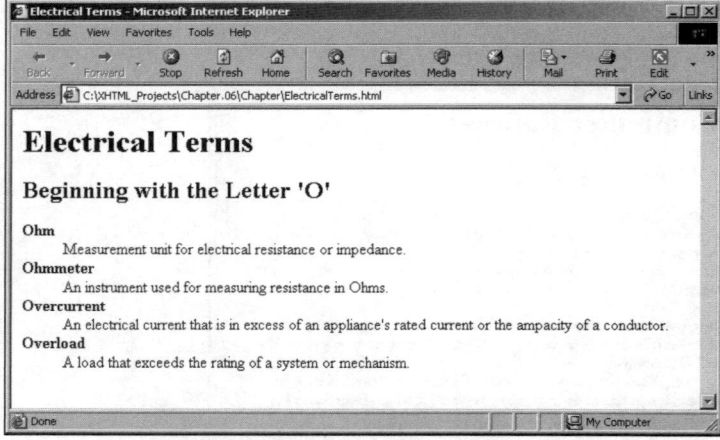

Figure 6-41   Definition list of electrical terms

CHAPTER SUMMARY

- Tables are collections of rows and columns that you use to organize and display data.

- In a table, the intersection of any given row and column is called a cell.

- You create tables using the `<table>` element.

- You create a cell within the `<table>` element using the `<td>` element.

❐ Table cells are declared within table row elements that you create with the `<tr>` element.

❐ Table cells can contain two types of information: data that you define with the `<td>` element and heading information that you define with the `<th>` element.

❐ You create a caption for a Web page table using the `<caption>` element.

❐ The **summary** attribute of the `<table>` element allows you to provide a more detailed summary of a table's structure and content for use in non-visual user agents.

❐ You use the **width** attribute of the `<table>` element to specify the size of a table.

❐ You can create row groups in a table that consist of a table header, table body, and table foot.

❐ The `<thead>` element defines a table header.

❐ The `<tbody>` element defines the table body.

❐ The `<tfoot>` element defines the table footer.

❐ Column groups are used for applying default alignment, width, and Cascading Style Sheets (CSS) styles to groups of columns within a table.

❐ You use the `<colgroup>` element to create a column group in a table.

❐ The `<col>` element allows you to apply formatting to an individual column in a column group.

❐ You can adjust the widths of columns using the **width** attribute of the `<colgroup>` or `<col>` elements.

❐ You use the **border** attribute of the `<table>` element to add a border to a table.

❐ You include the **frame** attribute in the `<table>` element to specify which sides of the table should display a border.

❐ You can include the **rules** attribute in the `<table>` element to specify which rules should appear in a table.

❐ You can use a `<td>` element to create an empty cell, but you must include the non-breaking space character entity ( ) as each empty cell's content.

❐ The **cellspacing** attribute specifies the amount of horizontal and vertical space between table cells.

❐ The **cellpadding** attribute specifies the amount of horizontal and vertical space between each cell's border and the contents of the cell.

❐ You can cause cells to span multiple rows or columns by including the **rowspan** or **colspan** attribute in the `<td>` or `<th>` elements.

❐ The **valign** attribute adjusts the vertical alignment of the contents of all table elements with the exception of the `<table>` and `<caption>` elements.

6

❑ An unordered list is a series of bulleted items.

❑ An ordered list is a series of numbered items.

❑ A definition list is a series of terms and their definitions.

REVIEW QUESTIONS

1. Tables are limited to displaying simple text. True or false?

2. Explain why the W3C discourages the use of tables to simulate frames and achieve other types of document layout.

3. Which of the following elements do you use to create table cells? (Choose all that apply.)

   a. `<table>`

   b. `<cell>`

   c. `<td>`

   d. `<th>`

4. Which of the following elements do you use to create table rows?

   a. `<row>`

   b. `<table_row>`

   c. `<tr>`

   d. `<rt>`

5. How do most Web browsers display a table's heading information?

6. Which of the following elements do you use to create a table caption?

   a. `<tc>`

   b. `<caption>`

   c. `<th>`

   d. `<heading>`

7. You use the **summary** attribute with which element?

   a. `<table>`

   b. `<caption>`

   c. `<th>`

   d. `<tc>`

8. A Web browser automatically sizes a table's width to 100% of the visible browser window. True or False?

9. Which values can you assign to the **align** attribute? (Choose all that apply.)

    a. left

    b. center

    c. right

    d. justify

10. You must include row group elements in a table. True or False?

11. Which elements are required when you include row groups in a table? (Choose all that apply.)

    a. `<thead>`

    b. `<trows>`

    c. `<tbody>`

    d. `<tfoot>`

12. Where must you place the `<colgroup>` element?

13. Which attribute of the `<colgroup>` and `<col>` elements determines the number of columns that are part of the group?

    a. `group`

    b. `cols`

    c. `span`

    d. `colspan`

14. Explain how you use a table to simulate frames.

15. What is the default width in pixels of the **border** attribute?

    a. 0

    b. 1

    c. 2

    d. 5

16. What value do you assign to the **frame** attribute for the frame to appear only on the left side of a table?

    a. left

    b. table_left

    c. rhs

    d. lhs

17. What value do you assign to the **rules** attribute for the table gridlines to appear only between a table's columns?

   a. vertical

   b. cols

   c. hgrid

   d. vgrid

18. Explain how to format an empty cell so it appears in a Web browser.

19. Which attributes of the **<table>** element adjust the margins of a table's cells? (Choose all that apply.)

   a. **spacing**

   b. **padding**

   c. **cellspacing**

   d. **cellpadding**

20. In which elements can you use the **rowspan** and **colspan** attributes? (Choose all that apply.)

   a. **<table>**

   b. **<th>**

   c. **<td>**

   d. **<tr>**

21. What attribute adjusts the vertical alignment of cell contents?

   a. **vertical**

   b. **valign**

   c. **span**

   d. **rowspan**

22. Which of the following elements is used with both unordered and ordered lists?

   a. **<ul>**

   b. **<ol>**

   c. **<li>**

   d. **<dl>**

HANDS-ON PROJECTS

Project 6-1

In this exercise, you create a document that contains a price list table for a barbershop.

1. Create a new document in your text editor.

2. Type the `<!DOCTYPE>` declaration, `<html>` element, document head, and `<body>` element. Use the Strict DTD and "Haircut Price list" as the content of the `<title>` element.

3. Add the following heading element to the document body.

    ```
    <h1>Bernie's Barbershop</h1>
    ```

4. Add the following table after the heading element:

    ```
    <table border="1" width="100%">
      <caption>Price List</caption>
      <tr>
        <td> </td>
        <td>Haircut</td>
        <td>Crew Cut</td>
        <td>Trim</td>
      </tr>
      <tr>
        <td>Men</td>
        <td>$11.99</td>
        <td>$9.99</td>
        <td>$6.99</td>
      </tr>
      <tr>
        <td>Boys</td>
        <td>$8.99</td>
        <td>$6.99</td>
        <td>$4.99</td>
      </tr>
    </table>
    ```

5. Save the file as **HaircutPrices.html** in the Chapter.06\Projects folder.

6. Close the **HaircutPrices.html** file in your text editor, and then use the W3C Markup Validation Service to validate it. Once the file is valid, open it in your Web browser.

7. Close your Web browser window.

Project 6-2

In this exercise, you create a document that contains a table of dog breeds by group, such as hounds and terriers.

1. Create a new document in your text editor.

2. Type the `<!DOCTYPE>` declaration, `<html>` element, document head, and `<body>` element. Use the Strict DTD and "Dog Breeds" as the content of the `<title>` element.

3. Add the following heading element to the document body.

    ```
    <h1>Dog Breeds</h1>
    ```

6

4. Add the following table after the heading element:

```
<table border="1" width="100%">
  <caption>Organized by Group</caption>
  <tr>
    <td>Herding Group</td>
    <td>Hound Group</td>
    <td>Terrier Group</td>
    <td>Sporting Group</td>
  </tr>
  <tr>
    <td>Collie</td>
    <td>Afghan Hound</td>
    <td>Bull Terrier</td>
    <td>Chesapeake Bay Retriever</td>
  </tr>
  <tr>
    <td>German Shepherd</td>
    <td>Basset Hound</td>
    <td>Cairn Terrier</td>
    <td>Golden Retriever</td>
  </tr>
  <tr>
    <td>Welsh Corgi</td>
    <td>Beagle</td>
    <td>Fox Terrier</td>
    <td> </td>
  </tr>
  <tr>
    <td> </td>
    <td>Bloodhound</td>
    <td>Scottish Terrier</td>
    <td> </td>
  </tr>
  <tr>
    <td> </td>
    <td>Greyhound</td>
    <td> </td>
    <td> </td>
  </tr>
</table>
```

5. Save the file as **DogBreeds.html** in the Chapter.06\Projects folder.

6. Close the **DogBreeds.html** file in your text editor, and then use the W3C Markup Validation Service to validate it. Once the file is valid, open it in your Web browser.

7. Close your Web browser window.

Project 6-3

In this exercise, you create a document that contains three empty tables.

1. Create a new document in your text editor.
2. Type the **<!DOCTYPE>** declaration, **<html>** element, document head, and **<body>** element. Use the Strict DTD and "Empty Tables" as the content of the **<title>** element.
3. Add three tables to the document body. Create the first table with one column and three rows; create the second table with one row and three columns; and create the third table with three rows and three columns. Use empty cells in each table. Place a simple border around each table. Size each table so it fills 60% of the screen.
4. Save the file as **EmptyTables.html** in the Chapter.06\Projects folder.
5. Close the **EmptyTables.html** file in your text editor, and then use the W3C Markup Validation Service to validate it. Once the file is valid, open it in your Web browser.
6. Close your Web browser window.

6

Project 6-4

In this exercise, you create a document with a table that lists major medical health insurance rates.

1. Create a new document in your text editor.
2. Type the **<!DOCTYPE>** declaration, **<html>** element, document head, and **<body>** element. Use the Strict DTD and "Major Medical Health Insurance Rates" as the content of the **<title>** element.
3. Add to the document body the headings and table shown in Figure 6-42. Use column groups to align the table cells and adjust their widths. Also add row groups to the table.
4. Save the file as **InsuranceRates.html** in the Chapter.06\Projects folder.
5. Close the **InsuranceRates.html** file in your text editor, and then use the W3C Markup Validation Service to validate it. Once the file is valid, open it in your Web browser.
6. Close your Web browser window.

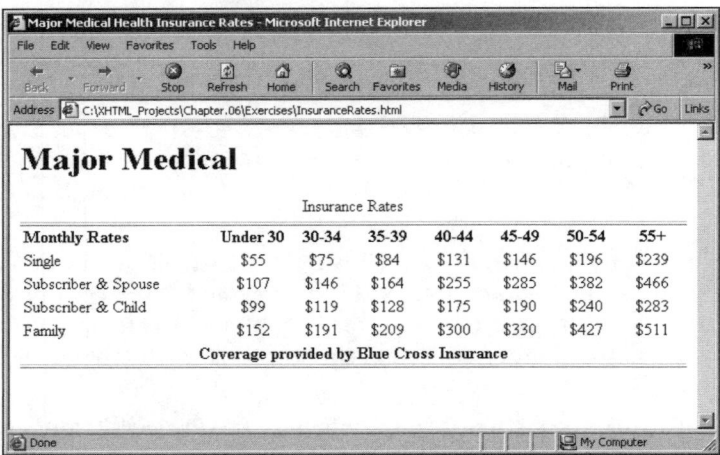

Figure 6-42   Insurance rates table

Project 6-5

In this exercise, you create a document with a table that lists the prices of premium exterior latex satin paint according to its sheen (flat, semi-gloss, and so on).

1. Create a new document in your text editor.

2. Type the **<!DOCTYPE>** declaration, **<html>** element, document head, and **<body>** element. Use the Strict DTD and "Exterior Latex Satin Paint Prices" as the content of the **<title>** element.

3. Add to the document body the headings and table shown in Figure 6-43. Use column groups to align the table cells and adjust their widths. Also add row groups to the table.

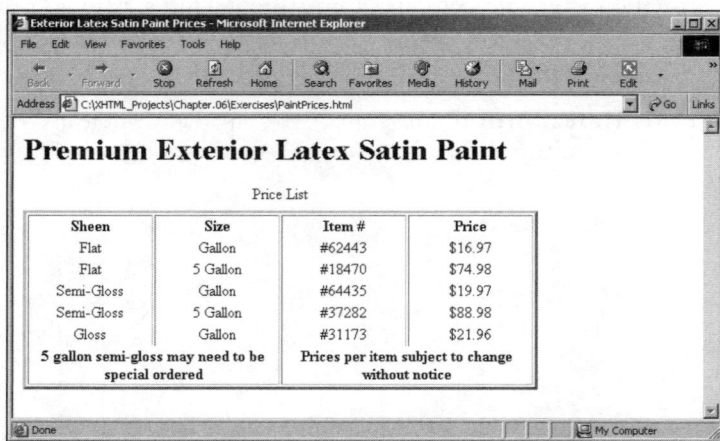

Figure 6-43   Exterior latex satin paint prices table

4. Save the file as **PaintPrices.html** in the Chapter.06\Projects folder.

5. Close the **PaintPrices.html** file in your text editor, and then use the W3C Markup Validation Service to validate it. Once the file is valid, open it in your Web browser.

6. Close your Web browser window.

Project 6-6

In this exercise, you create a document with a table that lists the credit terms for a credit card company.

1. Create a new document in your text editor.

2. Type the **<!DOCTYPE>** declaration, **<html>** element, document head, and **<body>** element. Use the Strict DTD and "Credit Terms" as the content of the **<title>** element.

3. Add to the document body the table shown in Figure 6-44. Use column groups to align the table cells and adjust their widths. Also add row groups to the table.

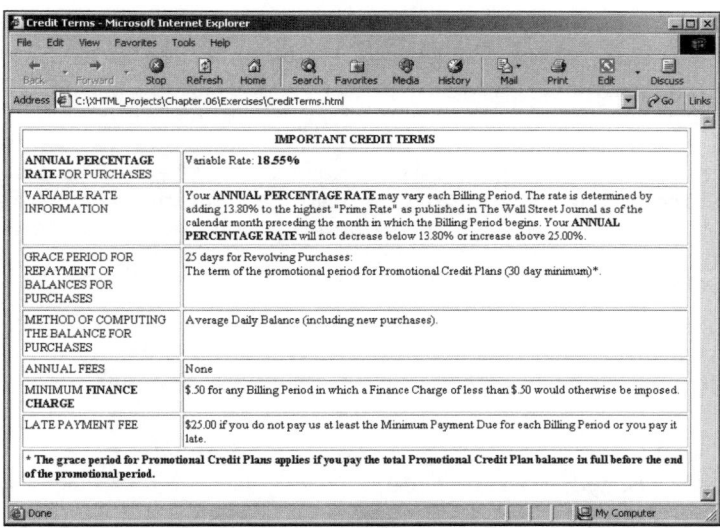

Figure 6-44   Credit terms table

4. Save the file as **CreditTerms.html** in the Chapter.06\Projects folder.

5. Close the **CreditTerms.html** file in your text editor, and then use the W3C Markup Validation Service to validate it. Once the file is valid, open it in your Web browser.

6. Close your Web browser window.

Project 6-7

In this exercise, you use tables to simulate a frameset document for a construction company. The frame simulation tables list information about home styles that the company offers. The tables simulate a two-column frameset. The left frame lists home styles, and the right frame displays an image of the home style along with available features. Your Chapter.06/Projects folder contains three images, chalet.jpg, ranch.jpg, and cottage.jpg that you can use for this exercise.

1. Create a new document in your text editor.

2. Type the `<!DOCTYPE>` declaration, `<html>` element, document head, and `<body>` element. Use the Strict DTD and "Home Styles" as the content of the `<title>` element.

3. Add the following heading elements to the document body.

```
<h1>Central Valley Construction</h1>
<h2>Home Styles</h2>
```

4. Add to the end of the document body the following parent table. The first cell contains a list of home styles. You will add information about each home style to the second cell.

```
<table border="1" frame="hsides" width="100%">
  <colgroup span="1" width="200" />
  <colgroup span="1" align="center" width="400" />
  <tr>
    <td valign="top"><a href="chalet.html">Chalet</a><br />
      <a href="ranch.html">Contemporary Ranch</a><br />
      <a href="cottage.html">Country Cottage</a></td>
    <td>
    </td>
  </tr>
</table>
```

5. Add to the second cell in the parent table the following text and elements for the Chalet style:

```
<img src="chalet.jpg" alt="Image of a chalet"
    height="113" width="200" />
<p><strong>Square feet</strong>: 1305<br />
<strong>Bedrooms</strong>: 3<br />
<strong>Baths</strong>: 2</p>
```

6. Save the file as **Chalet.html** in the Chapter.06\Projects folder, then immediately save it as **Ranch.html** in the Chapter.06\Projects folder.

7. Replace the text and elements for the Chalet style in the parent table's second cell with the following text and elements for the Contemporary Ranch style:

```
<img src="ranch.jpg" alt="Image of a ranch house"
    height="53" width="200" />
<p><strong>Square feet</strong>: 1670<br />
```

```
<strong>Bedrooms</strong>: 4<br />
<strong>Baths</strong>: 3</p>
```

8. Save the **Ranch.html** file, then immediately save it as **Cottage.html** in the Chapter.06\Projects folder.

9. Replace the text and elements for the Contemporary Ranch style in the parent table's second cell with the following text and elements for the Country Cottage style:

```
<img src="cottage.jpg" alt="Image of a cottage"
    height="113" width="200" />
<p><strong>Square feet</strong>: 1240<br />
<strong>Bedrooms</strong>: 2<br />
<strong>Baths</strong>: 1</p>
```

10. Save and close the **Cottage.html** file in your text editor, and then use the W3C Markup Validation Service to validate it along with the Chalet.html and Ranch.html files. Once the files are valid, open one of them in your Web browser and test the links.

11. Close your Web browser window.

Project 6-8

In this exercise, you create a document that contains a definition list of some weather-related terms.

1. Create a new document in your text editor.

2. Type the `<!DOCTYPE>` declaration, `<html>` element, document head, and `<body>` element. Use the Strict DTD and "Weather Terms" as the content of the `<title>` element.

3. Add the following heading elements to the document body.

```
<h1>Weather Terms</h1>
<h2>Definition List</h2>
```

4. Add to the end of the document body the following definition list:

```
<dl>
    <dt><b>Anemometer</b></dt>
    <dd>An instrument that measures the speed or force of
    the wind.</dd>
    <dt><b>Baroclinity</b></dt>
    <dd>The state of stratification in a fluid in which
    surfaces of constant pressure intersect surfaces
    of constant density. </dd>
    <dt><b>Celestial Equator</b></dt>
    <dd>The projection of the plane of the geographical
    equator upon the celestial sphere.</dd>
</dl>
```

5. Save the file as **WeatherTerms.html** in the Chapter.06\Projects folder.

6. Close the WeatherTerms.html file in your text editor, and then use the W3C Markup Validation Service to validate it. Once the file is valid, open it in your Web browser.

7. Close your Web browser window.

CASE PROJECTS

For the following projects, save the files you create in the Chapter.06\Cases folder. Create the files so they are well formed according to the Strict DTD. Be sure to validate the files you create with the W3C Markup Validation Service.

Project 6-1

Create a set of documents that use tables to simulate frames for a metric conversion center Web site. Include pages containing conversion tables for common measurements such as centimeters, inches, miles, kilometers, and so on. One page should present tables for converting from inches to centimeters, another should present tables for converting from gallons to liters, and so on. Use document names that describe the currently displayed conversion table. For instance, the inches to centimeters page should be named InchesToCentimeters.html, the gallons to liters page should be named GallonsToLiters.html, and so on.

Project 6-2

Create a set of documents that use tables to simulate frames for a math tables Web site. Include pages that contain math tables such as multiplication tables, prime number tables, and square root tables. Use document names that describe the currently displayed math table. For instance, the multiplication tables page should be named Multiplication.html, the prime number tables page should be named PrimeNumbers.html, and so on.

Project 6-3

Create a set of documents that use tables to simulate frames for an online photo calendar. The parent table should contain a single row with two cells. The left cell should display a list of links for the twelve months of the year. The right cell should display a calendar created with a table for the currently selected month. Create the first row in the calendar table so it spans all of the other rows in the table and place within it an image that is appropriate for the current month. For instance, the image for April may be some spring flowers. Search the Internet for images you can use for each month. Use the name of the currently displayed month as the document name. For instance, the January document should be named January.html.

Project 6-4

Create a document that contains a list of hyperlinks to your favorite recipes. Clicking each hyperlink should open another document, which then displays the selected recipe. Use unordered lists for the recipe ingredients and ordered lists for the preparation instructions. Name the main document Recipies.html, and name each recipe document according to the recipe name. For example, if you have a recipe for apple pie, name its associated document ApplePie.html.

7

FORMS

In this chapter, you will:

◆ Study <form> elements

◆ Learn about input fields

◆ Use the <button> element

◆ Create selection lists

◆ Create multiline text fields

◆ Learn how to submit form data via e-mail

◆ Create labels, access keys, and field sets

Many Web sites use **forms** to collect information from users and transmit it to a server for processing. Typical forms you may encounter on the Web include order forms, surveys, and applications. Figure 7-1 shows a form that people can use to register a new mailing address with the United States Postal Service.

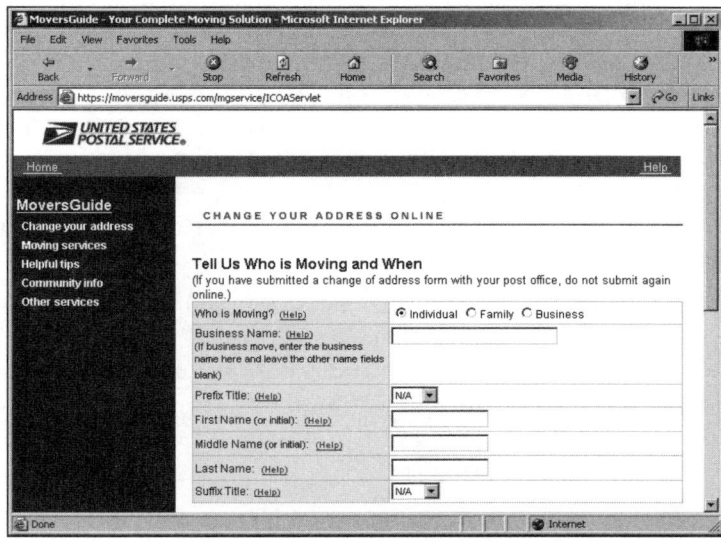

Figure 7-1   United States Postal Service change-of-address form

Another type of form frequently found on Web pages gathers search criteria from a user. After the user enters search criteria, the data is sent to a database on a Web server. The server then queries the database, using the data gathered in the search form, and returns the results to a Web browser. Figure 7-2 shows an example of a form from the Yahoo!Finance Web site that allows you to look up the symbol for a security (an invest-ment). Once you select the market, enter the security, company, or index name whose symbol you want to look up, select the security type, and then click the Search button, the Web server returns the results shown in Figure 7-3.

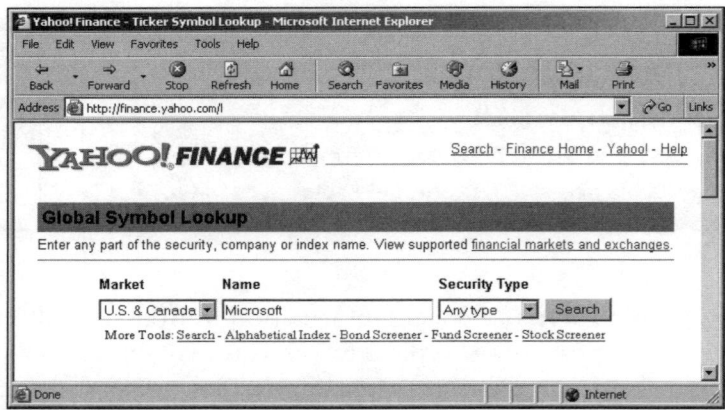

Figure 7-2 Yahoo!Finance Global Symbol Lookup page

Forms are usually set up so that the data collected is transmitted to either a server-side scripting language program on a Web server or to an e-mail address. A **server-side scripting language program** processes data that is transmitted from a form to a server. Some of the more popular server-side scripting languages include Common Gateway Interface (CGI), Active Server Pages (ASP), and Java Server Pages (JSP). The programs you create with server-side scripting languages are called **scripts**. Because the main focus of this book is XHTML, you will not study server-side scripting languages used for pro-cessing form data that is sent to a server. Later in this chapter you will learn how to sub-mit form data to an e-mail address.

Before learning how to submit form data to an-e-mail address, you will submit your forms to a file named FormProcessor.html, located in your Chapter.07\Chapter folder. The FormProcessor.html file uses JavaScript code to display the values submitted from a form. The only purpose of the FormProcessor.html file is to display form data and pro-vide a simple simulation of the response you would normally receive from a program created with a server-side scripting language.

Figure 7-3   Web page returned after clicking the Search button

If you would like to learn about some of the server-side scripting languages you can use to process form data, refer to *Web Warrior Guide to Web Programming*, published by Course Technology. If you would like to learn more about JavaScript programming, refer to *JavaScript, Second Edition*, also published by Course Technology. In addition, the comprehensive edition of this book contains several chapters that discuss JavaScript.

FORM ELEMENTS

You use the following primary elements to create forms in XHTML:

- <form>
- <input>
- <button>
- <select>
- <textarea>
- <label>

With the exception of the <form> element, all of the elements used to create forms are inline elements that must be contained within a block-level element such as the <p> element.

The <form> Element

The **<form> element** designates a form within a Web page and contains all the text and elements that make up a form. You can include as many forms as you like on a Web page, although you cannot nest one form inside another. Table 7-1 lists the attributes you can use with the <form> element.

To help ensure that your Web pages are well formed, you should always type the opening <form> tag and the closing </form> tag at the same time, and then go back and fill in the elements and content that you want to appear in the form.

Table 7-1   Attributes of the <form> element

Attribute	Description
action	Required attribute that specifies a URL to which form data will be submitted. If this attribute is excluded, the data is sent to the URL that contains the form. Typically you would specify the URL of a program on a server or an e-mail address.
method	Determines how form data will be submitted. The two options for this attribute are "get" and "post". The default option, "get", appends form data as one long string to the URL specified by the action attribute. The "post" option sends form data as a transmission separate from the URL specified by the action attribute. Although "get" is the default, "post" is considered the preferred option, because it allows the server to receive the data separately from the URL.
enctype	Specifies the Multipurpose Internet Mail Extensions (MIME) type of the data being submitted. The default value is application/x-www-form-urlencoded.
accept-charset	Specifies a comma-separated list of possible character sets that the form supports.

The **enctype** attribute is important because a server-side scripting program will use its value to determine how to process the form data. The default MIME type of *application/ x-www-form-urlencoded* specifies that form data should be encoded as one long string. The only other MIME types allowed with the **enctype** attribute are multipart/form–data, which encodes each field as a separate section, and text/plain, which is used to upload a file to a Web server or to submit form data to an e-mail address. With the exception of when you submit form data to an e-mail address, you should use the default MIME type of *application/x-www-form-urlencoded*.

Examine the True Aquarium Plants Web page shown in Figure 7-4 to see an example of how to send data to a URL. The document contains a very simple form consisting of a single text box and a button that you use to subscribe to "The Plant Report" newsletter.

Figure 7-4   True Aquarium Plants newsletter subscription page

If you examine the source of the Web page shown in Figure 7-4, you will see code similar to the following that creates the form.

```
<form name="subscribe" action="subscribe.asp" method="post">
<table width="100%" border="0" cellpadding="0" cellspacing="0">
  <tr>
    <td align="center">Subscribe to The Plant Report!<br>
      Your e-mail address:
      <input type="hidden" name="frmaction" value="yes">
...
  </table>
  </form>
```

Notice that the form in the preceding example is contained within a table. Many Web page authors use tables to control the layout of forms on Web pages.

The **<form>** element in the preceding code contains an **action** attribute that sends the form data to the URL *subscribe.asp*, which specifies an ASP script that will process the form data. The **method** attribute of the **<form>** element specifies that the form data will be sent using the **post** method instead of the default **get** method. Because the enctype attribute is omitted, the form data will be encoded with the default *application/ x-www-form-urlencoded* format. Let's assume that a user submits the form using the Subscribe button. After the server receives the data, the *subscribe.asp* script adds the e-mail address to a database, then returns the message shown in Figure 7-5.

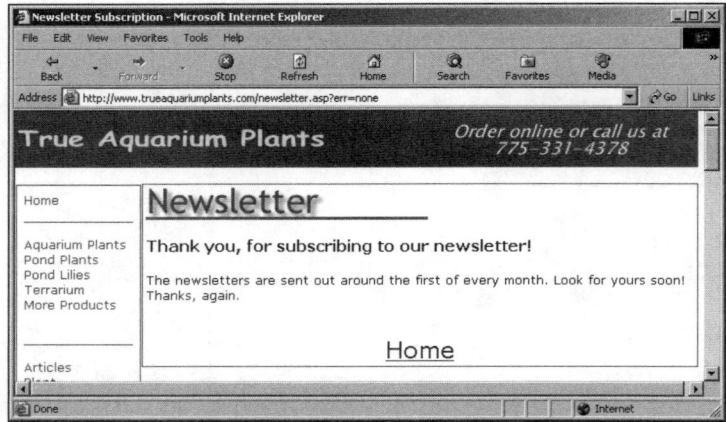

Figure 7-5　Response returned after subscribing to "The Plant Report"

Next, you start creating a similar subscription form for a newspaper called the "Coast City Gazette".

To start creating the Coast City Gazette Subscription form:

1. Start your text editor and create a new document.

2. Type the `<!DOCTYPE>` declaration, `<html>` element, document head, and `<body>` element. Use the Strict DTD and "Coast City Gazette Subscription Form" as the content of the `<title>` element. Your document should appear as follows:

```
<!DOCTYPE html PUBLIC
"-//W3C//DTD XHTML 1.0 Strict//EN"
"http://www.w3.org/TR/xhtml1/DTD/xhtml1-strict.dtd">
<html xmlns="http://www.w3.org/1999/xhtml" lang="en"
xml:lang="en" dir="ltr">
<head>
<title>Coast City Gazette Subscription Form</title>
<meta http-equiv="content-type"
content="text/html; charset=iso-8859-1" />
</head>
<body>
</body>
</html>
```

3. Add the following heading elements to the document body:

```
<h1>Coast City Gazette</h1>
<h2>Newspaper Subscription</h2>
```

4. Add the following two tags to the end of the document body to create the form section. Throughout the following sections of this chapter, you will add form elements between these tags. Notice that the form's `action` attribute submits the form data to the FormProcessor.html file and the `method` attribute submits the form data using the "get" option in order to append the form data as one long string to the FormProcessor.html URL. This will allow the JavaScript code within the FormProcessor.html file to display the data in the Web browser.

```
<form action="FormProcessor.html" method="get"
enctype="application/x-www-form-urlencoded">
</form>
```

5. Save the file as **Subscription.html** in the Chapter.07\Chapter folder. Do not open the Subscription.html file in a Web browser, because it does not yet contain any form elements.

Form Controls

There are four primary elements used within the `<form>` element to create form controls: `<input>`, `<button>`, `<select>`, and `<textarea>`. The `<input>` and `<button>` elements are used to create input fields that users interact with. The `<select>` element displays choices in a drop-down menu or scrolling list known as a selection list. The `<textarea>` element is used to create a text field in which users can enter multiple lines of information. Any form element into which a user can enter data, such as a text box, or that a user can select or change, such as a radio button, is called a **field**.

The `<input>`, `<textarea>`, and `<select>` elements can include `name` and `value` attributes. The `name` attribute defines a name for an element, and the `value` attribute defines a default value. When you submit a form to a Web server, the form data is submitted in name=value pairs, based on the `name` and `value` attributes of each tag. For example, for a text `<input>` field created with the statement `<input type="text" name="company_info" value="ABC Corp.">`, a name=value pair of *company_info=ABC Corp.* will be sent to a Web server (unless the user types something else into the field). If you intend to submit your form to a Web server, you must include a `name` attribute for each `<input>`, `<textarea>`, and `<select>` element.

You are not required to include a `value` attribute or enter a value into a field before the form data is submitted.

How form controls render depends on the type of Web browser as well as operating system. You may notice differences in how form controls appear between Windows and Macintosh operating systems and between different versions of the same operating system. For instance, there is a noticeable difference in how form controls render in Windows 2000 and how they render in Windows XP. The figures in this chapter were generated using Internet Explorer 6 running on Windows 2000.

INPUT FIELDS

The empty `<input>` element is used to create **input fields** that create different types of interface elements to gather information. Table 7-2 lists common attributes of the `<input>` element.

Table 7-2   Common attributes of the `<input>` element

Attribute	Description
alt	Provides alternate text for an image submit button
checked	Determines whether or not a radio button or a check box is selected; a Boolean attribute
maxlength	Accepts an integer value that determines the number of characters that can be entered into a field
name	Designates a name for the element; part of the name=value pair that is used to submit data to a Web server
size	Accepts an integer value that determines how many characters wide a text field is
src	Specifies the URL of an image
type	Specifies the type of element to be rendered; `type` is a required attribute. Valid values are text, password, radio, checkbox, reset, button, submit, image, file, and hidden
value	Sets an initial value in a field or a label for buttons; part of the name=value pair that is used to submit data to a Web server

One of the most important attributes of the `<input>` element is the `type` attribute, which determines the type of element to be rendered and is a required attribute. Valid values for the `type` attribute are text, password, radio, checkbox, reset, button, submit, image, file, and hidden. You will study each of these elements next.

Text Boxes

An `<input>` element with a type of *text* (`<input type="text">`) creates a simple **text box** that accepts a single line of text. You can include the `name`, `value`, `maxlength`, and `size` attributes with the `<input type="text">` element. When you include the `value` attribute in a text `<input>` element, the specified text is used as the default value when the form first loads, as shown in Figure 7-6.

```
<form action="FormProcessor.html" method="get">
<p>Name<br />
<input type="text" name="name"
    value="The White House" size="50" /></p>
<p>Address<br />
<input type="text" name="address"
    value="1600 Pennsylvania Ave." size="50" /></p>
<p>City, State, Zip<br />
<input type="text" name="city"
    value="Washington" size="38" />
<input type="text" name="state"
    value="DC" size="2" maxlength="2" />
<input type="text" name="zip"
    value="20500" size="5" maxlength="5" /></p>
</form>
```

Figure 7-6 Form with several text `<input>` elements

Next, you add text `<input>` elements to the Subscription form that collect basic customer data.

To add form text `<input>` elements to the subscription:

1. Return to the **Subscription.html** file in your text editor.

2. Within the `<form>` element, add the following text `<input>` elements, which gather a customer's name, address, city, state, zip, and e-mail address:

```
<p>Name<br />
<input type="text" name="customer_name" size="50" /><br /></p>
<p>Address<br />
<input type="text" name="address" size="50" /></p>
<p>City, State, Zip<br />
<input type="text" name="city" size="34" />
```

```
<input type="text" name="state" size="2" maxlength="2" />
<input type="text" name="zip" size="5" maxlength="5" /></p>
<p>E-Mail<br />
<input type="text" name="email" size="50" /></p>
```

3. Save the **Subscription.html** file and then open it in your Web browser. The text `<input>` elements you entered should appear as shown in Figure 7-7.

Figure 7-7 Subscription form after adding text `<input>` elements

4. Close your Web browser window.

Password Boxes

An `<input>` element with a type of *password* (`<input type="password">`) creates a **password box** that is used for entering passwords or other types of sensitive data. Each character that a user types in a password box appears as an asterisk or bullet, depending on the operating system and Web browser, in order to hide it from anyone who may be looking over the user's shoulder. You can include the `name`, `value`, `maxlength`, and `size` attributes with the `<input type="password">` element. The following code creates a password box with a maximum length of eight characters. Figure 7-8 shows how the password box appears in a Web browser after entering some characters.

```
<form action="FormProcessor.html" method="get"
enctype="application/x-www-form-urlencoded">
<p>Please enter a password of 8 characters or less:<br />
<input type="password" name="password" maxlength="8" /></p>
</form>
```

Figure 7-8   Password box in a Web browser

Next, you add a password `<input>` element to the Subscription.html file that prompts users to enter a password that they use to manage their subscriptions online.

To add a password `<input>` element to the Subscription.html file:

1. Return to the **Subscription.html** file in your text editor.

2. After the last `<input>` element, add the following lines for the password `<input>` element, which prompts users for a password:

```
<p>Enter a password that you can use to manage your subscription
online<br />
<input type="password" name="password" size="50" /></p>
```

3. Save the **Subscription.html** file, and then open it in your Web browser. Test the password field to see if the password you enter appears as asterisks or bullets. Figure 7-9 shows how the form appears in a Web browser after typing a password.

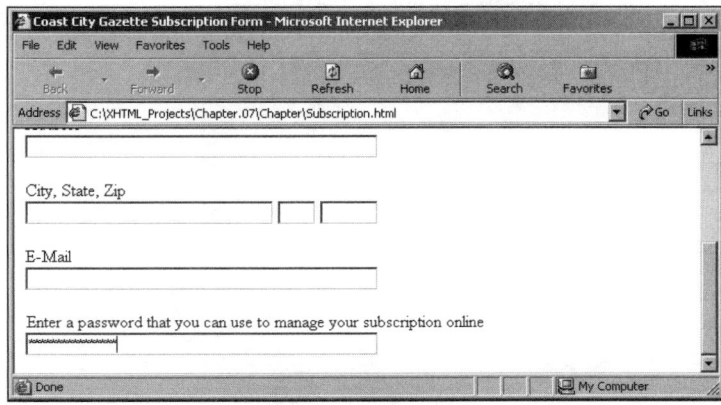

Figure 7-9   Subscription form after adding a password `<input>` element

4. Close your Web browser window.

Radio Buttons

An <input> element with a type of *radio* (`<input type="radio">`) is used to create a group of **radio buttons**, or **option buttons**, from which you can select only one value. To create a group of radio buttons, all radio buttons in the group must have the same **name** attribute. Each radio button requires a **value** attribute. Only one selected radio button in a group creates a name=value pair when a form is submitted to a Web server. You can also include the **checked** attribute in a radio <input> element to select an initial value for a group of radio buttons. If the **checked** attribute is not included in any of the <input type="radio"> elements in a radio button group, then none of the buttons in the group are selected when the form loads. The following code creates a group of five radio buttons. Because the "18–34" radio button includes the **checked** attribute, it will be selected when the form first loads. Figure 7-10 shows how the radio buttons appear in a Web browser.

```
<form action="FormProcessor.html" method="get"
enctype="application/x-www-form-urlencoded">
<p>Please select your age range:<br />
<input type="radio" name="age_range"
      value="Under 18" />Under 18<br />
<input type="radio" name="age_range"
      value="18-30" checked="checked" />18-30<br />
<input type="radio" name="age_range"
      value="31-45" />31-45<br />
<input type="radio" name="age_range"
      value="46-64" />46-64<br />
<input type="radio" name="age_range"
      value="65 and older" />65 and older</p>
</form>
```

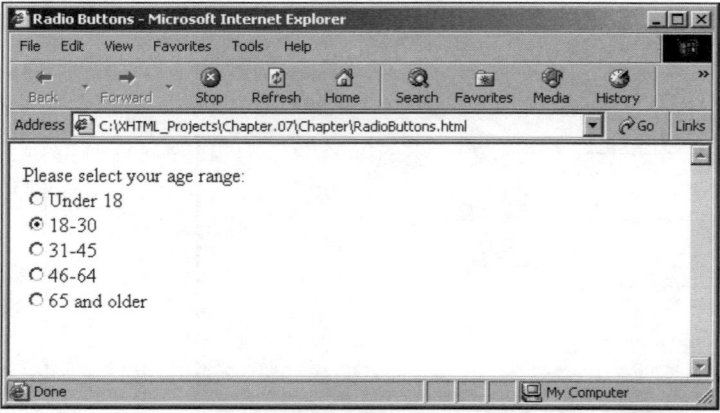

Figure 7-10   Form with radio buttons

Next, you add radio buttons to the Subscription.html file that allow users to select their desired delivery option. The radio buttons you add are created within a table to make it easier to align the radio buttons on the page.

 Recall from Chapter 6 that the W3C discourages using tables for document layout because tables can be difficult for non-visual user agents, such as Braille and speech devices, to interpret. Instead, the W3C encourages the use of CSS for document layout. However, it's much easier to lay out forms using tables, so the recommendation of the W3C is largely ignored.

To add radio buttons to the Subscription.html file:

1. Return to the **Subscription.html** file in your text editor.

2. After the password `<input>` element, add the following `<p>` element along with the opening `<table>` element and the table's header information:

```
<p>Delivery Rates</p>
<table border="0" cellpadding="3" cellspacing="0">
<colgroup align="left" width="100" />
<colgroup span="4" align="center" width="100" />
<tr><th> </th>
<th>4 weeks</th>
<th>13 weeks</th>
<th>26 weeks</th>
<th>52 weeks</th></tr>
```

3. Next, add the following table row elements that include payment options for delivery Monday through Saturday. Notice that each radio button's `name` attribute is assigned the same name of "delivery" so that the radio buttons are part of the same group.

```
<tr><td><b>Mon-Sat</b></td>
<td><input type="radio" name="delivery"
    value="12.60" />$12.60</td>
<td><input type="radio" name="delivery"
    value="40.95" />$40.95</td>
<td><input type="radio" name="delivery"
    value="81.90" />$81.90</td>
<td><input type="radio" name="delivery"
    value="156.00" />$156.00</td></tr>
```

4. Next, add the following table row elements that include payment options for delivery every day of the week:

```
<tr><td><b>Every Day</b></td>
<td><input type="radio" name="delivery" value="13.56"
/>$13.56</td>
<td><input type="radio" name="delivery" value="44.07"
/>$44.07</td>
<td><input type="radio" name="delivery" value="88.14"
/>$88.14</td>
```

```
<td><input type="radio" name="delivery" value="159.74"
/>$159.74</td></tr>
```

5. Type the closing **</table>** tag.

6. Save the **Subscription.html** file, and then open it in your Web browser. Test the radio buttons to see if you can select only a single button at a time. Figure 7-11 shows how the radio buttons appear in a Web browser.

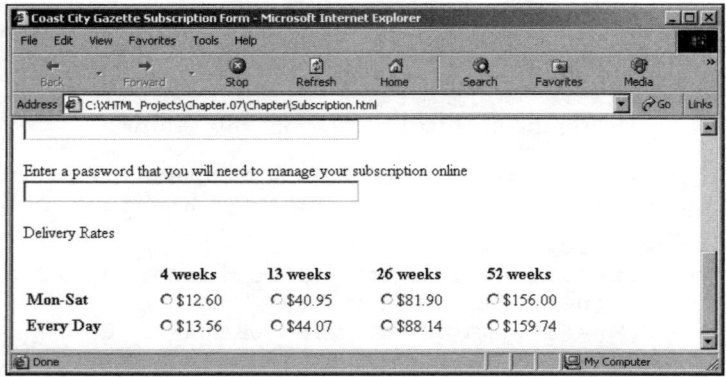

Figure 7-11   Subscription form after adding radio buttons

7. Close your Web browser window.

Check Boxes

An **<input>** element with a type of *checkbox* (**<input type="checkbox">**) creates a box that can be set to yes (checked) or no (unchecked). You use **check boxes** when you want users to select whether or not to include a certain item or to allow users to select multiple values from a list of items. Include the Boolean **checked** attribute in a checkbox **<input>** element to set the initial value of the check box to *yes*. You can also include the **name** and **value** attributes with the checkbox **<input>** element. If a check box is selected (checked) when a form is submitted, then the check box name=value pair is included in the form data. If a check box is not selected, a name=value pair will not be included in the data submitted from the form.

The following code creates several check boxes. Note that the Science Fiction check box will be checked when the form first loads because it includes the **checked** attribute. Figure 7-12 shows how the check boxes appear in a Web browser.

```
<form action="FormProcessor.html" method="get"
enctype="application/x-www-form-urlencoded">
<h3>What type of books do you like to read?</h3>
<p><input type="checkbox" name="books"
    value="fiction" />Fiction<br />
```

```
<input type="checkbox" name="books"
    value="science_fiction" checked="checked" />Science
Fiction<br />
<input type="checkbox" name="books"
    value="romance" />Romance<br />
<input type="checkbox" name="books"
    value="mysteries" />Mysteries</p>
</form>
```

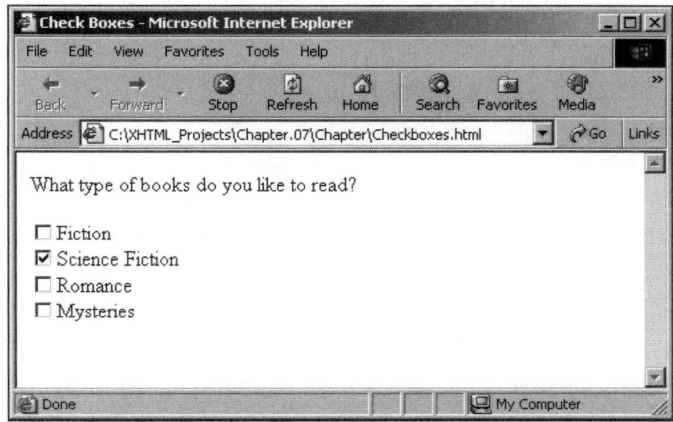

Figure 7-12   Form with check boxes

Like radio buttons, you can group check boxes by giving each check box the same name value, although each check box can have a different value. Unlike radio buttons, users can select as many check boxes in a group as they like. When multiple check boxes on a form share the same name, then multiple name=value pairs, each using the same name, are submitted to a Web server. In the preceding example, if the Fiction and Romance check boxes are selected, then two name=value pairs, books=fiction and books=romance, are submitted. Note that you are not required to group check boxes with the same **name** attribute. Although a common group name helps identify and manage groups of check boxes, it is often easier to keep track of individual values when each check box has a unique **name** attribute.

Next, you add check boxes to the Subscription.html file that allow users to select any other newspapers to which they are currently subscribed.

To add check boxes to the Subscription.html file:

1. Return to the **Subscription.html** file in your text editor.

2. After the closing </table> tag, add the following checkbox elements:

```
<p>Do you subscribe to any other newspapers?</p>
<p><input type="checkbox" name="newspapers"
    value="nytimes" />The New York Times<br />
```

```
<input type="checkbox" name="newspapers"
    value="bostonglobe" />The Boston Globe<br />
<input type="checkbox" name="newspapers"
    value="sfchronicle" />San Francisco Chronicle<br />
<input type="checkbox" name="newspapers"
    value="miamiherald" />The Miami Herald<br />
<input type="checkbox" name="newspapers"
    value="other" />Other</p>
```

3. Save the **Subscription.html** file, and then open it in your Web browser. Figure 7-13 shows how the check boxes appear in a Web browser.

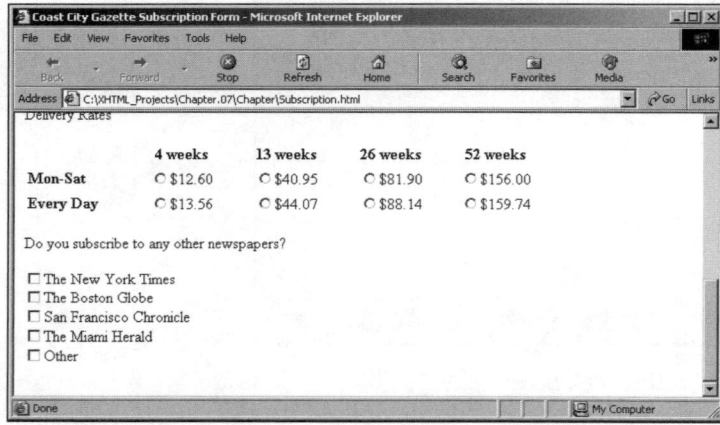

Figure 7-13   Subscription form after adding check boxes

4. Close your Web browser window.

Reset Buttons

An **<input>** element with a type of *reset* (**<input type="reset">**) creates a **reset button** that clears all form entries and resets each form element to the initial value specified by its **value** attribute. Although you can include the **name** attribute for a reset button, it is not required because reset buttons do not have values that are submitted to a Web server as part of the form data. The text you assign to the reset button's **value** attribute will appear as the button label. If you do not include a **value** attribute, then the default label of the reset button, *Reset*, appears. The width of a button created with the reset **<input>** element depends on the number of characters in its **value** attribute.

The following code creates a form with a reset button. Figure 7-14 shows the resulting Web page after entering some data.

```
<h3>Billing Information</h3>
<form action="FormProcessor.html" method="get"
enctype="application/x-www-form-urlencoded">
```

```
<p><b>Name</b><br />
<input type="text" name="name" size="50" /></p>
<p><b>Address</b><br />
<input type="text" name="address" size="50" /></p>
<p><b>City, State, Zip</b><br />
<input type="text" name="city" size="34" />
<input type="text" name="state" size="2" maxlength="2" />
<input type="text" name="zip" size="5" maxlength="5" /></p>
<p><b>Credit Card</b><br />
<input type="radio" name="creditcard" checked="checked" />VISA
<input type="radio" name="creditcard" />MasterCard
<input type="radio" name="creditcard" />American Express<br />
<input type="radio" name="creditcard" />Discover
<input type="radio" name="creditcard" />Diners Club</p>
<p><b>Credit Card Number</b><br />
<input type="text" name="cc" size="50" /></p>
<p><b>Expiration Date</b><br />
<input type="text" name="expdate" size="50" /></p>
<p><input type="reset" /></p>
</form>
```

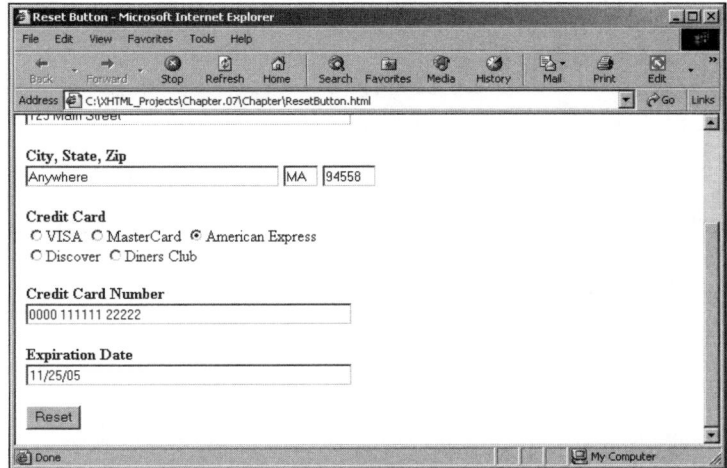

Figure 7-14   Form with a reset button

If you click the reset button in the form shown in Figure 7-14, the content of each field clears or resets to its default value, as shown in Figure 7-15.

Next, you add a reset button to the Subscription.html file.

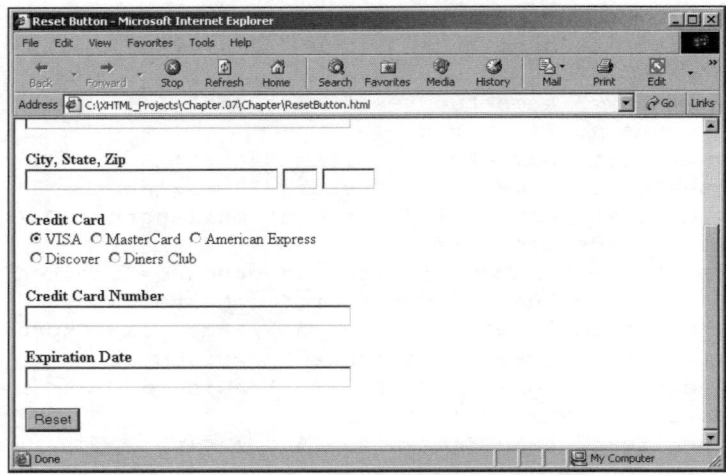

Figure 7-15   Form after clicking the Reset button

To add a reset button to the Subscription.html file:

1. Return to the **Subscription.html** file in your text editor.

2. After the last checkbox **<input>** element, add the following elements to create the reset button:

   ```
   <p><input type="reset" /></p>
   ```

3. Save the **Subscription.html** file, and then open it in your Web browser. Enter some data in the form's fields and test the reset button to see how it works. Figure 7-16 shows how the reset button appears in a Web browser.

Figure 7-16   Subscription form after adding a reset button

4. Close your Web browser window.

Push Buttons

An `<input>` element with a type of *button* (`<input type="button">`) creates a **push button** that is similar to the OK and Cancel buttons you see in dialog boxes. Push buttons are also similar to submit and reset buttons. However, push buttons do not submit form data to a Web server as submit buttons do, nor do they clear the data entered into form fields as reset buttons do. Instead, push buttons execute JavaScript code that performs some type of function, such as a calculation. Because the main purpose of a push button is to execute JavaScript code, they are essentially useless unless you know how to use JavaScript. (JavaScript programming is discussed in the comprehensive edition of this book.)

Push buttons are also called command buttons.

You can use the `name` and `value` attributes with a push button `<input>` element. The text you assign to a push button's `value` attribute is the text that will appear on the button face. The width of a push button created with the `<input type="button">` element is based on the number of characters in its `value` attribute.

You are not required to include the `name` and `value` attributes, because a user cannot change the value of a push button. If you include the `name` and `value` attributes, then the default value set with the `value` attribute is transmitted to a Web server along with the rest of the form data. The following code creates a push button that uses JavaScript code to display a simple dialog box:

```
<p><input type="button" name="push_button"
    value="Click Here"
    onClick="alert('You clicked a push button');" /></p>
```

The code for the `<input>` element creates a button with a value of *Click Here* and a name of *push_button*. As shown in Figure 7-17, if you click the push button, you will see a dialog box containing the text *You clicked a push button*.

Figure 7-17   A push button in a Web browser

Submit Buttons

An `<input>` element with a type of *submit* (`<input type="submit">`) creates a **submit button** that transmits a form's data to a Web server. The `action` attribute of the `<form>` element that creates the form determines to what URL the form is submitted. You can include the `name` and `value` attributes with the submit `<input>` element, the same as with a push button `<input>` element. The width of a button created with the submit `<input>` element is based on the number of characters in its `value` attribute. If you do not include a `value` attribute, then the default label of the submit button, *Submit Query*, appears.

The following code creates a Web page with a submit button:

```
<h1>DVD of the Month Club</h1>
<h3>Select the types of movies you like to see and
click the Join button.<br />
A new movie will be sent to you every month.</h3>
<form action="FormProcessor.html" method="get"
enctype="application/x-www-form-urlencoded">
<p><input type="checkbox" name="genre" value="action" />
Action<input type="checkbox" name="genre" value="adventure" />
Adventure<br />
<input type="checkbox" name="genre" value="comedy" />
Comedy
<input type="checkbox" name="genre" value="drama" />
Drama<br />
<input type="checkbox" name="genre" value="sci_fi" />
Science Fiction
<input type="checkbox" name="genre" value="western" />
Westerns</p>
<p><input type="submit" name="submit_button" value="Join" /></p>
</form>
```

Next, you add a submit button to the Subscription.html file.

To add a submit button to the Subscription.html file:

1. Return to the **Subscription.html** file in your text editor.

2. Before the reset `<input>` element's closing paragraph tag, add the following elements to create the submit button:

```
<p><input type="reset" />
<input type="submit" value="Subscribe" /></p>
```

3. Save the **Subscription.html** file, and then open it in your Web browser. Figure 7-18 shows how the subscription button appears in a Web browser.

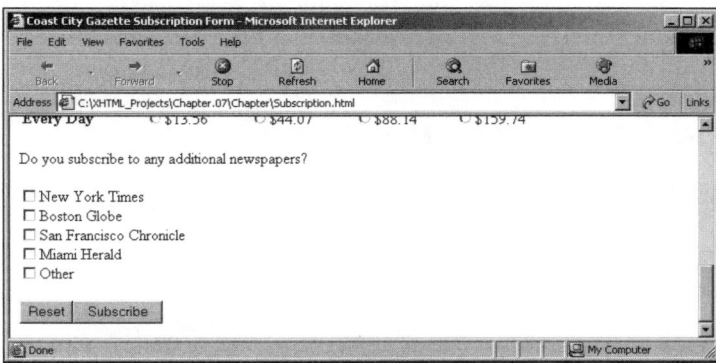

Figure 7-18   Subscription form after adding a submit button

4. Fill in the form fields and then click the **Subscribe** button. The FormProcessor.html file should open and display the data you entered. Notice in your Web browser's address bar that a question mark and the form data have been appended to the Web page's URL. This is how form data is sent to a server when the `method` attribute is assigned a value of "get". When the `method` attribute is assigned a value of "post", the form data is sent to the Web server as a separate transmission. Figure 7-19 shows how the FormProcessor.html file appears in a Web browser.

5. Close your Web browser window.

Image Submit Buttons

An `<input>` element with a type of *image* (`<input type="image">`) creates an **image submit button** that displays a graphical image and transmits a form's data to a Web server. The image `<input>` element performs the same function as the submit `<input>` element. You include the `src` attribute to specify the image to display on the button. You can also include the `name` and `value` attributes with the image `<input>` element, with the `alt` attribute to define alternate text for user agents that do not display images. The following code creates the Web page with an image `<input>` element shown in Figure 7-20. Notice that the image `<input>` element also includes the `alt` attribute.

Figure 7-19   FormProcessor.html after submitting the Subscription form

```
<h1>DVD of the Month Club</h1>
<h3>Select the types of movies you like to see and
click the image.<br />
A new movie will be sent to you every month.</h3>
<form action="FormProcessor.html" method="get"
enctype="application/x-www-form-urlencoded">
<p><input type="checkbox" name="genre" value="action" />
Action<input type="checkbox" name="genre" value="adventure" />
Adventure<br />
<input type="checkbox" name="genre" value="comedy" />
Comedy
<input type="checkbox" name="genre" value="drama" />
Drama<br />
<input type="checkbox" name="genre" value="sci_fi" />
Science Fiction
<input type="checkbox" name="genre" value="western" />
Westerns</p>
<p><input type="image" alt="Graphical image of a movie camera"
src="camera.jpg" /></p>
</form>
```

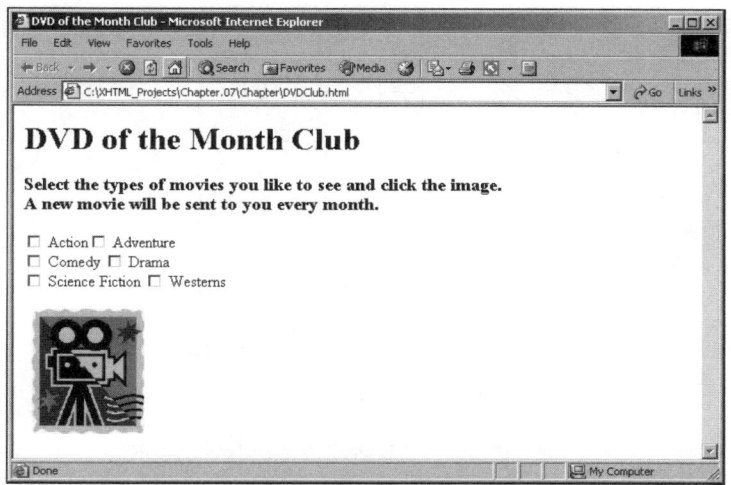

Figure 7-20   Form with an image `<input>` element

Image `<input>` elements are also used to create server-side image maps, which are similar to the client-side image map you created in Chapter 3. The primary difference between server-side and client-side image maps is that with server-side image maps, most of the work is done on the server; for client-side image maps, most of the work is done in a Web browser.

File Boxes

An `<input>` element with a type of *file* (`<input type="file">`) creates a **file box**, which is a text box control along with a push button labeled with "Browse..." that you can use to upload a file to a Web server. You can type either the drive, folder, or filename you want to upload directly into the text box or search for the file on your computer by clicking the Browse button. This is the same control on the W3C MarkUp Validation Service's upload page that you have used thus far to validate your documents. A `<form>` element that contains a file box control must assign a value of "post" to its `action` attribute and "multipart/form-data" to its `enctype` attribute. The following code shows an example of a form with a file box that a job candidate might use to upload his or her resume to an employer's Web site. Figure 7-21 shows how the form appears in a Web browser.

```
<h2>Resume Submission Form</h2>
<form action="FormProcessor.html" method="get"
enctype="multipart/form-data">
<p>Please attach your resume and press the Submit button.<br />
<input type="file" />
<input type="submit" value="Submit" /></p>
</form>
```

Figure 7-21   Form with a file `<input>` element

You can use the `value` attribute to specify the default name of a file to include in the file box, although most current browsers ignore this attribute for security reasons. If you use the `value` attribute with a file `<input>` element, a persistent hacker could find some way to access files on the computer of a visitor to your Web site without his or her knowledge.

Hidden Form Fields

A special type of form element, called a **hidden form field**, allows you to hide information from users. You create hidden form fields with the `<input>` element. A Web browser does not display hidden form fields. Hidden form fields temporarily store data that needs to be sent to a server along with the rest of a form, but that a user does not need to see. Examples of data stored in hidden fields include the result of a calculation or some other type of information that a program on the Web server might need. You create hidden form fields using the same syntax used for other fields created with the `<input>` element: `<input type="hidden">`. The only attributes that you can include with a hidden form field are the `name` and `value` attributes.

As an example of a hidden form field, you may have a form that a script on a Web server processes. Once the script processes the form fields, you want it to send the results to an e-mail address (probably your own) that is contained within the form. However, you do not want everyone who accesses the form to view your private e-mail address. Therefore, you could place your e-mail address in a hidden form field, as follows:

```
<form action="FormProcessor.html" method="get"
enctype="application/x-www-form-urlencoded">
...form fields...
<input type="hidden" name="email"
    value="your_email_address@domain.com" />
<input type="submit" /></p>
</form>
```

Remember that although you may place a hidden form field on your Web page, it is never visible within a browser that renders the page. In other words, visitors to the Web page that contains the preceding elements never see the hidden form field containing the e-mail address rendered on the Web page. However, visitors to the Web page can view the default value assigned to a hidden form field by viewing the source file.

THE <button> ELEMENT

Because the <input> element is an empty element, you must use the **value** attribute to define the text that appears as the label for push buttons, submit buttons, and reset buttons. Instead of using the <input> element, you can use the **<button> element** to create push buttons, submit buttons, and reset buttons. Table 7-3 lists the attributes of the <button> element.

Table 7-3   Attributes of the <button> element

Attribute	Description
name	Designates a name for the button.
type	Specifies the button type to be rendered. Valid values are submit, reset, and button.
value	Assigns a value that will be submitted to a Web server.

You specify the type of button to create by assigning the appropriate value to the **type** attribute. The buttons you create with the <button> element are virtually identical to the buttons you create with the <input> element. The big difference, however, is that you create the <button> element using an opening and closing tag pair, which allows more flexibility in the labels you can create for a button. You can include the **name** and **value** attributes with the <button> element, the same as with the submit <input> element and the push button <input> element. However, the value you assign to the **value** attribute is not used as the button's label (although it will be sent to the Web server as part of the control's name=value pair). Instead, the content placed within the <button> element tag pair determines the button label. You can embed an <img> element within the <button> tag or use text formatting and phrase elements to modify the appearance of the text that appears as a button's label. For instance, the following code uses the <strong> element to add emphasis to the label in a <button> element and adds an <img> element to the button label. Figure 7-22 shows how the button appears in a Web browser.

```
<form action="FormProcessor.html" method="get"
enctype="application/x-www-form-urlencoded">
<p><button type="button">Click for <strong>Flight
Information</strong><br /><br />
<img src="airplane.gif" alt="Graphical image of an airplane." />
</button></p>
</form>
```

7

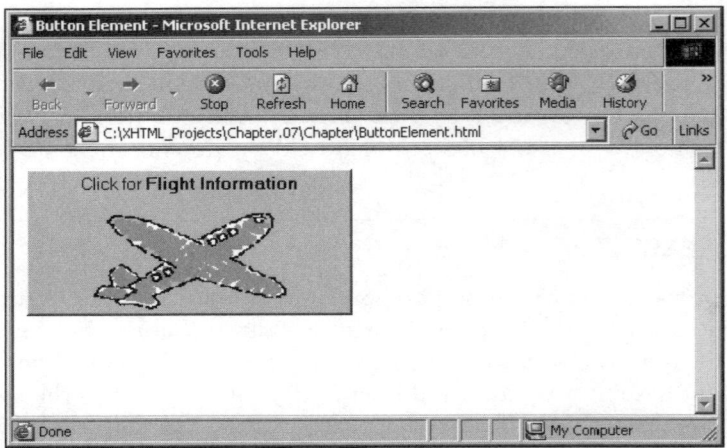

Figure 7-22   Button created with the `<button>` element

Next, you modify the Subscription.html file's reset and submit buttons so they are created with the `<button>` element instead of the `<input>` element. The Chapter.07\Chapter folder contains two image files, Eraser.gif and Newspaper.gif, that you use to create the reset and submit buttons.

To modify the Subscription.html file's reset and submit buttons:

1. Return to the **Subscription.html** file in your text editor.

2. Replace the `<p>` and `<input>` elements that make up the reset button with the following `<button>` element.

   ```
   <p><button type="reset"><strong>Reset Form</strong><br /><br />
   <img src="eraser.gif" alt="Graphical image of an eraser." />
   </button>
   ```

3. Next, replace the `<p>` and `<input>` elements that make up the submit button with the following `<button>` element.

   ```
   <button type="submit"><strong>Subscribe</strong><br /><br />
   <img src="newspaper.gif" alt="Graphical image of a newspaper on a
   doorstep." />
   </button></p>
   ```

4. Save the **Subscription.html** file, and then open it in your Web browser. Figure 7-23 shows how the buttons appear. Enter some data in the form fields and test the Reset Form button. Enter some data again and click the Subscribe button. The data you entered should display in the FormProcessor.html document.

5. Close your Web browser window.

Figure 7-23   Subscription form after adding <button> elements

SELECTION LISTS

The **<select> element** creates a **selection list** that presents users with fixed lists of items from which to choose. The items displayed in a selection list are created with <option> elements, which you will study next. As with other form elements that create controls, the **<select>** element must appear within a block-level element such as the **<p>** element. The selection list can appear as an actual list of choices or as a drop-down menu. Depending on the number of items in the list, a selection list can also include a scroll bar. Table 7-4 lists frequently used attributes of the **<select>** element.

Table 7-4   Attributes of the <select> element

Attribute	Description
multiple	Specifies whether a user can select more than one item from the list; a Boolean attribute
name	Designates a name for the selection list
size	Determines how many lines of the selection list appear

Like other form controls, the **<select>** element includes a **name** attribute that is submitted to a Web server. However, the value portion of a **<select>** element's name=value pair will be the value assigned to an item that is created with the **<option>** element (which you study next). If a **<select>** element includes the Boolean **multiple** attribute, which specifies whether a user can select more than one item from the list, and a visitor selects more than one item in the list, then multiple name=value pairs for the **<select>** element are submitted with the form. Each instance of a **<select>** element's name=value pair includes a value assigned to one of the selected list items created with the **<option>** element.

The `size` attribute designates how many lines of the selection list appear when the form renders in a Web browser. If this attribute is excluded or set to one, then the selection list is a drop-down style menu. You see examples of the `size` and `multiple` attributes in the next section.

Menu Options

You use **`<option>` elements** to specify the items that appear in a selection list. The content of an `<option>` element appears as a menu item in a selection list. Table 7-5 lists the attributes of the `<option>` element.

Table 7-5   Attributes of the `<option>` element

Attribute	Description
label	Designates alternate text to display in the selection list for an individual option
selected	Determines if an item is initially selected in the selection list when the form first loads; a Boolean attribute
value	Specifies the value submitted to a Web server

You place `<option>` elements as the contents of a `<select>` element to specify the selection list's menu options. Each selection list must contain at least one `<option>` element. For example, the following code creates two selection lists. Figure 7-24 shows the code in a Web browser. Notice that the "West Indian Manatee" option is the selected value in the first list. Also notice that because the second list's `<select>` element includes the `multiple` attribute, you can select multiple options, as shown in the figure.

```
<h1>U.S. Fish and Wildlife Service</h1>
<h2>Threatened and Endangered Florida Species</h2>
<form action="FormProcessor.html" method="get"
enctype="application/x-www-form-urlencoded">
<h3>Mammals and Birds</h3>
<p><select name="mammals_birds">
<option value="panther">Florida Panther</option>
<option selected="true" value="manatee">West Indian
Manatee</option>
<option value="jay">Florida Scrub Jay</option>
<option value="sparrow">Cape Sable Seaside Sparrow</option>
</select></p>
<h3>Reptiles and Amphibians</h3>
<p><select multiple="true" name="species" size="3">
<option value="alligator">American Alligator</option>
<option value="sea_turtle">Hawksbill Sea Turtle</option>
<option value="salamander">Flatwoods Salamander</option>
</select></p>
</form>
```

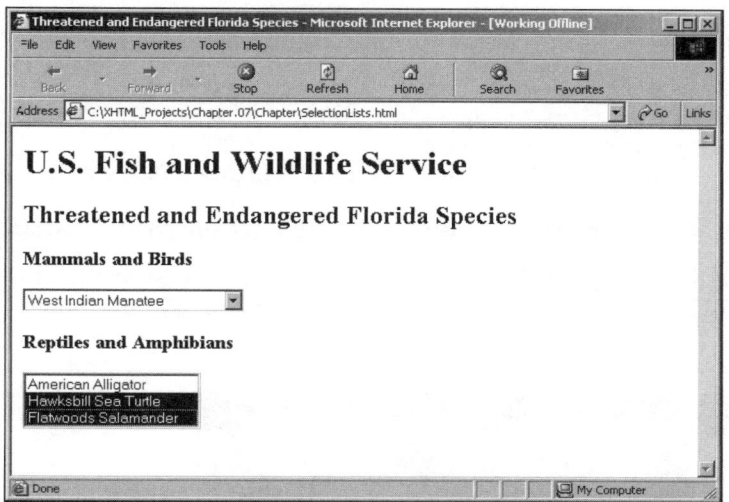

Figure 7-24 Two selection lists

The `label` attribute of the `<option>` element allows you to specify alternate text to appear as the menu item in a selection list. When an `<option>` element includes a `label` attribute, a user agent is supposed to render its value as the menu item in the selection list, although most current Web browsers ignore this requirement.

Next, you add a selection list and some text `<input>` elements to the Subscription.html file that a subscriber uses to enter payment information.

To add a selection list to the Subscription.html file:

1. Return to the **Subscription.html** file in your text editor.

2. Above the opening `<p>` tag for the reset `<button>` element, add the following elements to create the selection list:

```
<p>Payment Method<br />
<select name="payment">
<option value="check">Check</option>
<option value="moneyorder">Money Order</option>
<option value="visa">Visa</option>
<option value="mastercard">MasterCard</option>
<option value="amex">American Express</option>
<option value="discover">Discover</option>
<option value="dinersclub">Diners Club</option>
</select></p>
```

3. After the closing `</p>` tag that follows the closing `</select>` tag, add the following text `<input>` elements for the subscriber's credit card information:

```
<p>Name as it appears on credit card<br />
<input type="text" name="cc_name" size="50" /><br /></p>
<p>Credit card number<br />
<input type="text" name="cc_num" size="50" /><br /></p>
<p>Expiration date<br />
<input type="text" name="expires" size="50" /><br /></p>
```

4. Save the **Subscription.html** file, and then open it in your Web browser. Figure 7-25 shows how the selection list appears in a Web browser after you open it.

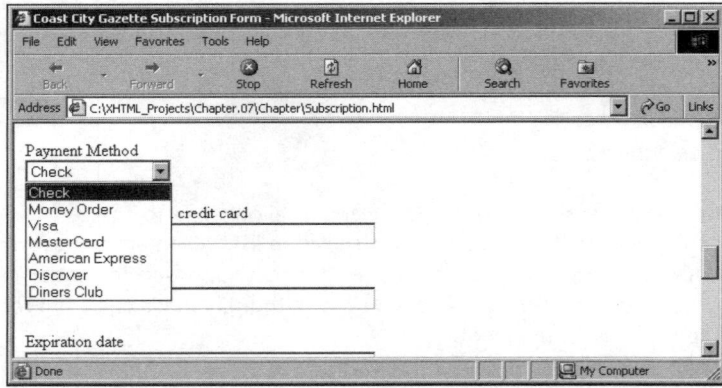

Figure 7-25   Subscription form after adding a selection list

5. Close your Web browser window.

Option Groups

You use the **<optgroup> element** to create **option groups** that organize groups of option elements that appear in a selection list. Option groups are not widely supported in older browsers, so be sure to use them only for Web pages that you are sure will only be opened in a current browser or higher. (At the time of this writing, Internet Explorer 6 and Netscape 6 are considered to be the most current Web browsers.) The `<optgroup>` element includes two attributes: `disabled` and `label`. The optional Boolean `disabled` attribute disables an option group, whereas the required `label` attribute defines the heading that will identify a specific option group. You nest the `<option>` elements that are part of an option group within the `<optgroup>...</optgroup>` tag pair. For example, the following code combines the two threatened and endangered Florida species lists and organizes them according to animal type. Figure 7-26 shows how the combined selection list appears in a Web browser.

```
<h1>U.S. Fish and Wildlife Service</h1>
<h2>Threatened and Endangered Florida Species</h2>
<form action="FormProcessor.html" method="get"
enctype="application/x-www-form-urlencoded">
<p><select name="species" size="12">
<optgroup label="Mammals">
<option value="panther">Florida Panther</option>
<option selected="true" value="manatee">West Indian
Manatee</option>
</optgroup>
<optgroup label="Birds">
<option value="jay">Florida Scrub Jay</option>
<option value="sparrow">Cape Sable Seaside Sparrow</option>
</optgroup>
<optgroup label="Reptiles">
<option value="alligator">American Alligator</option>
<option value="sea_turtle">Hawksbill Sea Turtle</option>
</optgroup>
<optgroup label="Amphibians">
<option value="salamander">Flatwoods Salamander</option>
</optgroup>
</select></p>
</form>
```

Figure 7-26   Selection list organized by option groups

Next, you add a single option group to the payment method selection list in the
Subscription.html file that contains the credit card names.

To add an option group to the payment method selection list:

1. Return to the **Subscription.html** file in your text editor.

2. Modify the selection list as follows so the credit card names are contained within an <optgroup> element with a label of "Credit Cards":

```
<p><select name="payment">
<option value="check">Check</option>
<option value="moneyorder">Money Order</option>
<optgroup label="Credit Cards">
<option value="visa">Visa</option>
<option value="mastercard">MasterCard</option>
<option value="amex">American Express</option>
<option value="discover">Discover</option>
<option value="dinersclub">Diners Club</option>
</optgroup>
</select></p>
```

3. Save the **Subscription.html** file and then open it in your Web browser. Figure 7-27 shows how the selection list appears in a Web browser after you open it.

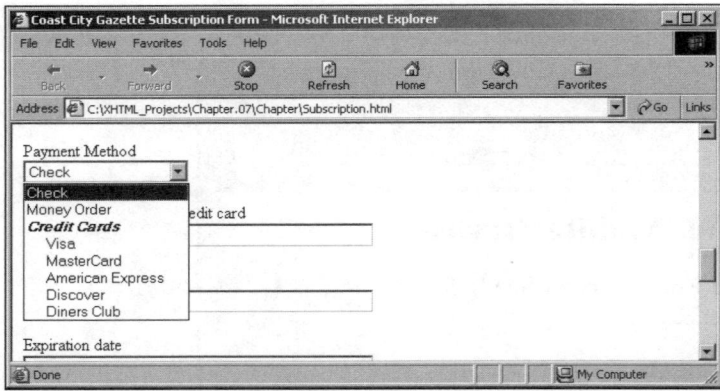

Figure 7-27   Payment Method selection list after adding an option group

4. Close your Web browser window.

MULTILINE TEXT FIELDS

The <textarea> element is used to create a field in which users can enter multiple lines of information. Fields created with <textarea> elements are known as **multiline text fields** or **text areas**. Table 7-6 lists the attributes of the <textarea> element.

Table 7-6   Attributes of the `<textarea>` element

Attribute	Description
name	Designates a name for the text area
col	Specifies the number of columns to be displayed in the text area
rows	Specifies the number of rows to be displayed in the text area
name	Designates a name for the text area

You can create the `<textarea>` element either as an empty element or using the `<textarea>...</textarea>` tag pair. The only items you include within a `<textarea>...</textarea>` tag pair are default text and characters you want to display in the text area when the form loads. Any characters placed between the `<textarea>...</textarea>` tags, including tab marks and paragraph returns, will be displayed as the text area default value. For example, a line of text that is indented with two tabs and placed between the `<textarea>...</textarea>` tags will be indented with two tabs when it appears in the text area on the Web page. Any XHTML elements you place within a `<textarea>` element will be rendered as plain text within the text area. Note that any text displayed in a text area when a form is submitted will be part of the control's name=value pair.

The following elements create a text area control consisting of 50 columns and 10 rows, with the default text of *Enter additional information here*. Figure 7-28 shows the output in a Web browser.

```
<form action="FormProcessor.html" method="get"
enctype="application/x-www-form-urlencoded">
<h3>Comments</h3>
<p><textarea cols="50" rows="10">
Enter additional information here
</textarea></p>
</form>
```

Next, you add a text area element to the Subscription.html file that subscribers can use to provide directions to their home or special delivery instructions.

To add a text area element to the Subscription.html file:

1. Return to the **Subscription.html** file in your text editor.

2. Above the opening `<p>` tag for the reset `<button>` element, add the following elements to create the text area:

```
<p>Directions or special instructions<br />
<textarea name="directions" cols="50" rows="10">
Enter directions to your home or any special instructions.
</textarea></p>
```

Figure 7-28   Text area control

     3. Save the **Subscription.html** file and then open it in your Web browser. Figure 7–29 shows how the text area appears in a Web browser.

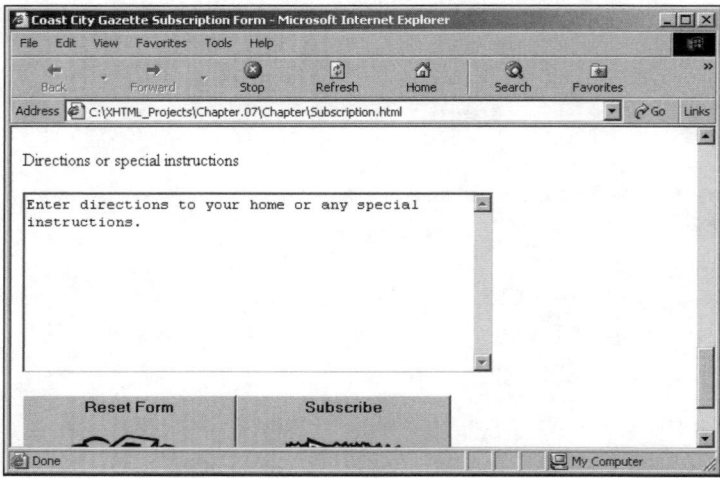

Figure 7-29   Subscription form after adding a text area

     4. Close your Web browser window.

E-MAILING FORM DATA

In most of the forms you have seen so far, the form is set up so that the data collected is transmitted to a Web server. Instead of submitting form data to a Web server, you can set up a form to send data to an e-mail address. Sending form data to an e-mail address is a much simpler process than creating and managing a script on a Web server. Instead of relying on a complex script on a Web server to process the data, you rely on the recipient of the e-mail message to process the data. For instance, a Web site may contain an online order form for some type of product. After the user clicks the Submit button, the data for the order can be sent to the e-mail address of whomever is responsible for filling the order. For large organizations that deal with hundreds or thousands of orders a day, e-mailing each order to a single individual is not an ideal solution. But, for smaller companies or Web sites that do not have a high volume of orders, e-mailing form data is a good solution.

To e-mail form data, you replace the Web server script's URL in the `<form>` element's `action` attribute with `mailto:email_address`. You add the mailto protocol and any optional mailto properties to the URL, the same as when you added it to an anchor element in Chapter 3. For instance, the following code generates an RSVP form for a fictitious wedding-planning company. The form's data is e-mailed to a fictitious e-mail address, rsvp@CentralValleyWeddings.com. Notice that the `mailto` attribute is placed at the start of the URL, separated by a colon, and that the optional subject property is appended to the end of the URL with a question mark. Figure 7-30 shows the form in a Web browser.

```
<h1>Jose and Melinda's Wedding</h1>
<h2>RSVP Form</h2>
<p><strong>Please send your reply by 3/15/2005.</strong></p>
<form action="mailto:rsvp@CentralValleyWeddings.com?subject=RSVP"
    method="post" enctype="text/plain">
<h3>Your Name</h3>
<p><input type="text" size="50" /></p>
<p><input type="radio" name="attending"
    value="yes" />Will attend<br />
<input type="radio" name="attending"
    value="no" />Will not</p>
<p><input type="hidden" name="wedding" value="Jose and Melinda"
/></p>
<p><button type="reset">Reset</button>
<button type="submit">RSVP</button></p>
</form>
```

Notice that the preceding code includes a hidden element that stores the name of the couple having the wedding.

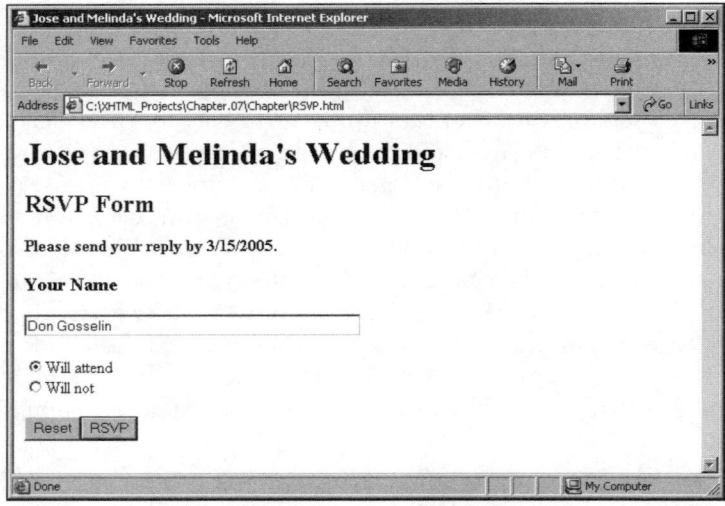

Figure 7-30   RSVP form

When you send form data to an e-mail address, use the **enctype** of *text/plain*. The **enctype** of *text/plain* ensures that the data arrives at the e-mail address in a readable format. Figure 7-31 shows an example of the e-mail message received by rsvp@CentralValleyWeddings.com after the form generated by the preceding code is submitted. The e-mail message appears in Microsoft Outlook.

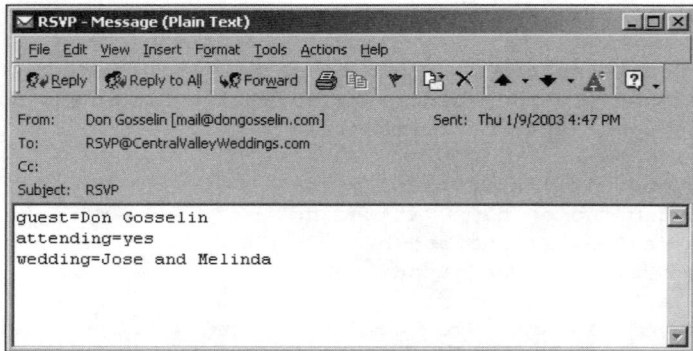

Figure 7-31   Data e-mailed from a form

The drawback to e-mailing form data is that some older Web browsers do not support the **mailto:***email_address* option with the **<form>** element **action** attribute. In addition, the performance of the mailto:*email_address* option is unreliable. Some Web browsers that support the e-mailing of form data do not properly place the data within the body of an e-mail message. If you write a Web page that e-mails form data, be sure to test it thoroughly before using it.

Data that is transferred between Web browsers and Web servers cannot include spaces or certain special characters such as a percent sign (%). When you transmit data, most Web browsers will convert spaces to plus signs (+) and special characters into their equivalent hexadecimal American Standard Code for Information Interchange (ASCII) values, preceded by a percent sign. Hexadecimal ASCII is a special code for representing English characters as numbers. For example, 25 is the hexadecimal ASCII equivalent of a percent sign (%). Most e-mail programs, including Microsoft Outlook, will convert the plus signs back into spaces and any hexadecimal ASCII values back into their character equivalents. However, some e-mail programs do not perform this conversion. If you see any plus symbols or hexadecimal ASCII characters in data that is e-mailed from a form, then your e-mail program does not automatically perform this conversion. You will either need to write a special program to perform the conversion or use a different e-mail program.

 When users click the Submit button for a form that is e-mailed, they may receive a security warning or be given a chance to edit the e-mail, depending on how their e-mail application is configured.

Next, you change the `<form>` element of the Subscription form so that the form data is sent to your e-mail address whenever it is submitted.

To change the Subscription form so that the form data is sent to your e-mail address:

1. Return to the **Subscription.html** file in your text editor.

2. Modify the opening `<form>` element as follows; be sure to replace *email_address* with your own e-mail address:

   ```
   <form action="mailto:email_address" method="post"
   enctype="text/plain">
   ```

3. Save the **Subscription.html** file, and then open it in your Web browser. Fill in the form fields, and then submit it. Depending on your e-mail configuration, you may receive warning dialog boxes or be given a chance to edit the e-mail message.

4. Wait several minutes before retrieving the new message from your e-mail, because transmission time on the Internet can vary. After you receive the e-mail, examine the message to see how the form data appears.

5. Close your Web browser window.

LABELS, ACCESS KEYS, AND FIELD SETS

In this section, you learn how to make the controls on your forms more accessible by using labels and access keys. You also learn how to visually organize your controls with field sets.

Labels

So far, the labels you have created for your form controls have consisted of text that is unrelated to the control itself. In other words, the text that describes the control is in no way associated with the control itself, other than that it happens to appear next to the control when it renders in a browser. In other types of programming languages, the label for a control is actually part of the control itself. This allows you to select the control by clicking the control's label instead of clicking the control itself. In XHTML, you use the **<label> element** to associate a label with a form control. You can associate a particular <label> element with only one form control. The content of the <label> element appears as the label for a control. You can include other elements, such as the **<strong>** and **<em>** elements, within the <label> element to modify the appearance of the label. In addition to allowing you to select controls by clicking a label, the <label> element allows you to select and deselect controls such as check boxes by clicking the control label. Another benefit of the <label> element is that it provides control descriptions to non-visual browsers, helping ensure that a Web page is compatible with the widest number of user agents.

You can use two attributes with the <label> element: **accesskey** and **for**. You learn about the **accesskey** attribute later in this section. You use the **for** attribute to associate a <label> element with a target form control. You assign to the **for** attribute the same value that is assigned to the target control's **id** attribute. Throughout this chapter, you have used only **name** attributes with your form controls. But in order to associate a label with a form control, the control must include an **id** attribute. The following code shows an example of the White House form you saw earlier. This time each **<input>** element includes a **<label>** element. In addition, each form control now includes an **id** attribute that is assigned the same value as the control's **name** attribute. Note that you are not required to assign the same value to the **name** and **id** attributes. In fact, if you want to associate a **<label>** element with a particular radio button or check box that is assigned the same **name** value as other radio buttons or check boxes that are part of the same group, you must assign a unique value to the control's **id** property in order for the code to be valid. However, for controls that have a unique value assigned to their **name** attributes, you can safely use the same value for the control's **id** attribute.

```
<form action="FormProcess.html" method="get"
enctype="application/x-www-form-urlencoded">
<p><label for="name">Name</label><br />
<input type="text" name="name" id="name"
    value="The White House" size="50" /></p>
<p><label for="address">Address</label><br />
<input type="text" name="address" id="address"
    value="1600 Pennsylvania Ave." size="50" /></p>
<p><label for="city">City</label>, <label
for="state">State</label>, <label for="zip">Zip</label><br />
<input type="text" name="city" id="city"
    value="Washington" size="30" />
```

```
<input type="text" name="state" id="state"
    value="DC" size="2" maxlength="2" />
<input type="text" name="zip" id="zip"
    value="20500" size="5" maxlength="5" /></p>
</form>
```

For a document with a form to be valid, a `<label>` element must either include a `for` attribute or contain as a nested element the form control with which it is associated. The following code shows the first two controls of the White House form nested within their associated `<label>` elements.

```
<form action="FormProcess.html" method="get"
enctype="application/x-www-form-urlencoded">
<p><label>Name<br />
<input type="text" name="name" id="name"
    value="The White House" size="50" /></label></p>
<p><label for="address">Address<br />
<input type="text" name="address" id="address"
    value="1600 Pennsylvania Ave." size="50" /></label></p>
...
```

Next, you add `<label>` elements to controls in the Subscription form. To keep the exercise simple, you add `<label>` elements only for the name, address, city, state, zip, e-mail, and password controls.

To add `<label>` elements to controls in the Subscription form:

1. Return to the **Subscription.html** file in your text editor.

2. Modify the name, address, city, state, zip, e-mail, and password controls as follows so they include `<label>` elements. The code you need to add is in boldface. Be sure to add `id` attributes to each of the `<input>` elements.

```
<p><label for="customer_name">Name</label><br />
<input type="text" name="customer_name" id="customer_name"
size="50" /><br /></p>
<p><label for="address">Address</label><br />
<input type="text" name="address" id="address"
size="50" /></p>
<p><label for="city">City</label>, <label
for="state">State</label>, <label for="zip">Zip</label><br />
<input type="text" name="city" id="city" size="34" />
<input type="text" name="state" id="state" size="2"
maxlength="2" />
<input type="text" name="zip" id="zip" size="5"
maxlength="5" /></p>
<p><label for="email">E-Mail</label><br />
<input type="text" name="email" id="email" size="50" /></p>
<p><label for="password">Enter a password that you can use to
manage your subscription online</label><br />
<input type="password" id="password" name="password" size="50"
/></p>
```

3. Save the **Subscription.html** file, and then open it in your Web browser. The labels for the `<input>` elements should appear the same as they did before you added the `<label>` elements.

4. Close your Web browser window.

Access Keys

All of the form control elements, with the exception of the `<select>` element, can also include the **accesskey attribute**, which designates a key that visitors to your Web site can press to jump to a control, or select and deselect a control such as a check box. You assign to the `accesskey` attribute the keyboard character that you want to use as a control's access key. How you execute an access key depends on the platform on which the Web browser is running. On Windows systems, you select an access key by holding down the Alt key and simultaneously pressing the access key. On Macintosh systems, you select an access key by holding down the Control key and simultaneously pressing the access key. For instance, if you assign an access key of 'W' to a control, you can access the control by pressing Alt+W on a Windows system or Control+W on a Macintosh system. The following code shows access keys assigned to the first two elements in the White House form:

```
<form action="FormProcess.html" method="get"
enctype="application/x-www-form-urlencoded">
<p><label for="name">Name</label><br />
<input type="text" name="name" id="name" accesskey="N"
    value="The White House" size="50" /></p>
<p><label for="address">Address</label><br />
<input type="text" name="address" id="address" accesskey="A"
    value="1600 Pennsylvania Ave." size="50" /></p>
. . .
```

Be sure not to assign to a form control an access key that is already used by the Web browser. For instance, the access key that opens the File menu in Internet Explorer running on a Windows platform is 'f'. If you assign 'f' as an access key to one of your form controls, then the control's access key overrides the File menu's 'f' access key. You can tell what access keys are assigned to a Web browser menu by holding down your Alt key and examining the menu names. Each menu's access key appears as an underlined letter in the menu name.

Access keys are not case sensitive.

The <label> element can also be assigned an access key, which either jumps to the label's associated control or selects and deselects controls such as a check box. One benefit to assigning access keys to <label> elements is they allow you to assign an access key to a <select> element, which cannot use the accesskey attribute on its own. Note that in order to assign an access key for a control to its label, the <label> element must include the for attribute. The following code shows access keys assigned to the first two <label> elements in the White House form:

```
<form action="FormProcess.html" method="get"
enctype="application/x-www-form-urlencoded">
<p><label for="name" accesskey="N">Name</label><br />
<input type="text" name="name" id="name"
    value="The White House" size="50" /></p>
<p><label for="address" accesskey="A">Address</label><br />
<input type="text" name="address" id="address"
    value="1600 Pennsylvania Ave." size="50" /></p>
...
```

Regardless of whether you assign an access key directly to a control or to its associated <label> element, you should identify the access key for Web page visitors. Windows platforms use underscores to identify access keys. However, in Web page authoring, you should not use underscores or underlines because visitors to your Web site may confuse them with links. An alternative is to use an element such as <strong> to make the access key stand out, as shown in the following code for the first two elements of the White House form. Figure 7-32 shows the form in a Web browser.

```
<form action="FormProcess.html" method="get"
enctype="application/x-www-form-urlencoded">
<p><label for="name"
accesskey="N"><strong>N</strong>ame</label><br />
<input type="text" name="name" id="name"
    value="The White House" size="50" /></p>
<p><label for="address"
accesskey="A"><strong>A</strong>ddress</label><br />
<input type="text" name="address" id="address"
    value="1600 Pennsylvania Ave." size="50" /></p>
...
```

Access keys are of somewhat limited use due to the mouse-oriented nature of Web pages. With long or complex forms, you may find it counterproductive to assign access keys to every control on the form. Therefore, you may want to consider using access keys only on short or simple forms, or where they would be of most benefit. In this chapter's Subscription form, access keys would be useful for helping users select the check boxes for any newspapers to which they already have subscriptions.

Next, you add <label> elements and access keys to the check boxes in the Subscription form.

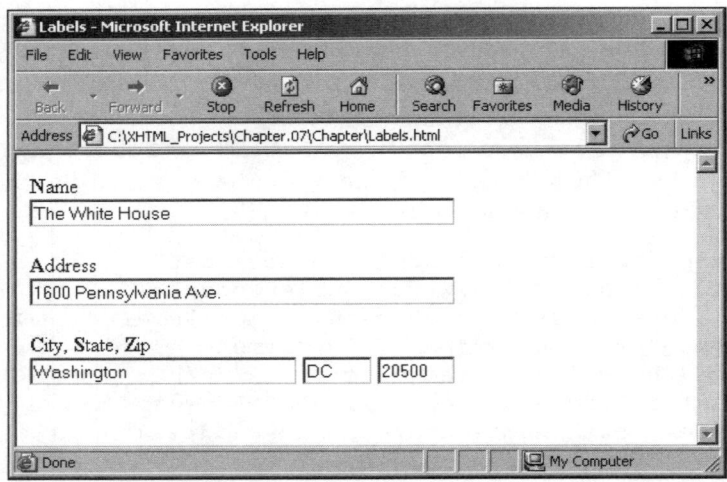

Figure 7-32   Form with access keys

To add `<label>` elements and access keys to the check boxes in the Subscription form:

1. Return to the **Subscription.html** file in your text editor.

2. Modify the checkbox `<input>` elements as follows so they include `<label>` elements and **accesskey** attributes. The code you need to add is identified in boldface. Also add `<strong>` elements to identify the access key for each control. Notice that new `id` attributes have been added to the `<input>` elements. Because all of the checkbox `<input>` elements have the same value ("newspapers") assigned to their `name` attributes, each `id` attribute is assigned a unique name in order to clearly identify with which control each `<label>` element should be associated.

```
<p><input type="checkbox" name="newspapers" id="nyt"
    value="nytimes" /><label for="nyt" accesskey="n">The
<strong>N</strong>ew York Times</label><br />
<input type="checkbox" name="newspapers" id="bg"
    value="bostonglobe" /><label for="bg" accesskey="b">The
<strong>B</strong>oston Globe</label><br />
<input type="checkbox" name="newspapers" id="sfc"
    value="sfchronicle" /><label for="sfc"
accesskey="s"><strong>S</strong>an Francisco Chronicle</label><br
/>
<input type="checkbox" name="newspapers" id="mh"
    value="miamiherald" /><label for="mh" accesskey="m">The
<strong>M</strong>iami Herald</label><br />
<input type="checkbox" name="newspapers" id="ot"
    value="other" /><label for="ot"
accesskey="o"><strong>O</strong>ther</label></p>
```

3. Save the **Subscription.html** file, and then open it in your Web browser. Test the access keys for the newspaper check boxes. Also, try clicking the label for each check box to see if it selects and deselects the associated check box control. The check boxes should appear the same, except that the access key for each control should appear bold.

4. Close your Web browser window.

Field Sets

A time may arise when you want to clearly identify controls in a form as being part of the same group. You can use a **field set** to visually group related controls on a form. A field set draws a box around a group of controls. You create a field set by nesting a group of related controls within the **<fieldset>** element. The first element in a **<fieldset>** must be a **<legend> element**, which provides a caption or description for the group of controls.

 Like option groups, field sets are not widely supported in older browsers, so be sure to use them only for Web pages that you are sure will only be opened in a current browser or higher.

The following code shows how to place a group of check boxes within a field set that is identified by the caption "What type of books do you like to read?". Figure 7-33 shows the field set in a Web browser.

```
<fieldset>
<legend>What type of books do you like to read?</legend>
<p><input type="checkbox" name="books"
    value="fiction" />Fiction<br />
<input type="checkbox" name="books"
    value="science_fiction" checked="checked" />
    Science Fiction<br />
<input type="checkbox" name="books"
    value="romance" />Romance<br />
<input type="checkbox" name="books"
    value="mysteries" />Mysteries<br /></p>
</fieldset>
```

The radio buttons for the Subscription form's delivery rates would be easier to read if they were part of the same field set. Therefore, you now add a field set to the delivery rate radio buttons in the Subscription form.

To add a field set to the delivery rate radio buttons:

1. Return to the **Subscription.html** file in your text editor.

7

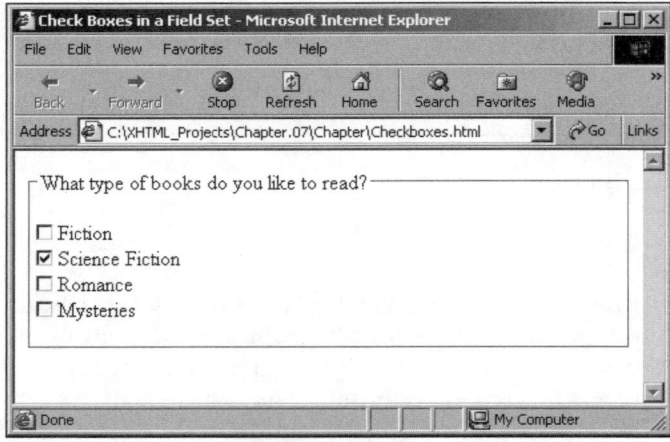

Figure 7-33   Check boxes in a field set

2. Replace the `<p>Delivery Rates</p>` statement that starts the delivery rates radio button group with the following `<fieldset>` and `<legend>` elements:

```
<fieldset>
<legend>Delivery Rates</legend>
```

3. Add a closing `</fieldset>` tag after the closing `</table>` tag.

4. Save and close the **Subscription.html** file, and then open it in your Web browser. Figure 7-34 shows how the radio buttons appear in the field set.

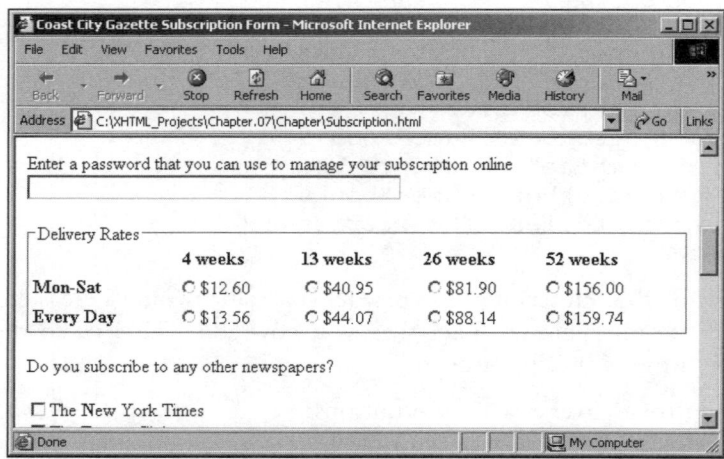

Figure 7-34   Field set added to the Subscription form

Finally, you validate the Subscription.html file.

To validate the Subscription.html file:

1. Start your Web browser and enter the URL for the upload page of the W3C MarkUp Validation Service: **validator.w3.org/file-upload.html**.

2. Open and validate the **Subscription.html** file. If you receive any errors, fix them, and then revalidate the document.

3. Close your Web browser window, text editor, and e-mail program.

CHAPTER SUMMARY

7

❏ Forms are used to collect information from users and transmit that information to a server for processing.

❏ Server-side scripts process data that is transmitted from a form to a server.

❏ The <form> element designates a form within a Web page and contains all text and elements that make up a form.

❏ Any form element into which a user can enter data, such as a text box, or that a user can select or change, such as a radio button, is called a field.

❏ The empty <input> element is used to create different types of input fields that gather information.

❏ An <input> element with a type of *text* (<input type="text">) creates a simple text box that accepts a single line of text.

❏ An <input> element with a type of *password* (<input type="password">) creates a password box that is used for entering passwords or other sensitive data.

❏ An <input> element with a type of *radio* (<input type="radio">) is used to create a group of radio buttons, or option buttons, from which you can select only one value.

❏ An <input> element with a type of *checkbox* (<input type="checkbox">) creates a check box that allows users to specify whether or not to include a certain item or allows users to select multiple values from a list of items.

❏ An <input> element with a type of *reset* (<input type="reset">) creates a reset button that clears all form entries and resets each form element to its initial value specified by the value attribute.

❏ An <input> element with a type of *button* (<input type="button">) creates a push button that is similar to the OK and Cancel buttons you see in dialog boxes.

❏ An <input> element with a type of *submit* (<input type="submit">) creates a submit button that transmits a form's data to a Web server.

❏ An <input> element with a type of *image* (<input type="image">) creates an image submit button that displays a graphical image and transmits a form's data to a Web server.

❑ An <input> element with a type of *file* (<input type="file">) creates a file box, which is a text box control and a push button labeled with "Browse" that you can use to upload a file to a Web server.

❑ An <input> element with a type of *hidden* (<input type="hidden">) creates a special type of form element, called a hidden form field, which allows you to hide information from users.

❑ You can also use the <button> element to create push buttons, submit buttons, and reset buttons.

❑ The <select> element creates a selection list that presents users with fixed lists of values from which to choose.

❑ You use <option> elements to specify the menu items that appear in a selection list.

❑ You use the <optgroup> element to create option groups that organize groups of option elements that appear in a selection list.

❑ The <textarea> element is used to create a multiline text field, or text area, in which users can enter multiple lines of information.

❑ Instead of submitting form data to a Web server, another option is to send the form data to an e-mail address.

❑ You use the <label> element to associate a label with a form control.

❑ The accesskey attribute designates a key that Web site visitors can press to jump to a control or to select and deselect a control such as a check box.

❑ A field set draws a box around a group of controls.

❑ You create a field set by nesting a group of related controls within the <fieldset> element.

❑ The first element in a <fieldset> must be a <legend> element, which provides a caption or description for the group of controls.

REVIEW QUESTIONS

1. Explain how forms are used on Web pages.

2. Which of the following are server-side scripting languages? (Choose all that apply.)

   a. Common Gateway Interface (CGI)

   b. Active Server Pages (ASP)

   c. Java Server Pages (JSP)

   d. Extensible Markup Language (XML)

3. Which of the following are block-level elements? (Choose all that apply.)

   a. `<form>`

   b. `<input>`

   c. `<select>`

   d. `<textarea>`

4. You can nest one form inside another form. True or False?

5. What is the default value of the `<form>` element's `enctype` attribute?

   a. text/plain

   b. multipart/form-data

   c. application/x-www-form-urlencoded

   d. image/gif

6. Describe the two ways in which form data can be submitted to a Web server.

7. In what form is form data submitted to a Web server?

   a. in value,name pairs

   b. in name=value pairs

   c. as values separated by commas

   d. as values separated by paragraph marks

8. The text `<input>` element _____.

   a. displays a static label

   b. creates input fields that use different types of interface elements to gather information

   c. creates a simple text box that accepts a single line of text

   d. creates either a submit or a reset button

9. The `size` attribute is used with the _____ `<input>` element.

   a. button

   b. image

   c. text

   d. submit

10. Each character entered into a text box created with a password `<input>` element appears _____.

   a. with the ampersand (&) symbol

   b. with the number (#) symbol

   c. as a percentage (%)

   d. as an asterisk (*)

11. Which attribute is used to designate a single button in a radio group as the default?

    a. `checked`

    b. `check`

    c. `selected`

    d. `default`

12. Which of the following statements about check boxes is true?

    a. You can select only one check box in a group at a time.

    b. You can select as many check boxes as necessary.

    c. When you select one check box, all other check boxes in the same group are also selected.

    d. Check boxes are not used for user input.

13. What is the purpose of the reset `<input>` element?

    a. to reload the current Web page

    b. to reset the contents of a single form element to its default value

    c. to reset all form elements in the current form to their default values

    d. to close and restart the Web browser

14. What type of `<input>` element creates a push button similar to the OK and Cancel buttons found in dialog boxes?

    a. radio

    b. ok_cancel

    c. dialog

    d. button

15. What is the default value of a submit button label?

    a. Submit

    b. Query

    c. Submit Query

    d. Execute

16. Which type of elements can be used to submit form data to a Web server? (Choose all that apply.)

    a. image `<input>` element

    b. radio `<input>` element

    c. submit `<input>` element

    d. submit `<button>` element

17. The contents of a selection list are determined by which element?

 a. `<select>`

 b. `<contents>`

 c. `<items>`

 d. `<option>`

18. Which is the correct syntax for creating a text area?

 a. `<text cols="50" rows="10">default text</text>`

 b. `<textarea cols="50" rows="10">default text</textarea>`

 c. `<text size="50">default text</text>`

 d. `<textarea size="50">default text</textarea>`

19. Explain the benefits of using a `<label>` element to associate a label with a form control.

20. The first element in a `<fieldset>` must be a `<legend>` element. True or False?

HANDS-ON PROJECTS

For the following exercises that require the FormProcessor.html file, a copy of the file is saved in your Chapter.07\Projects folder.

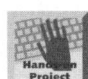

Project 7-1

In this exercise, you create a contact information form for an online company that sells patio furniture.

1. Create a new document in your text editor.

2. Type the `<!DOCTYPE>` declaration, `<html>` element, document head, and `<body>` element. Use the Strict DTD and "Contact Us" as the content of the `<title>` element.

3. Add to the document body the following heading elements.

```
<h1>Coast City Patio Furniture</h1>
<h2>Contact Us</h2>
```

4. Add to the end of document body the following `<form>` element that submits the form to the FormProcessor.html file:

```
<form action="FormProcessor.html" method="get"
enctype="application/x-www-form-urlencoded">
</form>
```

5. Add to the `<form>` element that following `<input>` and `<textarea>` fields. The text `<input>` fields are created in a table to make it easier to lay them out on the page.

```
<table width="100%">
<colgroup span="1" width="100" />
<tr><td>Name</td><td><input type="text" size="75" name="name"
/></td></tr>
<tr><td>Address</td><td><input type="text" size="75"
name="address" /></td></tr>
<tr><td>City</td><td><input type="text" size="75" name="city"
/></td></tr>
<tr><td>State</td><td><input type="text" size="75" name="state"
/></td></tr>
<tr><td>Zip</td><td><input type="text" size="75" name="zip"
/></td></tr>
<tr><td>Telephone</td><td><input type="text" size="75"
name="phone" /></td></tr>
</table>
<p>Question or comment<br />
<textarea rows="6" cols="70">Enter your question or comment
here</textarea></p>
```

6. Add the following reset and submit buttons using `<input>` elements:

```
<p><input type="reset" /><input type="submit" /></p>
```

7. Save the file as **ContactUs.html** in the Chapter.07\Projects folder.

8. Close the **ContactUs.html** file in your text editor, and then use the W3C Markup Validation Service to validate it. Once the file is valid, open it in your Web browser. Test the form and submit the data to the FormProcessor.html file.

9. Close your Web browser window.

Project 7-2

In this exercise, you create an airline survey form.

1. Create a new document in your text editor.

2. Type the `<!DOCTYPE>` declaration, `<html>` element, document head, and `<body>` element. Use the Strict DTD and "Airline Survey" as the content of the `<title>` element.

3. Create the airline survey form shown in Figure 7-35. Design the form using a table and `<input>` elements to create the radio buttons. The `<input>` elements in each row of radio buttons should be assigned the same **name** attribute in order for them to be part of the same group. Assign the appropriate value (Excellent, Good, Fair, Poor, No Opinion) to the **value** attribute of each `<input>` element. For example, you create the radio button for the first "Excellent" button using this statement: `<input type="radio" name="wait_time" value="Excellent" />`.

Airline Survey

Wait time for check-in?	○ Excellent	○ Good	○ Fair	○ Poor	○ No Opinion
Friendliness of customer staff?	○ Excellent	○ Good	○ Fair	○ Poor	○ No Opinion
Space for luggage storage?	○ Excellent	○ Good	○ Fair	○ Poor	○ No Opinion
Comfort of seating?	○ Excellent	○ Good	○ Fair	○ Poor	○ No Opinion
Cleanliness of aircraft?	○ Excellent	○ Good	○ Fair	○ Poor	○ No Opinion
Noise level of aircraft?	○ Excellent	○ Good	○ Fair	○ Poor	○ No Opinion

Done   My Computer

Figure 7-35   Airline survey form

4. Add reset and submit buttons to the airline survey form. The submit button should submit the survey data to the FormProcessor.html file.

5. Save the file as **AirlineSurvey.html** in the Chapter.07\Projects folder.

6. Close the **AirlineSurvey.html** file in your text editor, and then use the W3C Markup Validation Service to validate it. Once the file is valid, open it in your Web browser. Test the form and submit some data to the FormProcessor.html file.

7. Close your Web browser window.

Project 7-3

Forms on Web pages commonly use selection lists to allow users to select dates. In this exercise, you create a simple form that uses selection lists to create date fields.

1. Create a new document in your text editor.

2. Type the `<!DOCTYPE>` declaration, `<html>` element, document head, and `<body>` element. Use the Strict DTD and "Date Fields" as the content of the `<title>` element.

3. Add to the document body the following `<form>` element that submits the form to the FormProcessor.html file:

```
<form action="FormProcessor.html" method="get"
enctype="application/x-www-form-urlencoded">
</form>
```

7

4. Next, add to the **<form>** element the following selection list with **<label>** elements that allows users to select a month:

```
<p><label for="month">Month </label><select name="month"
id="month">
<option selected="selected" value="Jan">Jan</option>
<option value="Feb">Feb</option>
<option value="Mar">Mar</option>
<option value="Apr">Apr</option>
<option value="May">May</option>
<option value="Jun">Jun</option>
<option value="Jul">Jul</option>
<option value="Aug">Aug</option>
<option value="Sep">Sep</option>
<option value="Oct">Oct</option>
<option value="Nov">Nov</option>
<option value="Dec">Dec</option>
</select>
```

5. Now add to the end of the **<form>** element the following selection list for the date of the month:

```
<label for="date">Date </label><select name="date"
id="date">
    <option selected="selected" value="01">01</option>
    <option value="02">02</option>
    <option value="03">03</option>
    <option value="04">04</option>
    <option value="05">05</option>
    <option value="06">06</option>
    <option value="07">07</option>
    <option value="08">08</option>
    <option value="09">09</option>
    <option value="10">10</option>
    <option value="11">11</option>
    <option value="12">12</option>
    <option value="13">13</option>
    <option value="14">14</option>
    <option value="15">15</option>
    <option value="16">16</option>
    <option value="17">17</option>
    <option value="18">18</option>
    <option value="19">19</option>
    <option value="20">20</option>
    <option value="21">21</option>
    <option value="22">22</option>
    <option value="23">23</option>
    <option value="24">24</option>
    <option value="25">25</option>
    <option value="26">26</option>
```

```
        <option value="27">27</option>
        <option value="28">28</option>
        <option value="29">29</option>
        <option value="30">30</option>
        <option value="31">31</option>
    </select>
```

6. Finally, add to the end of the **<form>** element the following **<label>** and text **<input>** elements for the year, along with submit and reset buttons created with the **<button>** element:

```
<label for="year">Year </label><input type="text"
name="year" id="year" value="Year" size="4" /></p>
<p><button type="reset">Reset</button>
<button type="submit">Submit</button></p>
```

7. Save the file as **DateFields.html** in the Chapter.07\Projects folder.

8. Close the **DateFields.html** file in your text editor, and then use the W3C Markup Validation Service to validate it. Once the file is valid, open it in your Web browser. Test the form and submit it to the FormProcessor.html file.

9. Close your Web browser window.

Project 7-4

In this exercise, you create a reservation form for a surfboard rental company.

1. Create a new document in your text editor.

2. Type the **<!DOCTYPE>** declaration, **<html>** element, document head, and **<body>** element. Use the Strict DTD and "Coast City Surfboard Rentals" as the content of the **<title>** element.

3. Add to the document body the following heading elements:

```
<h1>Coast City Surfboard Rentals</h1>
<h2>Reservations</h2>
```

4. Add to the end of document body the following **<form>** element that submits the form to the FormProcessor.html file:

```
<form action="FormProcessor.html" method="get"
enctype="application/x-www-form-urlencoded">
</form>
```

5. Use **<input>** elements to create contact information fields in the **<form>** element, including name, address, and telephone number.

6. Use the date selection lists you created in Exercise 7-3 to add two date reservation fields to the end of the form, one for the date a user will pick up his or her surfboard and another for the date he or she will return it.

7. Now, add two selection lists from which users can select the number of guests to reserve surfboards for. One selection list should be for the number of adults and the other for the number of children.

8. Next, add a text area where users can enter questions or comments.

9. Finally, use **<button>** elements to add reset and submit buttons to the document.

10. Save the file as **SurfboardRentals.html** in the Chapter.07\Projects folder.

11. Close the **SurfboardRentals.html** file in your text editor, and then use the W3C Markup Validation Service to validate it. Once the file is valid, open it in your Web browser. Test the form and submit it to the FormProcessor.html file.

12. Close your Web browser window.

Project 7-5

In this exercise, you create a form with some radio button fields from a product survey for a software company.

1. Create a new document in your text editor.

2. Type the **<!DOCTYPE>** declaration, **<html>** element, document head, and **<body>** element. Use the Strict DTD and "Product Survey" as the content of the **<title>** element.

3. Create the form with the radio buttons shown in Figure 7-36. Use **<label>** elements and create access keys for each of the radio button options.

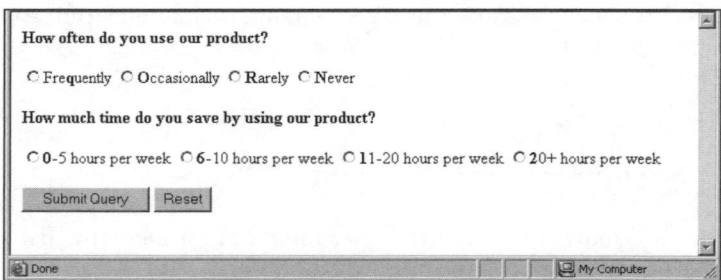

How often do you use our product?

○ Frequently ○ Occasionally ○ Rarely ○ Never

How much time do you save by using our product?

○ 0-5 hours per week ○ 6-10 hours per week ○ 11-20 hours per week ○ 20+ hours per week

[Submit Query] [Reset]

Figure 7-36 Product survey form

4. Use **<button>** elements to add reset and submit buttons to the product survey form. The submit button should submit the survey data to your e-mail address.

5. Save the file as **ProductSurvey.html** in the Chapter.07\Projects folder.

6. Close the **ProductSurvey.html** file in your text editor, and then use the W3C Markup Validation Service to validate it. Once the file is valid, open it in your Web browser. Test the form and submit some data to your e-mail address.

7. Close your Web browser window.

Project 7-6

In this exercise, you create a fitness survey form for a health club.

1. Create a new document in your text editor.

2. Type the `<!DOCTYPE>` declaration, `<html>` element, document head, and `<body>` element. Use the Strict DTD and "Fitness Survey" as the content of the `<title>` element.

3. Create the form shown in Figure 7-37.

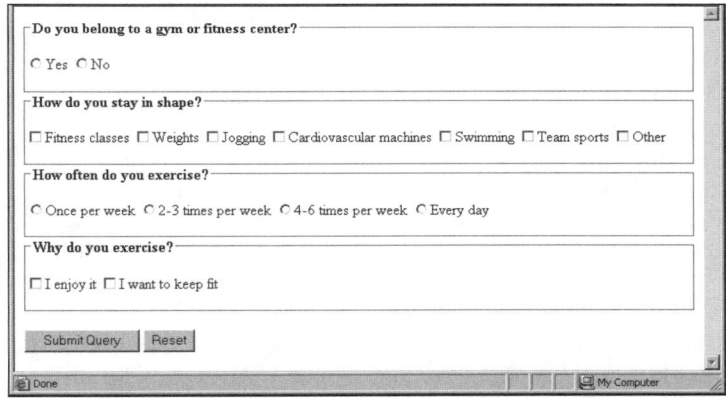

Figure 7-37   Fitness survey form

4. Use `<button>` elements to add reset and submit buttons to the product survey form. The submit button should submit the survey data to your e-mail address.

5. Save the file as **FitnessForm.html** in the Chapter.07\Projects folder.

6. Close the **FitnessForm.html** file in your text editor, and then use the W3C Markup Validation Service to validate it. Once the file is valid, open it in your Web browser. Test the form and submit some data to your e-mail address.

7. Close your Web browser window.

CASE PROJECTS

For the following projects, save the files you create in the Chapter.07\Cases folder. Create the files so they are well formed according to the Strict DTD. Be sure to validate the files you create with the W3C Markup Validation Service. For the projects that require the FormProcess.html file, a copy of the file is saved in your Chapter.07\Cases folder.

Project 7-1

Create a form to be used as a software development bug report. Create two radio buttons, open and closed, for the status of the bug. Include fields such as short and long descriptions of the bug, severity, the date the bug was opened, diagnosis of the problem, and the actions taken to fix the bug. Use `<label>` elements for each control and create the date fields using selection lists. Place the radio buttons within a field set. Submit the form to the FormProcessor.html file. Save the document as BugReport.html.

Project 7-2

Create a form to be used for tracking, documenting, and managing the process of interviewing candidates for professional positions. Create three field sets: Interviewer Information, Candidate Information, and Candidate's Skills/Presentation. Within the Interviewer Information field set, include fields for the interviewer's first name, last name, position, and date of interview. Create the date field using selection lists. Within the Candidate Information field set, include fields for the candidate's first and last name, a selection list containing the interviewer's overall recommendation (Don't Hire, Maybe Hire, and so on), and a comment field. Within the Candidate's Skills/Presentation field set, include the following selection lists: Intellect, Communication Skills, Business Knowledge, and Computer Skills. Include within each selection list values such as Average, Above Average, and so on. Use `<label>` elements for each of the form controls. Submit the form to the FormProcessor.html file. Save the document as Interview.html.

Project 7-3

Create a consent form for a school trip. Create three field sets: Description of Trip, Student Information, and Parental Information. Within the Description of Trip field set, include fields for the destination, date of the trip, and purpose of the trip. Also, include three radio buttons for the duration of the trip, Half Day, Full Day, and Overnight. Within the Student Information field set, include fields for the student's name, home telephone, physician's name and telephone, and any special medical requirements. Within the Parental Information field set, include fields for the name of the student's mother and father, along with their work telephone numbers. Include two radio buttons that read "Permission is Granted" and "Permission is NOT Granted" that parents can use to grant or deny permission for the field trip. Use `<label>` elements for each of the form controls. Also assign access keys to each of the form's radio buttons. Submit the form to your personal e-mail address. Save the document as ConsentForm.html.

Project 7-4

Create a documentation evaluation form for a software company. Include check boxes to allow visitors to select the documents to which their comments apply along with a text area where they can type their comments. Also, include a survey that allows visitors to rate the documents they selected. The survey should include questions that allow visitors to rate the document in areas such as technical accuracy, clarity of writing, usefulness, and so on. Use radio buttons for each survey question that allow users to select one of five choices that describe a specific survey question. The five radio buttons should provide one of the following ratings: Excellent, Good, Fair, Poor, and Very Poor. Also include in the form a section that allows visitors to enter their contact information. Submit the form to your personal e-mail address. Save the document as DocEval.html.

8

CASCADING STYLE SHEETS

> **In this chapter, you will:**
> - Study basic Cascading Style Sheet (CSS) syntax
> - Work with internal and external style sheets
> - Learn about CSS values
> - Set color and background properties
> - Set text properties
> - Set font properties
> - Validate style sheets

Thus far, you have studied the importance of separating an Extensible Hypertext Markup Language (XHTML) document's content from the way it displays in a user agent. One of the primary reasons for this is to allow all user agents to be able to correctly render the contents of a Web page, even if the user agent does not support formatting characteristics such as fonts, colors, or images. This is equally important for user agents for the visually impaired, mobile phones, and Personal Digital Assistants (PDAs). One way you learned to separate document content from display is through using phrase elements, which describe text content, instead of text-formatting elements, which determine how the text should appear in a traditional Web browser. You have also learned that it is important to provide alternate text that describes an image to user agents that are incapable of displaying images.

Although you should always strive to create Web pages that are compatible with all user agents, you should also design and format them so they are visually pleasing when rendered in a traditional Web browser. To design and format the display of Web pages for traditional Web browsers, you use Cascading Style Sheets (CSS), which you study in this chapter. As you work through this chapter, notice that the Cascading Style Sheet design and formatting techniques are independent of the content of a Web page, unlike text-formatting elements, such as the <b> and <i> elements. Cascading Style Sheets allow you to provide design and formatting specifications for well-formed documents that are compatible with all user agents.

Remember as you work through this chapter that although CSS are a vital part of Web page design, this book teaches Web page authoring, not design. Therefore, this chapter focuses on the skills necessary for using CSS to format Web pages, not on design techniques and concepts.

INTRODUCTION TO STYLES AND PROPERTIES

In Chapter 1 you learned that the Hypertext Markup Language (HTML) language was originally designed to define the elements in a document independently of how they would appear, the same as its predecessor, Standard Generalized Markup Language (SGML). However, HTML has gradually evolved into a language that is capable of defining how elements should appear in a Web browser. This occurred when display and formatting extensions to HTML were added to each Web browser in order to provide functionality for displaying and formatting Web pages.

To ensure that future Web page authoring separates the definition of the elements in a document from how they appear, many of the display and formatting extensions that were added to the HTML language, such as the <font> element, were deprecated in HTML 4.0 and in XHTML 1.0 in favor of CSS. **Cascading Style Sheets (CSS)** are a standard set by the World Wide Web Consortium (W3C) for managing the design and formatting of Web pages in a Web browser. A single piece of CSS formatting information, such as text alignment or font size, is referred to as a **style**. Some of the style capabilities of CSS include the ability to change fonts, backgrounds, and colors, and to modify the layout of elements as they appear in a Web browser. CSS information can be added directly to documents or stored in separate documents and shared among multiple Web pages. The term "cascading" refers to the Web pages' ability to use CSS information from more than one source. When a Web page has access to multiple CSS sources, the styles "cascade," or "fall together," based on some rules that you will study later in this chapter.

It bears repeating that your primary goal as a Web page author is to write well-formed documents that separate content from the way it appears in a user agent. Your first step in achieving this goal was to learn how to use XHTML to create well-formed documents that are focused on content instead of design. Your second step is to learn how to apply styles using CSS. Today, virtually every professionally designed Web site is created with CSS. CSS is not only used in separating a Web page's content from its appearance, but also in providing much greater design and formatting capabilities than are available with standard HTML and XHTML elements and attributes. For example, the text formatting, colors, and layout in the National Geographic Society Web page shown in Figure 8-1 would be difficult (if not impossible) to achieve without CSS.

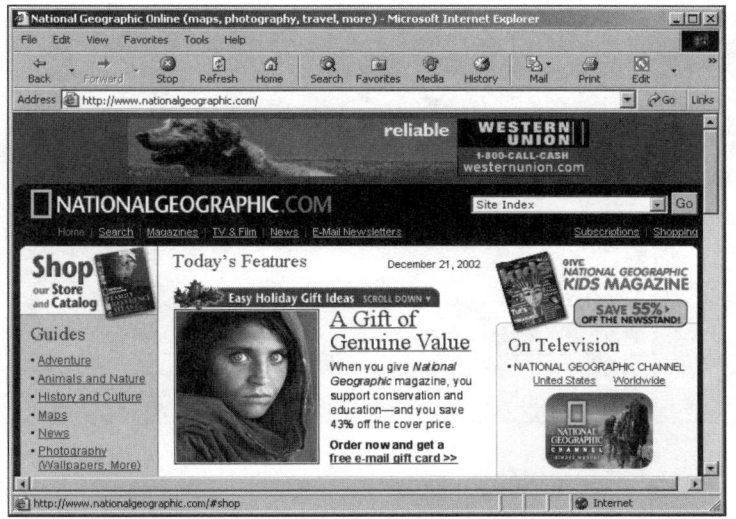

Figure 8-1   Web page designed with CSS

CSS Properties

CSS styles are created with two parts separated by a colon: the **property**, which refers to a specific CSS style, and the value assigned to it, which determines the style's visual characteristics. Together, a CSS property and the value assigned to it are referred to as a **declaration** or **style declaration**. Figure 8-2 shows a simple style declaration for the `color` attribute that changes the color of an element's text to blue.

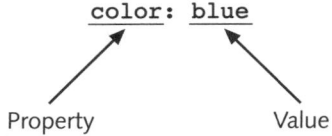

Property   Value

Figure 8-2   Style declaration

Table 8-1 contains descriptions and examples of some common CSS properties.

Table 8-1   Common CSS properties

CSS Property	Description	Code Example
background-color	Specifies a background color for the document	background-color: blue
color	Specifies the text color of an element	color: blue
font-family	Specifies the font name	font-family: arial
font-style	Specifies the font style: normal, italic, or oblique	font-style: italic
margin-left	Adjusts the left margin	margin-left: 2in
margin-right	Adjusts the right margin	margin-right: 2in
text-align	Determines the alignment of text: center, justify, left, or right	text-align: center

 You can find a listing of CSS1 properties in Appendix D.

You can define numerous properties for a single element, and you can format each CSS property with different values, depending on the property. For example, the <p> element can use any of the properties listed in Table 8-1, and many others.

The W3C published its first CSS recommendation, Level 1, in 1996, and it is commonly referred to as CSS1. Current Web browsers (Internet Explorer 6 and Netscape 6) provide excellent support for most of the properties in CSS1, although support in older browsers is sketchy. The properties available in CSS1 are grouped into the following categories:

- Color and background properties
- Font properties
- Text properties
- Box properties
- Classification properties

CSS recommendation, Level 2 (CSS2) was released in 1998. CSS2 builds on the properties in CSS1 and includes new features such as table properties and the ability to change the appearance of the mouse pointer.

At the time of this writing, no Web browser provides complete support for the properties available in CSS2. For this reason, in this chapter you study only properties that are available in CSS1. If you decide to use properties from CSS2, be sure that you only use styles supported by the browsers in which you anticipate your Web pages will be opened. To be on the safe side, you should only use CSS1 properties until Web browser manufacturers catch up with the W3C CSS2 recommendation.

At the time of this writing, CSS recommendation, Level 3 (CSS3) is in final draft and should be released soon as a recommendation by the W3C. You may need to wait awhile before Web browsers are available that support all of the new properties and features in CSS3.

Because there are more than 100 CSS1 properties, this chapter does not examine each and every property in detail. Instead, you focus on learning how to add CSS styles to documents and how to work with styles in three of the most commonly used property categories: color and background, text, and font and list. Once you understand the basics of how to work with CSS, it's fairly easy to use the various types of available properties. The ways in which you use CSS are limited. CSS properties are used almost exclusively for setting two primary aspects of your Web pages: the display of elements and their position on the screen.

Entire books are devoted to CSS. This chapter provides only enough information to get you started. For books that cover CSS more fully, search for "css" on the Course Technology Web site at *http://www.course.com*. You can also find the latest information on CSS at the W3C's Web site: *http://www.w3.org/Style/CSS/*.

8

There are three ways in which you can apply CSS styles to a document: inline styles, internal style sheets, and external style sheets. First, you learn how to use inline styles to apply style information to individual elements on a Web page.

Inline Styles

When you design a Web page, you often want the elements on your page to share the same formatting. For example, you may want all of the headings to be formatted in a specific font and color. Later in this chapter, you learn how to use internal and external style sheets to apply the same formatting to multiple elements on a Web page. However, there may be times you want to change the style of a single element on a Web page. The most basic method of applying styles is to use **inline styles**, which allow you to add style information to a single element in a document. You use the **style attribute** to assign inline style information to an element. You assign to the **style** attribute a property declaration enclosed in quotation marks. Suppose you want to modify a single paragraph in a document so it uses the Verdana font instead of the browser's default font. You can modify the default font using the following statement, which uses an inline style declaration for the **font-family** property. Figure 8-3 shows how the paragraph appears in a Web browser.

```
<p>This paragraph does not use CSS.</p>
<p style="font-family: Verdana">Paragraph formatted with
inline styles.</p>
```

Figure 8-3   Paragraph formatted with an inline style declaration

The styles you assign to an element are automatically passed to any nested elements it contains. For example, if you use the `font-family` style to assign a font to a paragraph, that font is automatically assigned to any nested elements the paragraph contains, such as `<strong>` or `<em>` elements.

> You learn more about how styles are applied to elements when you study the cascading order of styles later in this chapter.

Next, you start working on the home page for a fictional company named Western Kayak Adventures. Your Chapter.08\Chapter folder contains an existing copy of the home page, named WesternKayak.html, but without any style formatting. You add style formatting to the file throughout this chapter. First, you add the `font-family` property to each element in the file using inline styles.

To add inline styles:

1. In your text editor, open the **WesternKayak.html file**, which is located in your Chapter.08\Chapter folder, and immediately save it as **WesternKayakInline.html**.

2. Add the following inline style declaration to the file's `<h1>` and `<h2>` elements: **style="font-family: Garamond"**. For example, the opening tag for the `<h1>` element should read as follows:

   ```
   <h1 style="font-family: Garamond">Western Kayak
   Adventures</h1>
   ```

3. Now add the following inline style declaration to each of the file's `<p>` elements: **style="font-family: Trebuchet MS"**. The modified opening tags for each of the paragraph elements should read as follows:

   ```
   <p style="font-family: Trebuchet MS">
   ```

4. Save the file and then open it in your Web browser. Your file should appear similar to Figure 8-4.

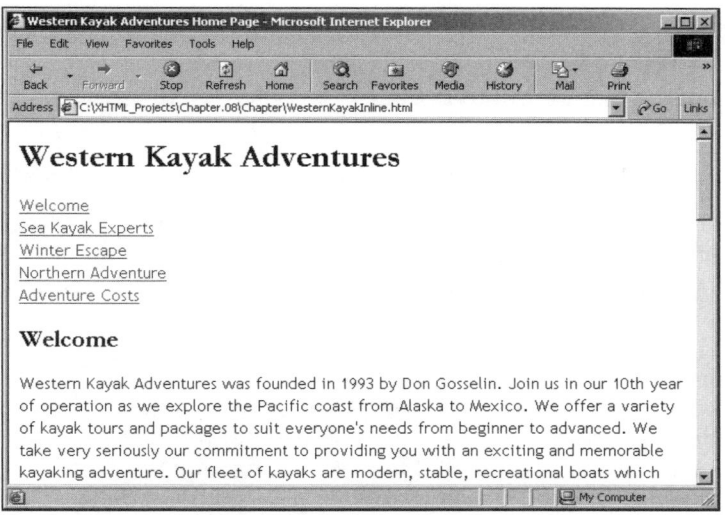

Figure 8-4   Western Kayak Adventures home page after adding inline styles

5. Close your Web browser window.

You can include multiple style declarations in an inline style by separating each declaration with a semicolon. The following statement shows the paragraph element you saw earlier, but this time with two additional style declarations: one for the `color` property, which sets an element's text color to blue, and one for the `text-align` property, which centers the paragraph in the middle of the page. Notice that the `<strong>` element, which is nested in the paragraph element, automatically takes on the paragraph element's style elements. Figure 8-5 shows how the paragraph appears in a Web browser.

```
<p style="font-family: Verdana; color: blue;
text-align: center">Paragraph formatted with
<strong>inline styles</strong>.</p>
```

Figure 8-5   Paragraph formatted with multiple inline style declarations

Next, you add `color` property declarations to the inline styles in the Western Kayak Adventures home page.

To add `color` property declarations to the inline styles in the Western Kayak Adventures home page:

1. Return to the **WesternKayakInline.html** file in your text editor.

2. Add the following `color` property declaration to the inline styles for each of the heading elements: `color: maroon`. You need to add the declaration to six headings in all. The modified opening tag for the `<h1>` element should appear as follows:

   `<h1 style="font-family: Garamond; color: maroon">`

3. Now add the following `color` property declaration to the inline styles for each of the paragraph elements: `color: olive`. You need to add the declaration to eight paragraphs in all. The modified opening tags for each of the paragraph elements should read as follows:

   `<p style="font-family: Trebuchet MS; color: olive">`

4. Save the **WesternKayakInline.html** file and open it in your Web browser. The file should appear the same, except for the new colors that should display for the heading and paragraph elements.

5. Close your Web browser window.

One of the great advantages to using CSS is that you can share styles among multiple Web pages, making it easier to create and maintain a common look and feel for an entire Web site. Inline styles, however, cannot be shared by other Web pages or other elements on the same page (except by elements that are nested within other elements). Plus, it is extremely time-consuming to add inline styles to every element on a Web page. Inline styles are only useful if you need to make a one-time change to a single element on a page. If you want to apply the same formatting to multiple elements on a page or share styles with other Web pages, then you need to use internal or external style sheets, which you will study later in this chapter.

CSS VALUES

The values you can assign to a CSS property depend on what type of property it is. Some properties can be assigned a range of values. For instance, you can assign any font name that is available on a user's system to the `font-family` property. For other properties, you must assign a value from a specific set of values. For example, you can only assign to the `text-align` property one of the following four values: left, center, right, or justify. (You learn more about the `font-family` and `text-align` properties later in this chapter.)

In addition to unique and specific values, there are three types of common values that are assigned to properties: length units, percentage units, and color units.

Length Units

Length units refer to the units of measure that you can use in a style declaration to determine the size or positioning of an element. Whether a length unit is used for sizing or positioning depends on the property and the element to which it is assigned. For example, the length unit value you assign to the `font-size` property determines the font size for an element. The length unit value you assign to the `text-indent` property adjusts positioning by determining how far to indent an element from the document's left margin. Table 8-2 lists the length units you can use with CSS.

Table 8-2   CSS length units

Unit	Name	Description
cm	Centimeters	Measures values in centimeters
em	Em space	Measures values according to width of the uppercase letter *M* for the font that is being used
ex	x-height	Measures values according to the height of the lowercase letter *x* for the font that is being used
in	Inches	Measures values in inches
mm	Millimeters	Measures values in millimeters
pc	Picas	Measures values in picas, which are equal to ⅙ of an inch
pt	Points	Measures values in points, which are equal to ½ of an inch
px	Pixels	Measures values in pixels

Although an em space length unit is usually defined as being equal to the width of a font's uppercase letter *M*, in practice it actually represents the point size of the current font. For example, if the font size for a paragraph is set to 12 points, then 1 em is equal to 12 points, 2 em is equal to 24 points, and so on.

You assign a measurement value to a property by assigning the number that represents the measurement, immediately followed by the unit of measure. For instance, the second paragraph in the following code increases an element's font size to 16 points and indents its first line by 1.5 inches. Notice that there is no space between "16" and "pt" or between "1.5" and "in". Figure 8-6 shows how the styles appear in a Web browser.

```
<p>This paragraph does not use CSS.</p>
<p style="font-size: 16pt; text-indent: 1.5in">
Paragraph is formatted with length units.</p>
```

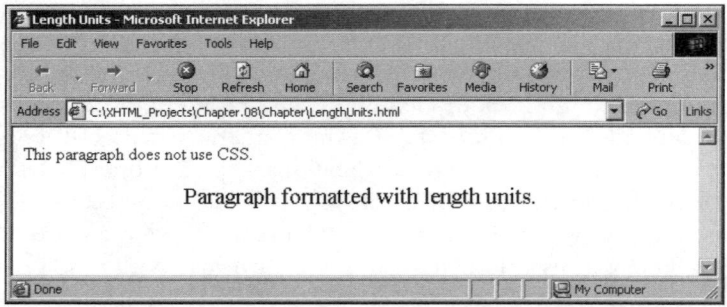

Figure 8-6   Paragraph formatted with length units

Do not include a space between the number and length unit assigned to a property, or most browsers will ignore the style. For instance, the styles in the following code include spaces between the number and the length unit assigned to the properties. As you can see in Figure 8-7, the Web browser ignores the styles.

```
<p>This paragraph does not use CSS.</p>
<p style="font-size: 16 pt; text-indent: 1.5 in">
This paragraph is formatted with length units.</p>
```

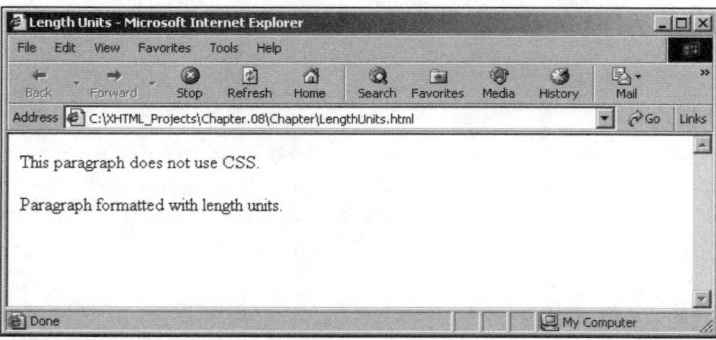

Figure 8-7   Paragraph with incorrectly formatted length units

Next, you modify the paragraph elements in the Western Kayak Adventures home page so the point size is 10.

To modify the point size for the paragraph elements:

1. Return to the **WesternKayakInline.html** file in your text editor.

2. Add the following `font-size` property declaration to the inline styles for each of the paragraph elements: **`font-size: 10pt`**. Be sure not to include a space between 10 and pt. The modified opening tags for each of the paragraph elements should read as follows:

```
<p style="font-family: Trebuchet MS; color: olive;
font-size: 10pt">
```

3. Save the **WesternKayakInline.html** file and open it in your Web browser. The point size of the paragraph elements should appear smaller, as shown in Figure 8-8.

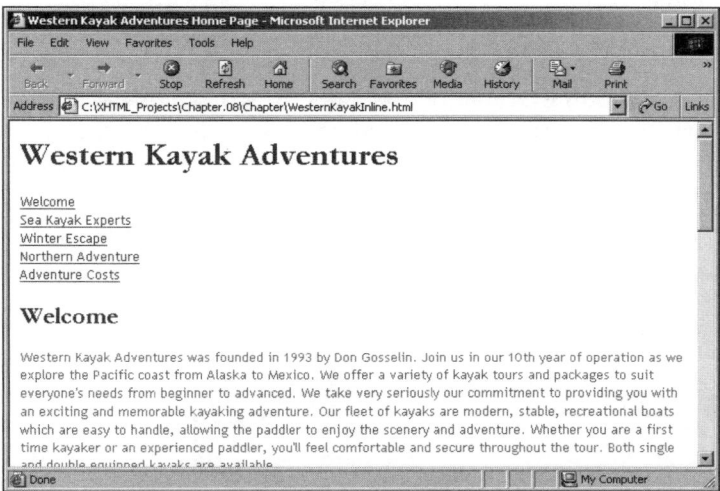

Figure 8-8   Western Kayak Adventures home page after modifying the point size of the paragraph elements

4. Close your Web browser window.

CSS length units are either absolute or relative. **Absolute length units** use an exact measurement to specify the size or placement of an element. The following CSS length units are absolute:

- cm (centimeters)
- in (inches)
- mm (millimeters)
- pc (picas)
- pt (points)

Absolute length units are not a good choice for Web page design because they do not automatically adjust to different screen sizes. **Relative length units** are preferred because they adjust properties according to screen size or user preferences. The following CSS length units are relative:

- em (em space)
- ex (x-height)
- px (pixels)

Consider the em and ex length units, which adjust font size in relation to the font size of the current element or the default font size of an element that is set by a browser. If a user with visual disabilities sets his or her monitor to display larger fonts, any elements with font sizes that are assigned with the em and ex units will automatically be sized larger for that user's monitor. However, if the font sizes are assigned values with the absolute pt measurement, the elements will not be resized.

The following code shows an example of a paragraph with a `font-size` property set to 18 points. The paragraph includes a nested `<strong>` element with a `font-size` property set to 1.5em. Because the paragraph's font is set to 18 points, assigning a value of 1.5em to the nested `<strong>` element formats its content to 27 points, as shown in Figure 8-9.

```
<p style="font-family: Arial; font-size: 18pt">
We're having a <strong style="font-size:
1.5em">sale</strong>!</p>
```

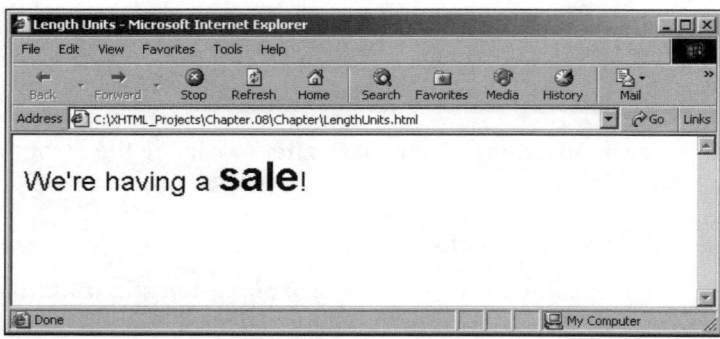

Figure 8-9   Paragraph formatted with pt and em length units

Next, you modify the pt length units in the inline styles to em length units for each of the paragraph elements.

To use em length units in the inline styles for each of the paragraph elements:

1. Return to the **WesternKayakInline.html** file in your text editor.

2. Change the value assigned to the `font-size` properties in each paragraph element's inline style from 10pt to **.8em**. The modified opening tags for each of the paragraph elements should read as follows:

   ```
   <p style="font-family: Trebuchet MS; color: olive;
   font-size: .8em">
   ```

3. Save the **WesternKayakInline.html** file and open it in your Web browser. The point size of the paragraph elements should appear the same as it did before you modified the length units assigned to the `font-size` properties.

4. Close your Web browser window.

Percentage Units

An alternative to relative length units is **percentage units**, which adjust properties relative to other values. You assign a percentage unit value to a property by assigning a number that represents the percentage, immediately followed by the percent symbol (%).

The following code shows two paragraph elements that contain nested `<strong>` elements. The font of the `<strong>` element in the first paragraph is resized to 150% of the size of the paragraph font, whereas the font of the `<strong>` element in the second paragraph is resized to 50% of the size of the paragraph font. Figure 8-10 shows the resulting styles in a Web browser.

```
<p style="font-family: Arial; font-size: 18pt">
We're having a <strong style="font-size:
150%">sale</strong>!</p>
<p style="font-family: Arial; font-size: 18pt">
Are you feeling <strong style="font-size:
50%">down</strong>?</p>
```

Figure 8-10   Elements resized with percentage units

Next, you modify the em length units in the inline styles to percentage length units for each of the paragraph elements.

To modify the em length units in the inline styles to percentage length units for each of the paragraph elements:

1. Return to the **WesternKayakInline.html** file in your text editor.

2. Change the value assigned to the `font-size` properties in each paragraph element's inline style from .8em to **80%**. The modified opening tags for each of the paragraph elements should read as follows:

```
<p style="font-family: Trebuchet MS; color: olive;
font-size: 80%">
```

8

3. Save and close the **WesternKayakInline.html** file and open it in your Web browser. The point size of the paragraph elements should appear the same as they did before you modified the length units assigned to the `font-size` properties.

4. Close your Web browser window.

Color Units

A **color unit** represents a color value that you can assign to a property. You can assign a color unit to a property using any one of 16 color names defined in the CSS1 specification.

The 16 color names defined in the CSS1 specification are listed in Table 8-3.

Table 8-3   CSS1 color name values

aqua	gray	navy	silver
black	green	olive	teal
blue	lime	purple	white
fuchsia	maroon	red	yellow

Assigning a color unit using one of the color names listed in Table 8-3 is simple. You have seen examples of color names several times throughout this chapter. As you have seen, you assign the color name to a property, as shown in the following code, which assigns the color name "navy" to the `color` property, which specifies the text color of an element:

```
<p style="color: navy">
Paragraph formatted with a color name.</p>
```

The 16 color names you can use are nowhere near sufficient for most professional Web page authors, especially considering that most computer systems can display millions of colors. Although computer systems can display so many colors, the display of colors is the result of combining just three colors, red, green, and blue. Most graphical computer systems, such as Windows, use the **red**, **green**, **blue**, or **RGB color system** for specifying colors. You can also assign a color using the RGB color system. Refer to Appendix D for information on assigning colors with the RGB color system.

CSS STRUCTURE

You now understand the basics of working with CSS. In this section, you learn how to structure the CSS used by your documents. After this section, you study in detail the various types of properties available in CSS.

Internal Style Sheets

As you learned earlier, inline styles are only useful if you want to add style information to a single element in a document. You use an **internal style sheet** to create styles that apply to an entire document. You create an internal style sheet within a `<style>` element placed within the document head. The `<style>` element must include a `type` attribute, which is assigned a value of "text/css", as follows:

```
<style type="text/css">
style declarations
</style>
```

 You can also use an optional `media` attribute with the `<style>` element, which you use to select the destination medium for the style information. Valid values you can assign to the `media` attribute are screen, tty, tv, projection, handheld, print, braille, and aural.

Within the `<style>` element you create any style instructions for a specific element that are applied to all instances of that element contained in the body of the document. The element to which specific style rules in a style sheet apply is called a **selector**. You create a style declaration for a selector in an internal style sheet by placing a list of declarations within a pair of braces { } following the name of the selector. Figure 8-11 shows a style declaration for the `<p>` element, the selector, that changes the `color` property to "blue".

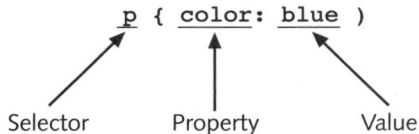

Selector   Property   Value

Figure 8-11 Selector style declaration

As with inline styles, you separate multiple properties for a selector by semicolons. The following code shows a portion of the head and the body of a document that includes a style sheet for the h1, h2, and p selectors. A pair of braces containing style instructions follows each selector. All instances of the associated elements in the body of the document are formatted using these style instructions. Figure 8-12 shows how the document appears in a Web browser.

```
...
<head>
...
<style type="text/css">
h1 {color: navy; font-size: 2em; font-family: serif }
h2 { color: red; font-size: 1.5em; font-family: Arial }
body {color: blue; font-family: Arial;
      font-size: .8em; font-weight: normal }
```

8

```
</style>
</head>
<body>
<h1>Coast City Kites</h2>
<h2>Airfoils</h2>
<p>Supported by the wind itself, these kites have nothing
to break or assemble. They pack down small enough to fit in
a pack, purse, or pocket, so you can always be ready to go
fly a kite.</p>
<h2>Deltas</h2>
<p>Traditional Deltas are easy to fly and make great first
kites. Flying on the wind rather than against it, they take
off in the lightest of breezes and soar with bird-like
grace.</p>
</body>
```

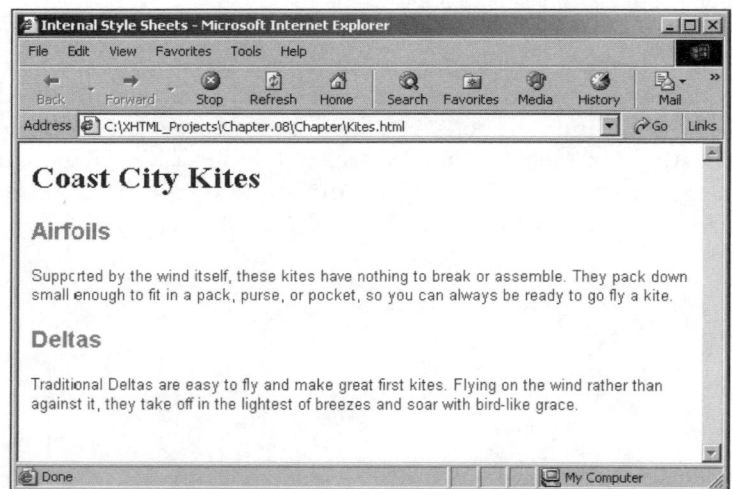

Figure 8-12   Document with an internal style sheet

You can group selectors so they share the same style declarations by separating each selector with a comma. For example, you use the following single declaration to format all of a document's <h1>, <h2>, and <h3> elements to use the same color:

```
<style type="text/css">
h1, h2, h3 {color: navy }
</style>
```

Next, you create a new version of the Western Kayak Adventures home page, but with an internal style sheet instead of inline styles.

To create a new version of the Western Kayak Adventures home page, using an internal style sheet:

1. Open the **WesternKayak.html** file in your Chapter.08\Chapter folder and immediately save it as **WesternKayakInternal.html** file in your text editor.

2. Above the closing **</head>** tag, add a **<style>** element, as follows:

```
<style type="text/css">
</style>
```

3. Add to the **<style>** element the following grouped selectors and declaration for the **<h1>** and **<h2>** elements that format the headings using the Garamond font and the color maroon.

```
h1, h2 { font-family: Garamond; color: maroon }
```

4. Now add to the end of the **<style>** element the following selector and declaration for the **<p>** element that sets the font to Trebuchet MS, the color to olive, and the font size to 80%.

```
p { font-family: Trebuchet MS; color: olive;
font-size: 80% }
```

5. Save the **WesternKayakInternal.html** file and open it in your Web browser. The style formatting for each of the elements should appear the same as they did with the inline styles version of the document.

6. Close your Web browser window.

Contextual Selectors

A **contextual selector** allows you to specify formatting for an element, but only when it is contained within another element. You create a contextual selector by including two or more selectors in a declaration within a **<style>** element separated by spaces. For example, the following **<style>** element creates a contextual selector that formats any **<em>** elements contained with a **<blockquote>** element as green and bold. Figure 8-13 shows how the document appears in a Web browser. Notice in Figure 8-13 that the **<em>** element in the paragraph does not include the formatting in the contextual selector; only the **<em>** element within the **<blockquote>** element contains the formatting.

```
...
<style type="text/css">
...
blockquote { color: navy }
blockquote em { color: green; font-weight: bold }
</style>
</head>
<body>
...
```

```
<p>Choose an open, treeless area. <em>Hills can be great
places to fly kites.</em> Stand on the windward side to
avoid turbulence created by the hill itself.
<blockquote><p>Trees or buildings upwind can cause ground
turbulence and make your kite hard to launch. Downwind,
these <em>kite eating</em> obstacles can cause turbulence
that attracts kites.</p></blockquote>
</body>
```

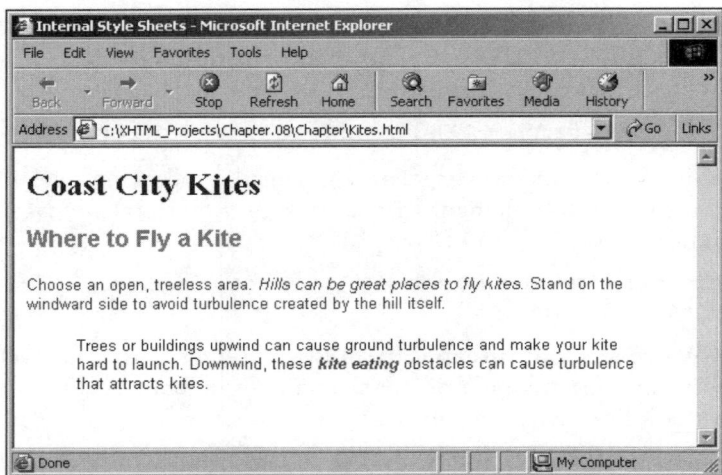

Figure 8-13   Document with a contextual selector

Next, you add a contextual selector to the Western Kayak Adventures home page. The contextual selector consists of a `<strong>` element inside a `<blockquote>` element. Anytime the `<strong>` element appears within a `<blockquote>` element, it is formatted in purple.

To add a contextual selector to the Western Kayak Adventures home page:

1. Return to the **WesternKayakInternal.html** file in your text editor window.

2. Above the closing `<style>` element, add the following declaration for a contextual selector that formats the `<strong>` element in purple anytime it appears within a `<blockquote>` element.

```
blockquote strong { color: purple }
```

3. Next, add the following `<blockquote>` element immediately above the Sea Kayak Experts `<h2>` element. Notice that the `<blockquote>` element contains several `<strong>` elements.

```
<blockquote><p>"My trip with Western Kayak Adventures is
one of the <strong>memorable experiences of my
life</strong>. Their kayak equipment is of the
<strong>highest quality</strong>, their employees are
<strong>well trained</strong> and
<strong>personable</strong>, and their safety record is
<strong>impeccable</strong>."</p></blockquote>
```

4. Save the **WesternKayakInternal.html** file and open it in your Web browser. Figure 8-14 shows how the `<blockquote>` element appears.

Figure 8-14   `<blockquote>` element formatted with a contextual selector

5. Close your Web browser window.

Class Selectors

Another method of applying styles is to use **class selectors**, which allow you to create different groups of styles for the same element. You create a class selector within a `<style>` element by appending a name for the class to a selector with a period. You then assign the class name to the standard `class` attribute of elements in the document that you want to format with the class's style definitions.

The following code defines a class selector named `danger` that formats paragraph text as red and bold. The class selector is applied to two of the paragraphs in the document body. Figure 8-15 shows the document in a Web browser.

```
...
<style type="text/css">
...
p.danger { color: red; font-weight: bold }
</style>
</head>
<body>
<h1>Coast City Kites</h2>
<h2>Safety Tips</h2>
<p>Never fly over people.</p>
<p>Never fly near trees or buildings.</p>
<p>Never fly near the airport.</p>
<p class="danger">Never fly in rain or thunderstorms.</p>
<p>Never fly near busy streets or roadways.</p>
<p class="danger">Never fly near power lines.</p>
</body>
```

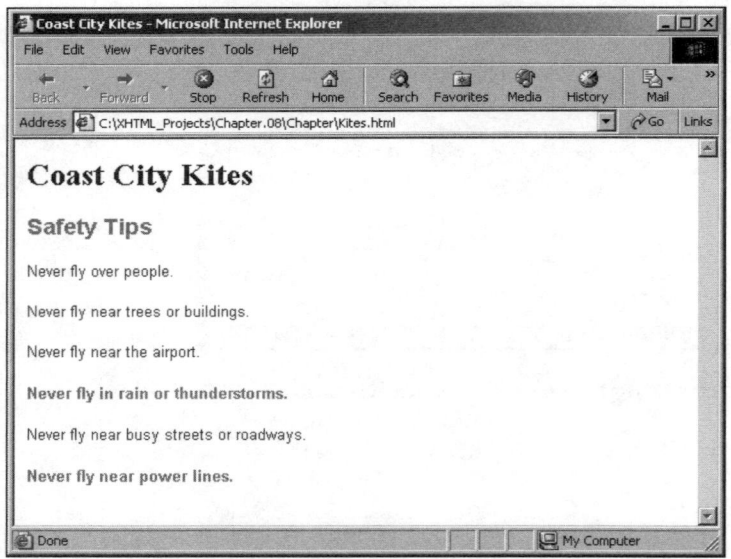

Figure 8-15   Document with a class selector

Next, you add to the Western Kayak Adventures home page a class selector for the `<h2>` element. The class selector formats any `<h2>` elements that include the class selector name in the color blue. You apply the new class selector to the Winter Escape and Northern Adventure headings to draw more attention to them.

To add to the Western Kayak Adventures home page a class selector for the `<h2>` element:

1. Return to the **WesternKayakInternal.html** file in your text editor window.

2. Add to the end of the `<style>` element the following class selector declaration for the `<h2>` element, which formats any `<h2>` elements that include the class selector in the color blue:

   ```
   h2.trip { color: navy }
   ```

3. Add to the Winter Escape and Northern Adventure headings the following `class` attribute that specifies the "trip" class selector: **class="trip"**. The opening `<h2>` tag for both headings should read as follows:

   ```
   <h2 class="trip">
   ```

4. Save the **WesternKayakInternal.html** file and open it in your Web browser. The Winter Escape and Northern Adventure headings should appear in the color navy. The other `<h2>` headings in the document should still be formatted in the color maroon.

5. Close your text editor window.

When you create a class selector by appending a name for the class to a selector with a period, you can only use that class selector with the element for which it was created. For instance, you can only use the `danger` class selector in the preceding example with `<p>` elements.

You can also create a generic class selector that it is not associated with any particular element. You create a generic class selector to use with any element by defining a class name preceded by a period, but without appending it to an element. The following code shows an example of the `danger` class selector, but this time it is not appended to the p selector. Notice that in the document body, the `danger` class selector is now applied to two different elements: `<p>` and `<strong>`. Figure 8-16 shows the document in a Web browser.

```
...
<style type="text/css">
...
.danger { color: red; font-weight: bold }
</style>
</head>
<body>
<h1>Coast City Kites</h2>
<h2>Safety Tips</h2>
<p>Never fly over <strong class="danger">people</strong>.
<p>
<p>Never fly near <strong class="danger">trees</strong>
or <strong class="danger">buildings</strong>.</p>
<p>Never fly near the <strong class="danger">airport
</strong>.</p>
```

8

```
<p class="danger">Never fly in rain or thunderstorms.</p>
<p>Never fly near busy <strong class="danger">streets
</strong> or <strong class="danger">roadways</strong>.</p>
<p class="danger">Never fly near power lines.</p>
</body>
```

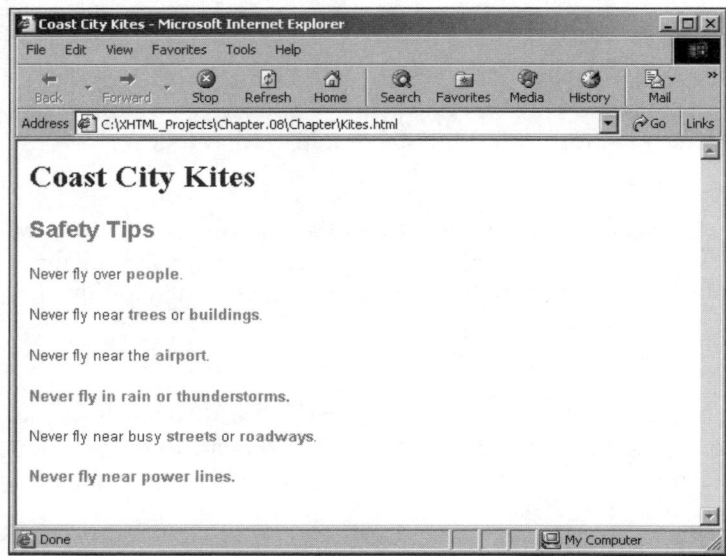

Figure 8-16   Document with a generic class selector

Next, you modify the `trip` class selector you created in the last exercise so it is a generic class selector that it is not associated with any particular element. You then apply the `trip` class selector to the paragraphs that appear beneath the Winter Escape and Northern Adventure headings in order to draw more attention to both trips.

To modify the `trip` class selector so it is a generic class selector:

1. Return to the **WesternKayakInternal.html** file.

2. Remove the h2 selector from the declaration for the `trip` class selector. The modified class selector should read as follows:

   `.trip { color: navy }`

3. Now add to each of the paragraphs beneath the Winter Escape and Northern Adventure headings a `class` attribute with "trip" assigned as its value.

4. Save the **WesternKayakInternal.html** file and open it in your Web browser. The paragraphs beneath the Winter Escape and Northern Adventure headings should now appear in the color navy.

5. Close your Web browser window.

ID Selectors

An **ID selector** is similar to an inline style in that it allows you to create style declarations that are only applied to a single element in the document. As with inline styles, you use an ID selector when you want to change the style of a single element on your Web page. The benefit to using ID selectors over inline styles is that they allow you to maintain all of your style declarations in a single location within the `<style>` element, as opposed to inline style declarations, which you must create within each element.

Recall that the value assigned to an element's `id` attribute must be unique in that it cannot be assigned to any other element's `id` attribute. You create an ID selector using the value assigned to an element's `id` attribute, but preceded by the # symbol. For example, the following code shows how to declare an ID selector for a paragraph with the value "p1" assigned to its `id` attribute.

```
...
<style type="text/css">
#p1 { font-family: Verdana; color: blue;
text-align: center }
</style>
<p id="p1">Paragraph formatted with an ID selector.</p>
```

 Elements can include both class and ID selectors. This gives you greater flexibility by allowing you to apply class formatting to an element while also adding custom style declarations to the element using an ID selector.

Next, you add to the Western Kayak Adventures home page an ID selector for a `<blockquote>` element that contains the name, city, and state of the person who made the quote that you added earlier. You create this additional `<blockquote>` element to align the name, city, and state with the other `<blockquote>` element. The ID selector formats the new `<blockquote>` element so it is right aligned with the `text-align` property.

To add an ID selector for a `<blockquote>` element:

1. Return to the **WesternKayakInternal.html** file in your text editor window.

2. Add to the end of the `<style>` element the following declaration for an ID selector named "b1". The selector includes a single style declaration that uses the `text-align` property to right align the element.

   ```
   #b1 { text-align: right }
   ```

3. Now add the following `<blockquote>` element immediately after the existing `<blockquote>` element. Notice that the opening `<blockquote>` tag includes an `id` attribute that is assigned the value of the ID selector.

   ```
   <blockquote id="b1"><p>Dan McClellen, Seattle, Washington
   </p></blockquote>
   ```

4. Save the **WesternKayakAdventure.html** file and open it in your Web browser. Figure 8-17 shows how the new `<blockquote>` element appears.

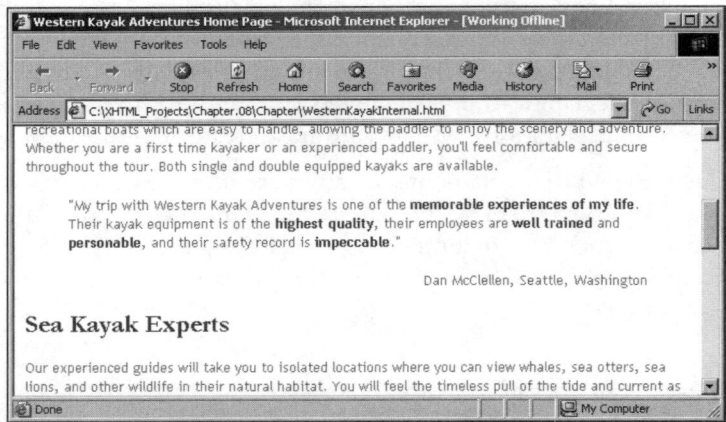

Figure 8-17   Western Kayak Adventures home page formatted after adding an ID selector

5. Close your Web browser window.

External Style Sheets

Inline styles are useful if you only need to format a single element, whereas internal style sheets are useful for creating styles that apply to an entire document. However, most companies want all of the documents on a Web site to have the same look and feel. For this reason, it's preferable to use **external style sheets**, which are separate text documents containing style declarations that are used by multiple documents on a Web site. You should create an external style sheet whenever you need to use the same styles on multiple Web pages on the same site.

You create an external style sheet in a text editor, the same as when you create XHTML documents. However, you should save the document with an extension of .css. The style sheet document should not contain XHTML elements, only style declarations. Use the same rules for creating style declarations in an external style sheet as you use in an internal style sheet. The contents of a typical external style sheet may appear as follows. Notice that the code contains no XHTML elements.

```
h1 {color: navy; font-size: 2em; font-family: serif }
h2 { color: red; font-size: 1.5em; font-family: Arial }
body {color: blue; font-family: Arial;
    font-size: .8em; font-weight: normal }
```

You can add comments to an external style sheet by adding /* to the start of the first line that is to be included in the comment and */ after the last text to be included in the comment. These are the same types of comments found in C++, Java, and other programming languages.

The most popular way of accessing the styles in an external style sheet is to use the empty `<link>` element to link a document to a style sheet. You place the `<link>` element in the document head. You include three attributes in the `<link>` element: an `href` attribute that is assigned the Uniform Resource Locator (URL) of the style sheet, an `rel` attribute that is assigned a value of "stylesheet" to specify that the referenced file is a style sheet, and the `type` attribute, which is assigned the same "text/css" value as the type attribute used in the `<style>` element. For example, to link a document to a style sheet named company_styles.css, you include a link element in the document head, as follows:

```
<head>
...
<link rel="stylesheet" href="company_styles.css"
type="text/css" />
</head>
```

When a Web browser formats a document that links to an external style sheet, it formats the document using style declarations for each selector in the external style sheet, including contextual, class, and ID selectors.

CSS also includes an @import statement that allows a document to import a style sheet instead of linking to it. However, the @import statement is primarily used as a "hack" to prevent Web browsers that don't support CSS from seeing any CSS style declarations. If you anticipate that your Web pages with CSS will open in browsers that do not support CSS, then you should add comments to your `<style>` elements (as you learned earlier in the chapter) and continue using the `<link>` element to access style declarations in an external style sheet.

Next, you modify the Western Kayak Adventures home page so it is formatted with an external style sheet.

To use an external style sheet with the Western Kayak Adventures home page:

1. Return to the **WesternKayakInternal.html** file in your text editor and immediately save it as **WesternKayakExternal.html**.

2. Copy the style declarations within the `<style>` element to your Clipboard and create a new document in your text editor. Be sure not to copy the `<style>` or comment tags.

3. Paste the contents of your Clipboard into the new file.

4. Save the file as **adventure_styles.css** in your Chapter.08\Chapter folder.

5. Return to the **WesternKayakExternal.html** file in your text editor.

6. Replace the `<style>` element with the following `<link>` element that links to the adventure_styles.css external style sheet:

```
<link rel="stylesheet" href="adventure_styles.css"
type="text/css" />
```

7. Save the **WesternKayakExternal.html** file and open it in your Web browser. The file should appear the same as it did before you linked it to the external style sheet.

8. Close your Web browser window.

The `<div>` and `<span>` Elements

You can use the `<div>` and `<span>` elements to apply styles to a document. The **`<div>` element** formats a group of block-level and inline elements with styles, whereas the **`<span>` element** formats a group of inline elements. The only difference between these two elements is that the `<div>` element can contain block-level elements and also adds a line break after its closing tag.

Both the `<div>` and `<span>` elements can contain inline styles or be formatted with internal or external style sheets. The following code contains both `<div>` and `<span>` elements. Notice that the `<div>` element gets its style formatting from a class selector in an internal style sheet, whereas the `<span>` element uses inline styles. Also notice that the `<div>` element contains block-level elements (the `<h1>` and `<p>`) elements, whereas the `<span>` element contains only text and another inline element. Figure 8-18 shows the code in a Web browser.

```
...
<style type="text/css">
body { color: black; font-family: arial;
      font-size: .8em; font-weight: normal }
.new { color: blue }
</style>
...
<h2>Bicycle Tours</h2>
<p>A bicycle tour allows you to pedal through the world's
most scenic highways and byways, where a ribbon of new
sights, scents, and sounds are revealed. <span style=
"color: olive"><strong>Head off on your own or ride with
fellow travelers if you choose!</strong></span></p>
<div class="new"><h2>Walking Tours - New!</h2>
<p>Our new walking tours transform the small details of
the region into a mosaic of unforgettable encounters and
cultural revelations. There's simply no better way to
discover the simple beauty of a landscape, the
friendliness of the locals, or the camaraderie of fellow
travelers than by walking.</p></div>
```

Figure 8-18   Document with `<div>` and `<span>` elements

Next, you add a `<div>` element to the Western Kayak Adventures Web page that contains anchor elements at the top of the page. You will also add a class selector to the style sheet that formats the anchor elements in the `<div>` element.

To add a `<div>` element to the Western Kayak Adventures Web page:

1. Return to the **adventure_styles.css** file in your text editor.

2. Add the following class selector to the end of the file. The class selector includes the `font-family` property to format the links with the same font properties as the paragraph elements.

   ```
   .links { font-family: Trebuchet MS; font-size: 80% }
   ```

3. Save the **adventure_styles.css** file.

4. Return to the **WesternKayakExternal.html** file in your text editor.

5. Replace the `<p>` element that surrounds the links at the top of the page with a `<div>` element that includes the `class` attribute assigned a value of "links" for the class selector you just created. The elements should appear as follows:

   ```
   <div class="links">
   <a href="#wel">Welcome</a><br />
   <a href="#ske">Sea Kayak Experts</a><br />
   <a href="#we">Winter Escape</a><br />
   <a href="#na">Northern Adventure</a><br />
   <a href="#ac">Adventure Costs</a>
   </div>
   ```

6. Save the **WesternKayakExternal.html** file and open it in your Web browser. The file should appear the same as it did before you added the `<div>` element.

7. Close your Web browser window.

Cascading Order

Earlier in this chapter, you learned that when a Web page has access to multiple CSS sources, the styles "cascade," or "fall together," based on some rules. Styles from different sources (inline styles, internal style sheets, or external style sheets) that apply to the same selector fight for control over the element. There are several rules that a browser applies to determine which style source wins the fight between competing style declarations from multiple sources. First, a more specific style declaration outweighs a more general style one. For example, in the following code, two style declarations set the `color` property. The color declaration in the `<body>` element is more general than the color declaration in the `<p>` element. Therefore, any `<p>` elements in the document are formatted in red instead of the blue color that is declared in the `<body>` element. However, any other elements in the document that do not have a color specified through a style will be formatted in blue.

```
<style type="text/css">
body { color: blue }
p { color: red }
```

CSS also uses an order of precedence to determine which styles to apply when a selector is formatted in different sources. The least important style formatting is the browser's default style settings. The most important style formatting, or the one that wins out over other sources, is inline styles that are applied to an element. The cascading order of precedence for styles, starting with the least important to the most important, is as follows:

1. Browser default
2. External style sheets
3. Internal style sheets
4. Inline styles

SETTING COLOR AND BACKGROUND PROPERTIES

In this section, you study the color and background properties that are available to CSS. You already know that the **color property** sets the text color of an element. You have seen several examples of how to set the color for individual elements such as the `<h1>` and `<p>` elements. To set the text color for all of the text in a document, you add the `color` property to the `<body>` element, either as in inline style or using the `body` selector.

Background properties set the background color or image that appears behind an element. Table 8-4 lists the CSS1 background properties.

Table 8-4   CSS1 background properties

Property	Description	Values
background	Sets all the background properties in one declaration	*background-color* | *background-image* | *background-repeat* | *background-attachment* | *background-position*
background-attachment	Determines whether an image specified with background-image will scroll with a Web page's content or be in a fixed position	scroll | fixed
background-color	Sets the background color of an element	*color* | transparent
background-image	Sets the background image of an element	none | url(*url*)
background-position	Specifies the initial position of an image specified with background-image	*percentage unit* | *length unit* | top | bottom | left | right | top left | top center | top right | center left | center center | center right | bottom left | bottom center | bottom right
background-repeat	Determines how an image specified with background-image is repeated on the page	repeat | repeat-x | repeat-y | no-repeat

In Table 8-4, the | symbol means "or" and is used to separate the different values that can be applied to a property. For instance, the background-attachment property can be assigned a value of "scroll" or "fixed". Values that appear in italics designate values that can vary. For instance, the color value you assign to the background-color property will vary, depending on the color you want to use.

Next, you study each of the background properties.

Foreground and Background Color

You have already seen examples of how to use the **color** property to change the color of an element's text. The color you apply with the color element is also referred to as the **foreground color**. Another type of color you can add to elements is **background color**, which you create with the **background-color** property. The foreground color that is applied to an element's text appears on top of an element's background color. For example, the following inline style formats a paragraph's foreground color (its text) as white, and its background color as black. Figure 8-19 shows how a paragraph formatted with the style appears in a Web browser.

```
p { color: white; background-color: black;
font-family: Arial }
```

Figure 8-19   Foreground and background colors

The W3C strongly recommends that whenever you use the `color` property, you also include the `background-color` property to ensure that the foreground color text is placed on a suitable background. If you fail to include the `background-color` property, you could create some unpleasant results. For example, if you failed to include the background color of black in the preceding example, the foreground color of white would be unreadable in a Web browser.

There may be times when you do not need a background color for an element. For example, when you want to include an image as the document background (which you will study next), you would not want to set a color for an element's `background-color` property or the image will not be visible behind the element. In these cases, you can assign a value of "transparent" to the `background-color` property and still comply with the W3C's recommendation.

You have almost certainly seen Web pages with a background color or image. In order to set background properties for the Web page itself, you declare them for the `<body>` element. For example, the following code uses the `background-color` property to set the background color for the document body to gray.

```
body { background-color: gray }
```

Next, you add a document background color to the Western Kayak Adventures home page. You also add `background-color` properties to each of the style declarations that include `color` properties in order to conform to the W3C's recommendation. The color you use for the document background is aqua. You assign a value of transparent to the `background-color` properties for each of the style declarations that include the `color` property.

To add background color to the Western Kayak Adventures home page:

1. Return to the **adventure_styles.css** file in your text editor.

2. Add the following declaration for the **body** selector to the end of the file. The declaration contains a single property, **color**, to which you assign the color aqua.

   ```
   body { background-color: aqua }
   ```

3. Now add the **background-color: transparent** to each of the other style declarations that include a color declaration. You should add five **background-color** properties in addition to the one you added for the **body** selector. For example, the style declaration for the **p** selector should appear as follows:

   ```
   p { font-family: Trebuchet MS; color: olive;
   font-size: 80%; background-color: transparent }
   ```

4. Save the **adventure_styles.css** file and then open the **WesternKayakExternal.html** file in your Web browser. The background of the Web page should appear in aqua.

5. Close your Web browser window.

Background Images

You have probably also seen an image used as a document's background. To set an image to appear as the document background, you use the **background-image** property and assign to it a URL using the format url(*url*). For example, the following code sets the background image for a document to an image file named simple_kite.gif. Figure 8-20 shows how the background image appears in a Web browser.

```
body {color: navy; font-family: Arial;
    font-size: .8em; font-weight: normal;
    background-image: url(simple_kite.gif) }
```

When you assign a relative URL to the background-image property, the image file is located in relation to the external style sheet—not the XHTML document. In other words, a Web browser will look for the image file in the same folder as the external style sheet instead of the folder in which the Web page is located.

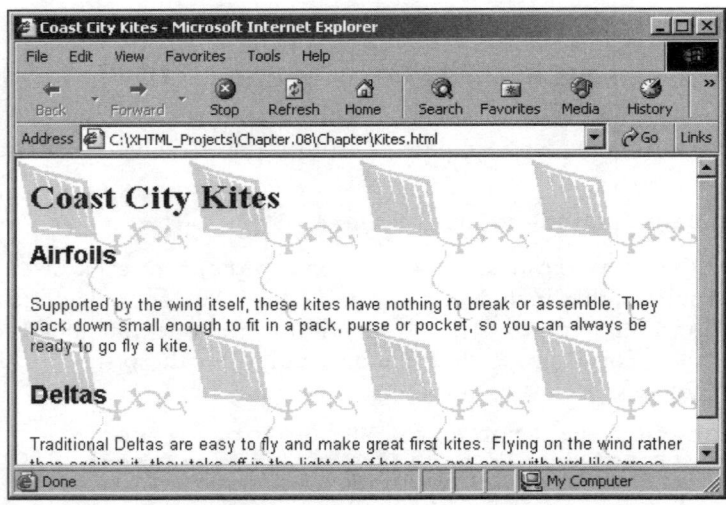

Figure 8-20   Document with a background image

The kite image that displays in Figure 8-20 is actually a single image. By default, CSS places the image in the top left of the screen and repeats it so it appears as if the image were "wallpapering" the document. You can change where the image is initially placed with the `background-position` property and how it repeats with the `background-repeat` property. The following code shows how to change the image so that it is placed at the top of the page in the center and repeats only along the *y*-axis (from top-to-bottom). Figure 8-21 shows the document in a Web browser.

```
body {color: navy; font-family: Arial;
      font-size: .8em; font-weight: normal;
      background-image: url(simple_kite.gif);
      background-position: top center;
      background-repeat: repeat-y }
```

Next, you add a repeating background image to the Western Kayak Adventures home page. Your Chapter.08\Chapter folder contains an image, kayak.gif, that you can use.

To add a repeating background image to the Western Kayak Adventures home page:

1. Return to the **adventure_styles.css** file in your text editor.

2. Change the value assigned to the `background-color` property from aqua to transparent. Also, add a style declaration that assigns the kayak.gif file to the `background-image` property.

```
body { background-color: transparent;
background-image: url(kayak.gif) }
```

3. Save the **adventure_styles.css** file and then open the **WesternKayakExternal.html** file in your Web browser. Figure 8-22 shows how the file appears after adding the background image.

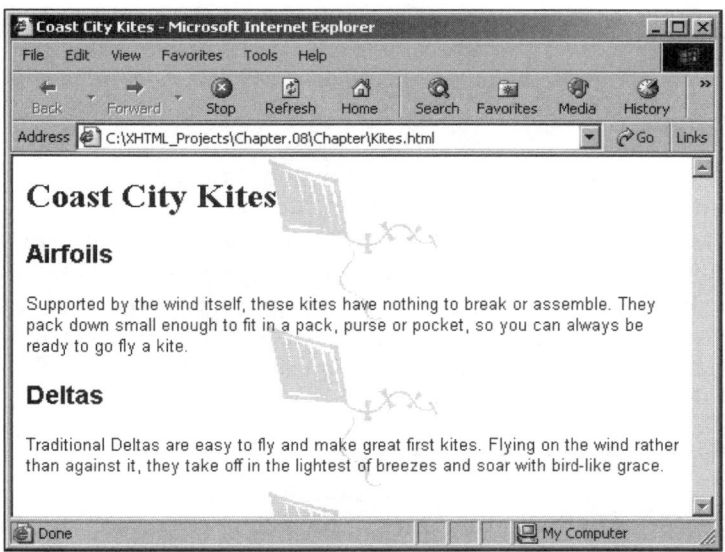

Figure 8-21   Document with a background image positioned at the top of the page and repeated along the *y*-axis

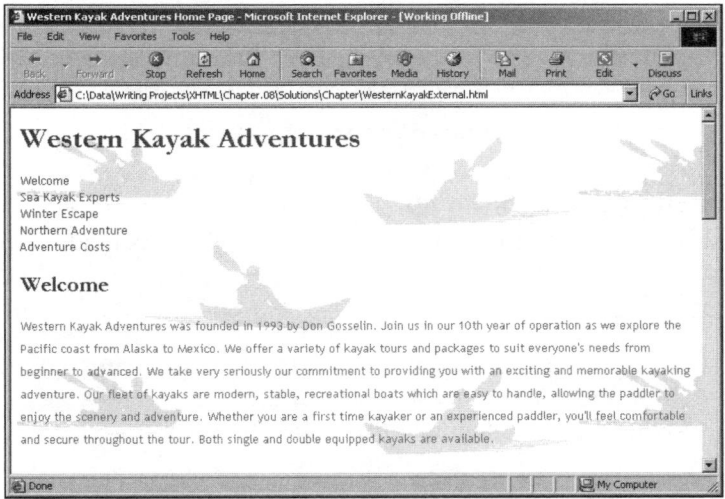

Figure 8-22   Western Kayak Adventures home page after adding a background image

4. Close your Web browser window.

The background Shorthand Property

Several of the property categories include a special property called a **shorthand property** that allows you to set all of the properties in a category using one declaration. The shorthand property for the background properties category is the `background` property. Many of the properties for each category have unique values that are assigned to them. The `background-attachment` property, for instance, can be assigned the values "scroll" or "fixed"; neither of these values can be assigned to any other background property. With this in mind, you can set any background property by assigning just its property value to the `background` property. Multiple property values are separated by spaces. For example, to use the `background` property to set the `background-image`, `background-position`, and `background-repeat` properties from the preceding example, you use the following declaration:

```
background: url(simple_kite.gif) top repeat-y }
```

Next, you replace the `background-color` and `background-image` properties in the adventure_styles.css file with the `background` property.

To replace the `background-color` and `background-image` properties in the adventure_styles.css file with the `background` property:

1. Return to the **adventure_styles.css** file.

2. Replace the `background-color` and `background-image` properties in the style declaration for the **body** selector with the following `background` property:

   ```
   body { background: transparent url(kayak.gif) }
   ```

3. Save the **adventure_styles.css** file and then open the **WesternKayakExternal.html** file in your Web browser. The background color and image should look the same as it did before you added the `background` property.

4. Close your Web browser window.

Remember that background properties are not limited to the document background. You can also use them in other elements, as shown in the following declaration for the h2 selector. Figure 8-23 shows the document in a Web browser.

```
h2 { color: navy; font-size: 1.5em; font-family: Arial;
     background-image: url(kites.gif);
     background-position: center center;
     background-repeat: no-repeat }
}
```

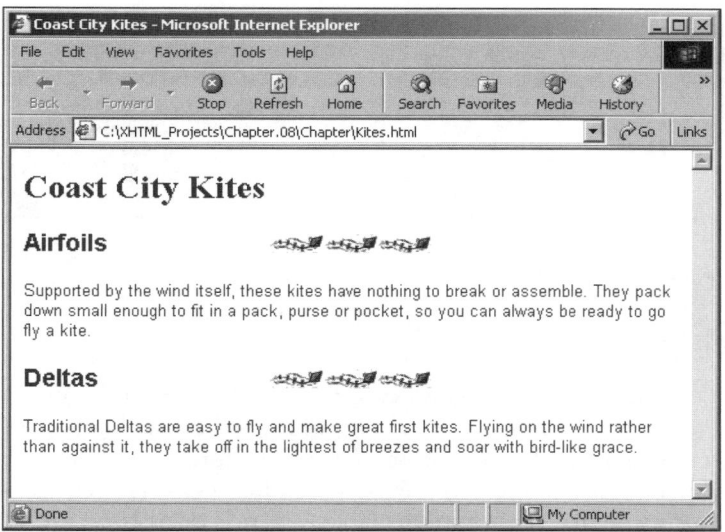

Figure 8-23   <h2> elements with a background image

SETTING TEXT PROPERTIES

You use **text properties** to specify the placement and appearance of text. The difference between text properties and font properties (which you study next) is that text properties do not change the appearance of an element's font. Rather, text properties adjust visual aspects such as word and letter spacing, text alignment, indentation, and so on. Table 8-5 lists the CSS1 text properties.

Table 8-5   CSS1 text properties

Property	Description	Values
word-spacing	Adjusts spacing between words	*length unit*
letter-spacing	Adjusts spacing between letters	*length unit*
text-decoration	Adds decorations to an element's text	none | underline | over-line | line-through | blink
vertical-align	Determines the vertical positioning of an element	baseline | sub | super | top | text-top | middle | bottom | text-bottom | *percentage unit*
text-transform	Changes the letter case of an element's text	none | capitalize | uppercase | lowercase
text-align	Determines the horizontal alignment of an element's text	left | center | right | justify

8

Table 8-5   CSS1 text properties (continued)

Property	Description	Values
text-indent	Specifies the indentation of an element's text	*length unit | percentage unit*
line-height	Determines the line height of an element's text	*length unit | percentage unit*

Next, you study each of the text properties.

Word and Letter Spacing

Word spacing refers to the amount of space between words, whereas letter spacing refers to the amount of space between letters. You set word spacing with the **word-spacing** property and letter spacing with the **letter-spacing** property. Manipulating word spacing and letter spacing is common in publishing and typesetting. Increasing the space between these items can make text more readable, whereas decreasing the space can be useful for getting more text to fit within a line or paragraph. The amount of space between words and letters varies according to the typeface you are using. Therefore, you should always use a relative length unit, such as ems or percentages, when you assign a value for each of these items.

As an example of word and letter spacing, consider the paragraph in Figure 8-24, which does not include the **word-spacing** or **letter-spacing** properties. The paragraph is created with the following style declaration, which uses the Arial Narrow font:

```
<style type="text/css">
p { font-family: "Arial Narrow" }
</style>
```

Figure 8-24   Paragraph that uses the Arial Narrow font

The word and letter spacing of the Arial Narrow font is fairly tight. You can expand the spacing of the word and character of the font by adding **word-spacing** and **letter-spacing** properties to the style declaration, as follows. Notice that only a small value, .1em, is assigned to each property. Figure 8-25 shows how the paragraph appears in a Web browser after adding the properties.

```
<style type="text/css">
p { font-family: "Arial Narrow";
word-spacing: .1em; letter-spacing: .1em }
</style>
```

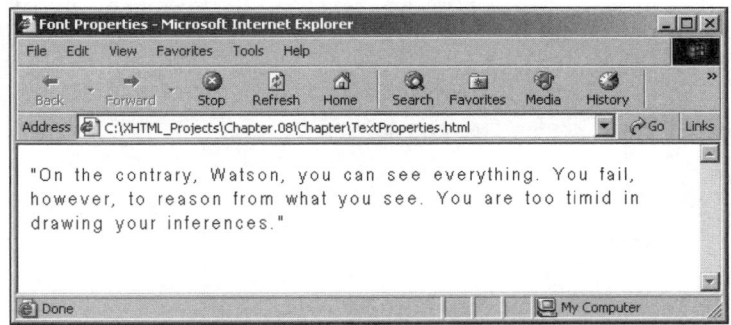

Figure 8-25   Paragraph that uses word-spacing and letter-spacing properties

Text Decorations

The **text-decoration** property modifies the appearance of text by adding the following "decorations" to the text: none, underline, overline, line-through, and blink. An underline value underlines the text, an overline value places a line over the text, and a line-through value places a line through the text, the same as the **<del>** element.

A value of "blink" should cause text to appear and disappear. Usability experts recommend that you avoid using blinking text, mainly because most people find it annoying. Additionally, some user agents, such as those for the visually impaired, have no way of rendering blinking text. A final reason for not using blinking text is because it is not supported by Internet Explorer and other browsers.

You should avoid using underlined text on your Web pages because users may confuse the text with hyperlinks.

One of the more common uses of the **text-decoration** property is to turn off the underline that appears beneath links for design purposes. To turn off the underline for a hyperlink, you assign a value of "none" to the `text-decoration` property for the anchor (`<a>`) element. For example, the `a` selector declaration in the following code turns off underlining for the document's `<a>` elements. Figure 8-26 shows how the paragraphs appear in a Web browser.

```
...
<style type="text/css">
p { font-family: Arial; color: olive }
a { text-decoration: none; color: blue }
</style>
...
<p><a href="http://abcnews.go.com">ABC News</a> provides
news around the globe.</p>
...
```

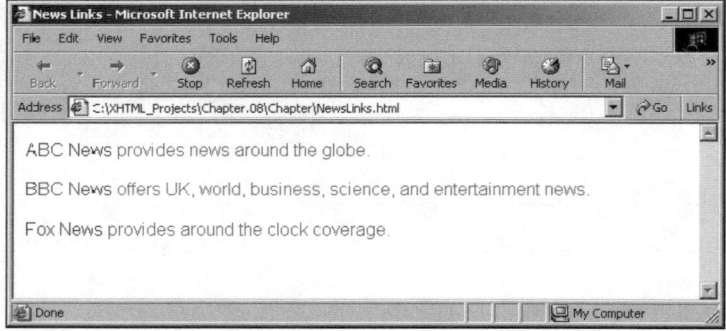

Figure 8-26   Document with underlining turned off for its `<a>` elements

Next, you add a style declaration to the adventure_styles.css file that turns off the underlining for the anchor elements.

To add a style declaration to the adventure_styles.css file that turns off the underlining for the anchor elements:

1. Return to the **adventure_styles.css** file in your text editor window.

2. Add the following style declaration for the anchor element to the end of the file:

   `a { text-decoration: none }`

3. Save the **adventure_styles.css** file and then open the **WesternKayakExternal.html** file in your Web browser. The anchor elements should no longer be underlined.

4. Close your Web browser window.

Line Height

By default, the line height in a document is set to single-space. You use the `line-height` property to change the default line of an element from single-spacing to something else. The `line-height` property can accept a length unit or percentage unit value. If you use a length unit, be sure to use a relative unit such as ems or a percentage unit.

The following style declaration formats a document's paragraph elements to double-space by assigning a value of 200% to the `line-height` property. Figure 8-27 shows how the paragraphs for the Coast City Kites Web page appear when it includes the following declaration.

```
p { line-height: 200% }
```

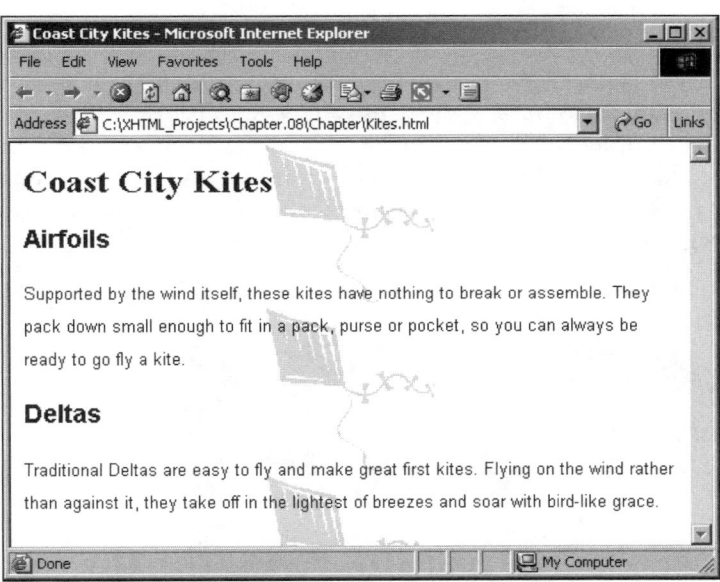

Figure 8-27   Coast City Kites Web page with paragraph line heights formatted to 200%

Next, you modify the style declaration for the **p** selector so paragraph text is formatted with double-spacing.

To modify the style declaration for the **p** selector so paragraph text is formatted with double-spacing:

1. Return to the **adventure_styles.css** file in your text editor window.

2. Modify the style declaration for the p selector so it includes a `line-height` property that changes the line height of the paragraph to double. The modified style declaration for the p selector should appear as follows:

```
p { font-family: Trebuchet MS; color: olive;
font-size: 80%; background-color: transparent;
line-height: 200% }
```

3. Save the **adventure_styles.css** file and then open the **WesternKayakExternal.html** file in your Web browser. The paragraph text should appear double-spaced.

4. Close your Web browser window.

Indenting

The `text-indent` property indents the first line of a paragraph according to the value you specify. You may be tempted to use an absolute measurement such as inches or centimeters with the `text-indent` property. Instead, be sure to use a relative length unit or a percentage unit in order to allow the indent to scale according to the element's font. For example, the following p selector style declaration indents the paragraph text by 5% of the total width of the paragraph. Figure 8-28 shows how the paragraphs for the Coast City Kites Web page appear when it includes the following declaration.

```
p { text-indent: 5%; line-height: 200% }
```

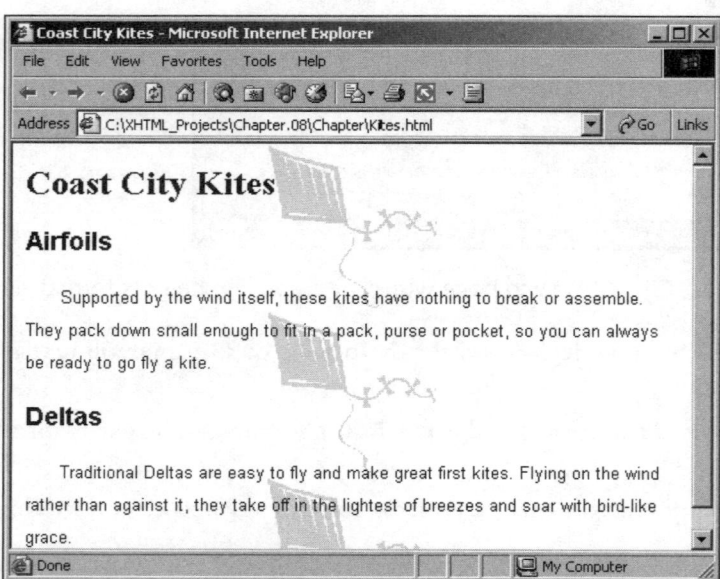

Figure 8-28   Coast City Kites Web page with paragraphs indented 5%

To indent all of the lines in an element, not just the first line, use the `margin-left` property. You can also use the `margin-right` property to set the right margin of an element and `margin-top` and `margin-bottom` properties to set the top and bottom margins of an element. The `margin-left`, `margin-right`, `margin-top`, and `margin-bottom` properties are part of the box properties category.

Next, you modify the style declaration for the **p** selector so paragraph text is indented by 5%.

To modify the style declaration for the **p** selector so paragraph text is indented by 5%:

1. Return to the **adventure_styles.css** file in your text editor window.

2. Modify the style declaration for the **p** selector so it includes a `text-indent` property that indents the first line of the paragraph by 5%. The modified style declaration for the **p** selector should appear as follows:

```
p { font-family: Trebuchet MS; color: olive;
font-size: 80%; background-color: transparent;
line-height: 200%; text-indent: 5% }
```

3. Save the **adventure_styles.css** file and then open the **WesternKayakExternal.html** file in your Web browser. The first line of each paragraph should appear indented.

4. Close your Web browser window.

Text Alignment

You have seen how to align text horizontally using the `text-align` property. Although the examples you have seen have been with inline styles, you can also use the `text-align` property with selectors. For example, to center align a document's `<h1>` and `<h2>` elements, you include the following declarations for each element's selector. Figure 8-29 shows how the headings appear for the Coast City Kites Web page when it includes the following declarations.

```
h1 { text-align: center }
h2 { text-align: center }
```

The `vertical-align` property is a little more complicated in that it changes the vertical alignment of an element in relation to its parent element. One common use of the `vertical-align` property is to adjust the position of images, such as toolbar buttons, that are placed inside a line of text. For example, the following statement places an image named home.jpg within the paragraph. Figure 8-30 shows how the paragraph appears in a Web browser.

```
<p>In Internet Explorer, you press the <img src="home.jpg"
/> button to return to your home page.</p>
```

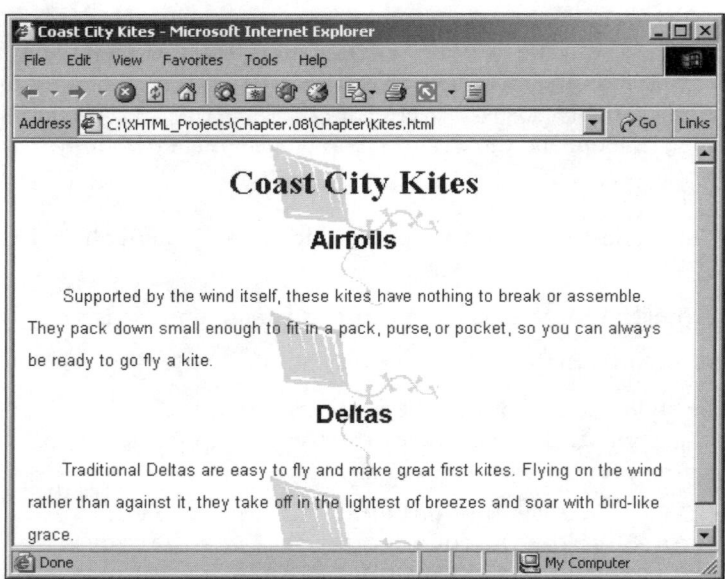

Figure 8-29 Coast City Kites Web site with headings center aligned

Figure 8-30 Paragraph with an inline image

Notice in Figure 8–30 that the image is aligned to the bottom of the line, which is the default setting. To format the image so it is positioned in the middle of the line, you add the **vertical-align: middle** style declaration to the **<img>** element, as shown by the inline style in the following code. Notice in Figure 8-31 that the image now appears in the middle of the line.

```
<p>In Internet Explorer, you press the <img style=
"vertical-align: middle" src="home.jpg" /> button to return
to your home page.</p>
```

Figure 8-31   Paragraph with an inline image formatted with the `vertical-align` property

SETTING FONT PROPERTIES

You use **font properties** to specify the typeface, size, and style of an element's text. Table 8-6 lists the CSS1 font properties.

8

Table 8-6   CSS1 font properties

Property	Description	Values
font	Sets all the font properties in one declaration	*font-family | font-size | font-style | font-variant | font-weight*
font-family	Specifies a list of font names or generic font names	*font family* | serif | sans-serif | cursive | fantasy | monospace
font-size	Specifies the size of a font	xx-small | x-small | small | medium | large | x-large | xx-large | smaller | larger | *length unit* | *percentage unit*
font-style	Sets the style of a font	normal | italic | oblique
font-variant	Specifies whether the font should appear in small caps	normal | small-caps
font-weight	Sets the weight of a font	normal | bold | bolder | lighter | 100 | 200 | 300 | 400 | 500 | 600 | 700 | 800 | 900

Next, you study each of the font properties.

Font Name

The `font-family` property is a critical font property because it sets the font that an element displays. When you select a font for an element, be sure to use a font that you know is installed on a user's computer. Your best bet is to assign a list of font names to the `font-family` property, separated by commas. When a Web browser renders the document, it looks for the first font name in the list, and uses it if it is available. If the first font name in the list is not available, the browser looks for the second name in the list, and so on. The following code specifies that the `<p>` element should use the Arial typeface if it is available. If Arial is not available, it uses the Helvetica typeface.

```
p { font-family: Arial, Helvetica }
```

For font names that do not include spaces, as in the preceding example, assign the names to the `font-family` property. However, you must place any font names that include spaces in quotation marks, as follows:

```
p { font-family: "Times New Roman", "New Century
Schoolbook", Garamond }
```

If you use an inline style to specify a font name with spaces, place the font name in single quotation marks, as follows:

```
<p style="font-family: 'Times New Roman'">Paragraph
formatted with Times New Roman.</p>
```

Generic font families represent the five major font families available in typography: serif, sans serif, cursive, fantasy, and monospace. Serif fonts include short lines and strokes, called serifs, like the ones found in the Times New Roman or New Century Schoolbook typefaces. Sans serif fonts are plainer and do not include text adornments. Examples of sans serif fonts include Arial and Helvetica. Cursive fonts look similar to cursive writing or handwriting. Fantasy fonts include various types of artistic fonts, like Algerian or Impact. Monospace fonts resemble typewriter fonts. Examples of monospace fonts are Courier and Courier New. The W3C recommends that you end a font list with one of the five generic font names. If the fonts you specify in the font list are not available on a user's machine, the Web browser will find the first font in the user's font list that is part of the generic font family. For example, a font list that specifies serif fonts, such as Times New Roman, should end with the serif generic font family, as follows:

```
p { font-family: "Times New Roman", "New Century
Schoolbook", Garamond, serif }
```

 If none of the fonts in a font list are available, not even the generic font family, then a user agent will display its own default font.

Next, you add font lists and a generic font family to each of the style declarations in adventure_styles.css that include a `font-name` property.

To add font lists and a generic font family to each of the style declarations that include a `font-name` property:

1. Return to the **adventure_styles.css** file in your text editor window.

2. For the `h1` and `h2` selectors, add Times New Roman and serif to the `font-family` property list. Be sure to place the Times New Roman font name in quotation marks. The modified style declaration should appear as follows:

```
h1, h2 { font-family: Garamond, "Times New Roman",
serif; color: maroon; background-color: transparent }
```

3. For the `p` and `links` selectors, place the Trebuchet MS font in quotation marks, and add Arial, Helvetica, and sans-serif to the font-family property list. The modified style declarations for both selectors should appear as follows:

```
p { font-family: "Trebuchet MS", Arial, Helvetica,
sans-serif; color: olive; background-color: transparent;
font-size: 80%; line-height: 200%; text-indent: 5% }
.links { font-family: "Trebuchet MS", Arial, Helvetica,
sans-serif; background-color: transparent; font-size: 80% }
```

4. Save the **adventure_styles.css** file and then open the **WesternKayakExternal.html** file in your Web browser. The Web page should appear the same as it did before you added the font lists.

5. Close your Web browser window.

Font Size

You have seen examples of how to specify font size using the `font-size` property. When specifying font size, be sure to use a relative length unit such as ems or a percentage unit. Alternately, you can use one of the following predefined values to set font size: xx-small, x-small, small, medium, large, x-large, xx-large, smaller, or larger. Each of these predefined values are called absolute sizes and are somewhat limited because they do not adjust automatically to the browser or parent font, as do font sizes specified with relative length units. Figure shows 8-32 how each of the absolute sizes appear in a Web browser. Each of the lines shown in Figure 8-32 is created using a statement similar to the following:

```
<p style="font-size: xx-small">Paragraph formatted with
the <code>xx-small</code> absolute value.</p>
```

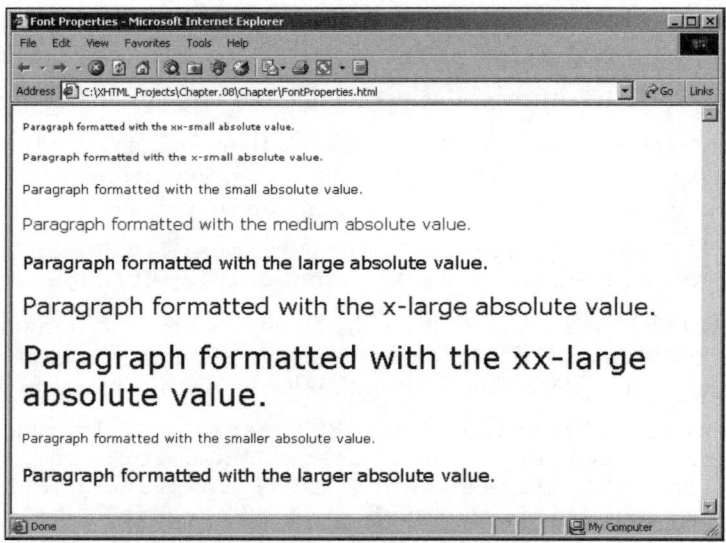

Figure 8-32   Paragraphs formatted with absolute font sizes

Font Appearance

In addition to the font family and the font size, you can change the appearance of a font using the `font-style`, `font-variant`, and `font-weight` properties. The `font-style` property allows you to make text italicized or oblique, which is a slanted font, similar to an italicized font. The `font-variant` property causes text to appear as small capital letters, LIKE THIS. The `font-weight` property determines how bold text appears or how light it appears.

The `font` Shorthand Property

Just as the `background` property is the shorthand property for the background properties category, the `font` property is the shorthand property for the font properties category. Using the `font` shorthand property, you can set values for all of the font properties in a single declaration. In addition to setting the `font-style`, `font-weight`, `font-variant`, `font-size`, and `font-family` properties, you can also use the `font` shorthand property to set the `line-height` property from the text properties category. As with the `background` property, you can set any `font` property or the `line-height` property by assigning just the property value to the `font` property. You separate multiple property values with spaces. Note that the values for the `font` property must be set in the following order:

- `font-style` (optional)
- `font-weight` (optional)

- font-variant (optional)

- font-size (required)

- line-height (optional)

- font-family (required)

You must include the font-size and font-family property values, although you can safely exclude the rest. However, if you exclude the optional property values, be sure that the properties you use follow the correct order.

Note that the font-size and line-height property values must be separated by a forward slash (/). For example, to use the font property to set the font-weight, font-size, line-height, and font-families properties, you use the following declaration. Notice that although the declaration does not include the font-style or font-variant properties, the values still follow the correct order.

```
p { font: normal 1em/200% Arial, Verdana, sans-serif }
```

 Do not include spaces on either side of the forward slash that separates the font-size and line-height values or some browsers, including Internet Explorer, will ignore the line-height value.

Next, you replace the font-family, font-size, and line-height properties in the style declaration for the p selector with the font shorthand property.

To use the font shorthand property in the style declaration for the p selector:

1. Return to the **adventure_styles.css** file in your text editor window.

2. Replace the font-family, font-size, and line-height properties in the style declaration for the p selector with the font shorthand property, as follows:

```
p { color: #808000; background-color: transparent;
text-indent: 5%; font: 80%/200% "Trebuchet MS", Arial,
Helvetica, sans-serif }
```

3. Save and close the **adventure_styles.css** file and then open the **WesternKayakExternal.html** file in your Web browser. The Web page should appear the same as it did before you added the font shorthand property.

4. Close your Web browser window and text editor.

VALIDATING STYLE SHEETS

Next, you will validate the WesternKayakExternal.html file.

To validate the WesternKayakExternal.html file:

1. Start your Web browser and enter the URL for the upload page of the W3C MarkUp Validation Service: **validator.w3.org/file-upload.html**.

2. Open and validate the **WesternKayakExternal.html** file. If you receive any errors, fix them, and then revalidate the document.

3. Close your Web browser window.

The W3C also offers a utility, the W3C CSS Validation Service, for validating CSS code. The W3C CSS Validation Service upload is primarily used for external style sheets. You can download a copy of the utility or validate your CSS code online, the same as you validate XHTML code with the W3C Markup Validation Service. You can access the main W3C CSS Validation Service at *http://jigsaw.w3.org/css-validator/*. The upload page for the W3C CSS Validation Service is located at *http://jigsaw.w3.org/css-validator/validtor-upload.html*.

You choose the external style sheet file you want validated by clicking the Browse button. The Warnings combo box allows you to select the severity of warnings you want displayed when your style sheet is validated. The Profile combo box allows you to select the type of styles used in your style sheet (CSS1, CSS2, and so on). The Medium combo box allows you to select the type of medium your styles are designed for, such as the screen, aural and Braille browsers, and handheld devices.

Now you will validate the adventure_styles.css file.

To validate the adventure_styles.css file:

1. Start your Web browser and enter the URL for the upload page of the W3C CSS Validation Service: **jigsaw.w3.org/css-validator/validator-upload.html**.

2. Open the **adventure_styles.CSS** file. Leave the Warnings combo box set to its default setting of Normal report and the Medium combo box to its default setting of all. However, change the setting in the Profile combo box from CSS version 2 to **CSS version 1**.

3. Click the **Submit this CSS file for validation** button to validate the file. You should receive a message of "No error or warning found", as shown in Figure 8-33. If you receive any errors, fix them, and then revalidate the style sheet.

4. Close your Web browser window.

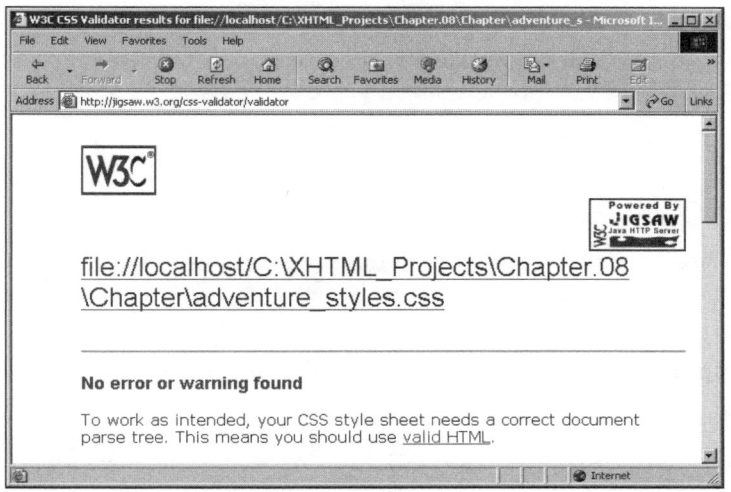

Figure 8-33   Results returned from validating the adventure_styles.css file

CHAPTER SUMMARY

❏ Cascading Style Sheets (CSS) are a standard set by the W3C for managing the design and format of Web pages in a Web browser.

❏ A single piece of CSS formatting information, such as text alignment or font size, is referred to as a style.

❏ The term *cascading* refers to the Web pages' ability to use CSS information from more than one source.

❏ CSS styles are created in two parts separated by a colon: the property, which refers to a specific CSS style, and the value assigned to it, which determines the style's visual characteristics.

❏ A CSS property and the value assigned to it are referred to as a declaration or style declaration.

❏ Inline styles allow you to add style information to a single element in a document.

❏ Length units refer to the units of measure that you can use in a style declaration to determine the size or positioning of an element.

❏ Percentage units adjust properties relative to other values.

❏ A color unit represents a color value that you can assign to a property.

❏ You use an internal style sheet to create styles that apply to an entire document.

8

❑ The element to which specific style rules in a style sheet apply is called a selector.

❑ A contextual selector allows you to specify formatting for an element, but only when it is contained within another element.

❑ A class selector allows you to create different groups of styles for the same element.

❑ An ID selector allows you to create style declarations that are applied to only a single element in the document.

❑ External style sheets are separate text documents containing style declarations that can be used by multiple documents on a Web site.

❑ The `<div>` element formats a group of block-level and inline elements with styles, whereas the `<span>` element formats a group of inline elements.

❑ The `color` property sets the text color of an element.

❑ Background properties set the background color or image that appears behind an element.

❑ Several of the property categories include a special property called a shorthand property that allows you to set all of the properties in a category using one declaration.

❑ You use text properties to specify the placement and appearance of text.

❑ You use font properties to specify the typeface, size, and style of an element's text.

REVIEW QUESTIONS

1. What is the correct syntax for creating an inline style that assigns Arial to the `font-family` property?

   a. `style="font-family, Arial"`

   b. `font-family=Arial`

   c. `style="font-family: Arial"`

   d. `font-family; Arial`

2. The styles you assign to an element are automatically passed to any nested elements it contains. True or False?

3. You can include multiple style declarations in an inline style by separating each declaration with a _____.

   a. colon

   b. semicolon

   c. comma

   d. forward slash

4. Explain when you should use inline styles.

5. Which of the following length units are relative? (Choose all that apply.)

    a. em (em space)

    b. ex (x height)

    c. px (pixels)

    d. pt (points)

6. The number and unit of measure you assign as a value to a property must be separated by a space. True or False?

7. Explain when you should use an internal style sheet.

8. A contextual selector allows you to specify formatting for an element, but only when it is contained within another element. True or False?

9. What is the correct syntax for creating a `class` selector named "emphasis" that can be used with any element?

    a. `styles.emphasis { color: greed; font-weight: bolder }`

    b. `all.emphasis { color: greed; font-weight: bolder }`

    c. `emphasis { color: green; font-weight: bolder }`

    d. `.emphasis { color: green; font-weight: bolder }`

10. Explain when you should use an external style sheet.

11. What value is assigned to the `rel` attribute in the `<link>` element?

    a. css

    b. external

    c. stylesheet

    d. stylesheets

12. Which of the following elements allow(s) you to apply style information to a group of elements? (Choose all that apply.)

    a. `<div>`

    b. `<css>`

    c. `<span>`

    d. `<styles>`

13. Which of the following style sources has the highest level of precedence?

    a. Internal style sheets

    b. External style sheets

    c. Inline styles

    d. Browser defaults

8

14. What is the default value applied to the **background-repeat** property?

    a. repeat

    b. repeat-x

    c. repeat-y

    d. no-repeat

15. Background properties can be applied only to the document body. True or False?

16. What is the correct format for assigning an image to the background-image property?

    a. `background-image: image.jpg`

    b. `background-image: "url(image.jpg)"`

    c. `background-image: url("image.jpg")`

    d. `background-image: url(image.jpg)`

17. Explain how you assign values to a shorthand property.

18. Which of the following values can be assigned to the **text-align** property? (Choose all that apply.)

    a. left

    b. center

    c. right

    d. justify

19. You must place any font names that include spaces in quotation marks. True or False?

20. If you have assigned to the **font-family** property a font list that includes the Arial and Helvetica fonts, what should the last entry in the font list be?

    a. serif

    b. sans-serif

    c. script

    d. fantasy

HANDS-ON PROJECTS

Project 8-1

In this project, you use inline styles to format a Web page for a relocation service. The file to which you will add the style information, Relocation.html, is located in your Chapter.08\Projects folder.

1. In your text editor, open the **Relocation.html** file from your Chapter.08\Projects folder. The document body contains two heading elements and three paragraph elements.

2. Add to the `<body>` element the following inline style declaration that changes the background color of the page to aqua:

   ```
   style="background-color: aqua"
   ```

3. Next, modify the two heading elements so they contain inline style formatting, as follows:

   ```
   <h1 style="font-
   family: 'Times New Roman', Times, serif; font-size: 2em;
   color: navy; background-color: transparent">
   Central Valley</h1>
   <h2 style="font-family: 'Times New Roman', Times, serif;
   font-size: 1.5em; text-spacing: 80%; color: navy;
   background-color: transparent">Relocation Service</h2>
   ```

4. Now, add the following inline style declaration to each of the paragraph elements:

   ```
   style="font-family: 'Times New Roman', Times, serif;
   font-size: .8em; color: navy; background-color: transparent"
   ```

5. Save the **Relocation.html** file.

6. Use the W3C Markup Validation Service to validate the Relocation.html file. Once the file is valid, open it in your Web browser and see how the new style formatting appears. Your Web page should look similar to Figure 8-34.

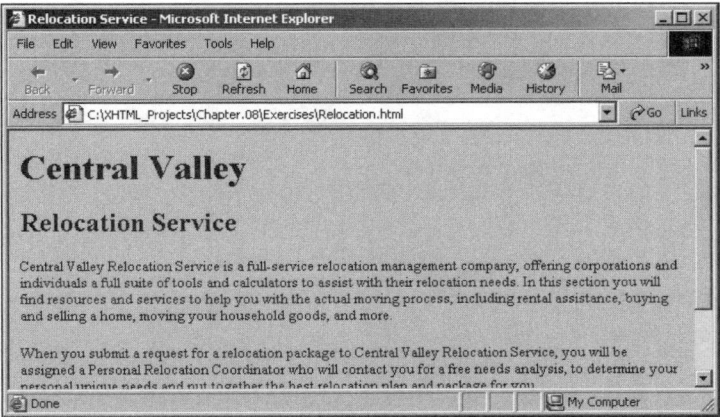

Figure 8-34   Relocation Web page

7. Close your Web browser window.

Project 8-2

In this project, you use an internal style sheet to add style information to a Web page that contains customer testimonials for an auto body shop. The file to which you add the style information, AutoBodyShop.html, is located in your Chapter.08\Projects folder.

1. In your text editor, open the **AutoBodyShop.html** file from your Chapter.08\Projects folder. The document body contains three `<blockquote>` elements, each of which includes text and `<em>` elements.

2. Add the following internal style sheet above the document's closing `</head>` element. The style sheet includes declarations for the h1, h2, and `blockquote` selectors, along with a contextual selector for the `<em>` element when located within a `<blockquote>` element.

```
<style type="text/css">
h1 { font-family: Verdana, Helvetica, sans-serif;
font-size: 1.5em; color: navy }
h2 { font-family: Verdana, Helvetica, sans-serif;
font-size: 1.2em; color: red }
blockquote { font-family: Verdana, Helvetica,
sans-serif; font-size: 1em; color: blue }
blockquote em { font-weight: bold; color: purple }
</style>
```

3. Save and close the file **AutoBodyShop.html** file.

4. Use the W3C Markup Validation Service to validate the AutoBodyShop.html file. Once the file is valid, open it in your Web browser. Figure 8-35 shows how the Web page should appear in a Web browser.

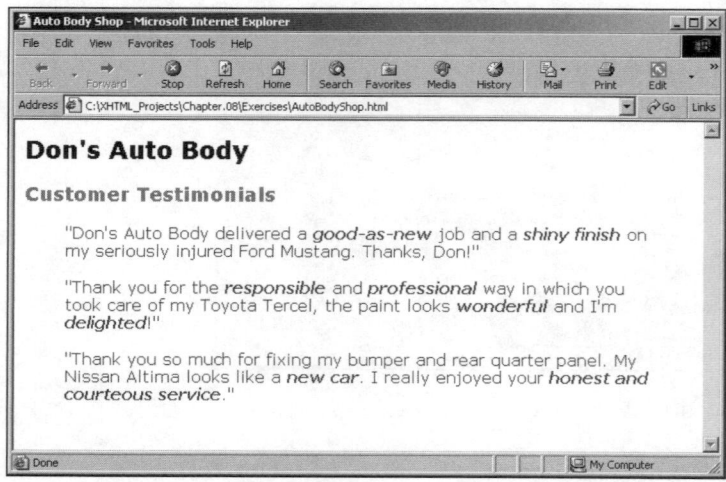

Figure 8-35   Auto Body Shop Web page

5. Close your Web browser window.

Project 8-3

In this project, you use inline styles to add background color, foreground color, and line height formatting to a paragraph on a Web page for a sailing school. The file to which you add the style information, SailingSchool.html, is located in your Chapter.08\Projects folder.

1. In your text editor, open the **SailingSchool.html** file from your Chapter.08\ Projects folder. The document body contains a single paragraph with information about the school.

2. Add inline styles to the paragraph so it matches Figure 8-36. Use whatever fonts you like, but be sure to create a font list. Format the paragraph so it is double-spaced. The background color should be navy, and the foreground color should be the hex value equivalent to white.

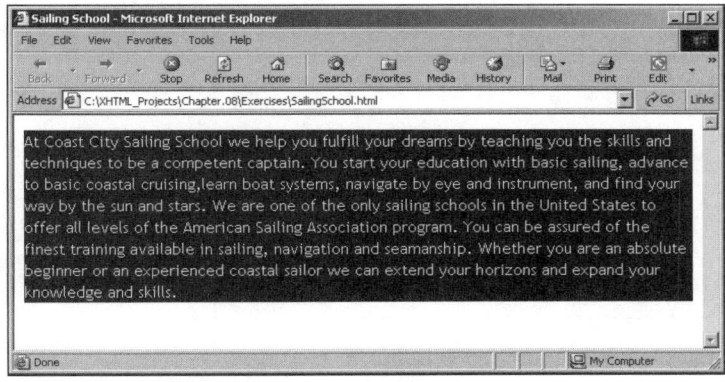

Figure 8-36   Sailing School Web page

3. Save the **SailingSchool.html** file.

4. Use the W3C Markup Validation Service to validate the SailingSchool.html file. Once the file is valid, open it in your Web browser and see how the colors look.

5. Close your Web browser window.

Project 8-4

In this project, you create a Web page for a petting zoo that includes an internal style sheet.

1. Create a new document in your text editor.

2. Type the `<!DOCTYPE>` declaration, `<html>` element, document head, and `<body>` element. Use the Strict DTD and "Noah's Ark Petting Zoo" as the content of the `<title>` element.

3. Create the document shown in Figure 8-37. Format the document using an internal style sheet. Create two class selectors in the style sheet for the `<p>` element: one for the first two indented paragraphs and another for the boldface, centered paragraph at the bottom of the page. Use the closest fonts you have to the fonts displayed in the figure, but be sure to create a font list.

4. Save the file as **PettingZoo.html** in the Chapter.08\Projects folder.

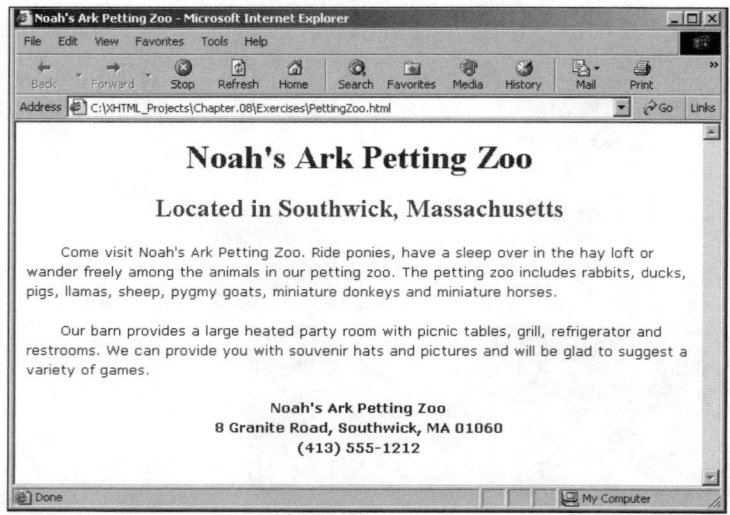

Figure 8-37   Noah's Ark Petting Zoo Web page

5. Close the **PettingZoo.html** file in your text editor, and then use the W3C Markup Validation Service to validate it. Once the file is valid, open it in your Web browser.

6. Close your Web browser window.

Project 8-5

In this project, you create a document that uses an ID selector to align a toolbar button in the middle of a line.

1. Create a new document in your text editor.

2. Type the `<!DOCTYPE>` declaration, `<html>` element, document head, and `<body>` element. Use the Strict DTD and "Free Shipping" as the content of the `<title>` element.

3. Add to the document body the following paragraph and inline image:

```
<p><img src="dollars.gif" alt="Graphic of a price tag with
a dollar symbol." /> Free shipping until January 1!</p>
```

4. Save the document as **FreeShipping.html** in your Chapter.08\Projects folder and open it in your Web browser window. The image should be raised too high on the line.

5. Close your Web browser window and return to the FreeShipping.html file in your text editor.

6. Add an internal style sheet to the document that includes an ID selector with the appropriate style declaration to align the image in the middle of the paragraph. Assign the ID selector to the **<img>** element that displays the image.

7. Save and close the **FreeShipping.html** file.

8. Use the W3C Markup Validation Service to validate the FreeShipping.html file. Once the file is valid, open it in your Web browser. Figure 8-38 shows how the Web page should appear in a Web browser.

Figure 8-38   Free Shipping Web page

9. Close your Web browser window.

Project 8-6

In this project, you use class selectors to add yellow highlighting to sections of a paragraph. The file to which you will add the highlighting, Highlighter.html, is located in your Chapter.08\Exercises folder.

1. In your text editor, open the **Highlighter.html** file from your Chapter.08\Projects folder. The document body contains a single paragraph from Leo Tolstoy's *Anna Karenina*.

2. Use an internal style sheet to add the yellow highlighting shown in Figure 8-39:

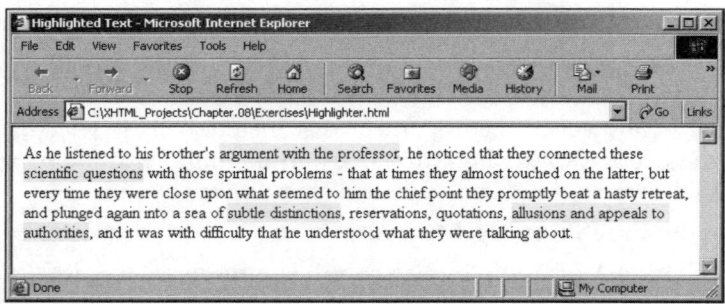

As he listened to his brother's argument with the professor, he noticed that they connected these scientific questions with those spiritual problems - that at times they almost touched on the latter; but every time they were close upon what seemed to him the chief point they promptly beat a hasty retreat, and plunged again into a sea of subtle distinctions, reservations, quotations, allusions and appeals to authorities, and it was with difficulty that he understood what they were talking about.

Figure 8-39   Paragraph with yellow highlighting

3. Save and close the **Highlighter.html** file.

4. Use the W3C Markup Validation Service to validate the Highlighter.html file. Once the file is valid, open it in your Web browser to see how the highlighted text appears.

5. Close your Web browser window.

Project 8-7

In this project, you create a document for a company that sells baseball team uniforms.

1. Create a new document in your text editor.

2. Type the `<!DOCTYPE>` declaration, `<html>` element, document head, and `<body>` element. Use the Strict DTD and "Team Uniform Sales" as the content of the `<title>` element.

3. Create the table shown in Figure 8-40. The three image files you need for the document—marlins.gif, braves.gif, and yankees.gif—are located in your Chapter.08\ Projects folder. Add the text formatting using an internal style sheet. For the text formatting in the right column, create three generic class selectors and apply them to each line using a `<span>` element. Name the class selector for the first line `.team`, the class selector for the second line, `.shipping`, and the class selector for the third line `.price`. Use the closest fonts you have to the fonts displayed in the figure, but be sure to create a font list. Also, use different colors for each of the three generic class selectors.

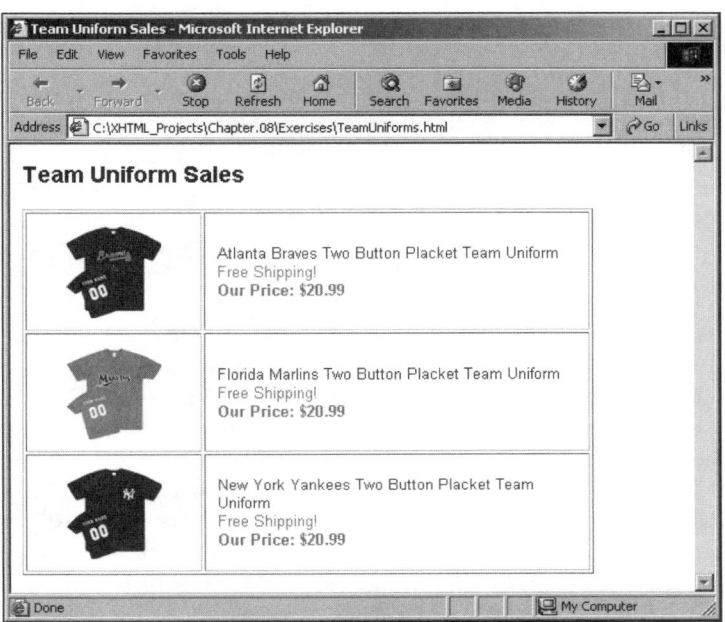

Figure 8-40   Team Uniform Sales Web page

4. Save the file as **TeamUniforms.html** in the Chapter.08\Projects folder.

5. Close the **TeamUniforms.html** file in your text editor, and then use the W3C Markup Validation Service to validate it. Once the file is valid, open it in your Web browser.

6. Close your Web browser window.

Project 8-8

In this project, you add a background image to the document body of a Web page for a chimney repair company. The files you will need, ChimneyRepairs.html and chimney.gif, are located in your Chapter.08\Projects folder.

1. In your text editor, open the **ChimneyRepairs.html** file from your Chapter.08\ Projects folder. The document body contains a heading and several paragraphs. The document head contains a `<style>` element that contains some font and color formatting properties for the heading and paragraphs.

2. Add the appropriate style declaration to the `<style>` element that will place the chimney.gif file in the document's background. The image should repeat.

3. Save and close the **ChimneyRepairs.html** file.

4. Use the W3C Markup Validation Service to validate the ChimneyRepairs.html file. Once the file is valid, open it in your Web browser.

5. Close your Web browser window.

CASE PROJECTS

For the following projects, save the files you create in the Chapter.08\Cases folder. Use external style sheets to add CSS formatting to each of the projects. Create the files so they are well formed according to the Strict Document Type Definition (DTD). Validate the Web pages you create with the W3C Markup Validation Service and the style sheets you create with the W3C CSS Validation Service.

Project 8-1

Create a Web page for a copy center. Format the heading level styles in olive and the paragraphs in blue. Format the heading and body elements using sans-serif fonts such as Arial and Helvetica. Include headings such as Services Offered, Hours of Operation, Copy Charges, and Accepted Forms of Payment. Within the Copy Charges heading, create a table that lists the cost of different types of copies such as black and white, color, and transparencies. Format the rows in the table so they alternate from white to gray. Within the gray rows, format the text to be white. Within the white rows, format the text to be black. You will need to set the `color` and `background-color` properties for the table's `<tr>` elements using class selectors. Save the Web page as CopyCenter.html and the style sheet as copies.css.

Project 8-2

Create a Web page for a company that rents snowmobiles. Format the heading elements in navy and the paragraphs in black. Use the body selector to format all of the text in the body using serif fonts such as Garamond and Times New Roman. Also, include as a repeating background image the snow.gif image located in your Chapter.08\Cases folder. Use whatever size you like for the heading and paragraph font sizes. Include at least three paragraphs that describe the services the company offers. Format each paragraph so its line height is spaced at 150%. Also, format the first word in every paragraph so it is 30% larger than the surrounding text, formatted in blue, and uses a sans-serif font such as Arial. Save the Web page as SnowmobileRentals.html and the style sheet as snowmobiles.css.

Project 8-3

Create a Web site for a tanning salon. Include a home page, a services page, and a frequently asked questions (FAQ) page. Create the Web page using a table that simulates a frame. Format the heading elements in Arial, with a font weight of bold, using the color lime. Also format the anchor elements in Arial, using the color lime, but with a font weight of normal. Format paragraph and table elements in Arial, but with a background color of black. Save the home page as TanningSalon.html, the services page as Services.html, the FAQ page as FAQ.html, and the style sheet as tanning.css.

XHTML 1.0 REFERENCE

STRICT DTD ELEMENTS

The `<!DOCTYPE>` declaration for the Strict Document Type Definition (DTD) is as follows:

```
<!DOCTYPE html PUBLIC
"-//W3C//DTD XHTML 1.0 Strict//EN"
"http://www.w3.org/TR/xhtml1/DTD/xhtml1-strict.dtd">
```

The following table lists the elements that are available in the Strict DTD.

The attributes available to elements vary according to the Extensible Hypertext Markup Language (XHTML) DTD that your document conforms to. For a detailed reference of XHTML elements and the attributes available to them according to DTD, visit the XHTML 1.0 reference that is available on the W3Schools Web site at *http://www.w3schools.com/xhtml/xhtml_reference.asp*.

Elements in the Strict DTD

Element	Description
`<!--...-->`	Adds non-rendering comments to a document
`<!DOCTYPE>`	Identifies the XHTML DTD to which the document conforms
`<a>`	Creates a hyperlink
`<abbr>`	Specifies abbreviated text
`<acronym>`	Identifies an acronym
`<address>`	Identifies address information
`<area />`	Identifies the coordinates within an image that will be recognized as hot zones
`<b>`	Formats text in boldface type
`<base />`	Specifies a base Uniform Resource Locator (URL) for all of a document's relative links
`<bdo>`	Determines text direction
`<big>`	Formats text in a larger font
`<blockquote>`	Defines a block quotation
`<body>`	Defines the document body
` `	Inserts a new line break
`<button>`	Creates push buttons, submit buttons, and reset buttons

Elements in the Strict DTD (continued)

Element	Description
`<caption>`	Defines a table caption
`<cite>`	Defines a citation
`<code>`	Identifies computer code
`<col>`	Defines a table column
`<colgroup>`	Defines a table column group
`<dd>`	Defines a definition list item
`<del>`	Identifies deleted text
`<dfn>`	Marks a definition
`<div>`	Formats a group of block-level and inline elements with styles
`<dl>`	Marks a definition list
`<dt>`	Defines a definition list term
`<em>`	Defines emphasized text
`<fieldset>`	Creates a field set that visually groups related controls on a form
`<form>`	Defines an interactive form
`<h1> to <h6>`	Heading level elements
`<head>`	Defines the document head
`<hr />`	Creates a horizontal rule
`<html>`	Identifies a document as a Hypertext Markup Language (HTML) or XHTML document
`<i>`	Formats text in italic type
`<img />`	Inserts an image
`<input />`	Creates input fields that create different types of interface elements to gather information
`<ins>`	Identifies inserted text
`<kbd>`	Indicates text that is to be entered by a visitor to a Web site
`<label>`	Associates a label with a form control
`<legend>`	Provides a caption or description for a group of controls in a field set
`<li>`	Defines a list item
`<link>`	Defines the relationship between linked documents
`<map>`	Specifies mapping coordinates for an image map
`<meta>`	Defines metadata about a Web page
`<noscript>`	Alternate script content
`<object>`	Defines an embedded object
`<ol>`	Defines an ordered list
`<optgroup>`	Creates option groups that organize groups of option elements that appear in a selection list

Elements in the Strict DTD (continued)

A

Element	Description
<option>	Specifies the items that appear in a selection list
<p>	Defines a paragraph
<param>	Defines a parameter for an object
<pre>	Preformatted text
<q>	Defines a quotation
<samp>	Identifies sample computer code
<script>	Contains commands for scripting languages such as JavaScript and VBScript
<select>	Creates a selection list that presents users with fixed lists of items from which to choose
<small>	Formats text in a smaller font
<span>	Formats a group of inline elements with styles
<strong>	Defines strongly emphasized text
<style>	Defines the style information for a specific element
<sub>	Formats enclosed text as a subscript
<sup>	Formats enclosed text as a superscript
<table>	Defines a table
<tbody>	Defines a table body
<td>	Defines table data
<textarea>	Creates a field in which users can enter multiple lines of information
<tfoot>	Defines a table footer
<th>	Defines a table heading
<thead>	Defines a table header
<title>	Contains text that appears in a browser's title bar
<tr>	Defines a table row
<tt>	Formats enclosed text as teletype or monospaced text
<ul>	Defines an unordered list
<var>	Defines a variable

TRANSITIONAL DTD ELEMENTS

The <!DOCTYPE> declaration for the Transitional DTD is as follows:

```
<!DOCTYPE html PUBLIC
"-//W3C//DTD XHTML 1.0 Transitional //EN"
"http://www.w3.org/TR/xhtml1/DTD/xhtml1-transitional.dtd">
```

The Transitional DTD includes all of the elements found in the Strict DTD, along with the elements listed in the following table:

Additional elements in Transitional DTD

Element	Description
`<applet>`	Executes Java applets
`<basefont />`	Specifies the base font size
`<center>`	Centers text
`<dir>`	Defines a directory list
`<font>`	Specifies a font name, size, and color
`<iframe>`	Creates an inline frame that displays another document within the body of the current document
`<isindex>`	Creates automatic document indexing forms
`<menu>`	Defines a menu list
`<noframes>`	Displays a message to users of Web browsers that are not capable of displaying frames
`<s>` or `<strike>`	Formats strikethrough text
`<u>`	Formats underlined text

FRAMESET DTD ELEMENTS

The `<!DOCTYPE>` declaration for the Frameset DTD is as follows:

```
<!DOCTYPE html PUBLIC
"-//W3C//DTD XHTML 1.0 Frameset//EN"
"http://www.w3.org/TR/xhtml1/DTD/xhtml1-frameset.dtd">
```

The Frameset DTD includes all of the elements found in the Strict and Transitional DTDs, along with the elements listed in the following table:

Additional elements in Frameset DTD

Element	Description
`<frame>`	Specify options for individual frames in a frameset
`<frameset>`	Divides a document into frames

STANDARD ATTRIBUTES

The standard XHTML attributes are listed in the following table:

Standard XHTML attributes

Attribute	Description
class	Identifies various elements as part of the same group
dir	Specifies the direction of text
id	Uniquely identifies an individual element in a document
lang / xml:lang	Specifies the language in which the contents of an element were originally written
style	Defines the style information for a specific element
title	Provides descriptive text for an element

The class, id, and title attributes are not valid in the <base>, <head>, <html>, <meta>, <param>, <script>, <style>, and <title> elements; the dir, lang, and xml:lang attributes are not valid in the <base>, <br>, <frame>, <frameset>, <hr>, <iframe>, <param>, and <script> elements; and the style attribute is not valid in the <html>, <head>, <title>, <meta>, <style>, <script>, <param>, and <base> elements.

B

NUMERIC CHARACTER REFERENCES AND CHARACTER ENTITIES

A numeric character reference inserts a special character using its numeric position in the Unicode character set. To display a character using a numeric character reference, you place an ampersand (&) and the number sign (#) before the character's Unicode number and a semicolon after the Unicode number. A character entity reference, or character entity, uses a descriptive name for a special character instead of its Unicode number. To display a character using a character entity, you place an ampersand (&) before the character's descriptive name and a semicolon after the Unicode number. Note that you do not include the number sign (#) after the ampersand as you do with numeric character references.

The following tables list the available numeric character references and character entities:

Latin 1 character set

Character	Description	Numeric Character Reference	Character Entity
	Space	&#32;	
!	Exclamation mark	&#33;	
"	Quotation mark	&#34;	&quot;
#	Number sign	&#35;	
$	Dollar sign	&#36;	
%	Percent sign	&#37;	
&	Ampersand	&#38;	&amp;
'	Apostrophe	&#39;	
(	Left parenthesis	&#40;	
)	Right parenthesis	&#41;	
*	Asterisk	&#42;	
+	Plus sign	&#43;	

Latin 1 character set (continued)

Character	Description	Numeric Character Reference	Character Entity
,	Comma	&#44;	
-	Hyphen	&#45;	
.	Period	&#46;	
/	Forward slash	&#47;	
0	Numeral 0	&#48;	
1	Numeral 1	&#49;	
2	Numeral 2	&#50;	
3	Numeral 3	&#51;	
4	Numeral 4	&#52;	
5	Numeral 5	&#53;	
6	Numeral 6	&#54;	
7	Numeral 7	&#55;	
8	Numeral 8	&#56;	
9	Numeral 9	&#57;	
:	Colon	&#58;	
;	Semicolon	&#59;	
<	Less than	&#60;	&lt;
=	Equals sign	&#61;	
>	Greater than	&#62;	&gt;
?	Question mark	&#63;	
@	At symbol	&#64;	
A	Capital A	&#65;	
B	Capital B	&#66;	
C	Capital C	&#67;	
D	Capital D	&#68;	
E	Capital E	&#69;	
F	Capital F	&#70;	
G	Capital G	&#71;	
H	Capital H	&#72;	
I	Capital I	&#73;	
J	Capital J	&#74;	
K	Capital K	&#75;	
L	Capital L	&#76;	
M	Capital M	&#77;	
N	Capital N	&#78;	

Latin 1 character set (continued)

Character	Description	Numeric Character Reference	Character Entity
O	Capital O	&#79;	
P	Capital P	&#80;	
Q	Capital Q	&#81;	
R	Capital R	&#82;	
S	Capital S	&#83;	
T	Capital T	&#84;	
U	Capital U	&#85;	
V	Capital V	&#86;	
W	Capital W	&#87;	
X	Capital X	&#88;	
Y	Capital Y	&#89;	
Z	Capital Z	&#90;	
[	Left square bracket	&#91;	
\	backslash	&#92;	
]	Right square bracket	&#93;	
^	Caret	&#94;	
_	Underscore	&#95;	
`	Acute accent	&#96;	
a	Small a	&#97;	
b	Small b	&#98;	
c	Small c	&#99;	
d	Small d	&#100;	
e	Small e	&#101;	
f	Small f	&#102;	
g	Small g	&#103;	
h	Small h	&#104;	
i	Small i	&#105;	
j	Small j	&#106;	
k	Small k	&#107;	
l	Small l	&#108;	
m	Small m	&#109;	
n	Small n	&#110;	
o	Small o	&#111;	
p	Small p	&#112;	
q	Small q	&#113;	

B

Latin 1 character set (continued)

Character	Description	Numeric Character Reference	Character Entity
r	Small r	&#114;	
s	Small s	&#115;	
t	Small t	&#116;	
u	Small u	&#117;	
v	Small v	&#118;	
w	Small w	&#119;	
x	Small x	&#120;	
y	Small y	&#121;	
z	Small z	&#122;	
{	Left brace	&#123;	
		Vertical bar	|	
}	Right brace	&#125;	
~	Tilde	&#126;	
	Nonbreaking space		
¡	Inverted exclamation	&#161;	&iexcl;
¢	Cent sign	&#162;	&cent;
£	Pound sterling	&#163;	&pound;
¤	General currency sign	&#164;	&curren;
¥	Yen sign	&#165;	&yen;
¦	Broken vertical bar	&#166;	¦ or &brkbar;
§	Section sign	&#167;	&sect;
¨	Diaeresis / Umlaut	&#168;	¨ or ¨
©	Copyright	&#169;	&copy;
ª	Feminine ordinal	&#170;	&ordf;
«	Left angle quote, guillemet left	&#171;	&laquo;
¬	Not sign	&#172;	&not;
	Soft hyphen	&#173;	&shy;
®	Registered trademark	&#174;	&reg;
¯	Macron accent	&#175;	¯ or &hibar;
°	Degree sign	&#176;	&deg;
±	Plus or minus	&#177;	&plusmn;
²	Superscript two	&#178;	&sup2;
³	Superscript three	&#179;	&sup3;
´	Acute accent	&#180;	&acute;
µ	Micro sign	&#181;	&micro;

Latin 1 character set (continued)

Character	Description	Numeric Character Reference	Character Entity
¶	Paragraph sign	&#182;	&para;
·	Middle dot	&#183;	&middot;
¸	Cedilla	&#184;	&cedil;
¹	Superscript one	&#185;	&sup1;
º	Masculine ordinal	&#186;	&ordm;
»	Right angle quote, guillemet right	&#187;	&raquo;
¼	Fraction one-fourth	&#188;	&frac14;
½	Fraction one-half	&#189;	&frac12;
¾	Fraction three-fourths	&#190;	&frac34;
¿	Inverted question mark	&#191;	&iquest;
À	Capital A, grave accent	&#192;	&Agrave;
Á	Capital A, acute accent	&#193;	&Aacute;
Â	Capital A, circumflex	&#194;	&Acirc;
Ã	Capital A, tilde	&#195;	&Atilde;
Ä	Capital A, diaeresis / umlaut	&#196;	&Auml;
Å	Capital A, ring	&#197;	&Aring;
Æ	Capital AE ligature	&#198;	&AElig;
Ç	Capital C, cedilla	&#199;	&Ccedil;
È	Capital E, grave accent	&#200;	&Egrave;
É	Capital E, acute accent	&#201;	&Eacute;
Ê	Capital E, circumflex	&#202;	&Ecirc;
Ë	Capital E, diaeresis / umlaut	&#203;	&Euml;
Ì	Capital I, grave accent	&#204;	&Igrave;
Í	Capital I, acute accent	&#205;	&Iacute;
Î	Capital I, circumflex	&#206;	&Icirc;
Ï	Capital I, diaeresis / umlaut	&#207;	&Iuml;
Ð	Capital Eth, Icelandic	&#208;	&ETH;
Ñ	Capital N, tilde	&#209;	&Ntilde;
Ò	Capital O, grave accent	&#210;	&Ograve;
Ó	Capital O, acute accent	&#211;	&Oacute;
Ô	Capital O, circumflex	&#212;	&Ocirc;
Õ	Capital O, tilde	&#213;	&Otilde;
Ö	Capital O, diaeresis / umlaut	&#214;	&Ouml;
×	Multiply sign	&#215;	&times;
Ø	Capital O, slash	&#216;	&Oslash;

Latin 1 character set (continued)

Character	Description	Numeric Character Reference	Character Entity
Ù	Capital U, grave accent	&#217;	&Ugrave;
Ú	Capital U, acute accent	&#218;	&Uacute;
Û	Capital U, circumflex	&#219;	&Ucirc;
Ü	Capital U, diaeresis / umlaut	&#220;	&Uuml;
Ý	Capital Y, acute accent	&#221;	&Yacute;
Þ	Capital Thorn, Icelandic	&#222;	&THORN;
ß	Small sharp s, German sz	&#223;	&szlig;
à	Small a, grave accent	&#224;	&agrave;
á	Small a, acute accent	&#225;	&aacute;
â	Small a, circumflex	&#226;	&acirc;
ã	Small a, tilde	&#227;	&atilde;
ä	Small a, diaeresis / umlaut	&#228;	&auml;
å	Small a, ring	&#229;	&aring;
æ	Small ae ligature	&#230;	&aelig;
ç	Small c, cedilla	&#231;	&ccedil;
è	Small e, grave accent	&#232;	&egrave;
é	Small e, acute accent	&#233;	&eacute;
ê	Small e, circumflex	&#234;	&ecirc;
ë	Small e, diaeresis / umlaut	&#235;	&euml;
ì	Small i, grave accent	&#236;	&igrave;
í	Small i, acute accent	&#237;	&iacute;
î	Small i, circumflex	&#238;	&icirc;
ï	Small i, diaeresis / umlaut	&#239;	&iuml;
ð	Small eth, Icelandic	&#240;	&eth;
ñ	Small n, tilde	&#241;	&ntilde;
ò	Small o, grave accent	&#242;	&ograve;
ó	Small o, acute accent	&#243;	&oacute;
ô	Small o, circumflex	&#244;	&ocirc;
õ	Small o, tilde	&#245;	&otilde;
ö	Small o, diaeresis / umlaut	&#246;	&ouml;
÷	Division sign	&#247;	&divide;
ø	Small o, slash	&#248;	&oslash;
ù	Small u, grave accent	&#249;	&ugrave;
ú	Small u, acute accent	&#250;	&uacute;

Latin 1 character set (continued)

Character	Description	Numeric Character Reference	Character Entity
û	Small u, circumflex	&#251;	&ucirc;
ü	Small u, diaeresis / umlaut	&#252;	&uuml;
ý	Small y, acute accent	&#253;	&yacute;
þ	Small thorn, Icelandic	&#254;	&thorn;
ÿ	Small y, diaeresis / umlaut	&#255;	&yuml;

Latin extended-A and Latin extended-B

Character	Description	Numeric Character Reference	Character Entity
Œ	Latin capital ligature oe	&OElig	&#338;
œ	Latin small ligature oe	&oelig	&#339;
Š	Latin capital letter S with caron	&Scaron	&#352;
š	Latin small letter s with caron	&scaron	&#353;
Ÿ	Latin capital letter Y with diaeresis	&Yuml	&#376;
ƒ	Latin small f with hook, =function, =florin	&fnof;	&#402;

Greek

Character	Description	Numeric Character Reference	Character Entity
A	Greek capital letter alpha	&Alpha;	&#913;
B	Greek capital letter beta	&Beta;	&#914;
Γ	Greek capital letter gamma	&Gamma;	&#915;
Δ	Greek capital letter delta	&Delta;	&#916;
E	Greek capital letter epsilon	&Epsilon;	&#917;
Z	Greek capital letter zeta	&Zeta;	&#918;
H	Greek capital letter eta	&Eta;	&#919;
Θ	Greek capital letter theta	&Theta;	&#920;
I	Greek capital letter iota	&Iota;	&#921;
K	Greek capital letter kappa	&Kappa;	&#922;
Λ	Greek capital letter lambda	&Lambda;	&#923;
M	Greek capital letter mu	&Mu;	&#924;
N	Greek capital letter nu	&Nu;	&#925;
Ξ	Greek capital letter xi	&Xi;	&#926;

Greek (continued)

Character	Description	Numeric Character Reference	Character Entity
O	Greek capital letter omicron	&Omicron;	&#927;
Π	Greek capital letter pi	&Pi;	&#928;
P	Greek capital letter rho	&Rho;	&#929;
Σ	Greek capital letter sigma	&Sigma;	&#931;
T	Greek capital letter tau	&Tau;	&#932;
Υ	Greek capital letter upsilon	&Upsilon;	&#933;
Φ	Greek capital letter phi	&Phi;	&#934;
X	Greek capital letter chi	&Chi;	&#935;
Ψ	Greek capital letter psi	&Psi;	&#936;
Ω	Greek capital letter omega	&Omega;	&#937;
α	Greek small letter alpha	&alpha;	&#945;
β	Greek small letter beta	&beta;	&#946;
γ	Greek small letter gamma	&gamma;	&#947;
δ	Greek small letter delta	&delta;	&#948;
ε	Greek small letter epsilon	&epsilon;	&#949;
ζ	Greek small letter zeta	&zeta;	&#950;
η	Greek small letter eta	&eta;	&#951;
θ	Greek small letter theta	&theta;	&#952;
ι	Greek small letter iota	&iota;	&#953;
κ	Greek small letter kappa	&kappa;	&#954;
λ	Greek small letter lambda	&lambda;	&#955;
μ	Greek small letter mu	&mu;	&#956;
ν	Greek small letter nu	&nu;	&#957;
ξ	Greek small letter xi	&xi;	&#958;
o	Greek small letter omicron	&omicron;	&#959;
π	Greek small letter pi	&pi;	&#960;
ρ	Greek small letter rho	&rho;	&#961;
ς	Greek small letter final sigma	&sigmaf;	&#962;
σ	Greek small letter sigma	&sigma;	&#963;
τ	Greek small letter tau	&tau;	&#964;
υ	Greek small letter upsilon	&upsilon;	&#965;
φ	Greek small letter phi	&phi;	&#966;
χ	Greek small letter chi	&chi;	&#967;
ψ	Greek small letter psi	&psi;	&#968;

B

Greek (continued)

Character	Description	Numeric Character Reference	Character Entity
ω	Greek small letter omega	&omega;	&#969;
ϑ	Greek small letter theta symbol	&thetasym;	&#977;
ϒ	Greek upsilon with hook symbol	&upsih;	&#978;
ϖ	Greek pi symbol	&piv;	&#982;

General punctuation

Character	Description	Numeric Character Reference	Character Entity
•	bullet, =black small circle	&bull;	&#8226;
…	horizontal ellipsis, =three dot leader	&hellip;	&#8230;
′	prime, =minutes, =feet	&prime;	&#8242;
″	double prime, =seconds, =inches	&Prime;	&#8243;
‾	overline, =spacing overscore	&oline;	&#8254;
/	fraction slash,	&frasl;	&#8260;
"	quotation mark	&quot	&#34;
&	ampersand	&amp	&#38;
<	less-than sign	&lt	&#60;
>	greater-than sign	&gt	&#62;
ˆ	modifier letter circumflex accent	&circ	&#710;
˜	small tilde	&tilde	&#732;
	en space		
	em space		
	thin space		
	left-to-right mark	&lrm	&#8206;
	right-to-left mark	&rlm	&#8207;
–	en dash	&ndash	&#8211;
—	em dash	&mdash	&#151;
'	left single quotation mark	&lsquo	&#8216;
'	right single quotation mark	&rsquo	&#8217;
‚	single low-9 quotation mark	&sbquo	&#8218;
"	left double quotation mark	&ldquo	&#8220;
"	right double quotation mark	&rdquo	&#8221;
„	double low-9 quotation mark	&bdquo	&#8222;
†	dagger	&dagger	&#8224;
‡	double dagger	&Dagger	&#8225;

General punctuation (continued)

Character	Description	Numeric Character Reference	Character Entity
‰	per mille sign	&permil	&#8240;
‹	single left-pointing angle quotation mark	&lsaquo	&#8249;
›	single right-pointing angle quotation mark	&rsaquo	&#8250;

Letter-like symbols

Character	Description	Numeric Character Reference	Character Entity
℘	script capital P, =power set, =Weierstrass p	&weierp;	&#8472;
ℑ	blackletter capital I, =imaginary part	&image;	&#8465;
ℜ	blackletter capital R, =real part symbol	&real;	&#8476;
™	trademark sign	&trade;	&#8482;
ℵ	alef symbol, =first transfinite cardinal	&alefsym;	&#8501;

Arrows

Character	Description	Numeric Character Reference	Character Entity
←	leftward arrow	&larr;	&#8592;
↑	upward arrow	&uarr;	&#8593;
→	rightward arrow	&rarr;	&#8594;
↓	downward arrow	&darr;	&#8595;
↔	left right arrow	&harr;	&#8596;
↵	downward arrow with corner leftward, =carriage return	&crarr;	&#8629;
⇐	leftward double arrow	&lArr;	&#8656;
⇑	upward double arrow	&uArr;	&#8657;
⇒	rightward double arrow	&rArr;	&#8658;
⇓	downward double arrow	&dArr;	&#8659;
⇔	left right double arrow	&hArr;	&#8660;

Mathematical operators

Character	Description	Numeric Character Reference	Character Entity
∀	for all	&forall;	&#8704;
∂	partial differential	&part;	&#8706;
∃	there exists	&exist;	&#8707;
∅	empty set, =null set, =diameter	&empty;	&#8709;
∇	nabla, =backward difference	&nabla;	&#8711;
∈	element of	&isin;	&#8712;
∉	not an element of	&notin;	&#8713;
∋	contains as member	&ni;	&#8715;
∏	n-ary product, =product sign	&prod;	&#8719;
∑	n-ary sumation	&sum;	&#8721;
−	minus sign	&minus;	&#8722;
*	asterisk operator	&lowast;	&#8727;
√	square root, =radical sign	&radic;	&#8730;
∝	proportional to	&prop;	&#8733;
∞	infinity	&infin;	&#8734;
∠	angle	&ang;	&#8736;
⊥	logical and, =wedge	&and;	&#8743;
⊢	logical or, =vee	&or;	&#8744;
∩	intersection, =cap	&cap;	&#8745;
∪	union, =cup	&cup;	&#8746;
∫	integral	&int;	&#8747;
∴	therefore	&there4;	&#8756;
~	tilde operator, =varies with, =similar to	&sim;	&#8764;
≅	approximately equal to	&cong;	&#8773;
≈	almost equal to, =asymptotic to	&asymp;	&#8776;
≠	not equal to	&ne;	&#8800;
≡	identical to	&equiv;	&#8801;
≤	less-than or equal to	&le;	&#8804;
≥	greater-than or equal to	&ge;	&#8805;
⊂	subset of	&sub;	&#8834;
⊃	superset of	&sup;	&#8835;
⊄	not a subset of	&nsub;	&#8836;
⊆	subset of or equal to	&sube;	&#8838;
⊇	superset of or equal to	&supe;	&#8839;

Mathematical operators (continued)

Character	Description	Numeric Character Reference	Character Entity
⊕	circled plus, =direct sum	&oplus;	&#8853;
⊗	circled times, =vector product	&otimes;	&#8855;
⊥	up tack, =orthogonal to, =perpendicular	&perp;	&#8869;
·	dot operator	&sdot;	&#8901;

Technical and geometric

Character	Description	Numeric Character Reference	Character Entity
⌈	left ceiling, =apl upstile	&lceil;	&#8968;
⌉	right ceiling	&rceil;	&#8969;
⌊	left floor, =apl downstile	&lfloor;	&#8970;
⌋	right floor	&rfloor;	&#8971;
⟨	left-pointing angle bracket, =bra	&lang;	&#9001;
⟩	right-pointing angle bracket, =ket	&rang;	&#9002;
◊	lozenge	&loz;	&#9674;

Miscellaneous symbols

Character	Description	Numeric Character Reference	Character Entity
♠	black spade suit	&spades;	&#9824;
♣	black club suit	&clubs;	&#9827;
♥	black heart suit	&hearts;	&#9829;
♦	black diamond suit	&diams;	&#9830;

C

LANGUAGE AND COUNTRY CODES

You designate the language of elements using the `lang`and `xml:lang` attributes. You assign to the `lang` and `xml:lang` attributes a two-letter code that represents a language. The available language codes are listed in the following table:

Language codes

Language	Code	Language	Code
Abkhazian	ab	Chinese (Simplified)	zh
Afar	aa	Chinese (Traditional)	zh
Afrikaans	af	Corsican	co
Albanian	sq	Croatian	hr
Amharic	am	Czech	cs
Arabic	ar	Danish	da
Armenian	hy	Divehi	dv
Assamese	as	Dutch	nl
Aymara	ay	Edo	No code defined
Azerbaijani	az	English	en
Bashkir	ba	Esperanto	eo
Basque	eu	Estonian	et
Bengali (Bangla)	bn	Faeroese	fo
Bhutani, Dzongkha	dz	Farsi, Persian	fa
Bihari	bh	Fijian	fj
Bislama	bi	Finnish	fi
Breton	br	Flemish	No code defined
Bulgarian	bg	French	fr
Burmese	my	Frisian	fy
Byelorussian (Belarusian)	be	Fulfulde	No code defined
Cambodian, Khmer	km	Galician	gl
Catalan	ca	Gaelic (Scottish)	gd
Cherokee	No code defined	Gaelic (Manx)	gv
Chewa	ny	Georgian	ka

Language codes (continued)

Language	Code	Language	Code
German	de	Lingala	ln
Greek	el	Lithuanian	lt
Greenlandic, Kalaallisut	kl	Macedonian	mk
Guarani	gn	Malagasy	mg
Gujarati	gu	Malay	ms
Hausa	ha	Malayalam	ml
Hawaiian	No code defined	Maltese	mt
Hebrew	he	Maori	mi
Hindi	hi	Marathi	mr
Hungarian	hu	Moldavian	mo
Ibibio	No code defined	Mongolian	mn
Icelandic	is	Nauru	na
Igbo	ig	Nepali	ne
Indonesian	id	Norwegian	no
Interlingua	ia	Occitan	oc
Interlingue	ie	Oriya	or
Inuktitut	iu	Oromo (Afan, Galla)	om
Inupiak	ik	Papiamentu	No code defined
Irish	ga	Pashto (Pushto)	ps
Italian	it	Polish	pl
Japanese	ja	Portuguese	pt
Javanese	jv	Punjabi	pa
Kannada	kn	Quechua	qu
Kanuri	kr	Rhaeto-Romance	rm
Kashmiri	ks	Romanian	ro
Kazakh	kk	Russian	ru
Kinyarwanda (Ruanda)	rw	Sami (Lappish)	No code defined
Kirghiz	ky	Samoan	sm
Kirundi (Rundi)	rn	Sangro, Sangro	sg
Konkani	No code defined	Sanskrit	sa
Korean	ko	Serbian	sr
Kurdish	ku	Serbo-Croatian	sh
Laotian	lo	Sesotho, Southern	st
Latin	la	Setswana, Tswana	tn
Latvian (Lettish)	lv	Shona	sn
Limburgish, Limburgan (Limburger)	li	Sindhi	sd

Language codes (continued)

Language	Code	Language	Code
Sinhalese	si	Tonga, (Tonga Islands)	to
Siswati, Swati	ss	Tsonga	ts
Slovak	sk	Turkish	tr
Slovenian	sl	Turkmen	tk
Somali	so	Twi	tw
Spanish, Castilian	es	Uighur	ug
Sundanese	su	Ukrainian	uk
Swahili (Kiswahili)	sw	Urdu	ur
Swedish	sv	Uzbek	uz
Syriac	No code defined	Venda	ve
Tagalog	tl	Vietnamese	vi
Tajik	tg	Volapük	vo
Tamazight	No code defined	Welsh	cy
Tamil	ta	Wolof	wo
Tatar	tt	Xhosa	xh
Telugu	te	Yi	No code defined
Thai	th	Yiddish	yi
Tibetan	bo	Yoruba	yo
Tigrinya	ti	Zulu	zu

Country Codes

The language code assigned to the `lang` and `xml:lang` attributes can be further defined to specify the language spoken in a particular country by adding a hyphen and a two–letter country code to the language code. The available country codes are listed in the following table:

Country codes

Country	Code	Country	Code
Afghanistan	AF	Antarctica	AQ
Albania	AL	Antigua and Barbuda	AG
Algeria	DZ	Argentina	AR
American Samoa	AS	Armenia	AM
Andorra	AD	Aruba	AW
Angola	AO	Australia	AU
Anguilla	AI	Austria	AT

Country codes (continued)

Country	Code	Country	Code
Azerbaijan	AZ	Cocos (Keeling) Islands	CC
Bahamas	BS	Colombia	CO
Bahrain	BH	Comoros	KM
Bangladesh	BD	Congo	CG
Barbados	BB	Congo, The Democratic Republic of the	CD
Belarus	BY	Cook Islands	CK
Belgium	BE	Costa Rica	CR
Belize	BZ	Côte D'Ivoire (Ivory Coast)	CI
Benin	BJ	Croatia	HR
Bermuda	BM	Cuba	CU
Bhutan	BT	Cyprus	CY
Bolivia	BO	Czech Republic	CZ
Bosnia and Herzegovina	BA	Denmark	DK
Botswana	BW	Djibouti	DJ
Bouvet Island	BV	Dominica	DM
Brazil	BR	Dominican Republic	DO
British Indian Ocean Territory	IO	East Timor	TP
Brunei Darussalam	BN	Ecuador	EC
Bulgaria	BG	Egypt	EG
Burkina Faso	BF	El Salvador	SV
Burundi	BI	Equatorial Guinea	GQ
Cambodia	KH	Eritrea	ER
Cameroon	CM	Estonia	EE
Canada	CA	Ethiopia	ET
Cape Verde	CV	Falkland Islands (Malvinas)	FK
Cayman Islands	KY	Faroe Islands	FO
Central African Republic	CF	Fiji	FJ
Chad	TD	Finland	FI
Chile	CL	France	FR
China	CN	French Guiana	GF
Christmas Island	CX	French Polynesia	PF

Country codes (continued)

Country	Code	Country	Code
French Southern Territories	TF	Japan	JP
Gabon	GA	Jordan	JO
Gambia	GM	Kazakhstan	KZ
Georgia	GE	Kenya	KE
Germany	DE	Kiribati	KI
Ghana	GH	Korea, Democratic People's Republic of	KP
Gibraltar	GI	Korea, Republic of	KR
Greece	GR	Kuwait	KW
Greenland	GL	Kyrgyzstan	KG
Grenada	GD	Lao People's Democratic Republic	LA
Guadeloupe	GP	Latvia	LV
Guam	GU	Lebanon	LB
Guatemala	GT	Lesotho	LS
Guinea	GN	Liberia	LR
Guinea-Bissau	GW	Libyan Arab Jamahiriya	LY
Guyana	GY	Liechtenstein	LI
Haiti	HT	Lithuania	LT
Heard Island and McDonald Islands	HM	Luxembourg	LU
Holy See (Vatican City State)	VA	Macao	MO
Honduras	HN	Macedonia, the Former Yugoslav Republic of	MK
Hong Kong	HK	Madagascar	MG
Hungary	HU	Malawi	MW
Iceland	IS	Malaysia	MY
India	IN	Maldives	MV
Indonesia	ID	Mali	ML
Iran, Islamic Republic of	IR	Malta	MT
Iraq	IQ	Marshall Islands	MH
Ireland	IE	Martinique	MQ
Israel	IL	Mauritania	MR
Italy	IT	Mauritius	MU
Jamaica	JM	Mayotte	YT

Country codes (continued)

Country	Code	Country	Code
Mexico	MX	Philippines	PH
Micronesia, Federated States of	FM	Pitcairn	PN
Moldova, Republic of	MD	Poland	PL
Monaco	MC	Portugal	PT
Mongolia	MN	Puerto Rico	PR
Montserrat	MS	Qatar	QA
Morocco	MA	Réunion	RE
Mozambique	MZ	Romania	RO
Myanmar	MM	Russian Federation	RU
Namibia	NA	Rwanda	RW
Nauru	NR	Saint Helena	SH
Nepal	NP	Saint Kitts And Nevis	KN
Netherlands	NL	Saint Lucia	LC
Netherlands Antilles	AN	Saint Pierre and Miquelon	PM
New Caledonia	NC	Saint Vincent and the Grenadines	VC
New Zealand	NZ	Samoa	WS
Nicaragua	NI	San Marino	SM
Niger	NE	Sao Tome and Principe	ST
Nigeria	NG	Saudi Arabia	SA
Niue	NU	Senegal	SN
Norfolk Islands	NF	Seychelles	SC
Northern Mariana Islands	MP	Sierra Leone	SL
Norway	NO	Singapore	SG
Oman	OM	Slovakia	SK
Pakistan	PK	Slovenia	SI
Palau	PW	Solomon Islands	SB
Palestinian Territory, occupied	PS	Somalia	SO
Panama	PA	South Africa	ZA
Papua New Guinea	PG	South Georgia and the South Sandwich Islands	GS
Paraguay	PY	Spain	ES
Peru	PE	Sri Lanka	LK

Country codes (continued)

Country	Code	Country	Code
Sudan	SD	Uganda	UG
Suriname	SR	Ukraine	UA
Svalbard and Jan Mayen	SJ	United Arab Emirates	AE
Swaziland	SZ	United Kingdom	GB
Sweden	SE	United States	US
Switzerland	CH	United States Minor Outlying Islands	UM
Syrian Arab Republic	SY	Uruguay	UY
Taiwan, Province of China	TW	Uzbekistan	UZ
Tajikistan	TJ	Vanuatu	VU
Tanzania, United Republic of	TZ	Vatican City State	See Holy See
Thailand	TH	Venezuela	VE
Timor-Leste	TL	Viet Nam	VN
Togo	TG	Virgin Islands, British	VG
Tokelau	TK	Virgin Islands, U.S.	VI
Tonga	TO	Wallis and Futuna	WF
Trinidad and Tobago	TT	Western Sahara	EH
Tunisia	TN	Yemen	YE
Turkey	TR	Yugoslavia	YU
Turkmenistan	TM	Zaire	See Congo, The Democratic Republic of the
Turks and Caicos Islands	TC	Zambia	ZM
Tuvalu	TV	Zimbabwe	ZW

C

APPENDIX

D

CSS LEVEL 1

This appendix lists the properties available to CSS recommendation, Level 1 (CSS1). You can find the latest information on CSS, including the properties available in CSS recommendation, Level 2 (CSS2) and CSS recommendation, Level 3 (CSS3), at the W3C's Web site: *http://www.w3.org/Style/CSS/*.

Color and background properties

Property	Description	Values
background	Sets all the background properties in one declaration	*background-color* | *background-image* | *background-repeat* | *background-attachment* | *background-position*
background-attachment	Determines whether an image specified with background-image will scroll with a Web page's content or be in a fixed position	scroll | fixed
background-color	Sets the background color of an element	*color* | transparent
background-image	Sets the background image of an element	none | url(*url*)
background-position	Specifies the initial position of an image specified with background-image	*percentage unit* | *length unit* | top | bottom | left | right | top left | top center | top right | center left | center center | center right | bottom left | bottom center | bottom right
background-repeat	Determines how an image specified with background-image is repeated on the page	repeat | repeat-x | repeat-y | no-repeat
color	Specifies the text color of an element	*color name* | *RGB value* | *Hex value*

Text properties

Property	Description	Values
word-spacing	Adjusts spacing between words	*length unit*
letter-spacing	Adjusts spacing between letters	*length unit*

Text properties (continued)

Property	Description	Values
text-decoration	Adds decorations to an element's text	none | underline | overline | line-through | blink
vertical-align	Determines the vertical positioning of an element	baseline | sub | super | top | text-top | middle | bottom | text-bottom | *percentage unit*
text-transform	Changes letter case of an element's text	none | capitalize | uppercase | lowercase
text-align	Determines the horizontal alignment of an element's text	left | center | right | justify
text-indent	Specifies the indentation of an element's text	*length unit* | *percentage unit*
line-height	Determines the line height of an element's text	*length unit* | *percentage unit*

Font properties

Property	Description	Values
font	Sets all the font properties in one declaration	*font-family* | *font-size* | *font-style* | *font-variant* | *font-weight*
font-family	Specifies a list of font names or generic font names	*font family* | serif | sans-serif | cursive | fantasy | monospace
font-size	Specifies the size of a font	xx-small | x-small | small | medium | large | x-large | xx-large | smaller | larger | *length unit* | *percentage unit*
font-style	Sets the style of a font	normal | italic | oblique
font-variant	Specifies whether the font should appear in small caps	normal | small-caps
font-weight	Sets the weight of a font	normal | bold | bolder | lighter | 100 | 200 | 300 | 400 | 500 | 600 | 700 | 800 | 900

Box properties

Property	Description	Values
margin-top	Sets the top margin of an element	*length unit* | *percentage unit* | auto
margin-right	Sets the right margin of an element	*length unit* | *percentage unit* | auto

Box properties (continued)

Property	Description	Values
margin-bottom	Sets the bottom margin of an element	*length unit*	*percentage unit*	auto
margin-left	Sets the left margin of an element	*length unit*	*percentage unit*	auto
margin	Sets all of the margin properties in one declaration	*margin-top*	*margin-right*	*margin-bottom*	*margin-left*
padding-top	Sets the top padding of an element	*length unit*	*percentage unit*
padding-right	Sets the right padding of an element	*length unit*	*percentage unit*
padding-bottom	Sets the bottom padding of an element	*length unit*	*percentage unit*
padding-left	Sets the left margin of an element	*length unit*	*percentage unit*
padding	Sets all of the padding properties in one declaration	*padding-top*	*padding-right*	*padding-bottom*	*padding-left*
border-top-width	Specifies the width of an element's top border	thin	medium	thick	*length unit*
border-right-width	Specifies the width of an element's right border	thin	medium	thick	*length unit*
border-bottom-width	Specifies the width of an element's bottom border	thin	medium	thick	*length unit*
border-left-width	Specifies the width of an element's left border	thin	medium	thick	*length unit*
border-width	Sets all of the border properties in one declaration	*border-top-width*	*border-right-width*	*border-bottom-width*	*border-left-width*
border-color	Sets the color of an element's four borders	*color unit*
border-style	Sets the style of an element's four borders	none	dotted	dashed	solid	double	groove	ridge	inset	outset
border-top	Sets all of the width, style, and color properties for an element's top border in one declaration	*border-top-width*	*border-style*	*color unit*
border-right	Sets all of the width, style, and color properties for an element's right border in one declaration	*border-right-width*	*border-style*	*color unit*
border-bottom	Sets all of the width, style, and color properties for an element's bottom border in one declaration	*border-bottom-width*	*border-style*	*color unit*
border-left	Sets all of the width, style, and color properties for an element's left border in one declaration	*border-left-width*	*border-style*	*color unit*

D

Box properties (continued)

Property	Description	Values
border	Sets all of the width, style, and color properties for all four of an element's borders in one declaration	*border-width* | *border-style* | *color unit*
width	Determines the width of an element	*length unit* | *percentage unit* | auto
height	Determines the height of an element	*length unit* | auto
float	Wraps text around an element	left | right | none
clear	Determines whether an element allows floating elements on its left or right sides	none | left | right | both

Classification properties

Property	Description	Values
display	Determines how an element is displayed in a browser	block | inline | list-item | none
white-space	Determines how an element handles white space	normal | pre | nowrap
list-style-type	Specifies the bullet or numbering style for an unordered or ordered list	disc | circle | square | decimal | lower-roman | upper-roman | lower-alpha | upper-alpha | none
list-style-image	Defines an image that will be used as a bullet in an unordered list	none | url(*url*)
list-style-position	Determines the indentation for the bullet or number in an unordered or ordered list	inside | outside
list-style	Sets all of the list-style-type, list-style-image, and list-style-position properties in one declaration	*list-style-type* | *list-style-position* | url(*url*)

Color Units

A **color unit** represents a color value that you can assign to a property. You can assign a color unit to a property using either one of 16 color names defined in the CSS1 specification or a red, green, blue (RGB) value.

The 16 color names defined in the CSS1 specification are listed in the following table.

CSS1 color name values

aqua	gray	navy	silver
black	green	olive	teal
blue	lime	purple	white
fuchsia	maroon	red	yellow

D

You assign the color name to a property, as shown in the following code, which assigns the color name "navy" to the **color** property, which specifies the text color of an element:

```
<p style="color: navy">
Paragraph formatted with a color name.</p>
```

The 16 color names you can use are nowhere near sufficient for most professional Web page authors, especially considering that most computer systems can display millions of colors. Although computer systems can display millions of colors, the display of colors is the result of combining just three colors, red, green, and blue. Most graphical computer systems, such as Windows, use the **red**, **green**, **blue**, or **RGB color system** for specifying colors. Using the RBG color system, you can assign a color unit in one of two ways: by using the color's RGB value or by using its hexadecimal value.

The syntax for assigning a color unit with an RGB value is `RGB(red, green, blue)`. Each color value accepts a number ranging from 0 to 255, which indicates its intensity. A value of 0 indicates that the color you are creating should include the minimum intensity of a primary color, and a value of 255 indicates that the color should include the maximum intensity of a primary color. By combining different intensities of the red, green, and blue primary colors, you can come up with millions of different hues. You create primary colors of red, green, or blue by using a full intensity value of 255 for one of the primary colors, and values of 0 for the two other primary colors. For example, you use an RGB value to assign the color red to the **color** property as follows: `color: RGB(255, 0, 0)`.

The colors represented by RGB values can also be represented as hexadecimal numbers. The decimal numbers you are most familiar with are based on a value of 10. In contrast, **hexadecimal**, or **hex**, **numbers** are based on a value of 16. In the hexadecimal system, numbers 0 through 9, are represented by the numerals 0 through 9, and the numbers 10 through 15 are represented by the letters *A* through *F*. A color represented by a hex number consists of the # symbol followed by six digits. The first two digits represent the red portion of the color, the second two digits represent the green portion of the color, and the last two digits represent the blue portion of the color. For example, the RGB value for yellow is represented as RGB(255, 255, 0). The decimal number 255 is equivalent to the hex number *FF*, and the decimal number 0 is equivalent to the hex number *0* or *00*. Therefore, the hex number for yellow is #FFFF00. You use a hex number to assign yellow to the **color** property as follows: `color: #FFFF00`. In the following code, the exact same color, red, is assigned to each paragraph. The first paragraph uses the RGB value for red, RGB(255, 0, 0), whereas the second paragraph uses the hex number for red, #FF0000.

```
<p style="color: RGB(255,0,0)">
Paragraph color formatted with an RGB value.</p>
<p style="color: #FF0000">
Paragraph color formatted with a hex value.</p>
```

The following table lists RGB values and hex values for the 16 color names defined in the CSS1 specification.

CSS1 color names and their corresponding RGB and hex values

Color Name	RGB Value	Hex Value
aqua	0, 25, 255	#00FFFF
black	0, 0, 0	#000000
blue	0, 0, 255	#0000FF
fuchsia	255, 0, 255	#FF00FF
gray	128, 128, 128	#808080
green	0, 128, 0	#008000
lime	0, 255, 0	#00FF00
maroon	128, 0, 0	#800000
navy	0, 0, 128	#000080
olive	128, 128, 0	#808000
purple	128, 0, 128	#800080
red	255, 0, 0	#FF0000
silver	192, 192, 192	#C0C0C0
teal	0, 128, 128	#008080
white	255, 255, 255	#FFFFFF
yellow	255, 255, 0	#FFFF00

There is a problem with being able to generate millions of colors: Monitors differ in the number of colors they are able to display. Most computer platforms are capable of displaying at least 256 colors. However, about 40 of these colors differ among platforms, which means that how your Web page renders can be unreliable. To ensure that colors on Web pages render the same on all monitors and platforms, most Web page authors limit the colors they use to those that are part of the Web palette. The **Web palette**, also known as the **Web-safe palette** and **browser-safe palette**, is a set of 216 colors that display reliably across platforms and on most computer monitors.

 You can find a list of browser-safe colors and their hex values, along with a utility that coverts RGB values to and from hex values, at *http://www.w3.org/ Markup/Guide/Style*.

Index